PREMIER LEAGUE
A HISTORY IN 10 MATCHES

Jim White has written for the *Independent*, the *Guardian* and the *Telegraph*. He is the author of *Manchester United: the Biography* and *You'll Win Nothing with Kids*.

JIM WHITE

PREMIER LEAGUE

A HISTORY IN **10** MATCHES

HEAD ZEUS

First published in 2013 by Head of Zeus Ltd
This paperback edition published in 2014 by Head of Zeus Ltd

1 3 5 7 9 10 8 6 4 2

A catalogue record for this book is available from the British Library.

ISBN (PB) 9781781854327
ISBN (E) 9781781854297

Printed and bound by CPI Group (UK) Ltd, Croydon, CR0 4YY

Head of Zeus Ltd
Clerkenwell House
45–47 Clerkenwell Green
London EC1R 0HT
WWW.HEADOFZEUS.COM

To H, E and B

CONTENTS

INTRODUCTION

It's football, Jim, but not as we know it

MANCHESTER CITY V. MANCHESTER UNITED

Etihad Stadium, Manchester

Sunday 9 December 2012

As the main course arrived in the Etihad's Mancunian Suite, one of my fellow diners leaned across the table and said: 'It's not a football match, this. It's the final of bloody *Masterchef*.'

In front of each of our party gathered to watch the 164th Manchester derby, waiters had just placed a large white plate. As they did so, a sudden burst of colour enlivened a dull, grey winter's lunchtime. Across each plate was smeared a smudge of vibrant-toned purée of butternut squash. In the middle of this, placed with such exactness a compass and spirit level must have been employed in its positioning, was a small tower constructed of alternating layers of pork, potato and some sort of brightly hued vegetable matter. It was topped with a spray of trimmed courgette batons, a small edible flower and a pencil-like strip of crisped crackling, which was so neat and well turned-out it looked like a pork scratching might after eighteen months at a Swiss finishing school. According to the menu, this was 'Deconstructed Sunday Roast'. It appeared to be less a meal than something Damien Hirst might have run up over a brandy, something to frame and hang on the wall.

The first time I had been to a derby game at City's ground, the food was not quite as elegantly presented. It was September 1977 and I was standing on the terrace segregated off for United fans in the rickety old Kippax Stand at the long-defunct Maine Road. Just after Mick Channon had scored City's third goal, someone lobbed a meat pie out of the City section. It was some throw, arcing over the line of police and stewards in the empty no-man's-land between the two groups of supporters. It also appeared to be laser-guided, perfectly seeking me out. The pie may have been more than half-eaten – they were clearly not wastrels, these City fans – but when it hit me on the shoulder there was sufficient gravy remaining within its pastry case to ensure, as it slipped to the ground, that it left a brown trail like an incontinent snail down the back of my parka.

Thirty-five years later and meat pies – aerially dispatched or not – were nowhere in sight as City took on United. I was sitting in the capacious hospitality area of the club's impressive Etihad Stadium, a guest of one of several dozen organizations happy to spend large sums of money entertaining at the football that afternoon. I'm no veteran of corporate hospitality, nor an expert on comparative levels of service, and have rarely watched a game with carpet under my feet. But it seemed to me this was a particularly civilized place to be. Everything about it was excellent. Beautiful food beautifully presented, elegant, airy surroundings, charming service. We had a visit to the table from Paul Lake, the former City midfielder who chatted amiably about the game ahead. No detail was left unattended. There was a jar of old-school sweets on the table; miniature bottles of milk shake; cookies and a cafetière of coffee at half-time. Everything was done with a flourish. Even the leather mats on which the plates of art were served had a bit of style. They were embossed with humorous sayings from celebrity City fans rhapsodizing Blue culture: self-mocking, ironic but proud. The one on mine was from the DJ Mark Radcliffe:

Sometimes we're good and sometimes we're bad but when we're good, at least we're much better than we used to be and when we are bad we're just as bad as we always used to be, so that's got to be good hasn't it?

The expansive, reclining seats in the stand, the free bar, the leather mobile-phone case decorated with the club crest, gift-wrapped on our place settings: I could only gawp at how much it must have all cost my host. What a contrast the comfort and ease of the Mancunian Suite offered to my early experiences of watching the football. Back when I was initiated into its rhythms you'd count yourself lucky if you were only hit by a meat pie. Never mind the pastry-hurling rival fans, supporters were routinely treated with disdain by the police, the football authorities and club owners, as if we were the annoying adjunct of the sport, something unpleasant fouling the soles of their well-heeled shoes.

Everything possible seemed to be done to put us off attending matches, to prevent us watching our heroes in action. The grounds in which we were penned every Saturday were dirty, dangerous and dilapidated. We were herded like cattle, treated like scum, our rights as routinely compromised as our well-being. On one visit to Wembley in 1979, I was obliged to pick my way through a torrent of urine cascading down the steps, had my view of the trophy presentation completely obscured by a pillar and, on making my way from the supposed temple of the English game, was verbally assaulted by a policeman. Spotting the badge on my lapel which read 'MUFC Reds Against Racism' he called me a 'coon-loving northern bastard'. Welcome to the football, lad.

Any pleasure we derived in those days was in spite of, rather than thanks to, those in charge of the game. Our enjoyment came from communality, the shared sense of resistance, of sticking it to the man. As Millwall fans would later insist about their own reputation, back then no-one liked us and we didn't care. There was certainly little empathy for the fans' position outside the fences in which we were kept caged (and we were caged – football grounds had no Mancunian Suites back then). In the media, in Parliament, in the wider popular mind we deserved nothing more. What did we expect with our wilful fondness for turning up to watch twenty-two men kick a ball around? According to an editorial in *The Sunday Times*, written in the aftermath of the Bradford City stadium fire in 1985 – in which fifty-six fans died when a neglected old wooden grandstand was incinerated in a fire probably started when a fan dropped a lighted cigarette or match through a hole in the stand onto rubbish that had accumulated below – football was a 'slum sport played in slum stadiums watched by slum people'.

No one was saying that in 2013. Certainly not *The Sunday Times*, part of the Murdoch media empire that has profited so handsomely from England's football revolution. But then in 2013 the game really is not the same as the target of that editorial's withering dismissal. Its procedures, processes and premises have changed beyond all recognition since first I started watching. There, on a plate at the Etihad, was all the evidence required of football's extraordinary metamorphosis. It is like someone suddenly switched the lights on.

And there is one simple reason for the quantum leap in the game's fortunes in this country: the Premier League. Sure, things like Paul Gascoigne's blubbing at Italia 1990 suddenly brought the game to the attention of a wider audience. Yes, Des Lynam's World Cup presentation and Pavarotti's warbling that same year romanticized the game, moved it close to the heart of the national conversation. But it was the arrival of the Premier League a couple of years later that changed everything. That's what altered the way football is perceived. As the advertising slogan insisted at the time of its launch, the Premier League really did make it a whole new ball game.

This is the Premier League's bottom line (and the bottom line has always, throughout its twenty-one-year existence, been the feature of which it is most proud): the formation in the summer of 1992 of a free-standing competition at the top of the English game meant those in control could exploit the coming of the digital age by providing television companies with content of enormous global value. More to the point, they could keep the incoming rush of money to themselves, feeling no obligation to share much of the bonanza with those residing lower down football's pyramid. From almost the first kick-off the élite were in financial clover and the revenue projections have maintained a vertiginous upwards trajectory ever since. Across double dips and worldwide banking crises, through recession and downturn, money has not stopped flowing into the Premier League's current account. For twenty-one years Cassandras like me have been predicting that football's bubble must burst, it simply cannot keep getting wealthier. And for twenty-one years we have been proved wrong with every freshly signed agreement.

In 1964, the BBC paid the Football League £5,000 for the right to screen highlights of its matches; the share for each club in the top division was £50, enough for a single deconstructed Sunday lunch at the Mancunian Suite. By 1992 things were very different. That year the twenty-two members of the new Premier League preened themselves with a broadcasting contract worth £52 million a year, more than 10,000 times greater than that 1964 contract. But that, it turns out, was just the start. In 2012, a three-year domestic deal was signed worth £3 billion, with £2.3 billion coming from Sky and £738 million from BT. No other business in the country has seen its income rise at such a prodigious rate.

In Spain, when the television money comes in, the top couple of clubs hog most of it. In England the Premier League operates what its chief executive Richard Scudamore calls 'an extremely regulated non-free market approach' to the distribution of its cash. Among the League's now twenty members the proceeds of success are equally shared. And with the never-ending increase in income it means that the team finishing bottom of the table in May 2014 will earn more than Manchester City did for winning the title in May 2012. And they got £60.6 million. Such is the popularity of the competition every televised match will earn £6.6 million. The overseas rights – still being negotiated at the time of writing – are anticipated to generate almost as much again. No wonder Anton Zingarevich, the Russian owner of Reading FC, says this of the game he has invested in: 'It was the television rights deal that made football a business.' And with £23 million gifted to a club from the League in a parachute payment when it plunges down into the Championship, even relegation does not alter its business-like condition. In the Premier League era, the wages of failure are eye-watering.

Why are television companies prepared to pay such staggering sums for Premier League football? The simple answer is because people want to watch it. Not just the games, either. They'll tune in even when they cannot see the action. One of the most bizarre by-products of the Premier League era has been Sky's *Gillette Soccer Saturday*. Effectively a televised radio show, it features Jeff Stelling introducing us to a bunch of former players sitting in front of monitors in a studio watching on monitors live action from various matches that contractual niceties prevent from being screened direct into the nation's living rooms. Stelling solicits their views, which are invariably punctuated by liberal use of their host's Christian name: 'Well, Jeff,' Matt or Charlie or Phil will say, 'he's come down the right-hand side and crossed to the far post where the big fella's come in and only gone and missed, Jeff.' And the incredible thing is, even in an age when illegal internet streaming of matches is widespread and we can, with a bit of careful searching, in fact watch what they are watching, we still tune in to the institutionalized Jeffing in our millions.

Not just in the home of the game, but across the world, the Premier League has proved to be broadcasting gold dust. Where once this was a pariah pursuit, now television has propelled English football across the planet. And corporations are prepared to pay huge sums to associate themselves with it; every man and his internet gaming site want to climb aboard. Just ahead of the derby, Manchester United revealed record revenues from the club's association with its commercial partners; from Malaysian potato-snack manufacturers to Bulgarian Telecoms providers, more than £170 million is now pouring annually into the club's coffers. Liverpool's four-year deal with the Asian banking group Standard Chartered to have their logo emblazoned on the team's shirts is worth £20 million a season alone.

And the bankers haven't made the deal in the hope of signing up new accounts in Merseyside. The corporate suits know people are watching on television, on tablets, on smart phones around the world. No fewer than 212 territories now buy the Premier League, while its fixtures are followed in 720 million households. Or to put that another way: there are currently but two nations on Earth where you cannot see Premier League fixtures on television. Only North Korea and Albania are beyond its reach. And a deal has been done with Albania. From the start of the 2013–14 season, the locals in Tirana will be able to watch West Bromwich v. West Ham.

That constant worldwide projection of the Premier League has changed the very manner in which the country itself is seen. In 1992, any British tourists in Bangkok, Kuala Lumpur or Cape Town announcing that they came from Stoke, Swansea or Sunderland would have been greeted with blank looks. Twenty-one years on, many of the locals will not only be fully aware of such places, but will engage the visitor in earnest debate about the relative merits of the striker newly signed by these cities' football clubs. Walk through a market in Abidjan, the capital of Ivory Coast, and you will see stalls submerged under tottering Himalayas of the replica shirts of English football clubs. In Addis Ababa screens are erected in public squares to show Premier League fixtures; thousands of Ethiopians turn up to watch, organizing themselves into gangs supporting one or other of the teams in action. Walking through the centre of Dar es Salaam in the autumn of 2011, I was stopped by a man in a Manchester United shirt. After establishing that I was English he had a pressing enquiry: would he ever see the day when the manager Sir Alex Ferguson signed an African player? Or was Fergie prejudiced against Africans? I told him I was sure one day an African player will be a prominent performer at Old Trafford. But then my powers of prophecy were not exactly working on full beam that day. I was there to interview Oscar Pistorius, who was in Tanzania on a charity visit, and I had just filed a piece predicting the Paralympic sprinter would rival Usain Bolt as the world's favourite athlete for the next five years.

According to David Miliband, who after serving as foreign secretary in the last Labour government secured a promotion on leaving office to become vice-chairman of Sunderland (he promptly quit the post in

April 2013 when the club appointed the self-confessed fascist Paolo di Canio as its manager), the Premier League is this country's major cultural export. Everywhere he went in an official capacity during his days at the Foreign Office he saw evidence of its growing prominence. When I spoke to him in February 2013 he used this expressive phrase to describe the Premier League: 'It's our Hollywood.' Once the products that gave Britain international recognition were the cars, motorbikes and locomotives we exported around the globe. Now it is our principal football competition, an international league played in England, featuring some of the world's best talent, the weekly World Cup. One moreover which is conducted in the English language, the world's second most widely spoken tongue.

Back in its homeland, everywhere you can see the fruits of the revolution. In the stadiums, now smart, modern, comfortable places to congregate. In the training grounds, now centres of sports-science excellence. In the academies, producing young players of touch and athleticism (albeit that many of the best graduates – like Cesc Fàbregas, Paul Pogba and Gerard Piqué – are foreigners, ineligible to play for England). Even the very pitches across which the ball is propelled are now firm, flat and grassy when they once could cheerfully have hosted the regional qualifiers of the world mud-wrestling championships. In the boardrooms, too, everything has changed. Where football used to be the domain of the local butcher or garage owner made-good, now foreign potentates queue up to buy into a competition that they hope will give them worldwide exposure. At the time of writing, half the Premier League clubs are owned by businessmen based overseas, several of whom have rarely set foot inside their property. Half the Championship clubs are foreign-owned too, bought up by those who think they are securing a cheap route into the Premier League and thereafter to global renown. Which might well be a little optimistic in the case of Peterborough.

Mainly, though, you can spot football's money in the car showrooms, designer clothes shops and estate agents' windows of the suburbs in which the players and their Marie Antoinette WAGs live. It is those engaged with the game on the pitch who have seen their lives most dramatically changed by the money. And how. In the spring of 2011, I was invited to Robbie Savage's house in the Cheshire village of Prestbury – Manchester's very own footballing ghetto – to interview him about his career as a pundit after retiring as a player. Savage is a chatty, hospitable bloke who has shown himself to be a sharp-tongued analyst on television and radio. But by his own admission he was not a world-class footballer. Yet when the electric gates at the end of his drive opened to let me in, I was confronted with a place that looked like something beamed in from Beverly Hills, a massive brand-new edifice in glass and steel, replete with home cinema and basement gym. For several years as an unexceptional regular with unexceptional Premier League clubs, Savage earned banker money. Now his playing days were at an end, he told me, he would have to start behaving as if he were once again in the real world. That might have to go, he said, pointing at the Italian sports car purring on his gravel drive (it was his, not mine). Now he was no longer on football's payroll, £300 a time to fill it up might prove a touch extravagant. 'Seriously, I never even thought about money when I was playing,' he told me. 'If I wanted something, I bought it. Not just watches or shoes, but cars. I'd go into a showroom and say: I'll have that one.'

As players like Savage enjoyed the bounty, so did their represent-atives. In 2002, Alan Sugar, the former chairman of Tottenham, gave this barbed assessment of football finance: 'the money has gone to Carlos Kickaball and slippery Giovanni, his agent.' And that was nine years before the 2011–12 season when £77,003,130 was shelled out by the twenty Premier League clubs in agents' fees. That was £25 million more than the entire first television deal flooding out of the game into the pockets of the men who contribute nothing beyond talking up their clients' contracts.

How indicative that is of the game's prevailing attitude to its income. It doesn't hang around long, the money. Investment is not an economic theory much pursued in football. Despite the incoming tide of cash, only six Premier League clubs made a profit in 2011–12.

A couple lost more than £100 million each, bailed out by their super-rich owners. Together, the clubs shared a debt of over £1 billion. Thirteen clubs, over the course of Premier League history, have bankrupted themselves in the desperate scramble to regain their place in its wealth-generating environs. Ten of the clubs that were in the first season of the competition in 1992–93 subsequently sank down to the third tier of the game, hamstrung by hangover debt. The money may be sloshing in at speed, but it is heading out at an even faster rate. What we have learned over the Premier League era is that – whatever the scale of its income – football obeys its own set of economic rules.

Plus we have witnessed an unhappy unintended consequence of all this wealth: however good the surface may be – and it is very good indeed – there is a sense of a growing disconnect between many of the clubs involved in the competition and the communities in which they were born. Football's glittering temples of avarice rise up out of some of the most deprived quarters of our inner cities, hovering there like alien mother ships. Tottenham, Liverpool, West Bromwich Albion: the streets surrounding their shiny headquarters are still pockmarked with deprivation. In the last five years those at the Premier League's headquarters have worked hard to promote corporate responsibility among its members. In 2011–12, 3.7 per cent of the television revenue (£45 million a year) was directed into community work. Some 1,603 staff (more than the Premier League players, managers and backroom staff put together) were employed by clubs in their community departments. Sunderland, Everton and Manchester City are among those actively using football's powerful lure to promote health and educational programmes; they run everything from pensioner walks to pop-up clinics testing for sexually transmitted diseases. Manchester United even support a community choir, some seventy or so locals gathering to enjoy the benefits of communal singing. Their repertoire largely consists of show tunes. Though presumably not – given its fans' antipathy to all things Scouse – 'You'll Never Walk Alone'.

Yet such admirable realities do little to alter a
game increasingly divorced from its roots. However
implore them on posters to test themselves for testic
can no longer relate to the multi-millionaire weari
colours. Stories told by older supporters about the tir
the bus to the ground with players sound like snapsh   ancient
history. The closest connection the fan makes with his hero these
days is sending him a vituperative posting on Twitter. And then being
blocked as a result.

Now they are internationally minded, the local is of diminishing
significance to clubs. For many, with their eyes cast on overseas
territories, there is little imperative to address the issues of the
customers on their doorstep, to engage with their concerns, even to
nurture the game at the level their fans play it. However Scudamore
tries to remind his members of their responsibilities, as the pinnacle
of the game grows ever more gilded, in England the grassroots fray
and wither. More than two decades of the Premier League have not
altered the fact that most of those who play the game in the country
of its birth are still likely to change in Portakabins. What do the game's
absentee foreign landlords care if local kids are obliged to spend half
an hour before they can play a match scooping dog shit off a potholed
mudbath of a pitch?

Like all revolutions, football's has had its collateral damage. As
the players and administrators relish their divorce from the financial
restraints of everyday life, thousands find themselves priced out of
live attendance. Those who still turn up are growing ever older, ever
more affluent. And they need to be. Whether it comes via subscription
television or the purchase of an XXXXL-sized replica shirt, the money
fuelling the Premier League revolution is ultimately sourced from the
pockets of fans. Take admission prices. In 2012–13 Arsenal charged
up to £126 for a ticket to a single game at the Emirates. That was not
a hospitality seat, and there was no accompanying smear of puréed
root vegetable; that was for simple, straightforward entry to the game.
For a season ticket, meanwhile, Arsenal demanded as much as £1,955.

pricing has had an inevitable effect on the audience at the event. Cast your eyes across the stands at any Premier League ground and it is immediately clear that women, ethnic minorities and the young are far less frequent consumers of the game's pleasures than middle-aged white blokes.

Yet, despite such attendant absurdities, the Premier League continues to dazzle. It is parked at the centre of our daily life, consuming more newsprint, airtime and webspace than anything else. There is always something to say about its rhythms. Good, bad or indifferent, there is a view to be taken: it has become a handy mirror to hold up; its nuances and leading characters providing easy generalizations about society's wider truths. Such a tabloid caricature has given rise to a joke at the competition's administrative headquarters that they are to blame for everything. Famine, war, banking collapse: it's the fault of the Premier League.

But while the papers fume about the supposed greed and oafishness of its leading practitioners, the Premier League's organizers acknowledge there is no such thing as bad publicity. Its pre-eminence means that as ticket prices head through the roof, so the stands have remained crammed, filled with those with a bit more cash than fans had when I first started watching, plus those prepared to scrape and scrounge to fund their weekly fix of the soap opera. In 1992, the average attendance at Premier League matches was just over 27,000. In 2012 it was more than 36,000.

For all our gripes, for all the lost opportunity, for all our righteous indignation about our obsession's ever more skewed priorities, of this those in control of the game can rest assured: we can't get enough of their product.

There is a simple reason for that: its quality. That day at the Etihad was a case in point. The food may have been delicious, the seats may have been lavish in their comfort, but it was the football that electrified. When Robin van Persie steered his free kick past a rapidly evaporating City wall to score the winning goal in the final seconds, it sealed ninety minutes of unrelenting excitement and drama. Full of skill, athleticism, power and effort, there could be no better way imaginable of spending a grimy winter's afternoon.

If we are to record the Premier League's coming of age, then, it is not the details of television contracts or the scale of the game's international penetration that should detain us. Because it is not contract negotiations or boardroom politics that keep us coming back for more. It is the football. And the football should remain at the heart of the history.

That is what this book attempts to do. I have chosen ten matches across the twenty-one years which, I think, between them tell us much of this astonishing competition's story. Through scanning the archive and talking to those who were involved, through the use of the contemporary record and viewing through the prism of hindsight, I have tried to draw out themes and details from these games which help piece together a narrative.

These ten are not necessarily selected because they were the best matches. Indeed the one which was selected by public vote as the finest during the League's twentieth birthday celebrations is not included. Liverpool against Newcastle in April 1996 was a breathless pageant of skill and endeavour, the Mersey Spice Boys at their joyous peak, Stan Collymore hammering home the winner at the last as the Newcastle manager Kevin Keegan hung his head in disbelief. But I'm not sure that game tells us as much about the League's development as Leeds against Charlton in 2004, or Manchester City against Spurs in 2010, or Portsmouth against Reading in September 2007, matches which had a resonance beyond the quality of the finishing on display.

The choices I have made inevitably mean I have been obliged to miss some of the subplots. Sadly I found myself without the room to examine the exemplary decade-long managerial reign of David Moyes at Everton, or the against-the-odds struggle of Dave Whelan's Wigan Athletic, or the attempt by a couple of pornographers to use West Ham as a laundry for their social reputation. Nor is there room for the rise of Newcastle under Keegan in the mid-1990s. What a thrilling ride he provided on Tyneside, as, for a couple of seasons, his team threatened to break the North West hegemony that had dominated the League since its inception. In the spring of 1996 he looked as if he might shift the very geographical axis of the game by bringing the title to the North East; a banner to hang on the Tyne Bridge announcing the title was even commissioned and made. But he didn't achieve it, ending up instead imploding on live television, jabbing his finger at the camera while wearing headphones and shouting how much he'd love it if Manchester United lost a game with Leeds. But United didn't lose. They kept winning, overhauling Newcastle long before the line was in view and consigning Keegan to a footballing slough of despond which ended up with him doing time as a pundit on ESPN's Premier League coverage.

Fear not, though, there are plenty of characters here. The leading figures in the Premier League soap opera are all examined through their actions. Fergie, 'Arry, José, Arsène and Roberto: men who have come to be as familiar in our daily lives as friends and family. Jack Walker, Roman Abramovich and Sheik Mansour too, men whose fortunes have shaped our fortune. The managers, the owners, the big – and small – businessmen, most have their moments. Plus – most importantly – there are the players, the ones whose actions lift us from our seats, the ones whose efforts have been seared onto our collective memory, their exploits playing on a loop on the screens of our mental multiplex.

Inevitably, by its very nature, this is a selective rather than comprehensive history. Anecdotal, opinionated and argumentative, too. Facts and figures are included, but not, I hope, to the exclusion of the real interest, the game. And if you don't agree with my choice, let me know. Maybe you think the match that tells us all we need to know about our times was Swindon against Oldham in August 1993. Or Southampton against Aston Villa in January 2013. If so, please argue the case: you never know, there might be a follow-up.

A brief word on nomenclature. I have referred to the competition by the name it took at the time of the match under discussion. It was called the Premiership between 1993 and 2007, and the Premier

League thereafter. Confusingly, the organizing body has always been known as the Premier League, and is called that throughout.

But back to the action, because after all that's what counts. Sitting in the stand at the Etihad that December afternoon, I was advised by my host to keep my allegiance to myself. This was a City-supporting section of the stadium. I might get a tower of roasted pork and potato hurled in my direction should I be identified as a follower of the other lot. And my host knew what he was talking about. In the interests of full disclosure, I should reveal I was there as a guest of Dan Johnson, the communications director of the Premier League. One of the very architects of English football's revolution had invited me along to witness at first hand the fruits of the transformation. And what a transformation it was.

For most of the ninety minutes I managed to observe the protocol. Though looking around the hospitality area, I got the feeling from the expressions on several other guests' faces that I wasn't the only interloper in enemy territory. As the tensions were tautened, I could sense those of red affiliation trying to keep the lid of discretion fastened. One woman on our row dug her nails into her hands and voicelessly mouthed the words 'don't score' every time City advanced into the United area in search of the winning goal. This was drama of the most unrelenting sort, a fizzing switchback of emotions as the momentum ebbed and flowed between two outstanding sides, jostling for supremacy. I wondered whether everyone would be able to hold it in should the visitors be the ones who emerged triumphant. Surely not. And so it proved: when van Persie made his decisive intervention and scored the winner in a 3–2 epic, a bloke sitting two rows in front of me could restrain himself no longer. He leapt from his seat, jumping about, flinging his arms above his head as he ran for the exit. There, for a moment he paused and did a giddy little dance on the spot, before heading away, whooping in delight.

Watching him perform his pirouette in celebration of a last-gasp victory, I was reminded of something I'd seen before. Something that had happened right at the beginning of the Premier League story...

Barclays Premier League

Etihad Stadium, Manchester

Sunday 9 December 2012

Manchester City   2 – 3   Manchester United

City scorers: Yaya Touré 60, Pablo Zabaleta 86

United scorers: Wayne Rooney 16, 29; Robin van Persie 90 + 2

Attendance: 47,166

Referee: Martin Atkinson

Teams:

Manchester City (4-4-2)

Joe Hart; Pablo Zabaleta, Vincent Kompany, Matija Nastasić, Gaël Clichy; Gareth Barry, Yaya Touré (Edin Džeko 83), David Silva, Samir Nasri; Mario Balotelli (Carlos Tévez 50), Sergio Agüero

Subs not used: Costel Pantilimon, Maicon, Joleon Lescott, Javi García, Kolo Touré

Manchester United (4-4-2)

David De Gea; Rafael da Silva, Jonny Evans (Chris Smalling 48), Rio Ferdinand, Patrice Evra; Antonio Valencia (Phil Jones 80), Michael Carrick, Tom Cleverley (Danny Welbeck 87), Ashley Young; Wayne Rooney, Robin van Persie

Subs not used: Sam Johnstone, Ryan Giggs, Javier Hernández, Paul Scholes

Match 1

If Fergie had his way they'd still be playing

MANCHESTER UNITED V. SHEFFIELD WEDNESDAY

Old Trafford, Manchester

Saturday 10 April 1993

Horatio Nelson would not have made much of a football man. I admit it would have been hard for Britain's greatest seafarer to forge any affiliation with the game, since he was fatally wounded during the Battle of Trafalgar – two decades before the first recorded instance of twenty-two young men charging around the playing fields of Shrewsbury School in pursuit of a ball, and a full fifty-eight years before the Football Association first crafted the laws of the game in a Holborn pub. But even if he hadn't been born a little too soon to spend his Saturday afternoons hopping around on the touchline, his telescope to his blind eye, moaning about the referee's eyesight, what makes it abundantly clear that the admiral had no proper sympathy for football's nuances was something he wrote in 1801, soon after his victory at the Battle of Copenhagen. 'Time is everything,' he declared. 'Five minutes makes the difference between victory and defeat.'

Anyone who knows anything about the game would quickly put him right. Certainly anyone who was in attendance on a bright Easter Saturday afternoon in Manchester in April 1993 would point out his fundamental error. It's not five minutes that makes the difference between victory and defeat, between immortality and ignominy, between winning the title and blowing it. It's six.

Such was the critical chronology that Eastertide. Six minutes:

long enough to boil up some pasta. Sufficient time to risk permanent damage to your frontal lobes by listening to Psy's 'Gangnam Style' not once but twice. About the time it takes to travel on the London Underground between King's Cross and Baker Street (signals permitting), or twice as long as it would take Sir Bradley Wiggins to cover the same distance on his bike. Six minutes: the difference between the box-fresh, all-new, game-changing Premier League starting with a whimper or with a bang. It was a span that etched itself into the sporting memory of the 40,102 people who had gathered at Old Trafford for a late-season fixture between Manchester United and Sheffield Wednesday. For them, it was to prove to be six minutes that changed their supporting lives.

Looking back, there seems little about Britain in 1993 that clamours for the historian's attention. This was the second year of John Major's second term as prime minister and the country experienced twelve months that were every bit as unremarkable as the occupant of 10 Downing Street. Here's how exciting it was: 1993 was the year that VAT was first introduced, the Ford Mondeo first went into production and Fermat's Last Theorem was ultimately resolved. Not that you would have read much about all that in the British tabloids. Britain's popular press was fixated on the news that the Princess of Wales had opened divorce proceedings against her errant husband. Which, if nothing else, suggested it was unlikely she would be buying Prince Charles a copy of the year's biggest-selling pop record: Whitney Houston's 'I Will Always Love You'.

Stirrings of revolution

In football, however, a revolution was underway. Seismic change was being fomented. And English football made the most unlikely revolutionary. In 1993 the game was only recently emerging from its bleakest years, a time riven with disaster and violence. It was only four years on from the horrors of Hillsborough, in which ninety-six Liverpool fans had been killed by institutional neglect, their reputation in death, as it would some twenty-three years later be officially admitted, shamelessly sullied in order to cover up culpability among those who should have been protecting them. It was only the season before that an English team had been allowed back into the European Cup, after UEFA's blanket ban imposed as punishment for Liverpool fans' complicity in the Heysel horror of 1986. And, rather than celebrating the return, Arsenal's campaign had ended in somehow appropriate anticlimax with a second-round defeat by Benfica.

This was not English football's greatest era, it was still a sport despised by those in power. Margaret Thatcher, Major's predecessor, had considered the game a national embarrassment. Or worse. 'She was a bully who despised football,' claims Graham Kelly, the FA's general secretary during her premiership. David Mellor, the former government minister, recalls that at cabinet meetings chaired by the Iron Lady he had to conceal the fact that he followed the game. 'I'd have to sit on my hands whenever it was mentioned and keep my enthusiasm secret,' he recalls.

He wasn't the only one: Major and Michael Howard too were keen fans sitting on their hands, knowing that to admit to a footballing affiliation in the late decades of the twentieth century was to court disdain. Even outside Conservative political circles, being a football fan was not something to boast about. I recall being at a social function in the late 1980s when, during a lull in conversation, I asked if anyone had seen *Match of the Day* the previous week. It was an enquiry greeted with curled lips. Apparently, I was informed by another guest, it was not an appropriate thing to talk about. When the evening ground to a halt (unlike football, there's only so much to be said about house prices) I was approached on the way out by a chap who had been sitting opposite me but said nothing when I raised the pariah subject. 'I saw *Match of the Day*,' he confided, in a conspiratorial whisper. 'I just didn't like to say.'

How things have changed. Nowadays, an association with football – however tangential – is reckoned the best way to demonstrate a common touch, of showing that you are a regular guy. In Britain in the second decade of the twenty-first century, those seeking political office are obliged to demonstrate a fondness for football in the way in which candidates for the presidency of the United States have to affect a keenness for a round of golf.

As Chelsea lifted the Champions League trophy in May 2012, the British prime minister's image makers ensured that David Cameron was photographed at a G8 summit punching the air in celebration. His chancellor went one better: George Osborne, who attended the final in Munich's Allianz Arena, was snapped grinning in the background even as the cup was presented. And twenty-five years on, that secretive fan so embarrassed about admitting to watching *Match of the Day* was hosting a party at which the whole point was for guests to watch that Champions League final live on television.

Perhaps surprisingly, at its inception those who started the Premier League had no idea quite what they were unleashing. David Dein, the former Arsenal chief executive who was one of the architects of the competition, recalls that many of those involved in running English football in its unfashionable trough were hardly far-sighted. In those days, his was not a business run by visionaries. To most of them, abroad was a foreign country. Dein gives an insight into the prevailing mindset at that time:

I remember my first ever meeting [of football's leading club representatives] when I proposed there should be two substitutes instead of one. It got outvoted when one of the club chairmen on the committee said: 'we can't have that, it's an extra hotel room, an extra meal, an extra win bonus.' Honestly, much of the thinking in the game was more than antiquated. It was stuck in the dark ages.

What made many of these men in charge of the country's leading clubs change their ideas was an approach from Greg Dyke in the summer of 1991. The future Director General of the BBC (and future chairman of the FA), then in charge of ITV Sport, Dyke came in their direction flourishing the one thing certain to grab their attention: a wad of money. After years of resistance from chairmen who imagined it would lead to a diminution in crowds attending matches (the essence of their objection was: why would people pay when they could watch it for free on TV?) league football had at last begun to be shown live on television in 1983. Transmissions were, however, intermittent and irregular; a dispute prevented even highlights being made available during the 1985–86 season. And a cartel of BBC and ITV kept the price paid down to a minimum.

Dyke reasoned that consistency of broadcast was essential. If his company was going to draw advertisers to sell their wares in breaks around the matches, they had to be games people wanted to watch. Moreover, he insisted that the traditional system of paying for televised football was, like much of the way the game administered itself, archaic. He wondered why it should be that the clubs that might draw a television audience shared their income with the other members of the Football League. The twenty-two First Division clubs had to hand over a good chunk of their earnings to the seventy others in the lower divisions. Which seemed all the more bizarre when it was really only half a dozen of those in the top division who generated big viewing figures. But then, his dealings with the game had only made him the more astonished at how poorly it was administered, how lacking in ambition it was to make the most of its potential allure.

'People called it one, but football wasn't a business at all,' he recalls. 'I was once asked to speak at a conference entitled business and football. I said there is a connection between business and football; business is where you make your money and football is where you lose it.'

Visions for the future

Dyke sensed it could be different; he recognized there was a huge latent interest in the game that, if armchair access were properly exploited, could generate sizeable revenue. And he had the financial wherewithal to kickstart change. He was prepared to pay big money for live football matches – up to £1 million a game. But only for the ones which caught the public imagination, ones like Liverpool against Arsenal in

May 1989, which had dragged millions to their screens to watch the title being decided before their very eyes. He was not interested in the old-school type of deal which required that for every not-to-be-missed fixture screened, a couple of non-events were shown. He found he was not alone in his vision. When Dyke planted the idea of a breakaway division, splitting from the century-old Football League and re-forming itself as a new, sparky, must-watch television-friendly competition, it was the kind of thinking that appealed to some of those, like Dein, who wanted the game to embrace a more businesslike approach.

'When I joined Arsenal's board in 1983, total turnover was under £2 million, it wasn't a business in any sense of the word,' says Dein. 'What I saw was a chance to create something that would be attractive to investors, so we could upgrade our stadiums. To do that we had to make football a true event.'

By coincidence, at that precise moment the Football Association, the governing body of the game in England since 1863, also felt things had to change. Alarmed at how their sport was perceived in the national consciousness, the body commissioned a report into its possible future organization, written by Alex Fynn, an executive at Saatchi and Saatchi, the advertising agency that had successfully marketed Thatcher's Conservative Party. Fynn – a man whose observations about English football are as acute as anyone's – concluded that a top division of fewer clubs would benefit the game as a whole. His view was simply summarized: 'Less is more,' he claims. 'What the television audience wanted was Arsenal against Manchester United, not Coventry against Oldham, who were two clubs in the top division at the time.'

Fynn, however, did not counsel breaking away. Instead, he recommended that his smaller top division should sit at the pinnacle of a regionalized league pyramid. What he did not appreciate was how his report would lubricate the internal politics of the FA, historically always anxious to bloody the nose of its rival, the Football League (the governing body of the English league competition since 1888). 'I thought I was giving them a vision about how they could be the true custodian of the professional and amateur game,' he says of his report. 'In fact I was giving them the ammunition to do what they had long wanted: smash the power of the Football League.'

So when Dein and other representatives of the self-styled Big Five clubs at the time (Manchester United, Liverpool, Tottenham, Arsenal and Everton) approached the FA with the idea of revolution, the concurrence of thinking could not have been more timely. 'We went to the FA and said we believe English football is in the doldrums, the only way we're going to get change is if we create a new league,' recalls Dein. 'We want to start afresh. And they agreed, they said the timing is right and they opened the door for us.'

With the FA prepared to sanction breakaway – and with Fynn and his argument for main-taining continuity quietly sidelined – the leading clubs had the official backing they needed. The Premier League was created at a meeting of the First Division club chairmen on 20 Feb-ruary 1992. The divorce settlement maintained relegation to and promotion from the Football League. In a telling demonstration of football's shifting powerbase, two of the clubs who voted for the formation of the new competition have never benefited from its success. Luton Town and Notts County were relegated at the end of the final season of the First Division and have never been close to regaining a place at the top table since.

Sky-high profits

They were not the only ones who missed out. Although he had been the man who sowed the seed, Dyke never enjoyed the fruits of his idea. At the time, Rupert Murdoch's BSkyB satellite television service was stumbling and stuttering, haemorrhaging money; contemporary reports suggested losses were totalling more than a million pounds a day. Murdoch had initially believed that movies would be the best way to sell subscriptions to pay television, but uptake had been sluggish. Executives at his company sensed that football might be different. As Fynn had noted, the football supporter offered a distinctive commercial opportunity:

> Fans are different from customers. A customer can take his business elsewhere; even if he's loyal he will occasionally be promiscuous. But if you're a football fan you cannot change your allegiance. It's given to you.

Sky's executives recognized that the semi-religious affiliations the game engendered could be converted into subscriptions. Fans would be obliged by their passion to pay to watch their own team in live action. In short, love of football could be monetized.

Whole books have been written about what happened next, but here's the brief synopsis. When negotiations opened with the fledgling league about who would televise matches, Dyke was outflanked. It didn't help his cause that the chairman of Tottenham, Alan Sugar, was the man whose Amstrad company supplied the satellite dishes for Sky. He and Murdoch were old associates. Indeed, Murdoch had encouraged him to take over Tottenham in the first place. At the time Robert Maxwell, then Murdoch's great newspaper-owning rival, was circling the club. Murdoch rang Sugar and suggested he take the chairmanship at Maxwell's expense. He wanted, in his own elegant phrase, to 'see off that fat cunt'. In the midst of the boardroom scurry, Maxwell fell overboard from his luxury yacht and drowned off the Canary Islands. And Sugar moved into Spurs unopposed.

During those first television negotiations, Sugar remembered his old friend. Busily briefing on his fellow chairmen's strategy, he advised Murdoch that the best way to win over the group over was to 'blast the opposition out the water'. So Sky's negotiating team bid £302 million for a five-year deal for exclusive rights to cover live matches, way beyond what ITV had offered. With the BBC picking up the right to show highlights for a further £22.5 million across five years, it was the kind of combined sum that made the eyes of the chairmen of the twenty-two breakaway clubs water. Dein doesn't see it that way, however:

This was never really about money. The ambition was to create a league which could put English football back on the map and challenge the top clubs in Europe. And I think what Greg did was give us the courage to do something about it.

Never really about money? As he was speaking on the phone at the time, it is hard to know where Dein's tongue was in relation to his cheek. Although, in truth, not every broadcasting contract associated with the Premier League brought in a shedload. The radio rights to cover matches live were sold to the BBC for just £65,000 a year. Or less than a third of Yaya Touré's weekly wage two decades later.

Even at the elevated price it had paid, Sky found itself in possession of a bargain, broadcasting gold dust. At £5.99 a month, the company recruited a million subscribers within the first few weeks of broadcasting the League. Within a year, its vast losses had been transformed into a £62 million profit.

Perhaps more significantly, in its desire to proselytize the game, the Premier League had found the most proactive partner. Murdoch may have been regarded with contempt by those who recalled his role in breaking the power of the print unions in the early 1980s (many to this day refuse to buy his products), but they proved to be a dwindling minority. What mattered more to the League was that Sky could not only give the game far more space to breathe than the terrestrial broadcasters – several whole channels could be dedicated to detailing its nuances – but Murdoch's newspapers could also act as seven-day-a-week promoters of the new competition, pushing its content remorselessly in the drive to sell subscriptions. Even Dyke agrees that Sky was a far better fit for football. 'They gave it much greater impetus in the early days than ITV ever could have done,' he admits. 'Without Sky the Premier League would not be where it is now.'

A whole new ball game

When the Premier League opened up for business, Sky's innovations mirrored the freshness of the competition. The first live game, Manchester City v. QPR on 17 August 1992, featured fireworks, dancing girls and a fire-eater. Fireworks were soon abandoned after a game at Southampton when a stray rocket landed on a petrol station next door to the stadium; the cheerleaders didn't hang around much longer than the first season. But the technical improvements transformed the manner in which the game was broadcast. Multiple camera angles, clever graphics, for the first time a countdown clock projected in the top corner of the screen informing the viewer of how long had elapsed in the game: such fundamentals of the football broadcast all arrived for the first time.

Though when the competition started, on the pitch there was not much evidence to suggest we were in at the start of a revolution. As the new world order began, the football looked much as it had for the previous decade. For a start, it remained a business of much smaller order than it is today. The average attendance in the First Division in 1991–92 was 21,662, across 462 league games; twenty years later it was 34,486, across 380 matches. Leeds United, the previous season's champions, had enjoyed an average attendance of 27,668; in 2011–12 Manchester United drew an average 75,387 paying customers. Not that the clubs kept hold of much of any increased revenue through the turnstile. The combined playing budget for the twenty-two First Division clubs in 1992 was £75 million; the total for the twenty Premier League clubs in 2012 was over £1.5 billion.

In truth the football on offer in 1992–93 was traditional, insular, unambitious fare, much like it had been for the previous twenty years. After a brief dalliance with the sweeper system following Italy's triumph in the 1982 World Cup, everywhere, every team adhered to the old-school virtues of 4-4-2. Leeds had won the title the previous season with only one non-Briton in their first-team squad. The odd experiment – like the short-lived managerial tenure of the Hungarian Jozef Vengloš at Villa Park – notwithstanding, the occupants of the dug-out were overwhelmingly British too. At the start of the Premier League one Welshman, one Irishman, four Scots and sixteen Englishmen patrolled the top division's touchline (the technical area had yet to be introduced). Managers were largely unschooled in the new methodologies of coaching that were then becoming fashionable in Holland, Italy and Germany. Back then, badges were something students wore on their lapels; coaching was a matter of doing what had always been done. The FA's technical director was Charles Hughes, a coach who believed a move involving more than five passes was the mere expression of self-indulgence; get it in the mixer as soon as possible was his favoured principle.

While some bosses – like the great Brian Clough, then in his managerial dotage – were natural psychologists, most were angry shouters, whose grasp of sports science was limited to getting the first round in at the bar. The closest most managers came to recognizing their players' individuality was acknowledging that some needed a kick up the backside and others an arm round the shoulder. The game they presided over remained the lusty combination of muscularity and heft which had long defined the English way. Guile and craft were alien concepts. Something foreigners did.

One thing, though, did seem different about this newfangled Premier League: the identity of those clubs who emerged to contest the first title. Leeds followed up their success the previous year by sinking to within two points of relegation; the worst title defence in modern times. Of the Big Five who had agitated to create the new competition, only one finished high enough up its inaugural table to qualify for Europe. Indeed, Aston Villa, Manchester United and Norwich City, the three clubs who jostled for the top spot, promiscuously exchanging the lead no less than fifteen times during the season, had won only one championship between them in the previous twenty years. That was Villa in 1981.

This, the architects of the Premier League insisted, was evidence of the new competition's democratic possibilities. No longer would a single entity be able to dominate as it once had. No longer, as Liverpool had in the 1970s and 1980s, would we see one club win it for years on the bounce. With television income democratically spread amongst the participants, this was to be a competition that mirrored American football: at the start of the season anyone could win it, everyone was in with a chance.

It was a nice thought. But if there was ever a chance in those early days of revolution that the Premier League would prove more open a competition than its predecessor, it was dispelled by the identity of one of those clubs attempting to elbow their way to the top. Manchester United's arrival at a position of prominence as the Premier League was born was a handy coincidence for both entities. This was the club with the historic resonance and charisma to drive up interest across the footballing world. The most comatose of sleeping giants, its reawakening would have a convulsive effect. Propelled by its chairman Martin Edwards – a man whose affection for a set of accounts was unyielding – United were forceful advocates of change. Everyone at United considered the Premier League a wonderful innovation. Well, almost everyone at United. Their manager Alex Ferguson, in his younger days a firebrand union man, described the new competition as 'a piece of nonsense'. He added that it had 'sold supporters right down the river'. A traditionalist, he saw the break with history as a potentially fatal loss of continuity. Unaware he was poised to make his own, he cleaved to the idea that history mattered.

And for him there was one piece of history that dominated his job description: the club he managed had not won the title in twenty-six years. It had been made evident from the day he arrived in Manchester six seasons previously from a successful time in Aberdeen that it was incumbent on him to deliver the ultimate in domestic success. The previous April, the vivacious young United team that Ferguson had created came close to seizing the title, but faltered in a nervous collapse at the last, stumbling and staggering as Leeds took the trophy.

Desperately seeking a striker
The trauma of that surrender appeared still to be haunting Ferguson's

side; United started the first Premier League season as if determined to live up to their manager's scepticism about the new competition. Looking anything but champions in waiting, they lost 2–1 at Sheffield United, 3–0 at home to Everton, then drew 1–1 at Ipswich, accruing just the one point from the first potential nine. Dion Dublin – a £1-million signing from Cambridge, bought on the strength of a video sent to the club by his previous manager – was given his debut in the fourth game and scored the winner against Southampton, in the eighty-ninth minute. Muscular, intelligent and hard-working, if not over-endowed with pace, Dublin led the line convincingly in the next game, another victory away at Forest. Then, in just his third match in a United shirt, at home to Crystal Palace, he slid into an opposing defender in pursuit of a goal-scoring opportunity and shattered his right leg. His season – indeed his United career – was finished before the end of September.

There followed a miserable sequence. Over thirteen games only two were won as United found themselves dispatched from both the League and UEFA Cups. As his team slumped to eighth in the table, Ferguson identified the problem: without Dublin, just nine goals had been scored in those thirteen matches. He needed a forward badly. Though he was getting nowhere in his efforts to recruit one. He had attempted to sign the young Southampton striker Alan Shearer over the summer but had been rebuffed. Nor were Sheffield Wednesday interested in selling him their coveted number nine David Hirst.

Growing increasingly cantankerous, unable to fashion a change of fortune, Ferguson was recorded at a game by Sky's cameras raging up and down the touchline, his face a spluttering spume of fury. The footage was shown repeatedly. He didn't see the news value in the broadcast. Embarrassed, he fulminated that Sky were intruding on his privacy and rang his old Scottish television contact Andy Melvin, who was working on the football coverage: 'Right you stitched me up last night, you're barred.' He refused to speak to the organization's representatives almost until the end of the season. It may have been the first ban on media cooperation he had issued in the Premier League; it would not be the last. Banned United: it was to become a badge of honour, a rite of passage for reporters to face a Fergie injunction.

An inspired signing

But then, on Wednesday 25 November 1992, something happened which stalled Ferguson's growing conviction that the sporting gods were lining up against him. He was in Edwards's office when the Leeds chairman Bill Fogarty rang to enquire about the availability of the United full-back Denis Irwin. This was in the days before the transfer window and a free-for-all market enabled clubs to swap players through much of the season. Edwards quickly informed the Leeds owner that the Irishman was not for sale, but since Fogarty was on the line, Ferguson wrote down on a piece of paper a name and handed it to Edwards. The United chairman assumed Ferguson was joking, but asked the question anyhow. Might Eric Cantona be for sale? He was amazed when Fogarty said yes, he might well be.

The Frenchman had arrived at Leeds in the latter stages of the previous campaign and his cool finishing had steered them towards the title. But the Yorkshire club's manager Howard Wilkinson was always suspicious of his one foreign player's motives. Cantona had a name as a quixotic troublemaker in his homeland, and was only in England because he had effectively been exiled from employment in France. Although he had shown nothing but application in his nine months at Elland Road, Wilkinson mistook his brooding intensity for discontent and was fearful it was only a matter of time before he exploded. Better to cash in now, was his opinion.

Ferguson had taken soundings from Gérard Houllier, then manager of France, who told him that Cantona's problems arose not from caring too little about the game, but caring too much. After a sleepless night wondering if there was anything in that firebrand reputation, Ferguson reassured his chairman that Cantona was exactly what United needed to take advantage of new opportunity. Especially as they only paid £1.2 million for him.

What is more intriguing about Cantona's signing, however, was not his transfer fee but the salary he was offered by United. A basic £3,000 a week was his first contract. Nothing demonstrates the Premier League's changing values quite as much as that figure. Twenty years on, the Arsenal manager Arsène Wenger claimed that his star striker Robin van Persie was offered £300,000 a week to sign for Manchester City, an enticement he declined. Good as he is, there are not many even in the van Persie household who would reckon him a hundred times better than Cantona. But Cantona was signed before the wage explosion that peppered the game with multi-millionaires. And he travelled across the Pennines for the promise of £150,000 a year, the income at the time of a television newsreader.

By no means everyone thought United were getting the better side of the bargain. Emlyn Hughes, the late Liverpool stalwart, wrote in his *Daily Mirror* column that the deal would prove so disastrous it would be Alex Ferguson's 'last gamble as Manchester United manager'. Playing on the terrace chant which had sound-tracked the Frenchman's time at Elland Road, Hughes opined that the signing would prove a case of 'ooh aargh Cantona'.

As it transpired, on this punt Ferguson was bang on the money: Cantona turned out to be the player who made the difference to United. Not just a performer of skill, courage and vision, but a man whose attitude permeated the club, infecting colleagues and supporters alike with a sense of shared destiny. At twenty-six he arrived at the club at the same age George Best had left it. Unlike the Irishman, he believed his best days lay ahead.

Faltering hopes

And from the moment he stepped on the pitch, coming on as substitute for the coltish teenaged winger Ryan Giggs in the Manchester derby in early December 1992, Cantona set United on the path to victory. A surge of wins through the winter pushed Ferguson's men to the top of the table. But then came another stutter.

As the days began to lengthen, just as Norwich, under the progressive management of Mike Walker, and Aston Villa, organized by the former United boss Ron Atkinson, refused to wilt, United's form began to desert them. During March, their performance diminished. Defeat at Oldham on 9 March prefaced a sequence of three draws. From first place, following a goalless home draw with Arsenal on 24 March, they had slipped to third. For Ferguson, the student of the past, it appeared history was about to repeat itself.

The previous season he had come close to breaking the long drought that had undermined the club, but had faltered at the last, fading over the Easter holiday, dropping points at the season's critical juncture and seeing his ambition punctured, handing the title to Leeds by four points. As they lost successive games at Nottingham Forest, West Ham and Liverpool that year, United's players were seemingly crippled by tension, and their agitated, fractious manager, jumpy on the touchline, characterized the fraught condition of their morale. The striker Mark Hughes paints a picture of that stumbling, knock-kneed 1992 run-in:

We were going into every game apprehensive, everything was a worry, really. Though actually I don't think it was down to the Boss. He was about the only one who wasn't on edge, doing his best to calm everyone down. It just didn't work.

Never before had the words of football's poet laureate, John Toshack, appeared so apposite as they did over the bank-holiday period of 1992 as United shed points like a moulting dog does its coat. The former Welsh international liked a rhyme and, when he was Liverpool's centre-forward, the McGonagall of the penalty area wrote this:

Easter time is very vital,
That's when we decide the title.

And now, in 1993, as Easter hove into view again, there were many who predicted Ferguson's nervy charges would blow it once more. This might be a new competition, but old habits seemed about to prevail. In *The Sunday Times*, a profile of the Scot suggested his urgent ambition had communicated itself to the players as the most debilitating of nerves. A betting man, the item concluded, would be wise to invest in more secure runners. Like Atkinson or Walker. Even a victory at Carrow Road – in which Cantona orchestrated a thrilling demonstration of the sort of counterattacking football that was to become the trademark of Ferguson's first great United team – did little to assuage the growing sense that this was a side that was a victim of destiny.

When Saturday came

And so along came Easter Saturday. What twanged the nerves of those arriving at Old Trafford towards breaking point was the identity of the opposition. For many, Sheffield Wednesday were the best footballing side in the country at the time. What's more, the Owls held the psychological edge over United, having beaten them when still a second-division side at Wembley in the 1991 League Cup final. In contrast to what was to become Sky's familiarly reverential coverage, that day Yorkshire TV opted not to show Wednesday's victory celebrations in the club's home region, cutting away as the match overran to broadcast its scheduled programme, *War of the Monster Trucks*. So aggrieved were Sheffield's fans at what they perceived as the Leeds bias of their local television company that one Wednesday fanzine took as its name the title of the offending show.

To the side that had carried the club to third place in the First Division in 1992, the Wednesday manager Trevor Francis had made a superb addition. He had repatriated England's most creative player, Chris Waddle, from Olympique Marseille for £1 million. The slope-shouldered shuffler had pro-vided dynamic propulsion to Wednesday all season, his intelligence and craft taking them to both domestic cup finals, his excellence recognized by the Football Writers' Association who voted him their footballer of the year for 1992–93. With Waddle the constructive influence behind the forceful front line of Hirst, Paul Warhurst and Mark Bright, with John Sheridan, Danny

Wilson and the elongated Carlton Palmer providing midfield cover and with Chris Woods between the posts, Francis had developed a cogent, coherent side that appeared to be going places.

The two teams had already shared the points in what many regarded as the best game of the season so far – a pulsating 3–3 draw at Hillsborough on Boxing Day. In front of what was then regarded as a huge crowd of 37,708, Cantona had scuffled in the equalizer right at the last. A late fight-back by United: there was an omen. But whatever the final result, United had been second best for much of that game, outwitted by Waddle's deceptively languorous contribution. And now, the relaxed and flexible, ambitious and intelligent Wednesday were the very last team a nervy bunch like United wanted to entertain in such a crucial Easter fixture.

Those arriving at the match that sun-sparkled Mancunian Saturday afternoon were immediately confronted by physical evidence of change. All around Old Trafford the Premier League era was taking shape. The stadium was being refashioned to conform with the findings of the Taylor Report, commissioned after the Hillsborough disaster. Concluding that terraces were inherently dangerous and a fundamental cause of the crushing horror of Leppings Lane, Lord Justice Taylor had insisted that every ground in the Premier League be all-seater by August 1994. Money had been found from the pools via the Football Trust to finance the change. United were granted £1.5 million to help refashion their ground – as it turned out, not much more than 10 per cent of the eventual cost of rebuilding just the Stretford End Stand. Nevertheless, work had been relentless; in Trafford Park, the cranes had been in position for much of the year.

United had been the first club to introduce executive boxes to football – an idea borrowed by their manager Matt Busby from the new grandstand at Salford racecourse back in the late 1960s. The boxes had been accommodated in English football's first ever cantilever stand, which had opened for the 1966 World Cup. Now the process of gentrification was in full swing: the Stretford End, once the most fearsomely noisy terrace in the country, for more than a generation a cauldron of passionate support, was in the midst of conversion; seats were being screwed into the concrete steps where once lads in voluminous flares had stood atop their stack heels. Nor would youths dressed in logo-bedecked sweaters and pricey trainers be able any longer to taunt the visiting supporters from the paddock that ran along the front of the north stand. It had already been transformed into seating. Only the paddock at the Scoreboard End remained as a standing area. The single 'Sit Down' by the Manchester band James, which had been adopted as an anthem by the United faithful to acclaim their team's victory in the 1991 European Cup Winners' Cup final in Rotterdam, was all too soon to become the presiding edict at Old Trafford.

Mind, the arrival of seats seemed to pique the punters' interest. In 1993 a total of 667,731 paying customers could be accommodated in the twenty-two stadiums in the Premier League. In 2012, the total of the twenty top stadiums was 748,529. In 1993 stadiums operated at 69.6 per cent of their capacity. In 2012 it was up to 92.6 per cent. Clearly, whatever the opinion of the romantic and the traditionalist yearning for the vibrant atmosphere generated by the standing terraces of old, the newly converted sit-down stadiums have proved far more attractive to the football consumer. Though there was one element of the Taylor Report to which no one seemed to pay much attention: it insisted that clubs could not profiteer from the switch from terraces to seats.

That April afternoon, as the new cantilevered roof over the Stretford End cast a sharp shadow over the pitch, United's biggest home crowd of the season were ushered into the new seats, still then retailing at just £6 a time. A total crowd of 40,102, out of an eventual proposed capacity of 44,000, nervily found their way to their places. The memory of what had happened twelve months previously still raw, there were not many in there confident about what they were about to witness.

Fergie v. Francis

Things did not start in a manner likely to soothe frayed nerves.

Wednesday, beaten only twice in their last twenty-eight matches, had arrived in the midst of a spate of injuries. Without either of their first-choice centre-backs and obliged to field their fourth- and fifth-choice strikers, they deployed the scarecrow-limbed midfielder Carlton Palmer – mocked by the Dutch media during the Euros the previous summer as a man better physically suited to basketball – in the heart of their defence. But one player they did have fit was Waddle. Immediately dispelling the reputation he had unjustly earned for disappearing in big games, the hunched Geordie was in the ascendant throughout the first half. On one occasion, he outsprinted the pacy United full-back Paul Parker, dragged the ball back from the byline and executed a perfect Cruyff turn. Cantona, the home team's champion, on the other hand, was finding his attempts to exercise influence over the proceedings checked by dogged Wednesday defence.

Watching from the sideline as Cantona laboured, the Wednesday manager must have been relieved about the decision he had taken back in January 1992. Fleeing from French football, Cantona had turned up at Hillsborough for a trial. The weather at the time was rotten, snow was thick on the ground and all training was being conducted indoors. Nevertheless, the Frenchman played in a match at the Sheffield Arena, scoring in an exhibition against Baltimore Blast from America's Major Indoor Soccer League. Francis, though, had not yet seen enough to be convinced. 'I made a reasonable request for him to stay another week so we could take a look at him, give him a trial on grass,' he said at the time. 'He rejected my request.' Cantona thanked Francis for his offer and went instead to Leeds, where Howard Wilkinson signed him without a trial. 'He reads poetry, he reads philosophy, he paints, he likes fishing, yeah he's different,' said Wilkinson. 'I hope he's different out there on the pitch.'

Well, he wasn't on Easter Saturday 1993. Like the rest of the United team, he seemed initially subdued, as if cowed by the horrible possibility of history quickly repeating itself. Indeed, after sixty minutes of stalemate what provoked the biggest cheer so far among

United's supporters was not a piece of Cantona trickery, a pacy Ryan Giggs run, or a bullocking charge by Mark Hughes. It was when the referee Michael Peck suddenly tumbled to the turf, as if struck by sniper fire from atop the new Stretford End roof. There is nothing a football fan enjoys more than watching a referee in pain, and Peck was in pain all right: his hamstring had been tweaked and he was writhing. After a lengthy delay, which was timed throughout by Alex Ferguson, worriedly pacing the touchline, constantly referring to his wristwatch, Peck was replaced by his linesman Michael Hilditch. And after no more than four minutes in control of the whistle, Hilditch was required to make a significant decision.

Near the edge of the United area, Wednesday's Andy King passed to Waddle. The England man controlled the ball, hunched his shoulders and strode into the area. His every step was being tracked by his United counterpart Paul Ince. And although he was not heading goalwards, instead moving towards the corner flag, Ince went to ground, slid in from the side and, with the ball pushed well ahead, tripped Waddle. Not one United player complained as Hilditch blew his whistle and pointed to the penalty spot. It didn't matter that the ref had only been in charge a few seconds, no other decision was possible. As Waddle took the congratulations of his team-mates, Ince just looked crestfallen. On the touchline, Ferguson, never slow to point out a dubious refereeing decision, said not a word. He wore the expression of a man about to be steamrollered once more by forces beyond his control.

John Sheridan, a boyhood United fan, stepped up to face goal-keeper Peter Schmeichel. Despite a crescendo of whistles rising from the crowd, loud enough to terrify dogs as far away as Rotherham, he nervelessly scored. Behind the goal every occupant of the Scoreboard End terrace looked as if they were watching the title disappear again. As the Sky cameras picked out a fan sitting in the stands with eyes filling with tears, Ferguson could be seen gently shaking his head. All around the ground, United fans and players had the hangdog appearance of serial chokers.

Enter Captain Marvel

As United pressed for an equalizer, however, Wednesday's keeper Chris Woods demonstrated the sort of form that had seen him recently elevated to the England team, twice saving brilliantly from Brian Mc-Clair. It seemed the visitors simply would not yield.

With just twenty minutes remaining to put his season back on track, Ferguson sent on his substitute, Bryan Robson, to replace the full-back Parker. It was only his ninth league appearance of the season, but Ferguson reasoned that the former Captain Marvel, now well into his twilight years as a player, had a particular motivation.

Coming to the end of his distinguished, if injury-bedevilled, career, Robson was desperate to add the one gong that mattered to his collection. He had moved to United in 1981 from West Bromwich Albion with the specific ambition of leading them to the championship; that was the task he had undertaken in exchange for what was then the largest transfer fee in British football history. A dozen years on, this represented his last chance. And Ferguson knew he would apply his enormous will, drive and enthusiasm to the enterprise. More to the point, he would provide an urgent aggression to the centre of the midfield, where Wednesday had maintained control throughout.

But still, as Robson drove United forward, Wednesday stood firm. By now the baying from the crowd, insisting the home team attack, attack and attack, had taken on a desperate edge. As United pressed, the goalkeeper Schmeichel was striding out of his area towards the halfway line, flapping his arms in a forward motion, as if hoping to generate sufficient wind power to force an equalizer.

Then, in the eighty-fifth minute, Cantona, on the edge of the Wednesday area, flicked the ball forward. It was a stray, misdirected effort, which landed at Carlton Palmer's feet. But, as the Wednesday man increased his sizeable stride to move away, Hughes took the ball from him. The Welshman then waltzed into the Wednesday area, evading three tackles as he jinked. 'Still Hughes, still Hughes,' boomed Barry Davies on the BBC's commentary.

Level with the penalty spot, Hughes sent a left-foot shot towards the bottom corner. It was not particularly powerful, not particularly venomous. But it was well placed. Woods was alert to it, diving to his left, palming the ball away for a corner. 'Look at this for grit and de-termination,' announced Davies. 'And another good save.'

Denis Irwin took the corner. Robson piled in with reckless lack of concern for his own well-being, bundling towards the goal. Per-haps distracted by his aggression, the Wednesday defence moment-arily lost concentration. The ball swung towards Steve Bruce, on the edge of the area. Although marked by Palmer, he took three sizeable paces and met the ball full on the forehead. With a pulse of his neck muscles, he planted it wide of Woods's desperate stretch. It was his first goal for six months.

Cue pandemonium. In the cacophony, somebody managed to convey the message to Ferguson that Aston Villa's home game with Coventry had already finished: a goalless draw. So a point from this game would not be a disaster: United would still be second in the table, just one behind the Midlands club. Fergie tried to let Robson know, screaming instructions from the touchline for the team to calm down and not open themselves up to counterattack. Nobody could hear him. Alongside him, Francis was signalling to Hilditch that it should be over by now: he wanted this point to help Wednesday's pursuit of a European place.

The gods smile

What the Wednesday manager had not done was take account of the minutes to be added for the referee's injury. How many minutes, however, nobody knew. One of the later innovations of the Premier League was an electronic board, held up by the fourth official, to indicate how much additional time had been awarded. The board has become part of the game's theatre, its signals a chance for the fans to boo if added time is too short, or gasp if it is too long. And for those anxious to beat the traffic, its arrival offers them the perfect excuse to begin their getaway. But in 1993, the board was not around.

Information was scant. At Old Trafford, the crowd, the players, the managers on the touchline, had no indication of how long Hilditch had added. The assumption was the whistle could go at any moment. In a second it could be done. In a blast United's title drought would continue.

The urgency was now utterly infectious. From the stands the noise reached a stirring, boiling crescendo as United pressed and pressed, looking for the winning goal. How the crowd howled when, from a cross by Giggs, the former United defender Viv Anderson almost headed the ball into the Wednesday goal. As the referee signalled for a corner, Waddle could be seen angrily asking him how long was left. Surely it was bloody well over. Hilditch merely shook his head and said 'not over yet'.

He was right there. Giggs took the corner. It was headed clear off Bruce's head. The ball ricocheted back out to the Welshman. His cross, however, was too long, sailing over the heads of defence and attack alike. But the centre- back Gary Pallister, up for the corner, galloped after it, stopping it going out for a throw-in. He crossed it back in. Nigel Worthington, the nearest Wednesday defender, managed to get his head to the ball. But his clearance was not clean. He merely added a bit of height and distance to the cross, sending the ball spinning and fizzing into the middle of the area. It arrived where Bruce, Cantona and McClair were gathered in a tight group, marked by three Wednesday defenders. Bruce reacted first. With his feet on the ground giving extra purchase, he met the ball with real dispatch, heading it firmly into the top-right corner.

The goal had been timed as arriving in the sixth minute of added time. And its significance was immediately apparent. As Bruce ran joyfully towards the Stretford End, Ferguson engaged in a stamping jig of triumph and relief on the touchline. 'Alex Ferguson cannot contain himself. And that's totally understandable. What a phenomenal finish,' yelled Martin Tyler in the Sky commentary box.

The manager, though, turned out to be restrained in his celebration compared to his assistant. In the days before the technical area proscribed such movement, Brian Kidd dashed past Ferguson out onto the pitch. With his tracksuit riding up his back, Kidd went down on his knees, as if in thankful acknowledgement of the assistance of the footballing gods. Kidd, who had won the European Cup with United in 1968, perfectly articulated the fans' sense of relief mixed with disbelief. Well he would do. He was a United fan himself.

A brief history of Fergie Time

'There's still a bit to be done,' continued Barry Davies. 'Ferguson and Kidd are almost celebrating the championship. This could be the decisive point. At Easter last year it went away. At Easter this, Manchester United may have made the final move to end their search.' Then he added: 'Now they want the whistle blown, of course.'

And when it did sound the facts were simple: United had won in the sixth of seven minutes of added time. It was the first recorded instance of the narrow window of last-gasp opportunity that would soon come to be known throughout English football as 'Fergie Time'. On so many occasions subsequently did United come to find rescue or victory in added time that a theory developed that posits extra minutes are added when they most need them. This strange distorting of the space-time continuum is prompted by Ferguson's insistent dumb show on the touchline, pointing vigorously at his watch.

On this occasion, Ferguson was insistent that the proper amount had not been added. In his autobiography he gives insight into his own obsession when he reveals that he went home after the game and watched it all through again on tape, with his stopwatch running, and concluded that seven minutes was actually a miserly addition. 'It should have been twelve' was his verdict.

In 2012 the sports-data organization Opta conducted a survey of added time and concluded that the top teams in the Premier League really do gain advantage. The company's statistician Duncan Alexander found that more time is added when United are losing than when they are winning. Though that truth has not, over the years, diminished Ferguson in his vigilance. After a match against Tottenham in 2012, which United lost, he was furious about the add-on. 'They only gave us four minutes of injury time,' he fumed. 'That's an insult to the game.'

But it was not the arrival of Fergie Time that was so significant about the result on Easter Saturday 1993. It was the fact that on this occasion United had not wilted, had not fallen at the last. A year on from the stumble in the dash with Leeds they had found new reserves of resolve. Against a team as impressive as Wednesday they did not buckle. It was the first demonstration of an attitude which became fundamental to Ferguson's winning sides: they delivered. 'That team had such mental toughness. Real tough bastards,' Ferguson wrote of his first championship side in his autobiography.

As the season reached its climax, United, with belief coursing through their veins, skipped to the title. In the end, they were so buoyed by this win over Wednesday, they took it by ten points over Villa, with Norwich in third. At the celebratory final home game against Blackburn, the symbolism was everywhere. In the stands, Sir Matt Busby, the last man to manage the club to the title, watched dewy-eyed as the new trophy was lifted by Robson and Bruce. In the club mythology, the two eras were artfully conflated, as if Ferguson had been Busby's immediate successor, and the twenty-six years and five other managers that separated their successes had never intervened.

Although Rick Parry, the chief executive, was careful not to suggest such a thing, for the fledgling Premier League it was the ideal result. United's renown propelled news of the competition way beyond the boundaries that would have been set by a Villa victory. United's aggressive merchandising department was already rolling out the championship duvet covers and title-winning wallpaper across the country. A victorious United were the best possible cheerleaders for the new brand.

Contrasting fortunes

And what happened thereafter to the two clubs involved in that titanic Easter afternoon is in itself a tale of how the Premier League unfolded.

At the time, there was not much to choose between them in terms of scale. Hillsborough could hold almost as many fans as Old Trafford, the pair's history and potential were almost on a par, average home attendances that season were almost the same: United's was 33,898, Wednesday's 27,268. In 1993, at £25 million United's turnover – made up of £3.8 million television revenue, £10.7 million from gate receipts and £10.7 million from commercial and merchandise sales – was no more than twice as much as Wednesday's. The two competed if not as equals then pretty close.

For United, from there the only way was up. As trophies and titles kept on coming, so the stadium grew, more fans came to worship, a financial explosion took place. A fixture at the top of the Premier League, a regular in the Champions League, they learned how to exploit their market. A benevolent circle of development, investment and growth started rolling almost from the moment Bruce headed home that winner. As the Premier League expanded, United acted as ambassador to the brand, with mutually beneficial results. By 2013, their commercial headquarters – located not in Manchester but in Mayfair – employed seventy people pushing the club to corporate sponsors across the globe.

For Wednesday it was not quite like that. After losing both cup finals to Arsenal in 1993, Francis consolidated the following season. But in 1995, the impressive Devonian was sacked as manager after finishing thirteenth in the Premier League. If that was considered a failure, the club was never to achieve such heights of failure again.

By 2000 they were relegated to the Football League First Division. Worse was to follow. In 2003 they went down again. For the next few years this most proud of Yorkshire sporting institutions oscillated between the second and third tiers. And as Old Trafford grew and modernized, Hillsborough remained in a time warp. With no investment, it crumbled and faded. With such a premises to call home, commercial activity was threadbare, income enfeebled.

In 2010, the club faced a series of winding-up orders, driven by the Inland Revenue who were owed £600,000 in unpaid PAYE.

The Co-operative Bank, meanwhile, was agitating for a return of an overdraft of more than £21 million. Five years after the Glazer family bought United for £800 million (albeit most of it borrowed), in December 2010 the Serbian-American tycoon Milan Mandarić took control of Wednesday for just £1. The club was worth no more than a coin chucked in a beggar's cup. While they may not have joined the thirteen clubs that have sunk into administration following relegation from the Premier League over the past twenty years, Wednesday have come perilously close. As United's profits are pushed ever further northwards, the last published accounts reveal that in 2011 Wednesday had an operating loss of nearly £7 million.

Remember how close the two were in 1993? Twenty years of widening divide has spun the pair into completely different financial orbits. There were only 6,000 more regular paying customers at Old Trafford than Hillsborough in 1993. In 2012 the average attendance at Wednesday's home matches was 19,804. At United's it was 75,387. The weekly attendance gap has grown more than eightfold.

Meanwhile, United's turnover had accelerated to over £320 million in 2012. That same financial year, Wednesday's had actually declined from its 1993 figure to £9.4 million. From twice the size, United's income had grown across twenty years of Premier League stability to more than thirty-four times as great as Wednesday's. In football, as in the rest of British society, the decades around the turn of the century have been characterized by this presiding economic truth: while the rich get ever richer, the poor get left behind.

And all that stemmed from six minutes, the six minutes that re-booted Manchester United's first Premiership season. Without question, the most valuable six minutes in recorded football time.

Twenty years after the event, as Ferguson pursued yet another title, Francis was no longer employed on the touchline. After suffering a heart attack in April 2012, his principal involvement in the game is the occasional bit of punditry for Al Jazeera television. He was on duty at Reading for their Premier League fixture against Newcastle in the autumn of 2012 when I asked him what he remembered of that

Easter encounter and the six minutes that changed so much of the footballing landscape. 'Well what I know is this,' he said. 'If Fergie had got his way, we'd still be playing now.'

● ● ● ● ●

FA CARLING PREMIERSHIP
Old Trafford, Manchester

Saturday 10 April 1993

MANCHESTER UNITED   2 – 1   SHEFFIELD WEDNESDAY

United scorer: Steve Bruce 86, 90+6

Wednesday scorer: John Sheridan 65 (pen)

Attendance: 40,102

Referee: Mike Peck (John Hilditch 60)

TEAMS:

MANCHESTER UNITED (4-4-2)

Peter Schmeichel; Paul Parker (Bryan Robson 68), Steve Bruce, Gary Pallister, Denis Irwin; Ryan Giggs, Brian McClair, Paul Ince, Lee Sharpe;

Eric Cantona, Mark Hughes

Subs not used: Les Sealey (gk), Mike Phelan

SHEFFIELD WEDNESDAY (4-4-2)

Chris Woods; Viv Anderson, Roland Nilsson, Carlton Palmer, Nigel Worthington; Gordon Watson, John Sheridan, Andy King, Danny Wilson (Chris Bart-Williams 60); Chris Waddle, Nigel Jemson (Mark Bright 53)

Sub not used: Kevin Pressman (gk)

Match 2

If I want to kick a fan I do it

CRYSTAL PALACE V. MANCHESTER UNITED

Selhurst Park, London

Wednesday 25 January 1995

At half-time during Crystal Palace's game with Manchester United there were not many in Selhurst Park who could have thought they were about to witness one of the seminal events in the two-decade-long history of the Premier League. Actually, if pushed, few would be able to recall much of what they had just seen. On a dull, nondescript winter's evening, in a dull, nondescript atmosphere, the crowd had been served up forty-five minutes of dull, nondescript football. No goals, no chances, nothing. Or, as United's Ryan Giggs was to summarize it later: 'Horrible pitch, horrible game, horrible night.'

Manchester United had enjoyed themselves mightily in the first couple of seasons of Carling Premiership competition. Alex Ferguson may still have been checking his watch to ensure no one was stealing their time, but his team were successfully re-establishing themselves as the country's pre-eminent football outfit. In January 1995, they were in pursuit of a third successive title, chasing it with brio and panache, changing public perception of the competition as they went.

Yet, as a commercial for football's sexy new entertainment revolution, this match should have been referred to the Advertising Standards Authority. Although the numbers who would subsequently claim to be there would swell over the years to at least twice the official gate, given the choice, there were not many among the 18,224 people who had traipsed through the South London chill to watch this farrago of mediocrity who would not have happily headed home at half-time.

Indeed, for this spectator, it was not anything that had occurred on the pitch but an incident during the interval that looked likely to be the only thing to lodge itself in the mind. Sent by my mate to fetch the teas, I had stood in a growing crush at the refreshment stall under Selhurst's Arthur Wait Stand as a United fan had politely ordered burgers and hot dogs by the dozen from the young attendant. As they arrived, the goods were passed back over the pressing crowd to his mates. After about five minutes of solid ordering – beers, cokes, crisps, every item on the menu – he pointed to a bag of sweets on a high shelf at the back of the stall and asked the young woman if she would mind getting him some of those. As she turned to reach them, he quickly barged his way out of the throng and, with his now-refreshed mates, bundled off down the corridor. When she turned back to hand over the sweets and to ask him for the sixty-odd quid he had totted up, he was long gone, his sly runner executed to perfection. As she stood there, her mouth agape but no words emerging, she looked so crestfallen, so humiliated, one of the other United fans queuing up took pity on her and offered to cover her losses. She didn't hear him. She just spread her arms in exasperation and sighed. A look that mixed hurt at the injustice of the situation with annoyance at her own gullibility spread across her features. It was not the last time we were to witness such a look that evening.

A disappointing debut

They might have come by their supplies in underhand fashion, but you could understand why those scamsters felt the need for sustenance, if only to take their minds off forty-five minutes of football that for the United fans had been particularly dispiriting. The Carling Premiership was supposed to deliver something better than this. A whole new ball game? The footballing fare on offer here should have been more nourishing, should have tasted better than this. What had most disappointed those United fans not trying to plunder the stock at half-time was that this represented the first opportunity many had had to see Andy Cole in action for United since his signing from Newcastle a fortnight earlier. And they weren't entirely thrilled with what they had witnessed.

The electric-heeled twenty-two-year-old had been a central part of manager Kevin Keegan's emerging side at St James's Park, his goals lifting Newcastle from the First Division into the top flight, where his partnership with the clever Peter Beardsley had solidified their progress. The previous season, the Magpies' first in the Carling Premiership, he had scored an astonishing thirty-four times. Alex Ferguson, who had toyed with the idea of bringing in Stan Collymore from Nottingham Forest as a long-term replacement for the ageing 1980s stalwart Mark Hughes, had surprised everyone by instead snaffling Cole for £6 million plus the £1-million-rated Keith Gillespie, a then-record fee between British clubs. Though perhaps no one was quite as surprised as the Geordie fan who had learned of the transfer as he left a Tyneside tattoo parlour, where he had just spent five hours having an image of Cole in a Newcastle shirt permanently applied to his thigh.

The man with the redundant tattoo was probably among the angry collection of Newcastle fans who gathered at St James's Park on the day the sale was announced to voice their unhappiness at the departure. To his credit, Keegan had stood at the top of the steps leading up to the ground's main entrance to debate with the stroppy bunch. 'Newcastle are not a selling club,' one man shouted. 'So what we doing selling our best player?' Keegan was adamant that he had got the better part of the deal: £6 million plus Gillespie, he said, represented the shrewdest of business for the club. Particularly as he was convinced that United's young Irish winger would turn out to be the best of the batch of 1992 FA Youth Cup-winning protégés whose first-team forays at Old Trafford had so far been largely limited to the odd League Cup appearance. He sensed, what's more, that Cole was a player in decline, that Newcastle had seen the best of him, that the pace which was the source of his goal-scoring prowess was less frequently in evidence. He thought he had pulled off a coup. As things would later turn out, he was to be proven wrong on every count.

Another way of looking at it was that the forward's signing made it clear that Ferguson was a disciple of the management school that had flourished in the Anfield boot room during the previous decade. The first principle of the Liverpool dynasty was always this: buy in a position of strength; better still, as you solidify your own squad, try to undermine that of your rivals. Cole's purchase did that all right.

But whatever the long-term implications of the transfer, the evidence of the first half at Selhurst Park suggested that the Nottingham-born centre-forward was not going to settle quickly into the United attack. He and Eric Cantona, the wellspring of all United creativity, did not seem to have forged much of a bond. In those forty-five minutes the pair had not exchanged a glance, never mind a pass. A suspicion was forming in the minds of some United followers that Keegan might have been right in his assertions.

Stifling United's stars

And that sense of unease didn't just focus on Cole, either. No one else in United's sleek black away shirt was seeing the benefit of Cantona's imagination that night: he had barely had a decent kick of the ball. And with the Frenchman misfiring, United's spark was noticeably absent. They had looked soggy and uninspired against a team they might have thought was there for the taking. As it happened, there was a reason for their sluggish indisposition that went beyond the pitch's pockmarked surface. Destructive as it may have appeared, Palace manager Alan Smith's team selection had played United perfectly. Their full-backs had pushed back the visitors' wingers; organized by Gareth Southgate, their midfield had smothered any hint of invention; while their forwards – Iain Dowie in particular – had worked stoically to close down United's defenders when they had possession. And more to the point, their centre-back Richard Shaw had followed Smith's instructions to the letter in his shackling of Cantona. Shaw had followed him everywhere, never leaving an inch of space, tugging at his opponent's number seven shirt, breathing down his upturned collar. He was like a footballing stalker, always there, always on his case. Much to Cantona's chagrin, the referee Alan Wilkie had not noted any transgression in Shaw's work, leaving him free to go about his business untroubled by official sanction.

And the wind-up was working to perfection. Cantona had risen to the bait. Far from the coruscating figure he had cut for much of his United career, far from the player who had scored a delicious chipped goal in United's third-round FA Cup tie at Sheffield United ten days before, or scored the late winner against Blackburn in their previous league outing, he looked unhappy, distracted. He appealed constantly to the referee, his arms permanently spread in supplication, the injustice of it all written across his face. So much was he moaning, Wilkie quickly tired of his complaining. It was not a night, in short, in which Cantona's ability to win football matches was being exhibited. Which disappointed Paolo Taveggia, the general manager of Internazionale, who was a guest in Selhurst's directors' box, his purpose specifically to see Cantona in action. He had called United three days earlier to talk about the player's availability for transfer. Martin Edwards, the club chairman, had rebuffed him. But he had turned up at Selhurst in any case to see what the Frenchman might do.

Taveggia's presence was evidence that, just three short years after the Premier League had first come into being, clubs in other leagues elsewhere were beginning to covet its international array of talent. However much the football at Selhurst might suggest otherwise, the Premier League was establishing itself as the shop-window for the world's best. Though after that first half, it was likely the Inter cheque book would remain firmly in their man's pocket.

Watching from the dug-out, Ferguson quickly read the pattern of the game. He could see what was unfolding. He knew his lynchpin was stumbling headlong into the trap set by Smith and Shaw. Instead of concentrating on providing passes for Cole, instead of spraying the ball out to Giggs and Lee Sharpe on the wings, Cantona had become preoccupied with the Palace man, moaning, moaning, moaning about his close proximity.

So, even as the Arthur Wait snack bar was being pillaged at half-time, Ferguson went to work in the visitors' dressing room. He pointed out that Cantona needed to get his head right, get his purpose back into focus. Sure, the ref might not be protecting him. Yes, Shaw was getting far too up close and personal. There was no argument the Palace man should have been booked for a couple of his meatier challenges. But the best way to counter that was to score a couple of goals. Getting sidetracked by the referee's refusal to protect him would ultimately only prove counterproductive. And whatever he was to do, Ferguson told Cantona as the team made their way back to the pitch for the second half, he should not under any circumstances attempt to mete out justice on his own. With a busy few weeks ahead, with the FA Cup now underway, the last thing the team needed was their creative hub getting sent off and suspended. He was no good to them watching from the stands. 'Is that understood?' Ferguson asked. The Frenchman did not reply.

Ferguson knew what he was talking about. Cantona's fuse – short and liable to ignite at the merest spark of perceived wrong – had already seen him dismissed on four occasions in his two and a bit years at United. No one else – not even the spiky Irishman Roy Keane – could match that record. The manager loved what Cantona had brought to his team – the certainty, the sure-footedness, the sparkle. Not to mention the trophies. But he also knew that his talisman possessed a heightened sensitivity to injustice which often led to a combustible reaction. He was aware that temper had defined the player's earlier career in France where he had constantly grated against authority. He knew the fire in Cantona's belly needed careful husbanding. He hoped, as he made his way back to the dug-out, that he had said enough to direct the spark in a positive direction. That was what good management entailed: identifying future problems and acting quickly to forestall them.

But as the second half began, it was soon apparent that Ferguson's wise words had gone unheeded. The pattern had not changed. Palace's work rate was still restricting United's space. Still

Cole was isolated and under-used. And still Shaw was invading Cantona's personal space.

Eric explodes

It was in the fifty-sixth minute, as the manager was on his feet directing his midfielders to play the ball out wide to Giggs, that his worst fears were realized. The ball was played back to Peter Schmeichel who, under pressure from Dowie, was obliged to launch it long and high forward into the Palace half. Cantona gave chase, running from the halfway line as the ball arced over his head. Shaw, inevitably, was by his side. This time the Frenchman's temper ignited at his proximity. As the pair ran, Cantona flicked a sly kick which connected with his marker's shin. Shaw went down, the linesman, his sight-line clear, waved his flag and the Palace fans in the Main Stand at last had something to shout about. Twenty yards behind the action, referee Wilkie did not hesitate. As he arrived at the scene of the crime, with centre-back Chris Coleman confronting Cantona, he pulled the red card from his pocket. The laws of the game dictated that he had no other choice. In case Cantona did not get the message, he pointed towards the tunnel which, in those days at Selhurst Park, was not in the middle of the Main Stand, but in the corner, where it abutted the Whitehorse Lane Stand.

'There's the morning headline,' said the television commentator Clive Tyldesley, who was in the midst of a brief period working for the BBC, the rights holders for Carling Premiership highlights. He wasn't wrong. Cantona's sending-off was to generate rather more than just a headline, however. Indeed, footage of the dramatic events that unfolded following the Frenchman's dismissal would come perhaps second only to Geoff Hurst's fourth goal at Wembley in 1966 as the most oft-repeated moment in English football history.

The sending-off itself was pretty routine. It was the fifth time Cantona had been dismissed for United, the third while wearing their black away shirt. Against the Turkish side Galatasaray in November 1993 and Arsenal in March 1994 he might have been justified in feeling he had been wrongly punished. Against Swindon, also in the spring of 1994, when he had stamped on John Moncur, and against Rangers in a pre-season friendly in August 1994, when he had received a second yellow for a ripe challenge, he could have little cause for complaint. This time too, he was the agent of his own misfortune. The most red-eyed United apologist would be hard-pressed to argue he had been wronged.

Still, he gave the impression of being utterly dumbfounded by Wilkie's decision. As furore erupted around him, as Cole and Denis Irwin made their opinion known to the referee, as the Palace players tapped their temples and told each other to keep focused, he stood in the middle of the pitch, his chest out, his collar up, turning round in slow circles looking into the crowd, as if seeking a second opinion somewhere in the stands. He was wearing a look on his face of bewilderment and injured pride. With just the slightest hint of sheepishness at his own stupidity. Just like the woman in the re-freshment stall, his expression betrayed his feelings, the fact he knew he should never have allowed himself to become the victim of such malicious injustice.

Ferguson did not share his striker's sense of wounded innocence. He was furious that Cantona had been so easily tricked. He had warned him of the trap Palace had set and here he was only going and falling for it. The manager could not believe that his star player had done what he specifically instructed him not to. And now, with vital points to be earned, he was obliged to see out over half an hour of a tough, uncompromising game with only ten men on the pitch. Cantona was not merely being reckless and impetuous. He was, the manager felt at that moment, being unprofessional.

It was no surprise, then, as Cantona approached him, shaking his head ruefully, that Ferguson offered no show of consolation. His hands thrust deep in the pockets of his track coat, the manager said not a word, gave not a glance. He stared straight past the departing striker as he walked forlornly towards the technical area. The message was obvious: you have let me down. The only person on the United bench who acknowledged the Frenchman's existence was the club's kit man Norman Davies. Realizing that Cantona still had to walk half the length of the stand occupied by home fans and that the reaction was likely to be hostile (he had just kicked one of their favourites, after all), Davies sprang from the bench and told Ferguson he would chaperone the player to the dressing room.

We spectators in the Arthur Wait Stand on the opposite side of the pitch had an unobstructed view of what happened next. As was always the case when Cantona played, the eye was inevitably drawn to him as he began his walk of shame. There was no point looking at the Palace players up the other end of the pitch as they gathered round the resulting free kick. No reason to be diverted by Ferguson semaphoring to the remaining United contingent how they should now line up. Looking at what Paul Ince or Brian McClair were up to could wait. You just knew that to take your eyes off Cantona was to risk missing the main event.

From football to martial arts

And so it proved. As Cantona was passing the Palace family section, no more than fifteen yards beyond the dug-out, a twenty-year-old glazier called Matthew Simmons, a Palace regular, ran down the steps to the front of the stand, shouting at the player. Later he was to claim that what he said was no more provocative than 'it's an early bath for you, Mr Cantona'. Witnesses in the immediate vicinity recall his language was somewhat more direct, and that he deployed a vocabulary suggesting he might have got a job as John Terry's voice coach in later life. It was widely agreed that what Simmons in fact yelled was: 'Fuck you, you French bastard, fuck off back to France, you motherfucker.'

Offensive and inflammatory, for sure. But it was not unusual for footballers to be thus addressed. Every week the baying from opposition supporters was full of the personal and the insulting. Venom was as plentiful as it was spiteful. And the sound and fury was growing within the Premiership. As players' salaries began to rocket with the injection of television money, the gap between the fan and his representatives on the pitch was growing. And with that disconnect came an assumption that the admission price bought the right to issue the kind of vituperation that would be considered way beyond the pale in any other walk of life. Simmons assumed he was entirely within his rights to yell his opinion. And he did so without fear of consequence, wearing a broad grin.

As Cantona admitted when I interviewed him a dozen years after the event, he was not particularly surprised by what was shouted:

> Provocation we always had. Millions of times people say these things, and then one day you don't accept it. Why? It's not about words. It's about how you feel at that moment. One day you react, but the words are exactly the same as those you have heard a million times, so it is impossible to say why you react.

Impossible to say why, maybe. Impossible to know how he felt, perhaps. But react he certainly did. Cantona broke free from Davies, who, having heard what was shouted, had put a protective arm around his shoulder. He advanced towards Simmons and, employing the violent street-fighting methods he had learned as a kid in Marseilles, leapt the barrier between stand and pitch, feet forward in a perfectly executed martial-arts kick, to plant both sets of studs firmly in Simmons's chest. Then, after falling back onto the pitch side, he quickly picked himself up and threw a sharp right-hander at the gobby malcontent's leather-jacketed back.

At that point, the evening changed from one with little to stir the memory into one whose resonance extended way beyond mere football, one that would invite endless comment, one that would provoke questions in the House of Commons. As Andrew Cole recalls: 'I caught it out the corner of my eye. I thought, "What the fuck is going on here?"'

The referee Wilkie, who had been talking to several of the Palace players about how the game should be restarted and had no idea what was going on in the stand, suddenly noticed he was alone. 'Where's everyone gone? I thought,' he remembers. 'Then I realized where they went. And I thought: oh no, something has really gone off this time.'

Everyone on the pitch had dashed towards the noisy source of the fracas; the stewards and police jumped into the fray, as Schmeichel and Ince and several other United players tried to pile into the crowd, believing that what had happened was a fan attack, rather than a player assault. Up in the commentary gantry, Clive Tyldesley summed up the confusion:

> What's going on here? Cantona's getting involved with some sup-
> porters. Oh this is outrageous. It's all got wildly out of hand. And
> once more Eric Cantona is at the centre of a dramatic controversy.

That's what you might call an understatement. In the Arthur Wait Stand the analysis was somewhat more robust. 'Oh fuck,' said the man by now standing up in front of me as we all watched the sudden explosion of violence on the other side of the pitch. There really wasn't a lot more you could say.

It was not the first – or last – occasion that a sportsman had attacked a paying customer. In 1979, several members of the Boston Bruins ice-hockey team left the ice at Madison Square Gardens to scale the ten-foot glass barriers and engage in running battles with fans of the New York Rangers. And in 2004 the Indiana Pacers basketball player Ron Artest (who later, in a burst of contrition, changed his name to Metta World Peace) punched at least half a dozen Detroit Pistons fans during a mass scrap in Auburn Hills Michigan. It was not even the first time a Manchester United player had done it: after a match at Luton Town in 1960, Harry Gregg, the hero of the Munich aircrash, who had pulled a stricken air hostess from the burning plane in February 1958, had a brusque altercation with a lippy fan which was barely noticed at the time.

All publicity is good publicity

But this was different. Unlike when Gregg went walkabout, this time, as the invisible wall between player and spectator was broken, there were cameras to record the moment. That made it news. And those pictures, as they were repeated time and again in intimate slo-mo, were undeniably exciting, a study in unrestrained violence that produced the same kind of visceral response as attending a boxing match.

Cantona's assault became a story that engulfed the British media for days, migrating from the back pages to the front, filling broadcast time, jamming up the airwaves via that newly invented barometer of public opinion, the football phone-in. Already the most famous footballer in the British game, with that kick Cantona transformed himself to another level. He immediately became the most infamous.

Yet, notorious as his action was, in many ways this was the incident that made the Premier League, sealing it in the wider consciousness. Whether you love it or hate it, whether you regard football as a gift from the Almighty or evidence that civilization is going to hell in a handcart, this was the League's graduation moment.

And its paymasters seized on the opportunity. Rupert Murdoch's newspaper executives saw in the Cantona kick the perfect vehicle to promote the product being sold by his television division. They were not the game's moral defenders, they were pushing subscriptions to his satellite channel, so why worry if the image of player slugging it out with fan was not exactly wholesome? Especially when they had such brilliant pictures. That it showed the game's dark side made the incident so much more potent. This gave the Carling Premiership edge, spice, vibrancy. Sales of subscriptions the next week were the highest so far in Sky's short history. This was marketing gold dust. And Murdoch's newspapers went to town.

Besides, every drama needs a bad guy. And Cantona – playing for the club which had come to be loathed by followers of every other team in the country – came ready-made from central casting as the most charismatic of pantomime villains. Thus it was that in the week following the Palace brawl, Clive Tyldesley and the rest of the country could not avoid the headlines. *The Sun* in particular went to town on the story. On the Friday morning, its front page carried the headline 'I'll Never Forget His Evil Eyes' above an eyewitness account from a woman who was standing next to Simmons as the assault occurred. Below it was a panel: 'The Shame of Cantona: Full story pages 2, 3, 4, 5, 6, 22, 43, 44, 45, 46, 47 & 48.' Later that month, Simmons's story would be bought up, in what the journalist Ian Ridley called the first example of a tabloid 'kick and tell'.

The Sun's rivals, though less intent on driving television subscriptions, followed suit: the market demanded no less. The image of Cantona leaping, his name across the shoulders of his black shirt, printed out in gold letters, was on every front page, including those of the broadsheets. It was on the inside pages too, illustrating opinion pieces which speculated on what the episode told us about ourselves.

Looking at that shot, taken by a photographer gifted an unobstructed view across the field from the front of the Arthur Wait Stand, you can't help noticing the faces of the crowd standing round Simmons: they were open-mouthed in astonishment. The satirical magazine *When Saturday Comes* neatly summed it all up with their headline above the picture which read: 'The Shit Hits The Fan.'

For the next few days, as the story continued to dominate the headlines, a wide range of pundits gave their views. The kick polarized opinion. In *The Guardian*, Roy Hattersley, the former shadow home secretary, called it the most appalling thing ever to have happened at a British football ground (a piece of silly hyperbole which those who witnessed the 1971 Ibrox disaster, the 1985 Bradford City stadium fire or the 1989 Hillsborough tragedy could readily have challenged). Trevor Brooking, the epitome of the gentleman footballer, gave the slightly more qualified view that it was 'the most horrendous incident involving a player I have ever witnessed at an English football ground'. Brian Clough issued his sober verdict that Cantona should be castrated. 'I think there's something wrong with the man,' he added.

Yet as the moral opprobrium rained down on Cantona's head, accusing him of failing to fulfil his responsibilities as a role model and public figure, there were plenty who saw it differently. Jimmy Greaves wrote this in his newspaper column:

We've heard a lot about Cantona's responsibilities. What about analysing the responsibility of Simmons and every foul-mouthed yob who thinks his £10 admission gives him the right to say what he likes to a man… to abuse, taunt, spit and behave in a way that would get you locked up if you repeated it in the high street?

The fact that the piece appeared in *The Sun* was no surprise: the publishers had a financial motive in keeping the debate alive. All their columnists were instructed to write what they liked as often as they wished. As long as it was about Cantona there was no party line to peddle. Any view that generated heat about the issue was welcome. The man himself, incidentally, later told me what he thought of the idea that he should behave like a role model.

I didn't want to say to myself I am an example. I am not an example. I never felt more important than the people you can meet in the street. Maybe if we analyse it, journalists don't understand the reaction and so they just say, he shouldn't do that. He is a bad man. But journalists are the ones who make players think they are more important than the other ones. We are not.

He had a sympathetic supporter in Danny Baker, the maverick presenter of the BBC Radio Five football phone-in *606*, who asked this rather pertinent question: 'Why the moral outrage? Most football fans just found it incredibly funny.'

One thing was certain, however: Alex Ferguson did not find it remotely amusing. Looking towards the pitch, keeping his gaze deliberately away from his departing player, at the time he did not see what had happened as Cantona left the field. Only Schmeichel, alone at the far end of the pitch, got a good view. And even he, as he rushed across to lead Cantona away to the tunnel after the kick had been executed, assumed that his colleague was the victim not the perpetrator. 'All I saw was Eric in trouble,' Schmeichel recalls. 'We were a team. We were all in it together, whatever. So I went over to pull him away. It wasn't until I saw the pictures later that I realized what had happened.'

The crowd, though, knew immediately what had gone on. 'You dirty northern bastards,' they chanted, as Schmeichel gesticulated in their direction on his return from the tunnel. In the visitors' dressing room after the game, the atmosphere was heavy with anticipated recrimination. As the player himself sat shamefaced, silent, by now showered and dressed in his club blazer in the corner, his colleagues waited for the manager to complete his press duties and address them. They knew an explosion was imminent. It soon came. Ferguson himself later suggested it was the only time in their relationship that he lost his temper with Cantona. Lee Sharpe remembers it slightly differently. He has worked the incident up into an after-dinner comedy routine he still uses some seventeen years on.

'The gaffer comes in and is fuming' is Sharpe's recollection. 'He screams at David May and Gary Pallister "you effin this, you effin that". He turns to me and Giggsy "you effin pair of useless c...s what the eff were you doing out there?" Then he sees Cantona and he unleashes both barrels at him, really gives him what for: "Eric old son do you think maybe, on second thoughts, that wasn't such a good idea?"'

Dealing with the fallout

It was not until Ferguson returned home after a long, brooding coach trip that he became fully aware of what had happened. Arriving in Macclesfield in the early hours, he was confronted by his son Jason, who asked him if he realized the significance of it all. He was so shocked when he saw the footage Jason had recorded he immediately knew this was the most serious breach of discipline he had experienced in his entire career. The next morning, he met with Edwards and Maurice Watkins, United's legal adviser, and mapped out a response. In the immediate aftermath of the assault, Edwards had told David Davies, the FA's director of communications, that Cantona would be dismissed from the club's employment. But sleeping on the issue overnight, the United chairman modified his stance. The club would suspend him for the rest of the season and fine him £20,000. However important the player might be to the team, the image of Manchester United had to be protected. They hoped this would be sufficiently draconian a punishment to minimize the fallout. Certainly, they believed it would pre-empt an FA ban. They thought they were applying a full stop, wishing that attention might now turn to United's next game, an FA Cup tie that Saturday at home to Wrexham. Some hope.

Within hours, the incident had developed a life of its own, a runaway story that brooked no attempt to control it. For the media, Cantona was, as Ferguson once put it, like Christmas every day, a gift to write about. Loathed or loved, admired or reviled, he made people buy papers and brought listeners to the radio. More to the point, he sold television subscriptions. And with both the police and the FA involved, twists in the plot soon followed, to keep the story bubbling. First, on 24 February, at Sopwell House Hotel in Hertfordshire, Cantona was obliged to face an FA disciplinary committee.

The Premier League might have been the organizing body of the new system in England, but it had no remit to maintain discipline in the game. That remained with the FA, ostensibly the organizing authority of the League. And the governing body had made its attitude towards Cantona clear from the outset. The morning after his assault, the FA general secretary Graham Kelly had not held back.

'What happened last night was a stain on our game,' he said. 'The FA believes last night's incident was unprecedented in our game. It brought shame on those involved and worst of all on the game itself. We especially deplore the appalling example set to young supporters who are the game's future. It is our intention to do everything in our power to prevent such a disgraceful event ever happening again.'

But if Kelly and his colleagues wanted the hearing to reinforce the dignity of their game they were to be disappointed. Cantona, who had shown in his early days in France that he had little time for authority, turned up at the hotel with Maurice Watkins not expecting much sympathy. And he demonstrated little respect for the hearing. Asked if he had anything to say, Cantona said he wanted to apologize.

61

And off he went, giving a long, meandering list of those to whom he wished to say sorry. It stretched from Manchester United, through his manager, team-mates and the referee, to all the kids in England, to everyone he had ever met. He concluded by saying: 'And I want to apologize to the prostitute who shared my bed last night.'

One of the three FA blazers sitting in judgment did not catch precisely Cantona's words. 'What did he say?' Gordon McKeag said to Geoff Thompson, another panel member. 'He wants to prostrate himself to the FA?' Kelly, who had heard exactly what had been said, decided it was best not to elucidate. Davies recalls being astonished at the faux apology: 'Eric was taking the mick,' he says. 'I looked at Maurice and neither of us could believe what we'd just heard.'

The board then left to consider its judgment. The trio quickly returned to announce to Cantona that his ban would be extended to eight months, up to and including 30 September. And the ban was to be draconian. United had assumed he could play in reserve matches. The FA said no, the ban was worldwide and total. He could not be seen kicking a football until the end of September. Though that was not the final act of the hearing. Ian Stott, the third member of the disciplinary council, was so star-struck by the now renowned celebrity in front of him that at the end of proceedings he asked for Cantona's autograph. Thompson told him – in no uncertain terms – that he couldn't have it.

A Marmite player

The stringent nature of their disciplinary decision – the longest ban in English football in thirty years since Tony Kay and Peter Swan were banned for life for a betting scam in 1964 – further fuelled the tale. The immediate assumption was that the ban would draw a line under Cantona's career in England. In *The Sun*, columnist John Sadler wrote: 'we have seen the best of him, now's the time to see the back of him.' The received wisdom was that he would be sold to Inter and would play in Italy when his ban finished. He was, so almost everyone agreed, finished in England.

Such second-guessing was required because we had heard nothing from the drama's principal character. The FA hearing had taken place behind closed doors and Cantona had remained publicly aloof from comment. Nobody had an inkling about what he thought or why he had done it. That did not stop the speculation. The thing about Cantona's silence was that it allowed theories of all kinds to flourish like weeds after rain: it was a void that was to be filled with all manner of assumptions.

Mostly what people thought was this: Cantona was different. And in a sense he defined the different new football of the Carling Premiership. From the pariah game of the 1980s, football was finding a newer, wider, more affluent audience. While the burst of popularizing would reach its zenith the year after Selhurst at Euro 96, Cantona was the first to offer incontestible proof that the game was no longer a pursuit solely of the bone-headed. Though he had up to that point refused all requests to be interviewed, the Frenchman was assumed to be an intellectual. He read poetry and philosophy, he painted, he liked to listen to jazz, his rare public statements – most of them scripted by his commercial backers Nike – were enigmatic; he had once been spotted on a hotel balcony in Istanbul playing backgammon with Schmeichel. This was a footballer with a brain, with a cultural hinterland. Plus, he was French, which in a country historically infused with a collective sense of inferiority about anything drifting from over the Channel, lent him added mystique.

For the middle-class arriviste watching from the stands or more likely from the armchair, he was manna from footballing heaven, proof that the game was worth watching. He was the poster boy of the new Carling Premiership. Nike cunningly played up to the image of lofty intellectualism. He starred in a series of commercials that toyed ironically with the game's traditional iconography. '1966 was a great year for English football,' read one, over a typically enigmatic picture of the man, collar up as always. 'Eric was born.'

Also, he could play a bit. But while United fans loved him for his goals, they also enjoyed the fact that, in the absence of anything much known about him, they could mould him into an image that was a perfect reflection of how they saw themselves and their club: lofty, superior, different. Tony Wilson, the late music entrepreneur who was a lifelong United fan, once said of him: 'The deification of Cantona was a fiercely Mancunian thing. Nobody played like him and nobody could have worshipped him like we did. The relationship he had with us fans was unique.'

The player himself agreed about that association, that sense of shared destiny. When I spoke to him at length in 2007 he said this of the United fans who – more than fifteen years on from his departure from the club – still sing his name as often as they do that of any contemporary player:

> I don't want to explain it. It's like love. You know when you are in love, you don't need to explain how you feel or why you feel like that. I think if you want to explain what was going on between me and the United fans, it would take six months. Sometimes it's better not to explain.

Such talk did little to placate the growing body of those who loathed United, who were infuriated by the way in which its marketing reach was so all-encompassing, who hated the fact that the club had begun to suck in media attention with all the irresistibility of a black hole in space. For them Cantona became a symbol too. They saw him as being, like United, revoltingly pleased with himself; they regarded him as a fraud, a pseud, an empty vessel making an awful lot of noise.

On 31 March Cantona was due to appear at Croydon Magistrates' Court. Ince, who was subsequently cleared of charges of threatening behaviour and assault arising from his role in the Selhurst fracas, remembers that the Frenchman once again refused to be cowed by authority. 'We stayed at the Croydon Park Hotel and when we got up in the morning I'm all dolled up, got me suit and tie on,' he says. 'I knock on Eric's door and he's standing in just this white shirt, long collars, unbuttoned so you can see his chest. "Eric, you can't go to court like that", I told him and he says: "I can go as I want. I am Cantona."'

Eventually persuaded by Maurice Watkins that a tie might, after all, be advisable in the circumstances, Cantona walked from the hotel to the courthouse, flanked by United's newly appointed head of security Ned Kelly, squeezing through a sizeable contingent of mostly supportive fans. Inside he was to find the presiding authority did not take kindly to his actions. After listening to character references from United players and officials and others and after taking into account Cantona's plea of guilty to the charge of common assault, Mrs Jean Pearch, a former music teacher, mother of three, and the chairperson of Croydon Magistrates, presented her judgment. She announced he was to be sent to prison for a fortnight.

'Take him down,' she instructed, as Cantona stood in the dock. I was in the press gallery and remember the frisson of astonishment that swept round the courtroom as the sentence was passed. Everyone looked to the dock, where once more, just before he was led down to the court cells, Cantona wore that look of injured innocence. But this time he had due cause: a fortnight inside for a first offence which did not involve any damage beyond light bruising to Simmons's ego – it was unheard of. Watkins quickly lighted on this clear breach of precedent and launched an immediate appeal. Within an hour, Cantona's sentence was reduced to 120 hours of community service and another fine.

The philosopher speaks

At this point, as reporters besieged him for comment, Watkins felt a public statement was required, the first from the player since he had leaped into the national consciousness. Cantona wondered why, but the club's legal man was insistent. So he arranged for a room to be set aside at the hotel and the press filed in. As they prepared to come in and speak, Cantona asked Watkins a couple of questions about English vocabulary. 'What do you call the big boat that catches fish?' he said. And: 'what is the English for the big seabird?' Even as he told him, Watkins wondered what on Earth he was on about.

Inside the room, television cameras from networks across the globe were in position. Dozens of reporters from the sport, news and showbusiness sections of the press filled the rows of seats. When the two men entered, Watkins was the first to speak, explaining the court's new ruling and the club's acceptance of it. Then Cantona was asked if he had anything to say. He had something to say all right. He poured himself a glass of water, leaned back in his seat and uttered the words he had prepared with Watkins's unwitting assistance – words that were to become among the most notorious in footballing history: 'When seagulls follow the trawler it is because they hope sardines will be thrown into the sea.' And with that, he got up and left the room.

It seemed a pretty straightforward comment about the parasitic nature of press reporting, the way in which the media feed off titbits thrown from the celebrity's table. But that did not stop many being diverted by its cryptic phrasing and heavy French-accented delivery into absurdist levels of textual analysis. The humourists Willie Donaldson and Terence Blacker satirized such over-intellectualizing in a book, *The Meaning of Cantona: Meditations on Life, Art and Perfectly Weighted Balls*, published in 1997. That was the scale of the industry Cantona had spawned: there was even money to be made suggesting there was too much being said about him.

It wasn't, however, the words he used that really signalled Cantona's intent in that press conference. It was the fact that in mid-sentence he was obliged to take a drink of water to stop himself cracking up laughing. The truth was, he was enjoying himself enormously, relishing being at the centre of the ludicrous storm that had been whipped up around him. In short, he was on stage. He was in his element. As he later confided in me:

Yes, I played that moment. It was a drama and I was an actor. I do things seriously without taking myself seriously. I think Nike found that side of my character and used it very well. Even when I kicked the fan it is because I don't take myself seriously. I didn't think because of who I was I had a responsibility not to do it. No, I was just a footballer and a man. I don't care about being some sort of superior person. I just wanted to do whatever I wanted to do. If I want to kick a fan I do it. I am not a role model. I am not a superior teacher telling you how to behave. I think the more you see, the more you realize that life is a circus.

For the rest of that season, football's circus had lost its most marketable clown. What happened in the Premiership after that night in Selhurst is detailed in the next chapter. But for Cantona, the chance to win his fourth championship medal on the trot (he had won one with Leeds before he joined United) was over. He had blown the opportunity. More tellingly, the champions' most influential player could not exert any influence from the stands, or from United's training ground at the Cliff where he saw out his community service coaching youngsters in the indoor gym, away from the prying lenses of the paparazzi.

In his absence from the game for the rest of that season and beyond, the stories kept coming: he was off to Italy, he had stormed out of United, Ferguson had been obliged to dash across the Channel to talk him out of quitting altogether. Rumour, speculation and received wisdom became media currency. With no official statements, fans, fanzine writers and other journalists became sources. They didn't know anything, but they could guess. Newspapers printed stories about Cantona's future at United that enraged the manager and so served only to widen the communications gap.

Not that the manager himself was any the wiser about his star player's motivation. He wondered all summer why Cantona had taken a detour to the dressing room via Simmons's chest. And he's still wondering now:

Over the years since then I have never been able to elicit an explanation of the episode from Eric. But my own feeling is that anger at himself over the ordering-off and resentment of the referee's earlier inaction combined to take him over the brink.

As a summary, Ferguson's surmise was no closer to the truth than any other of our wild guesses. Cantona himself remains reluctant to rationalize what he did, leaving it to us to speculate on his motives. 'I play this game because I enjoy it,' he told me. And by 'this game', it was clear he meant his life. 'Just play, I love just playing. But then I think journalists play too sometimes. They help me say to myself that's life, that's not serious. One day it's like this, one day it's like that, one day you are God, one day the devil. It's a circus, like I said. You don't learn anything at the circus.'

From rebel to role model

After the seagulls comment, nothing more was heard from Cantona until he returned to the fray on 1 October, in a home fixture against Liverpool. His comeback was heralded in a series of commercials by Nike which mocked the idea that he might show contrition. 'I'm sorry,' ran one of the television ads. 'I'm sorry for scoring twice in the 1994 Cup Final. I apologize for only scoring once against Manchester City.' Then there was the poster displayed outside Old Trafford that day. Below a picture of Cantona in his number seven shirt was the tagline: 'He's been punished for his mistakes. Now it's somebody else's turn.' Notoriety, it seemed, only reinforced the myth.

Cantona did seem to learn one thing from that incident: self-control. When he donned the red shirt of United again in a glittering comeback that encompassed two championships and became the first foreign captain to lift the FA Cup, he did not once provoke so much as a yellow card. Instead of the simmering madness of his earlier career, he exhibited not a hint of deviation from sanity. Cool, aloof and unflustered, he acted as mentor for the young players emerging from United's academy, providing them with a model of dedication to training and effort. If David Beckham, Paul Scholes, Nicky Butt and the Neville brothers had arrived in the first-team dressing room five years earlier, their role models would have been the hard-drinking Bryan Robson, Norman Whiteside and Paul McGrath, men behaving badly. Now, their captain and the man they observed most closely was someone who spent hours on the training pitch, long after the formal sessions had ended, perfecting his craft.

'People say that Eric taught us about going the extra mile,' says Phil Neville. 'It wasn't that. We were used to working hard, we'd all done it since we were juniors. We all liked staying on. What Eric did was give us the permission to do so. We didn't look like goody-goodies or teacher's pet because he was already doing what we wanted to do. He made it OK to work hard.'

This man who claimed he was no role model unintentionally became the mother hen to the finest crop of home-grown talent to emerge in the Premier League's twenty-year history. His growing influence over the game was recognized in May 1996 when, on the eve of the FA Cup final, Cantona was voted Footballer of the Year by the very football writers who had railed against him fifteen months before. He had won over his fiercest critics. At the ceremony, he gave a short speech in which he endeared himself to the seagulls in attendance, by explaining his attitude to journalism. 'Every morning,' he said, 'I screw up the papers and flush them down the toilet.'

Of course, it couldn't last forever. The years caught up with him in the end. At the conclusion of the 1997 season, aged just thirty-one, Cantona publicly terminated his romance with Manchester United. Perhaps this most proud of men detected a diminution in his powers, a slowing of his instincts, the dulling of physical ability that inevitably comes with time. He also told me that he worried his reserves of self-control were finite, that if he played on any longer something would, eventually, make him snap. That he would go walkabout again.

Life after *le football*

Away from the game, after enjoying himself on the sets of commercials for Nike and Bic razors, he decided acting might be the thing. He made his first film, *Le Bonheur est dans le pré*, in 1995, while serving his suspension. At the time of writing, he has appeared in a further twenty: comedies, dramas, a couple of action movies. Although he has managed the French beach football team and taken up a position on the board of the New York Cosmos, when I met him, he indicated that football was no longer something he wished to engage with:

> It lost its excitement for me. That's why I retired. I didn't have to retire, I was still fit, I was still good... But I got a bit bored. So I began again. What's important to me is to have new experiences – to be a neophyte. Being an actor is not the most important thing, going on stage, it's feeling alive... at risk. I live to feel myself in danger.

As for the others involved that dangerous night, well, Simmons blames Cantona for every misfortune that subsequently befell him, the periods in prison, his inability to find a job, probably even the fact that, when up in court in May 1996 for threatening behaviour, he lost his temper, kicking Jeffrey McCann, the prosecuting counsel, and grabbing him by the throat. Presumably Cantona was to blame that it took six officers to restrain him as he was carried out of court, while shouting 'I'm innocent. I promise. I swear on the Bible.'

Fourteen years after the event, when Cantona took a starring role in Ken Loach's wonderful comedy *Looking for Eric* (in which he reprised the 'I am Cantona' line he'd uttered to Ince in the Croydon hotel), Simmons was interviewed again by *The Sun*. He claimed he still suffered harassment because of the incident. 'I get phone calls taunting me and threatening me,' he said. Few would have felt much sympathy.

'I could understand why Eric hit that lad,' says Cantona's teammate David May. 'There have been many times when I've wanted to chin a fan for giving personal abuse about my family. When Cantona did it I thought, "Fair play, Eric." The lad became famous for that, but then his life was apparently ruined. Good.'

At least Simmons was spared one torment, though. As he was led away in handcuffs by the local constabulary following the fracas on that January night, he did not have to sit through to the end of the match, like 18,223 other people did. It was not a good one, and

Cantona's departure did nothing to improve its quality. It remained mired in a scruffy kind of kick-and-rush. United took the lead some five minutes after Cantona left, only for Gareth Southgate to equalize with ten minutes to go. A point each: it seemed a suitably forgettable conclusion to what was, in footballing terms, an utterly unmemorable encounter.

Not everyone wishes the game to be eradicated from the collective memory, though. May, signed from Blackburn the previous summer to serve as understudy for the established centre-backs Steve Bruce and Gary Pallister, scored United's goal, his first for the club. He recalls:

> At full time the gaffer had a go at me for their equalizer. I thought, 'Eric's just jumped into the crowd and leathered someone and you're having a go at me for a goal that was nothing to do with me.' And I bloody well scored our goal too. It's a great pub quiz question though, isn't it? Who scored for United on the night of Cantona's Kung Fu kick?

● ● ● ● ●

FA CARLING PREMIERSHIP

Selhurst Park, London

Wednesday 25 January 1995

CRYSTAL PALACE 1 – 1 MANCHESTER UNITED
Palace scorer: Gareth Southgate 80
United scorer: David May 56
Attendance: 18,224
Referee: Alan Wilkie

TEAMS:

CRYSTAL PALACE (4-4-2)

Nigel Martyn; Dean Gordon, Chris Coleman, Richard Shaw, Darren
Pitcher; John Salako, Gareth Southgate, Darren Patterson, Ricky
Newman; Chris Armstrong, Iain Dowie (Andy Preece 78)

Subs not used: Rhys Wilmot (gk), Bobby Bowry

MANCHESTER UNITED (4-4-2)

Peter Schmeichel; Denis Irwin, Steve Bruce, Gary Pallister,
Lee Sharpe (Andrei Kanchelskis 78); Brian McClair, Paul Ince,
Roy Keane, Ryan Giggs; Eric Cantona, Andrew Cole

Subs not used: Gary Walsh (gk), Paul Scholes

Match 3

We weren't singing Shearer songs

LIVERPOOL V. BLACKBURN ROVERS

Anfield Stadium, Liverpool

Sunday 13 May 1995

If you're writing about this game, then do us a favour,' says Peter Hooton, the lead singer of the Merseyside band The Farm and a long-standing season-ticket holder at Anfield. 'Can you nail this myth that we Liverpool fans were all supporting Blackburn that day?'

If myth it be, it is one that has become embedded in Premier League folklore. Since this May afternoon in 1995, the legend has grown up that, such is their raging antipathy for Manchester United, Liverpool supporters turned club loyalty on its head and spent a spring afternoon cheering as one for Blackburn. But according to Peter Hooton that's all hokum. It never happened. That's history for you. Sometimes reality is not quite as memorable as legend.

Here is what we know to be true: Rovers were engaged in what had been a lengthy battle with United at the top of the Carling Premiership, a scrap that had to be resolved on this final Sunday of the season. When they arrived on Merseyside, Blackburn led the table by two points. All they needed to do was equal or better United's result at West Ham and the title was theirs. If United won and they lost, however – swallow hard, Merseyside – Liverpool's hated North West rivals could sneak it.

The assumption behind the myth of the Rovers-supporting Scousers is this: with their own club fifteen points adrift of the summit the next best thing for the Anfield fans was to relish Manc ambition being thwarted. And what made the Lancastrians apparently even more attractive to the Merseysiders was that they were at the time in the charge of the all-time Liverpool hero Kenny Dalglish, the only man to have won the title at Anfield both as player and as manager. It is perhaps understandable, therefore, that the idea has taken root in the collective memory that the Kop became – just for one day – a seething mass of blue-and-white halved shirts.

'But it's just not true,' insists Hooton. 'One tabloid was reporting that a JJB Sports branch in Liverpool city centre had sold out of Blackburn kit that week. Well, I went into that store to find out what was going on. And the manager said to me: "to be honest, mate, we've not sold any." I don't remember seeing one solitary Liverpool fan wearing a Blackburn shirt at that game. It's a myth.'

Yet if it is all a fabrication, then it's one promoted by no less central a figure in the drama than Dalglish himself, who said this of the match in his autobiography:

> It was a tremendous occasion, strange with it. During the first half the guy just behind the dug-out was wearing a Liverpool strip. When we came out for the second half he had a Blackburn kit on, shouting for us.

If Hooton's memory is accurate, Dalglish must have been witness to the only Liverpool fan in the ground to be thus attired, a supporter who clearly bought his second shirt at Sports Direct. But whatever the choice of attire, of this we can be certain: the home crowd was undoubtedly conflicted in its emotions. This was not a match that followed the normal patterns of support. Indeed, as the fans arrived ahead of kick-off, they must have wondered whether this was a game that might end in the most unusual of footballing results: with both teams ending up as losers.

Man of steel

Whatever the truth of this particular matter, things were changing for

Liverpool fans. Watching trophies being decided at Anfield without any prospect of their own club winning one was a new experience for them. This was the home of the outfit that had won the title eleven times in the preceding twenty-two years. They had dominated English football throughout the 1970s and 1980s, bestriding the game at home and in Europe, a colossus of progress and continuity. As Liverpool swanked, Blackburn had been nowhere. While Liverpool conquered the peaks of European football, Blackburn ambled along the gentler slopes of English football's lower divisions, the acceptance among their fans that theirs was not an institution that actually, you know, won things.

Blackburn had been founder members of the Football League back in 1888, but they had not won the championship since the eve of the First World War. In the years that followed, as football power migrated to the big conurbations, the hillside terraces of Blackburn that had once thrummed to the heartbeat of the game grew increasingly peripheral. While Liverpool swaggered, Blackburn wilted, their tumbledown stadium an apt architectural metaphor for their place in football's wider scheme. And then, in the late 1980s, Jack Walker came knocking at the door. Bringing his wallet with him.

Walker was a Blackburn boy made very good indeed. He and his brother Fred had taken over their father's sheet-metal and car-body works and turned a modest family business into the biggest steel stockholders in Britain. In 1956 the annual turnover was £46,000; by 1988, the annual profit was £48 million. When Walkersteel was sold to British Steel in 1989, the £360 million received represented at the time the highest price paid in Britain for a private company.

His pockets now comfortably lined, Walker set about spending his windfall. From 1974 onwards he lived as a tax exile in Jersey (where he later acquired the local airline – Jersey European – and transformed it into Flybe) but remained fiercely loyal to the town of his birth. What he wanted to do with his cash was to make Blackburn prosper. And the quickest way to improve its status, he reckoned, was to propel its football club to the top.

In 1986 he had been invited on to the board at Ewood Park and was asked by the chairman Bill Fox to facilitate the rebuilding of the woefully neglected ground. Within a couple of years he had financed the construction of the Walkersteel Stand. But his ambition was not satisfied by bricks and mortar (or indeed the corrugated steel of the new edifice). By 1991 he had become the sole owner of the club. And he set out to do something which had not been done for a generation: he determined to buy the title. With a successful football club at its heart, he believed, the economic benefits to Blackburn would be enormous. What a legacy that would represent, putting the town Jack Walker loved back on the map.

In the early days of the professional game, many a northern industrialist saw football as a vehicle for the expression of civic pride. John Henry Davies, the brewing tycoon who saved Manchester United from bankruptcy in Edwardian times, said that his motivation in funding an FA Cup and championship-winning side was to 'create a team of Manchester men to make Manchester proud'.

But not since the cantankerous butcher Bob Lord had propelled Burnley to the title in 1960 on the back of sales of fat and gristle had that trick been attempted. Latterly the game had become the business of the footballing corporations of Liverpool, Arsenal and Manchester United. Football, especially in the era of the Premiership, was for the big boys.

The difference between Walker and the average local trader made good, however, was simple: he didn't just have a lot of money, he had a steel-roofed shed chock-full of readies. Real and immediate capital, not stuff tied up in property, bonds or shares. Furthermore, there was no smoke, mirrors or false promises about his commitment to Blackburn Rovers; he was prepared to spend to achieve his dream.

To many an observer it seemed less a dream than a hopeless fantasy. When he became club president Blackburn were a middling second-division outfit. Like their near-neighbours Bolton, Blackpool, Preston and Burnley they were widely written off as a remnant of football's past, a club whose glory days were submerged in the murk of history. Renowned for the quality of the cakes on offer in the boardroom and the smile on the commissionaire's face at the main entrance, if it was known at all, this was a place celebrated for the friendliness of its people. Salt of the earth maybe, but not somewhere that would ever have need of silver polish.

As he visited on a Saturday, flying in from the Channel Islands on his private jet, chatting with the tea ladies, joshing with the lads manning the turnstiles, what Walker recognized was absent from his new enterprise was this: an ambition to match his own. So what he did was buy some in.

Courting King Kenny

In the autumn of 1991, he approached Kenny Dalglish about the idea of becoming manager at Ewood. Dalglish had resigned from Anfield the previous year, mentally shattered by the aftermath of the 1989 Hillsborough disaster. After taking a sabbatical and rediscovering his enthusiasm for the game, he had been pondering an offer from Olympique Marseille when Walker contacted him. At the pair's first meeting, the Scotsman was blunt in his requirements: if he was to decamp to damp, drear Lancashire rather than sun-dappled Provence, Walker needed to be serious. To achieve anything at Blackburn would necessitate sizeable quantities of money. Not just to build a team but to bring the infrastructure up to the standard now required of a top-flight club.

Ewood Park was at that time, frankly, a joke. The manager was obliged to hold his post-match press conferences in the front room of a terraced house over the road from the main stand. The club's training ground was a council-owned rec that appeared to double as a dogs' lavatory. As for the stadium itself, well, the Walkersteel Stand was a grand addition, but the rest of it looked unlikely to survive the next visit by Millwall fans.

Walker reassured Dalglish that all of these changes and improvements would be carried out. There would be a new training ground, the bulldozers were already in place outside the stadium and Walker would go on to spend some £20 million on ground redevelopment. In short, whatever resources were required to modernize the club would be made available. So Dalglish was persuaded, brought with him Ray Harford, the former Luton and Wimbledon manager as his assistant, and by the following May he had steered Blackburn to promotion via the play-offs.

In August 1992, Blackburn had reached the top division at the perfect moment: the Premier League had just been born. They would participate in its first season, an arriviste force in an arriviste league. Blackburn were undeniably back where they had started: together with Aston Villa and Everton they shared the distinction of being founder members of both the Football League and the Premier League. Though for their owner that was just the beginning.

What Walker liked best about his new employee was that they had a common ambition. Dalglish didn't simply want to be a member of the new league, he wanted to win it. And he set about recruiting a team to do so, happily flourishing Walker's cheque-book.

Comparing prices in the present-day footballing market with what Walker forked out to build his squad in the early 1990s reveals how much the concept of big spending has changed in the first two decades of the Premier League's existence – and the inflation that has afflicted English football's top tier. In his three years in charge, Dalglish spent £27.5 million of Jack Walker's cash on twenty-seven players; that is exactly the same amount as Manchester City spent on bringing just one player, Edin Džeko, from Wolfsburg in 2011. His biggest buy was Chris Sutton, who came from Norwich City in the summer of 1994 for £5 million; in January 2011 Roman Abramovich paid Liverpool ten times that sum to sign Fernando Torres for Chelsea. And Dalglish's most substantial earner was Alan Shearer, who was recruited on a basic of £5,000 a week; in 2013, Yaya Touré signed a new deal with Manchester City worth more than fifty times as much.

Another sign of changed realities as the Premier League enters its third decade is that an investment of the scale of Walker's produces a far less tangible footballing return. Peter Coates, the founder of the Bet 365 chain, has pumped significantly more than Walker ever did into his beloved Stoke City, £60 million at the last count. And the reward for his outlay has not been a pitch for the title. It has been nothing more than Premier League solidity.

'When Walker first entered the Premier League it was an aspirational vehicle, in the sense an outsider could win it,' says Professor Simon Chadwick of Coventry University Business School. 'Now the kind of aspiration you can buy with his wealth is, "well we can get into it and hope to stay there". Over the years the Premier League has grown, so has the price to enter it and then win it. The crucial thing for the teams who have been in since the start is that they accumulate big money year after year, which gives them sustainable competitive advantage. To match that is incredibly difficult and unbelievably expensive. As stakes have got higher, as accumulation of resources increased, it is no longer an opportunity open to the local boy made good. You have to be a member of the world's mega-rich. In 1995 you could be a steel magnate. In 2013 you have to be an oligarch or a sheikh.'

Walker may have been breaking Premier League ground in attempting to buy his way to the top, but he appreciated this single truth about football: it is not just to do with money. What Dalglish brought to the club was the kind of authority that cash alone could not deliver. For the generation of players plying their trade in the mid-1990s, the Scotsman was close to a footballing deity. Memory of his brilliant forward play – deft of touch, deadly of finish, with a backside wider than the Mersey which he employed to shield the ball – was still fresh in the collective memory. Then, on hanging up his boots, Dalglish had become a hugely successful young manager. His record at Liverpool was extraordinary: five League titles as a player, three as boss. He was a seemingly perpetual winner, a man who simply didn't fail, the coach with the Midas touch. A far cry from the out-of-touch, old-fashioned, somewhat marooned figure he would cut on the Anfield touchline in 2012.

Team-building exercise

It was his presence that ensured Blackburn made their single most important signing in July 1992. That summer, the young Southampton forward Alan Shearer was hot property. Alex Ferguson in particular admired his strength, pace and bravery and was anxious to bring him to Old Trafford. But it was Dalglish who most impressed the player. What swung it for Shearer was not just the myth of 'King Kenny', but the care, diligence and understanding that Dalglish displayed when they met. Ferguson assumed that Shearer would be smitten by the romance of United and head straight to Manchester. But the young player wanted to be wooed in negotiations, wanted to be reassured, wanted to feel really, really needed. And Dalglish wooed him all right, with his story of how he could be part of something transformative, how he could be the man who uplifted not just a football club, but a whole town. He and Harford – who had worked with the striker for England's under-21s – told Shearer how they would build a team round him. That was music to his ears. That and the small matter of the biggest salary then available in English football.

Once Shearer was at the club (bought for a record £3.3 million, including Blackburn's leading scorer David Speedie thrown in as a £400,000 makeweight) it became much easier to attract other players to Blackburn; his was the signature that opened the door. Now when Dalglish approached players with a view to signing, they listened.

'The best way I can describe it is that there was a noise the club emitted, like a well-tuned engine,' remembers Graeme Le Saux, who was bought from Chelsea in the summer of 1993.

I'd had offers from a few clubs, Manchester City being one of them. Blackburn had only just been promoted, on paper there was no way I should have joined them. But I knew Alan was there and Kenny was a huge hero of mine and from the first conversation we had I just got this feedback that was so positive. It wasn't to do with money, I was actually offered more elsewhere. But everything about the place exuded ambition and I wanted to be part of it. I have to admit, though, when I did agree to come up and talk to them I had to look at the map. I had no idea where Blackburn was. Literally.

And as he travelled north Le Saux was quickly made aware of the new ways of Premiership transfer negotiation. A well-read man who was later subject to a degree of ridicule by both fans and players for his habit of browsing *The Guardian*, Le Saux thought he understood the transfer market. As far as he was concerned, it was a matter of negotiating a salary and signing on. But then he discovered it was not so simple.

'Eric Hall rang me and said: "I'm doing the deal",' he recalls of the garrulous agent who was one of the first to recognize that there was a huge amount of money to be made for third parties in this new league. 'This is where players are vulnerable. This was a chance to progress and here was some chap I'd never heard of, who I had never spoken to never mind employed, barging in, insisting that he should get a cut of the deal. I was kind of bamboozled.' Hall, the man who described himself as 'The Monster' of transfer dealings, was the harbinger of a new breed, a new way of doing business. Many were to follow; the agent was to become a part of the Premier League landscape; Le Saux's experience was to become commonplace.

Along with his cohort of financial fellow-travellers, Hall was to be busy on the road to Blackburn. Dalglish remembers that when he made his first signing at Ewood – the full-back Alan Wright, bought from Blackpool – it prompted a flurry of nervous excitement in the club secretary's office. They soon got used to it. He brought back the former youth-team player Colin Hendry from Manchester City, Mike Newell was his first million-pound signing from Everton and Tim Sherwood's arrival from Norwich cheered the chairman up no end. How Walker admired Sherwood's industry. So much so that when Dalglish sought permission to chase the renowned French pair of Zinédine Zidane and Christophe Dugarry, legend has it Walker said to him: 'why do we need them when we've got Tim Sherwood?'

Dalglish now insists that, despite the flurry of spending required to bring the squad up to fighting strength, despite the agents sniffing around every deal, he was never profligate with Jack Walker's money. He treated it like his own in negotiations, refusing on several occasions to sign those he regarded as overstating their worth. 'Some players we talked to made financial demands that were just ridiculous,' he says in his autobiography. 'They just wanted a slice of Jack's fortune.'

He regarded character as the most important quality in a player. He was not constructing a team for aesthetic purposes, to advance the beauty of the game. This was not a Lancastrian Barcelona, tippy-tapping across the moors. He had more urgent requirements: he wanted to win. To do so, he needed players with nerve and mental strength.

Those qualities were present in the spine of his side, constructed of Walker-financed steel. Shearer was joined up front by Chris Sutton, the centre-back-turned-centre-forward who had the sharpest elbows in the game. In the middle of midfield were Sherwood and the aggressive, snappy David Batty, bought from Leeds. At centre-back were Hendry and the unflappable Norwegian Henning Berg. And in goal was Tim Flowers, the keeper Liverpool – among several other clubs – were anxious to sign from Southampton.

'Kenny was basically the player of my youth,' says Flowers, reflecting on why he chose Ewood over Anfield. 'But I think what really swung it for me was that Kenny always made me feel like I was wanted. He called me constantly, telling me how important I'd be to the team. Kind of makes you want to play for him.' One thing that Dalglish did not explicitly refer to during their discussions, however, was the presiding ambition of the club. 'He never said, "right, you've got to win this league",' Flowers recalls. 'I cannot remember Kenny ever saying to any of us we're going to do this, we're going to do that. Actually, we went from one game to the next, encouraged never to think about the game after the next one. I know that's boring, but it's true.'

It may have been unspoken, the elephant in the dressing room, but the sense of urgency to achieve infected the entire squad. Le Saux remembers that the training ground buzzed with purpose. At his previous club Chelsea he had always been made to feel a little awkward for wanting to work hard in preparation sessions, his eagerness mocked as if he were the class swat. At Blackburn, there was no such worry:

> I knew I was on to something when, the first day after training, I was absolutely exhausted. It was like playing a match. With the right tempo and competition, the intensity of it was something else. I just knew from the off this was a motivated bunch of guys, motivated coaches, motivated staff everywhere. The standards were very high. You couldn't hide. And we weren't carrying anyone.

Flowers agrees that this was the basis of Blackburn's success – the mental strength evident everywhere in the dressing room:

> It's something I've grown to realize about football: ultimately success comes from good recruitment. Kenny was very good at that, making sure he signed characters. There were loads of leaders in that dressing room, lads who would point fingers at each other, but who would accept criticism. We were absolutely honest with each other but rarely had massive barneys. We were people who would hold our hands up if we made a mistake. Then work twice as hard to make sure we didn't do it again.

And, Flowers adds, there was something else about Dalglish's recruitment policy. 'He did his homework, I know he did on me. He rang five or six people about me, he even rang my old school teachers, to find out what sort of attitude I had. I know some managers basically haven't a clue what type of person you are when you sign.'

Like Le Saux, Flowers – these days a coach at Northampton Town – enjoyed the training. 'I wouldn't say Kenny and Ray were old school, but their approach wasn't exactly revolutionary,' he says. 'There was a lot of eight v. eight, shooting practice, work on set pieces. It was straightforward stuff. Kenny loved to join in with us on our big Friday games, arguably he was still the best player at the club. It was like the FA Cup final on a Friday, lots of forfeits, proper tackles. I still try to get that sort of vibe in my coaching sessions.'

Mercenaries or magicians?

Propelled by the togetherness forged on the training ground, Blackburn had finished second to Premiership champions United in 1994, even beating the eventual double winners in an Eastertide epic at Ewood in which the weather switched constantly from bright sunshine to icy hail howling in from the moors. That day the hillside behind the Walkersteel Stand had been filled with fans without tickets, enjoying the best free view in football, even as they braced themselves against the chill. Runners-up in the top division represented the club's most elevated league finish in eight decades. And what that achievement shouted out was that everything was now in place for Blackburn's final push to the summit. Well, almost everything. 'The ground was still a building site,' remembers Le Saux:

We used to get changed in temporary dressing rooms in a Porta-kabin behind the Darwen End Stand. And three buses used to be there, one for us, one for the oppo and one for the ref and linesmen, to bus us through the crowd to the north stand, where we would go through, out on to the pitch. I'm pretty sure that intimidated a number of our rivals. It made them feel uncomfortable.

The buses were needed because things could get very crowded at Ewood. There was no chance of walking through the throng. A place that had been moribund for years had seen a huge upsurge in attendance: it became the only venue in town. As Dalglish pushed the team closer to the title, crowds had trebled, filling the ever-expanding new stands. More than 20,000 people were now regularly coming to matches, from a community with a total population of no more than 105,000. One in five of the locals: Walker's dream was evidently being shared by those who lived in his home town.

And Walker himself, a fan to his bootstraps, was always there at Ewood Park. 'He had a very warm rapport with the players,' says Le Saux. 'I come from Jersey, where he lived, and he'd make a lot of that connection. He'd phone my dad on random Saturdays and say "there's space on my plane, do you want to come over?" My dad on a private jet flying over for Blackburn matches, it was hilarious.'

Walker's matchday ritual included a visit to the dressing room. He'd ask Dalglish who was in the team, then shake hands with every player. 'He was so good at it,' recalls Le Saux. 'In everything he did, he came across as a good northern lad. Everywhere in the club, there was a real sense of everyone sharing his vision.'

But if his vision was to be realized in 1994–95 it soon became clear it would not be in cup competition. Blackburn found themselves quickly knocked out of the knock-outs. They were dispatched from the League Cup by the eventual winners Liverpool and were dismissed from the FA Cup by Newcastle. Even more disappointingly, their first ever venture into Europe had finished in embarrassment, as they fell at the first hurdle in the UEFA Cup to the Swedish part-timers Trelleborgs. During commentary, BBC Radio Five Live's Alan Green made disparaging remarks about the ease with which Blackburn's expensively assembled team were brushed aside by a bunch of Nordic insurance salesmen and bus drivers. He accused Dalglish of wasting Walker's money on inadequate, mercenary players. The manager did not take kindly to such a critique. After the game he sought Green out and the pair had a very public stand-up row.

Dalglish may have been touchy, but this was evidence that Blackburn were operating in what, for them, was new footballing territory. As an unheralded outfit suddenly propelled by money to the forefront of the game, their every stumble was a potential source of Schadenfreude for the rest. There was a sense among fans of other clubs that Blackburn's place at the top was artificial, unearned, unjustifiable. They were not universally loved. Dalglish routinely dismissed such opinion as driven by jealousy. Which fan would not relish the arrival of a man of Walker's generosity at their club? It was not the last time such a question would be asked in the history of the Premier League.

And it was in the League that Blackburn had looked strong from the start of the season. Shearer and Sutton – by now widely known by the soubriquet SAS – were scoring freely. Shearer, who had missed much of his first year at Ewood through injury, in particular looked like a man on a mission: aggressive, hungry, clinical in his finishing. Worth every penny of Walker's investment. By the turn of the year, the pair's goals had swept Blackburn up to a wholly unfamiliar position: top of the league. And their prospects were hugely assisted by two of their principal rivals suffering substantial self-inflicted wounds. At the end of January, Manchester United saw their playmaker Eric Cantona banned for the rest of the season for his impromptu martial-arts class at Selhurst Park (see previous chapter). Meanwhile in February, Arsenal sacked George Graham, the manager who had won them two titles in the previous six seasons.

It appeared Graham had become a little too closely involved in the new, agent-driven method of doing football transfer business. He was found to have accepted £425,000 worth of illegal payments from the Norwegian agent Rune Hauge three years earlier, a thank-you for facilitating Arsenal signing two of Hauge's clients, John Jensen and Pål Lydersen. As Graham was defenestrated from Highbury, a new term was coined by the press to describe a system whereby club managers accepted backhanders to lubricate the transfer process: the 'bung'. And such backhanders appeared to be gaining popularity in the Premiership. It wasn't just Graham; Brian Clough too, the European Cup-winning manager of Nottingham Forest and once – before the bottle took its toll – reckoned the country's brightest boss, was said by the Tottenham chairman Alan Sugar 'to like a bung'. It all added to a sense of a game whose moral compass had been disturbed by the arrival of money.

Blackburn, though, did not seem remotely destabilized by these events. They took advantage of their moment. By the early spring they were comfortably ahead in the table, with United damaged by

Cantona's exile and Arsenal faltering under the stewardship of an interim manager, Stewart Houston. The title was clearly Blackburn's to lose. Only they could blow it. And then, with the finishing line in sight, came a hint that that was precisely what they were in danger of doing. With but six games of the seasonal marathon remaining, Blackburn appeared to hit the wall. They lost at home to Manchester City and away at West Ham. 'We did wobble,' admits Le Saux. 'Looking back, I think what we lacked as a team was experience of winning. Only David Batty had ever won the title before, the rest of us were learning as we went along.'

By contrast, United shook off their Cantona dependency and kept on winning; in the final run-in they closed an eight-point gap to just two, with two games remaining. Even though they had blooded a number of youngsters during the season, the Red Devils seemed to be building the remorseless momentum of serial champions. Their relentless progress is etched on Le Saux's memory:

> They kept winning in the ninety-eighth minute. I remember we didn't have a game one Saturday and I was driving from London where my girlfriend – now my wife – lived, listening to the commentary of their match on the radio. I remember being ecstatic at Birmingham because they were behind and there wasn't long to go. Then by the next junction they'd equalized. By the next, they'd won.

Battle of the Glaswegians

With his team's reputation for tenacity growing, Alex Ferguson fanned the psychological embers. He and Dalglish had always had a competitive relationship. One a former Rangers player, the other a Celtic stalwart, neither shirked a scrap – it was there in their very Glasgow upbringing. In April 1988, they had clashed on live television when Ferguson was being interviewed after United had lost at Anfield and was complaining bitterly about referees' bias towards the home team. As Fergie was reaching the animated conclusion of his rant, insisting that visiting managers were obliged to retire from Liverpool's home 'choking on their own vomit, biting their tongue, afraid to tell the truth', Dalglish happened to be walking past, cradling his infant daughter Lauren. He sarcastically suggested to the television reporter that he would be 'better off talking to my baby. She's only six weeks old but you'd get more sense from her than him.' Ferguson was visibly not amused.

The United manager, a keen racehorse owner, retaliated with a wounding psychological comparison from the Sport of Kings. He likened Blackburn's recent stutter to that of Devon Loch, the Queen Mother's horse which had collapsed ignominiously while enjoying a healthy lead in the 1956 Grand National. Dalglish pretended not to understand his rival's pointed reference. 'What's Devon Loch?' he said, when asked about the analogy. 'Is that a lake in Scotland?'

But in his autobiography, he acknowledges that his players 'definitely had a touch of the jitters' in that final run of matches in the 1994–95 season. And a clear sign of how much his squad had been antagonized by Ferguson's taunts came after their penultimate game, at home to Newcastle on 8 May. 'The atmosphere was incredible, electric,' says Le Saux of that match, which had drawn a crowd of 30,425, an attendance of a scale rarely seen at Ewood since. 'That was a fixture we approached thinking: "this could do us. Lose this and it's gone." We were all really up for it.'

Particularly Tim Flowers. He saved brilliantly twice from Newcastle's Peter Beardsley, apparently defying all known laws of gravity as he preserved Blackburn's single-goal lead to the final whistle. Shearer's first-half strike was enough to see them through. But it was in an interview with Sky after he had been voted man of the match that Flowers unintentionally spoke volumes about the tension in the Blackburn dressing room. In a loud and overexcited monologue, he rounded on those who had accused the team of faintheartedness, particularly those from Manchester.

'Well we showed bottle tonight,' he shouted, goggle-eyed, at the camera. At least half a dozen times. In fact he used the 'b' word so frequently that on his return to the dressing room, his team-mates christened him 'Ernie, the Fastest Milkman in the West'. Reflecting on these events, Flowers comments:

> When you get a wee bit clear, then you start to dream. We got to a point thinking, if we keep going we're uncatchable. But that's dangerous. I remember Sir Alex talking about Devon Loch, and the wheels coming off, and he was right they did. One thing I learned about that season: don't waste your time fifteen games beforehand thinking about the title. It all kind of came to a head with that interview. I was so relieved we won that match. But yeah, it was a bit embarrassing.

Live and lucrative

So it was that the final set of fixtures of the season arrived. Blackburn travelled along the M62 to Liverpool two points in front of United, who were visiting West Ham. Such was the aura of invincibility surrounding United that most of the Blackburn squad were convinced they would win in London's East End. In which case, only a Blackburn victory would do. 'We knew if we lost at Anfield we were practically saying goodbye to the title,' recalls the skipper Colin Hendry.

Dalglish had spent the week leading up to the game trying to soothe nerves and relax the overwrought. Le Saux remembers him exuding a sense of calm, trying at all times to remain matter of fact and unflustered. He organized a match between the Blackburn backroom staff and the press corps and invited the players to watch. As a joke, Umbro, the club's kit manufacturers, sent Manchester United shirts for the pressmen to wear. After the game, Dalglish gave a short speech to the journalists. 'Fergie would have been proud of you. You've worn those red shirts with pride,' he said. The writers had lost 16–0.

But however hard the manager tried to still the sense of trepidation, Flowers remembers arriving at Anfield that final Sunday awash with nerves: 'The closer you get to the winning post, the further it seems to get away from you. I always had butterflies, I was always hyped for games, always on a knife edge, sometimes to my cost. But that last game, I was more nervous than ever. I was really shitting myself.' This was exactly the sort of dramatic, nerve-shredding conclusion to the Premiership season that the men behind the League had dreamt of. The first couple of seasons of the new competition had petered out into anticlimax. Manchester United had won in 1993 and 1994 without even playing. It was mathematics that had determined the outcome, not a heart-stopping late winning goal. Ferguson had heard the news of his first triumph when a fellow golfer interrupted his round on a Cheshire course to tell him that Aston Villa – the only team who might catch his side – had lost. An exciting moment for him, maybe. But hardly broadcasting gold dust.

What the new paymasters of the League were anxious to see repeated was the kind of dénouement that had electrified the nation on 26 May 1989, when Arsenal had snatched the old First Division title at the last at Anfield. That season, because of disruption to Liverpool's fixtures caused by the Hillsborough disaster, rearrangements had led to the two sides in the running meeting for the final game on a midweek evening late in May, a collision televised live on ITV.

When Michael Thomas tripped through the Liverpool defence to score the winner, sending the commentator Brian Moore into raptures about how it was 'all up for grabs now', the spike in those watching on the box had been enormous. So extraordinary – and potentially commercially valuable – was this arrival of cup-final rhythms into the League championship that, from the moment the Premier League was first mooted, there were influential voices lobbying for a play-off system to be introduced to decide the title. End the season with a Superbowl-style shoot-out, conclude with United against Liverpool, or Tottenham against Arsenal, their argument ran, and the worldwide television audience would soon match that of the NFL's annual showcase.

However, more traditional counsel held sway. With English football already undergoing such radical change, it was felt that to undermine the time-honoured structure of the league might prove counterproductive. Within just three seasons, the proponents of this conservative approach had been vindicated: in 1995 the title was going to the wire, a last-gasp conclusion was in the offing. And, although this was not a play-off, although the two teams in with a chance of lifting the trophy were not meeting directly, it gave Sky a glittering opportunity to demonstrate how its partnership with the Premiership had changed the way football was enjoyed in Britain.

With the matches kicking off simultaneously, the Sky cameras could bring the action together, meld it seamlessly into one grand-standing event. What was happening at one ground could add signi-ficant drama to what was taking place at the other. It was a two-for-one offer that the company executives hoped would be irresistible.

And so it proved. This final Sunday was to be the most lucrative yet for the commercial broadcaster. Though you might not think so from looking at the numbers. Over twenty-eight million viewers had watched the BBC's coverage of the Leeds v. Chelsea FA Cup final replay in 1970. Just over half of that number had watched on ITV as Liverpool played Arsenal for the title in 1989. Yet on this final Sunday of the 1994–95 season, broadcast on a subscription satellite service, no more than two million viewers tuned in at home. Even taking into account the unknown but sizeable number of fans who followed the new trend of watching the game live on TV down at the pub, it seems counterintuitive to suggest Sky's viewing figures made the game so much more valuable for the broadcaster than previous events, which had attracted far more substantial audiences. Yet they did.

'The thing is, the new way of consuming football on television brought a nucleus of an audience that is much more committed,' explains Alex Fynn, the ad man who had advised the FA at the time of the Premier League's formation. 'That nucleus is all that is required. Previously you had millions of non-committed fans because of the unusual, event-like nature of big games. Now it was watched by committed football fans, in the main free-spending young males, who advertisers find almost impossible to reach. You can promote mobile technology, alcohol, betting, cars, using an environment only football can deliver. The absolute numbers may be lower. But there is far less wastage and therefore much more commercial opportunity.'

In short, knowing that they would hit the target, Sky could charge premium prices for the adverts bookending the action. They were in the money. And such commercial opportunity was everywhere evident in the Premiership. The League was shrinking that season from twenty-two to twenty members. So four teams were relegated, with just two promoted. In the scramble to stay in the division, fifteen clubs changed their manager between May 1994 and August 1995. The financial incentive to cling on in the top flight was growing by the season. That year, a new deal with sponsors Carling guaranteed every club £136,363 per year.

There had been objections, as several clubs had individual sponsorship deals with other breweries (Liverpool's with Carlsberg was the most lucrative), but eventually the Premier League's chief executive Rick Parry forced the deal through. It was growing increasingly evident how much cold cash the new competition was attracting to the game. And no club wanted to be banished from it, thereby to lose out on the chance to enjoy its riches.

Countdown to the championship

Not that Blackburn were concerned with the money when they pitched up at Anfield on the afternoon of Sunday 13 May. For them something much more substantial was on offer: glory. 'I remember arriving at the ground feeling very anxious and distracted,' admits Le Saux. 'Kenny had been so successful as a player, but he knew whatever he said it was in our hands. So he tried to play everything down, keep us focused on the process. But to be honest, none of us were focused. We were pretty terrible that day. The enormity of where we were had unsettled us.'

For their hosts, the priorities were very different. Liverpool had already won a trophy that season, beating Bolton at Wembley to secure the League Cup. But that was not enough for the traditions of Anfield. At least, after finishing sixth, sixth and eighth in the last three unhappy seasons under Graeme Souness, there was a chance of demonstrating improvement by finishing fourth under the new manager Roy Evans. Peter Hooton recalls:

> The Kop had been demolished in 1994, the terracing had gone, the whole place was changing from the glory days. And we had nothing to play for, there was definitely an end-of-season feeling of pointless anticlimax in the air.

Liverpool fans, though, were conscious of accusations that they might throw the match that had sprung up during the course of the week. 'It was round about time of the Grobbelaar stuff in *The Sun* and we didn't want to be seen to be supporting match fixing,' says Hooton. Bruce Grobbelaar, the Reds' former keeper, had been caught that year in a tabloid sting offering to let in a goal in return for cash. He was cleared after two criminal trials, and took out a libel action against *The Sun*. He was awarded token damages of £1 and was instructed to pay the newspaper's costs of around £500,000.

What with Kung Fu kicks, bungs and now kickbacks and lengthy, ruinously expensive libel cases, it had not been a happy year for football's image. But Hooton was right: entirely unfounded stories about Liverpool players cheerfully accepting incentives to lose circulated in the build-up to this game. In the days before Twitter became the favoured grapevine for the dissemination of utterly groundless gossip, everyone knew of someone who had been in a taxi driven by a cabby who had given a lift to the bloke who had told him Liverpool were going to throw the game.

In his pre-match comments ahead of United's trip to West Ham, Alex Ferguson talked of Liverpool's affection for Dalglish, of their fans' antipathy to all things United. But he also suggested that Liverpool's players would be anxious not to be seen to be putting the integrity of the competition in doubt. He said their professional pride would be compromised if they lost. His purpose was to motivate Liverpool to do what was required to allow his young team to steal the title.

'Look, Kenny was popular in Liverpool, course he was,' says

Hooton. 'But there wasn't 100 per cent adulation. There was a feeling that he had left us in a bit of a fix, with no youth coming through. We were uncomfortable seeing him taking someone else close to the title. We'd have preferred him to have stayed and done it at Anfield.'

Hooton had no inkling of the years of frustration that lay ahead for Liverpool. 'We had a feeling we had a team about to challenge,' he maintains. 'My personal thought was that [John] Barnes was being groomed to be manager and he'd lead us back to the top. We weren't that despondent that we were forced to watch another team in contention. We just thought this is a temporary blip and we'd soon be back. Little did we know.'

The Liverpool manager Roy Evans was somewhat hampered in his selection by an injury to his top scorer Ian Rush. He pushed his midfielder Nigel Clough forward to partner Robbie Fowler, and with Barnes and Steve McManaman in the wide positions, played Jamie Redknapp in central midfield. Alongside him was Michael Thomas, a man who knew all about scoring title-winning goals. Souness had signed Thomas in the hope he might be able to bring a little bit of champions' lustre to the Liverpool team. It hadn't worked out. Thomas's finest day at Anfield was forever to be 26 May 1989, when he was wearing an Arsenal shirt.

Dalglish selected what was undoubtedly his strongest team, with Sutton and Shearer up front, Jason Wilcox out wide and an un-compromising midfield three of Jeff Kenna, Sherwood and Batty, who was playing only his ninth game of an injury-bedevilled sea-son. Meanwhile, in London, Ferguson selected a team packed full of goal-scorers. Andrew Cole, Mark Hughes, Brian McClair, Ryan Giggs, Andrei Kanchelskis: it seemed improbable that, with such power available, they could fail to beat West Ham. Blackburn's players were convinced they had to win. Le Saux elucidates:

I remember Kenny tried so hard to make us all think it was just an-other game. Beforehand he didn't give us the Al Pacino *Any Given Sunday* spiel. He was very good at being very calm. But behind that there was emotion, definitely. At the time it didn't register to me that he was emotional about Liverpool. But retrospectively it must have been massive for him, with all those Hillsborough memories running through his head.

Two games of twists and turns

As he took his unfamiliar position in the Anfield away dug-out, Dalglish noted that the Sky technicians had a monitor in the tunnel switched to the action at Upton Park. He made sure they kept him informed of the state of play in east London, so that he knew exactly what was required from his players. However, the Blackburn team found it difficult to know how to respond to the unique pressures of the occasion.

'It was a most bizarre game,' remembers Le Saux. 'The atmosphere was really strange, the crowd were supporting us and them. I always relish it when a crowd hates me, I find that a big motivation. And I was just confused by an away ground being so nice to us. I spent most of the game trying to get signs from the crowd and bench about how things were developing.'

And at first, they developed very favourably for Blackburn. They opened the scoring through – who else – Shearer. It was his thirty-fourth Premiership goal of the season, an astonishingly fecund total unmatched ever since. Sutton had scored fifteen. The SAS were the most lethal hit squad in the game. From east London, meanwhile, there was even better news: against the run of play, with United almost camped in their half, West Ham had taken the lead. Michael Hughes had scored soon after Shearer. Things could not have panned out better for the Blue and Whites.

Even so, Le Saux recalls the half-time break was ripe with tension. Blackburn were so near, yet still so far from achieving their goal. 'We were all so nervous,' he says. 'Jason Wilcox came in at half-time saying "my bloody legs won't work". But we did think that 1–0 lead had given us a cushion. And I remember us saying how bizarre it was that the Liverpool fans had reacted positively to our goal. Even their players, they didn't want United to win it. But it didn't help us, none of us were focused, God we were terrible. We were limping to the line.'

At West Ham, Ferguson delivered a passionate half-time talk, encouraging his players to keep making chances as they had in the first half. Eventually, he said, one of them would be converted. And then the dam would break. Dalglish, meanwhile, told the Blackburn boys to keep strong, keep focused, keep doing the things that had got them into this position in the first place. As they clattered their way back onto the pitch, he told them how much they deserved the prize that was beckoning. 'And we did,' agrees Le Saux. 'Christ we deserved it.'

As the second half unfolded, it was as well that Jack Walker, up in the directors' box, was not privy to the same information as his manager. Because if he had been, Dalglish believes he might not have made it through to the whistle without succumbing to the gut-buckling tension. Across the country, in pubs and front rooms, viewers were able to watch every moment of the unyielding drama, as the action switched from ground to ground. It was the finest forty-five minutes in Sky's short history. And the Premier League would not produce a final day this tense for another seventeen years.

The first twist in the plot came when, with just over an hour played, Barnes equalized for Liverpool. 'Yeah, we celebrated that goal,' says Pete Hooton. 'It was a Liverpool goal, course we did.' Then Dalglish heard from those following events at the Boleyn Ground that McClair had got one for United. If the games finished with both clubs drawing, the title would still be Blackburn's, but the margin of error was growing thinner by the second.

And for those watching at home it seemed it could only be a matter of time before United took the lead. They were encamped in the West Ham area. Cole, bought for his prowess as a finisher, kept finding himself perfectly positioned to score. But the ball wouldn't bounce right for him. It just wouldn't drop. Or if it did, and he dispatched it goalwards, the Hammers' keeper Luděk Mikloško kept making improbable saves.

'We absolutely battered West Ham,' recalls the United skipper

Steve Bruce. 'We had chance after chance after chance.' But none were converted. How Dalglish and Walker and the Blackburn fans could have done with their team getting a goal, just to make sure. Tension, however, had gripped the players in blue and white. Passes went awry, possession was routinely squandered, no one could put together a proper dribble. The SAS were starved of ammunition. As Tim Flowers recalls:

I didn't know what was going on. I got very little feedback from the crowd. The only time was when I was taking a goal kick, and because of my run-up I'd gone right back to the fence with the crowd behind me and someone shouted out that Man United had equalized at West Ham. I just thought, well they're 1–1, they're Man United, they're absolutely bound to get a bloody winner in the 93rd or 94th minute. There's no way they won't nick it.

Then, with both matches reaching their conclusion, in injury time Liverpool won a free kick on the edge of the Blackburn area. Jamie Redknapp shaped to take it. Le Saux was in the wall that Flowers had positioned in front of the kicker. 'As soon as he hit it, I knew it was in,' admits Le Saux. 'I didn't want to turn round. Just couldn't bear to. The Blackburn fans were in a right state. You could almost hear the air going out of them.'

Picking the ball out of the back of his net, Flowers was equally despondent. 'When Jamie scored, I thought we'd missed it,' he says. 'I was really down. I honestly thought that was it.' Blackburn were now losing 2–1. The club had waited eighty-one years for a title. And, with circumstances conspiring against them, it seemed the wait was going to continue. Flowers was not alone in his conviction that United were going to get a last-gasp winner and Walker's dream was back on hold. It was all over.

But then an extraordinary thing happened. The game at West Ham had reached its conclusion before the one at Anfield, and the result from London was not the one anybody expected: it was a draw.

'As we walked back to the halfway line after the Liverpool goal, I suddenly heard this roar travelling round the stadium,' says Le Saux. 'Then I saw our bench jumping up and down. We knew then they'd drawn. I remember saying to the ref: "just blow up – we've won the Premiership". But he said: "no you've got two minutes to play".'

Dalglish was delirious in the dug-out, leaping and high-fiving and hugging an endless succession of Liverpool fans and employees delighted for his success. There was, he says, nowhere better to win the league than at Anfield. 'I remember Kenny saying afterwards how relieved he was at the way the result panned out,' says Flowers. 'Liverpool had been utterly professional, done their bit to ensure the integrity of the competition. There could be no fingers pointed. It was United who had blown it.'

And Ferguson knew it, telling his players never to forget the crushing disappointment they felt as they walked off the Upton Park pitch. And then to make sure they never experienced such a sensation again. Still, he was generous in defeat, sending a letter to Dalglish congratulating him on his success and reminding him who Devon Loch was ('I'm sure your dad backed him,' he wrote, 'I know mine did'). The Kop too was more than happy at the way things had turned out. There was no need for any Blackburn shirts to be worn, no need for integrity to be compromised.

'I stayed behind to applaud them,' says Hooton. 'But then I'd stayed behind to applaud Arsenal in '89 too. It was the perfect result. There wasn't wild celebrations, people were pleased we'd won so there could be no accusations of throwing it, and pleased United hadn't won it. We were pleased for Kenny too. I went back to the pub, but no one was singing Shearer songs. Absolutely no chance. Anyway, if United had won people would have shrugged their shoulders and said hey, well, they deserved it. If anyone understood that the table doesn't lie, it's Liverpool fans.'

Flash in the pan

For the Blackburn players, the joy was undiluted. Liverpool's Neil

Ruddock brought a case of champagne into their dressing room to help them celebrate. But the moment when it dawned on them what they had achieved was when Walker came in to thank them. The tears in the owner's eyes were the clearest articulation of precisely what they had delivered. It would have been churlish in the circumstances to refuse his invitation to join him that night in a celebratory dinner at a friend's restaurant where the Drifters were the cabaret act. Even if it was in Preston.

'It was over in a whimper, if that makes sense,' says Le Saux of the celebrations. 'It was the journey that was the achievement. That was the experience, that's what lingers in the memory. You can't have a party that lives up to that. The aftermath was a bit disappointing, if I'm honest. We ended up in Preston, for goodness sake. Then we went away. You never really got to enjoy the success. It was over so quickly. Just this fleeting moment.'

He's right there: for Blackburn the success was fleeting indeed. After becoming only the third manager after Herbert Chapman and Brian Clough to win the title with two different clubs, after being named Manager of the Season, Dalglish resigned that summer, heading upstairs to become Director of Football. Harford took over in the dug-out. And Blackburn's decline from champions to also-rans began immediately.

Le Saux takes up the story:

Where the club got it horribly wrong was that they were so amazed at what had been achieved in such a short space of time they didn't have the infrastructure in place to sustain it. They remained very loyal to the group who won the title and didn't move on those who had passed their sell-by date. It was the one time in their history they could have attracted anyone. But they didn't. As quickly as it came, look how quickly the wheels fell off.

The evidence was there for all to see in Harford's signings the summer following the title win. He bought Matty Holmes from West Ham,

Graham Fenton from Aston Villa, Lars Bohinen from Nottingham Forest, Chris Coleman from Crystal Palace and Billy McKinlay from Dundee United. Hardly Shearer, Sutton or Le Saux, never mind Zidane or Dugarry. 'There were three eras of Jack Walker's Blackburn,' says Professor Simon Chadwick. 'The first period was relatively modest, up to '92–'93. The middle era was the big push for the title. And the third period was "Hey, look I can't keep bailing you out, this has got to be sustainable."'

And if it was to be sustained, if Blackburn were to remain a functioning football club without their owner's endless largesse, the biggest marketable asset had to be the players who had delivered the title. Thus it was that the team that had achieved Walker's dream was sold on for considerable profit. One by one they went, the most crushing departure being that of Alan Shearer, who moved to Newcastle in the summer of 1996 for a world-record £15 million. That was when the Blackburn fans knew once and for all that their time as championship contenders was over. 'I think I'm probably the best example of how the club operated,' says Le Saux. 'I was bought in for £300,000 and they sold me back to Chelsea for £5.5 million. That's good business.'

After a blip when they were relegated to the First Division for a season in 1999, it was good business that kept Blackburn in the Premier League for more than a decade, albeit never again coming close to the title. Good business practices even survived the death of the man who had made it all possible. Walker died on 17 August 2000 from cancer. He was seventy-one. Jack Straw, Labour home secretary and Blackburn's MP, gave him precisely the eulogy he might have wished for: 'Jack Walker did more than any other individual in the last century to enhance the self-confidence and the prosperity of his home town. I salute a great local hero and shall miss him very badly.'

Before his death, Walker had put in place a trust to maintain the football club. Under the canny chairmanship of John Williams, Blackburn remained a steady if unspectacular presence in the Premier League. 'They were an exceptionally well-run club, who understood the culture of English football,' maintains Alex Fynn. 'They had a very good chairman, a very good managing director, a series of very good managers, from Mark Hughes to Sam Allardyce. As an economic model it was one which was superior even to Arsenal.'

Decline and fall

Then, in November 2010, Blackburn were sold. The last trace of the Walker stewardship vanished when the V H Group – a vast Indian conglomerate specializing in chicken-meat processing and pharmaceutical products – bought the club. It is safe to say the poultry magnates of Venky's did not understand the nuances of English football culture. Catastrophic errors were made as key personnel were let go: Williams and Allardyce foremost among them. And in May 2012, the inevitable happened: Blackburn were relegated from the Premier League, in a tailspin of debt and unsustainable losses – £18 million a year and counting. Walker's legacy had been horribly traduced. It was a proper fowl-up.

'The roots and history of the club are small,' says Le Saux. 'Jack was the catalyst, all the component parts created this unbelievable momentum out of nowhere. And it's withdrawn back to nowhere. That's sad, but perhaps not surprising. There was a combination of so many factors that just made it work. Everything had to be aligned. It was a piece of wonderful coincidence.'

The story of Blackburn's demise – hiring and firing four managers in a season in 2012–13 as they scuffed around the lower reaches of the Championship, flirting with relegation to League One – reminds me of something the late music entrepreneur Tony Wilson once told me about football. When you are young, he said, you think success is entirely to do with the players. When you grow up a bit you think the manager is the one who creates the conditions for victory. But when you are older and wiser you realize what is really going on in football: it is the chairman who ultimately counts. Nowhere in the history of the game has that truth been better illustrated than in Blackburn Rovers' Premiership-winning season.

FA CARLING PREMIERSHIP

Anfield Stadium, Liverpool

Sunday 13 May 1995

LIVERPOOL 2 – 1 BLACKBURN ROVERS

Liverpool scorers: John Barnes 64; Jamie Redknapp 90

Blackburn scorer: Alan Shearer 20

Attendance: 40,014

Referee: David Elleray

TEAMS:

LIVERPOOL (4-4-2)

David James; Steve Harkness, John Scales (Dominic Matteo 82), Phil Babb, Mark Kennedy; Steve McManaman, Jamie Redknapp, Michael Thomas, John Barnes; Nigel Clough, Robbie Fowler

Subs not used: Tony Warner (gk), Mark Walters

BLACKBURN (4-3-3)

Tim Flowers; Henning Berg, Colin Hendry, Ian Pearce, Graeme Le Saux; Jeff Kenna, David Batty, Tim Sherwood; Jason Wilcox, Alan Shearer, Chris Sutton

Subs not used: Bobby Mimms (gk), Robbie Slater, Mike Newell

Match 4

He went to Man United and he won the lot

MANCHESTER UNITED V. TOTTENHAM HOTSPUR

Old Trafford, Manchester

Sunday 16 May 1999

It was the early hours of 27 May 1999 when a sudden explosion of energy filled Barcelona's Hotel Arts. Alex Ferguson was bundling through, his face split in a huge beam as he made his way to join colleagues now well ensconced in a celebratory party in the hotel ballroom. No wonder he was smiling: the manager had just witnessed his Manchester United team win the Champions League final with two goals scored in the extra minutes added at the end of the game by the referee, another triumph in 'Fergie Time'.

As he barrelled through the hotel to join the frolics Ferguson exuded good cheer, stopping constantly, telling everyone he bumped into how unlikely his achievement was. Porters and cleaners, a gaggle of ecstatic United fans, a female hotel guest who had taken a wrong turn on her way to the Ladies and had no idea who he was, never mind what he had just won: he was hugging them all. Even this member of his least favourite body of men – the British press – found himself wrapped in his embrace.

After disentangling myself from his hug, with a friend I followed the cheerfully triumphant manager into the party. The two of us spent half an hour in there, unnoticed, mingling with the victorious players, their friends and family, lining up for the buffet listening to a debate between Ronnie Johnsen, Henning Berg and the Manchester

United dietician Trevor Lea about the merits of coleslaw. We might have been there all night, testing first-hand how much champagne is required to fill football's biggest trophy, had the club's head of security not spotted my friend shoving half a dozen of the souvenir menus down the front of her trousers. 'Those are the property of Manchester United Football Club,' Ned Kelly – the man I had last seen escorting Eric Cantona into a Croydon magistrates' court – said as he removed them from her waistband, as if she was trying to walk off with the European Cup itself. This before applying his sizeable boot to my behind.

But the thing I remember most, more than the fact I couldn't sit down for a week, more than Ryan Giggs's uninhibited dancing, more than David May endlessly getting Nicky Butt to photograph him holding the trophy, was what Ferguson had said to me as we exchanged hugs. Not that I was party to some unique observation. He had said it to everyone else he'd embraced, indeed to anyone who would listen: 'Football, eh?' he kept repeating. 'Fucking hell!'

Albeit later cleaned up for wider public consumption, Ferguson's words were to become the motif not only of that evening's extraordinary result, but of the 1998–99 season as a whole. It was the only appropriate articulation of a footballing year of such improbable drama it would have been deemed absurd by any rational Hollywood script editor.

Throughout eight months of unexpected twists and last-minute turns, Ferguson's United had kept their dream alive in astounding, odds-defying fashion. Time and again it seemed their hopes had been dashed, their ambition curtailed, their Icarus wings scorched. But on every occasion, they had regained their purpose, maintained the pursuit, upheld the cause. Their manager's cause.

And that was what it was: a cause. As he emerged smiling from this swirling tumble-drier of a season, Ferguson appreciated that what he had done was make history. That was what he had set out to do as a football coach: leave his mark. But for him there was something more in the achievement than simply leaving his stamp on the game, something that made this feat all the more delicious. What he was relishing as he made his way to that party that night was vindication. Because this, this was personal.

Arsène d'Arsenal

Were we to identify what precisely had given the impetus to this triumphant dénouement to United's *annus mirabilis*, it lay not in Barcelona, or Old Trafford, or even in the Cliff – the intimate, venerable and soon-to-be-redundant Salford training ground where Ferguson had plotted his team's advance. Rather, it began in north London, two summers on from Blackburn's Premiership triumph. On 12 August 1996 Arsenal sacked their manager Bruce Rioch. And employed in his stead Arsène Wenger.

When he was appointed, the angular, ascetic Alsatian was not on the radar of many in English football. If Alan Shearer had been a regular on the *Match of the Day* sofa at that time he would doubtless have declared that no one had heard of the man. Wenger had achieved little as a player and none of Europe's great sides were listed on his coaching CV.

He had, admittedly, taken Monaco to the French title in 1988, but since January 1995 he had been working in Japan, as manager of Nagoya Grampus Eight, a backwater outfit in a backwater league.*

His good friend David Dein, Arsenal's chief executive, was not concerned with his lack of renown. He had wanted Wenger at Highbury to replace George Graham when the Scotsman was dismissed in 1995. But he had been outvoted by the board, who had gone for Rioch instead. Dein, though, had kept championing the Wenger cause. And when Rioch too had been removed, he persuaded his fellow directors to back his judgment. Even so, when the Frenchman finally came to London, the *Evening Standard* summed up the underwhelming nature of his arrival with the headline 'Arsène Who?'

---

* The club is best known in England for signing Gary Lineker after he retired from the Premiership; he played two seasons for them, in 1992–94, quitting just before Wenger's arrival.

Wenger did not feel diminished by such reporting; he happily admitted his background was not something to generate much excitement. Particularly in a footballing culture as insular as England's. Nor was he too surprised when his new charges quickly reached for a stereotype when weighing him up. He was a bit awkward physically and he was French, so the Arsenal players gave him an all-too-predictable nickname: Inspector Clouseau.

'One of the biggest bets [among the players] was how long I would last,' Wenger recalls. 'Everybody was betting I would be gone by January 1st.' There was no chance of that; Dein knew what he had. He was convinced he was hiring a manager fit for the increasingly rigorous demands of the Premiership, a man who would signal the necessary revolution needed to master a competition whose scale had grown far beyond anything anyone – even Dein, its chief architect – had envisaged at its inception.

And it quickly became apparent the forty-eight-year-old's arrival would have a profound effect not just on Arsenal, but on the club's rivals. There had been a few foreign managers in the Premiership before him, most notably Ruud Gullit at Chelsea and Osvaldo Ardiles at Spurs, but neither had translated their playing prowess into an ability to mould a title-winning team. Neither had lasted long. Wenger was the Premiership's first career coach, its first student of methodology, its first football professor. Just as the influx of foreign players attracted by television money had brought new attitudes, new focus, new professionalism to English football, so he now brought new systems, new approaches to preparation, a new appreciation of sports science. Not to mention an encyclopedic knowledge of dietary supplements.

Inheriting a stalwart though ageing defence of Tony Adams, Steve Bould, David Seaman, Lee Dixon, Martin Keown and Nigel Winterburn, Wenger immediately won them over with the promise that his approach would lengthen their careers (and thus, as football's wages suddenly began to spiral, prove beneficial to their current accounts). 'It is a modern saying "to buy into an idea",' says

Bob Wilson, a double-winner with Arsenal (from 1971) and Wenger's goalkeeping coach:

> But that is what the team Arsène inherited did: they bought into his way of thinking. You could see those guys realizing on a daily basis as they did what he showed them, wow this could add to my career. He wasn't and never has been tactile, chummy, hugging and kissing them, saying 'you played great today, Tony'. With Arsène it is a respect thing. It's an intelligence thing. They had to see that what he did worked. And it did. Every year he was there, they got better. And could carry on that bit longer.

Pre-match stretching, the regular use of osteopaths and massage, an energy-rich, vegetable-heavy, fat-free diet: such procedures may now be routine, but they were largely alien to the English game when Wenger introduced them. Also, despite being the son of a bar owner, he made clear his suspicion of alcohol to a group that hitherto had cheerfully regarded a bevvy or five as suitable reward for athletic endeavour.

The main thing, though, was the change of attitude. Graham was an old-fashioned chivvier, his management style that of the sergeant major. The atmosphere around the club reflected his aggression. Things often got heated in the dressing room, words were slung around, the sparring hostile. Wenger was very different. Martin Keown explains:

> He was just incredibly calm, respectful, the best word is nice. That was what was so great about him. In a sense he is proof that nice guys can win in this game. You wanted to play for him because you liked him. He made the club a happy place to be.

Wenger quickly forged a winning team by coupling English bulldog resolve to the continental technique of the French trio of Patrick Vieira, Emmanuel Petit and Nicolas Anelka, complemented by the guile of Holland's Dennis Bergkamp (a player signed by Rioch). It was a determined side, too. Just twenty months after he arrived, in spring of 1998, his Arsenal had made up a twelve-point deficit opened up by United and won the Carling Premiership. They also won the FA Cup. Ferguson had assumed doubles were his territory, but now a new tank had apparently been parked immovably on his lawn. No one was calling Wenger Clouseau now.

Mutual antipathy

The United boss, however, was not simply irked by the new competition. Unlike Martin Keown and the Arsenal players, he did not take to the newcomer as a man. From the first time Wenger spurned the Scotsman's invitation to share a handy little claret after a game, he considered him haughty, aloof, snobbish. The needle between the two men was almost immediately evident. In later years their relationship would thaw to a comradely respect, but according to Pat Crerand, the former United player who remained close to United's management, in those early days Ferguson's dislike of Wenger was profound.

'It's not like Alec, he usually gets on with other managers,' says Crerand. 'He's a union man, believes in sticking by your fellow workers. But this one, he really disliked him.' Ferguson certainly made no secret of his disdain. 'He's a novice – he should keep his opinions to Japanese football,' he said soon after he first met the Frenchman. 'They say he's an intelligent man, right? Speaks five languages? I've got a fifteen-year-old boy from the Ivory Coast who speaks five languages.'

The feeling was mutual. Wenger had no time for England's masonic order of football management of which the United boss had become the acknowledged godfather. When Ferguson claimed in an interview that his United played better football than Wenger's Arsenal, the Frenchman responded with his trademark raised eyebrow: 'Everyone thinks they have the prettiest wife at home.' But what riled Ferguson far more than a personal animus was the manner in which their rivalry had routinely come to be portrayed. As Arsenal began to gain ascendancy, it became a media commonplace that Wenger was the modernist, the quick-witted reformer, the quantum opposite of Ferguson. His professorial demeanour was contrasted with the Scot's barrack-room bluster. Wenger was the new broom, while Fergie was old school. It was Wenger, so the widely held theory went, who had the superior intellectual capacity demanded by a job that increasingly required PhD levels of knowledge in everything from physiology to psychology. Never mind that Ferguson took an interest in wine, politics, history, cooking, languages, horse-racing and the piano, never mind that he had a huge circle of friends in politics, entertainment and business, never mind that Wenger was a loner whose hinterland was confined largely to studying videos of German third-division matches, the studious incomer was reckoned the sharper brain. He was deemed the future, Ferguson the dinosaur. And Wenger's double triumph in 1998 seemed to signal the triumph of a new order. Ferguson's time was up.

During that season, I recall a senior executive at *The Guardian*, where I worked at the time, asking me if I could get an interview with Wenger to run as a cover story in the paper's G2 section. 'He's fascinating,' I was told. 'So much bigger than just football.' I failed, but by coincidence managed to secure one-on-one time with Ferguson. It was decided that that interview would be better placed in the sports section.

It may have been a media simplification, this idea that Wenger was the coming man, an easy characterization of a more complex narrative, but it infuriated Ferguson. He took it as a direct challenge, it made their rivalry something more than just a football spat, more than just the competitive gap between the two best teams in the country. While the United manager has always been spurred by confrontation, this one was special: it went to the heart of his sense of purpose as a football manager. He would later define it as one of the most significant of his career. And how he relished it. 'I know where to search for motivation,' he once said. 'It's a spur of the moment thing that you use as a key. In most things, a cause is the best key.'

After eclipsing the Old Firm with Aberdeen, and after setting out to knock Liverpool off their perch when he first came to United, now Ferguson had a new cause. In the summer of 1998, he reacted to Wenger's double with a determination to win back his reputation as the top man in English football. Beating that Frenchman became a priority. He needed to win the Premiership title to demonstrate he could outwit the upstart. He had to prove who was boss, show that, far from being yesterday's man, he was both the present and the future.

The first thing he recognized was that it could not be done without a serious investment in his playing resources. He had an outstandingly tenacious captain in Roy Keane, a fine pair of strikers in Ole Gunnar Solskjaer and Andrew Cole, plus a magnificent goalkeeper in Peter Schmeichel. Not to forget a youthful core of locally developed players, the 'Six Amigos' as Keane referred to them, of Giggs, Butt, Paul Scholes, David Beckham and the Neville brothers, Phil and Gary. But Ferguson felt a major spending spree was required to add skill and power, the impetus to catch the Gunners. And, more to the point, outwit Wenger.

Boardroom battles

Extracting the cash to fund such an assault on the market, though, he believed would not be easy. United may have been the club best placed to exploit the Premier League era, they might be inviting 55,000 paying customers through the turnstiles of their newly refurbished stadium at every home game, their commercial operation may have been so muscular that the marketing director once told me that he and the chairman Martin Edwards had a pre-match ritual of looking out of the window of his office at the queues lining up outside the United souvenir shop and smiling, but their recent financial history was one defined by caution.

The club had been floated on the London Stock Exchange in 1991 and Ferguson had come to believe that the necessity of paying dividends had stifled investment in the team, scuppering his chance of attaining continental supremacy. Though Edwards vigorously disputed such analysis (and he may have been right: the amount that departed from United's coffers to pay dividends in the time of the plc was less than a tenth that was spent on interest payments in the Glazer era), in the previous few years the manager had blamed the plc for his failure to land world-class talents like Patrick Kluivert, Gabriel Batistuta and Marcelo Salas. The one that really infuriated him was missing out on the Brazilian forward Ronaldo, whom the manager thought he had persuaded to sign for United in 1996. But, at a time when the ceiling for the weekly wage at Old Trafford was £23,000, the deal had collapsed when the board refused to countenance the South American's demand of £50,000 a week (those doughnuts don't buy themselves).

That summer, then, his negotiations with the men who held the cheque- book were critical. According to his biographer Michael Crick, in the initial budgetary meeting in July 1998 with Edwards and the plc chairman Roland Smith, Ferguson had been shocked by an opening question about whether, distracted by his new-found fondness for horse-racing, he had lost his focus. His response was to deploy the nuclear negotiating option: he threatened his own retirement. 'Do you want to call it a day?' he said.

So alarmed were the two directors by what such a move would do to their share price, they acquiesced: £14 million would be made immediately available to spend on reinforcements. Ferguson quickly used up that and more on the foursquare Dutch defender Jaap Stam (£10.6 million) and the Swedish winger Jesper Blomqvist (£4.4 million). But he also wanted the crafty Aston Villa striker Dwight Yorke, the player Patrick Barclay (another Ferguson biographer) reckons the most underrated of his generation. He argued vigorously for the extra money and eventually £12.6 million was released to land the forward.

Edwards insisted, however, that the deal must be part-financed by a sale. Negotiations were held to offload Solskjaer to Tottenham. United accepted a fee of £5 million, but the player refused to go. He and his wife liked living in Cheshire and had no enthusiasm for a move to London. Besides, he believed the side he watched frequently from the bench were poised on the very lip of greatness. He wanted to be part of it. Edwards may have cavilled at the time, but it was a recalcitrance that was to have profoundly beneficial consequences for Ferguson, his club and the fans. Not to mention the plc's bottom line.

Initially, though, the newcomers appeared to make no material difference to the newly established, Gunner-friendly status quo. Stam in particular was given the runaround in the 1998–99 season's opening Charity Shield, the jet-propelled Anelka twice embarrassing him for pace as Arsenal won 3–0. Despite Ferguson's spending spree, in the press box that afternoon at Wembley the certainty was that the balance of power had finally and irrevocably shifted down the M1 to Highbury. The headline in the *Evening Standard* had changed somewhat in tone from the days of Arsène Who? It now read: 'Wenger 3 Fergie 0'.

And away from the pitch, too, United appeared to be on the cusp of change. A hint of the Premier League's growing financial vigour came on 9 September 1998 when the competition's broadcaster BSkyB announced it had reached terms to take over Manchester United plc. A bid of £623.4 million had been accepted by the board (Edwards alone was to trouser some £85 million for his shares). It seemed only a few contractual Ts needed crossing before the television company took control of the country's most substantial football club.

For those seeking corporate synergy the move was an obvious one. Sky relied on its contract to cover football to sell subscriptions. With the most significant club in the Premiership not so much onside as inside the corporation, that deal could be protected; one vote in future negotiations was forever guaranteed. Plus, the move confirmed what José Angel Sanchez, director of marketing at Real Madrid, United's rivals for the position of the world's richest football club, had reflected about the Premiership: English football was now in the business of selling media content. These were moving pictures it peddled. This was now the sporting equivalent of Universal Studios. And the Theatre of Dreams was an entertainment brand as powerful as Disneyland. For Sky that was some proposition. They could not only control the means of delivery, they would have a stake in what was being shown.

But not everyone felt as comfortable with the deal as the buyers, or the soon-to-be-enriched directors. A group of United fans, alarmed at the prospect of their club falling into the hands of those without a true appreciation of its cultural importance, started a campaign against the takeover. For them, Sky's interest in their club began and ended with a fondness for the further procurement of money and power. And they didn't want the institution they loved to be thus exploited.

This was not the traditional terrace rebellion, with people chanting 'sack the board' from the stands and threatening to smash the windows at the chairman's house (though such a move was mooted at an early anti-takeover meeting). It was a sophisticated, modern operation whose organizers had a far better grasp of United's emotional pull than its putative owners. 'I think they saw us as a group of raggedy-arsed football fans,' remembers Andy Walsh, the protest leader. 'I think we surprised them.'

The truth is that the organization reflected the widening footballing constituency that had developed in the Premiership years. Sky had proselytized the game across the classes, had relentlessly promoted it as the smartest, sexiest show in town, a compelling lure for the kind of audience marketers craved. And now Sky's executives reaped what they had sown, finding themselves confronted by a campaign co-ordinated as much by lawyers, accountants, media men and advertising copywriters as by manual workers from football's traditional demographic. It was as much Oxbridge as Stalybridge. There were so many United fans within the City of London's financial institutions, for instance, that Sky's business advisers complained that many a detail of their progress was leaked to the anti-takeover campaign. Just six years after the Premiership had begun, everywhere you looked, old assumptions were being overturned.

All change at Old Trafford

With United distracted in the boardroom, things appeared to be in a state of flux in the dressing room, too. Ferguson's hopes of regaining ascendancy from his French counterpart were dealt a serious blow when, in November, Peter Schmeichel announced he would be leaving Old Trafford at the end of the season. The Dane was not the most popular figure among the players. Keane, for instance, routinely referred to him as the world's most boringly self-obsessed man and deliberately fired howitzer shots at him during training with the intention of bruising his palms if not his ego. But even the headstrong skipper recognized Schmeichel had legitimate claim to be the best goalkeeper of the Premiership era; his saves, his physical domination of his penalty area and his ability to organize a defence had underpinned the club's rise to pre-eminence. He would come to be missed like few others in the club's history.

Then, in December, came another major loss. The assistant manager Brian Kidd accepted a position as Blackburn manager, re-placing the sacked Roy Hodgson on an annual salary rumoured to be £1 million (more, the United boss couldn't fail to note, than Ferguson himself was earning at the time). Kidd had been influential in the development of the United team's youthful soul; good cop to Fergie's bad, he had been the young gang's emotional supporter, always encouraging, always on their side. Now he was off to Blackburn, aside from Arsenal the only club so far to challenge United's Premiership hegemony. That hurt. But beyond any perceived slight, Ferguson thought his former deputy was making a mistake. He doubted Kidd had the necessary steel to become a number one. 'All the players think he wants them in the team,' he once said of his erstwhile assistant. 'They all think he's their friend. You can get away with that when you're a number two, but not when you're in charge.'

When United lost 3–2 at home to Middlesbrough on 19 December, it seemed that the game was up: the edifice was crumbling, the Frenchman was on the march; Sky, it appeared, were about to splash out on the country's second most successful team. And Fergie? Well, he was just about to turn fifty-eight. The press speculated that time was imminently to be called on the Scotsman's career.

The man himself, however, refused to be cowed by such a notion. With Kidd gone, he resumed responsibility for day-to-day coaching. Aided by his new assistant Steve McClaren, recruited from Derby County, he instituted a new fitness regime at the club. With three of four trophies still to be played for (his side had been knocked out of the League Cup by Tottenham in December), he rightly deemed stamina to be key. There was to be zero tolerance of alcohol, diets were reassessed, rest became paramount. If, in his team talks, he was to preach a doctrine of never giving up, of fighting until the very last moment, then his players needed the physical tools to sustain such a challenge. The irony was, what he was doing was making the place more Wenger-like. Ever the pragmatist, Ferguson may not have liked the man, but if his methods worked, they would be embraced, not scorned. 'We'd always been brought up to do the extra, work your-selves that bit harder,' recalls Phil Neville. 'But that mid-season in training he nearly had us on our knees. And we loved it.'

This new focus worked. After the defeat to Middlesbrough, as the New Year turned, Ferguson's team went on a thirty-three-match unbeaten run through the rest of the season. During that time they knocked Liverpool, Chelsea, Internazionale, Juventus and Bayern out of cup competitions. Time and again, they did so after falling behind, they did so in the last second of added time even as Ferguson was in his technical area tapping at his watch. Almost every victory seemed to defy the odds.

Arsenal, too, found themselves caught up in the Manchester maelstrom. The two clubs met in the FA Cup semi-final. After a drawn game, they resumed battle on 14 April at Villa Park. And once again, United recovered from seeming oblivion. With the scores tied, in the last moments of normal time, Schmeichel produced an astonish-ing save from a Bergkamp penalty, thus preserving the dream of a treble of FA Cup, Champions League and Premiership titles even as it seemed to be disappearing before everyone's eyes.

Then, in extra time, with a conclusion of penalties looming, Giggs picked up a misplaced pass from Vieira, waltzed upfield, slipping past every member of the most vaunted defence in Europe in a mazy, pacy jig. On the touchline Ferguson bellowed at him to pass the ball. But Giggs weaved on, leaving Arsenal defenders panting in his wash, before slamming the ball over Seaman's shoulder high into the net. Wheeling away and removing his shirt in triumph, he ran the entire length of the touchline bare-chested and bellowing, his chest hair swishing in the breeze.

It was a goal from football's fantasy playground, one of unfettered joy. And it sent United's followers at Villa Park into a delirious pitch-invading frenzy, celebrating not just the fact that United were on their way to Wembley for the FA Cup final, but that they were doing so at the expense of their newest rivals. In the press box, the latest dispatch reporting United's demise had to be scrapped and rewritten. Onward they marched.

Giggs's goal, incidentally, was the last ever to be scored in an FA Cup semi-final replay – from the next season they became single-match affairs, their outcomes settled in extra time or a penalty shoot-out. But for Ferguson that wonder strike had symbolic resonance for United's 1998–99 season. 'It gathered everyone together, we became a force,' he reckoned. 'And that was down to Ryan's fantastic goal. He made us believe.'

Eyes on the prizes

It was after that game that Wenger, rueing Bergkamp's penalty miss, fuming about defeat, and incandescent about his failure to sustain Arsenal's upward trajectory, refused to shake Ferguson's hand. Ferguson took the snub badly, citing it in the post-match press conference as an example of how standards of courtesy within the game were declining. But unhappy though he may have been at Wenger's failure to observe protocol, the Scot could comfort himself with the clear evidence that he had drilled himself beneath his rival's skin. Plus he had won.

Soon after that pivotal semi-final, to the amazement of Sky's senior executives (and members of the United board) Stephen

Byers, the then Secretary of State for Industry, announced that the broadcaster's bid to buy the club had been found to breach the Monopoly and Mergers Commission's regulations on competitiveness. Sky withdrew, maintaining no more than a 9 per cent shareholding. The celebrations among the campaigners were as unrestrained as those at Villa Park: a huge commercial entity had been defeated by the efforts of a bunch of football fans. To their lasting regret, however, it was not a victory that would be repeated six years later when another corporate raider came calling.

But as United swaggered their way through the season, brushing aside all opposition in the FA Cup and Champions League, in the Premiership Arsenal kept snapping at their heels. Wenger was proving as stubbornly intransigent as Ferguson. Arsenal's unbeaten run in the league extended back even further than United's – all the way to 13 December 1998, when they had lost 3–2 at Aston Villa.

So when Arsenal beat Tottenham on 5 May as United were held to a draw by Liverpool and moved three points clear at the top, everyone was once more predicting that Ferguson's quest for three trophies was as good as over. Surely Arsenal wouldn't falter now; Wenger wouldn't let them. The treble was an impossible dream too far. And for the manager it was reckoned this would be the toughest blow: while he always enjoyed the FA Cup, while Europe offered gilding, it was the Premiership, he had always made clear, that truly defined a side's prowess. As he him-self put it in his autobiography: 'There is only one stamp of supremacy in our country's football and that is the Premiership title.'

But in this of all seasons, even with Arsenal occupying the top spot and the finishing line in sight, anyone dismissing United's hopes should have realized there would be a twist in the plot. Plenty of people who should have known better did just that: I wrote a piece that week suggesting the treble was an impossibility. No club could sustain a campaign on three fronts successfully, I argued – not even the great Liverpool side of the 1970s had managed that.

And then on 11 May, the day that piece was printed, in the Gunners' next game, as United were beating Middlesbrough, came the stutter. Jimmy Floyd Hasselbaink scored the only goal for Leeds and Arsenal were beaten. Three points we'd all assumed were Arsenal's had gone west. For the first time in six months, Wenger was on the losing side in a Premiership match. His defence, parsimonious to the point of miserliness, had been breached. But unlike his counterpart at United he did not have the attacking options to respond.

Fate had intervened on Ferguson's behalf once more: the race for the Premiership title was back on and now the maths had switched back in the Scot's favour. With two games of the season remaining, the numbers were simple: United required four points to secure their fifth title in seven seasons. No matter what Arsenal did, snaffle those four and United could not be caught. The position was exactly what Ferguson had always sought: he had control. With just two games remaining the title was his to lose.

The first of the four points was achieved when United went to Ewood Park and ground out a 0–0 draw. Watching that stodgy, turgid and dull game, few would have imagined that they were watching history-makers in action. The best that could be said of United was that they were efficient. As for their hosts, that was the match that relegated Blackburn and their new manager, Brian Kidd. Knowing his opponent had to win to remain in the financial uplands of the Premiership, Ferguson was astonished at Kidd's negative tactics. And amazed, too, at his former assistant's smiling demeanour after the game. In such circumstances the United manager confessed he would have gone home and buried his head in a pillow for the next fortnight. But Kidd appeared unperturbed, inviting his erstwhile boss to his office for a drink and wishing him all the best of luck for the next three games.

And what games they were: the last fixture in the Premiership, the FA Cup final and the Champions League final. Succeed in those and Ferguson would rewrite history. He would be the man who landed the treble, a distinction that had eluded the greatest of English club managers, from Bill Shankly, Bob Paisley and Matt Busby through to

Brian Clough and Don Revie. He would be in a class of his own. More to the point, Ferguson's treble would be one better than Wenger's double.

The enormity of what lay ahead finally dawned on the manager when he arrived at training the day before his final Premiership game to discover that Danny McGregor, United's commercial manager, was distributing T-shirts to all staff with the legend '3 to go' on the front. He informed Ferguson that he had shirts ready to hand out as each prong of the treble was achieved, '1 down 2 to go' morphing into '2 down 1 to go' before completing the set with '3 down 0 to go'. Ferguson winced at this wilful tempting of fate. A keen student of Sophocles, he knew it wasn't over until it was over.

That was undoubtedly the case in the Premiership; it all rested on the final game of the season. The requirement was straightforward: going into the fixture one point ahead, United knew victory would ensure they were champions. Any other result could prove terminal to their ambitions. If they stumbled and Arsenal won their home game with Aston Villa, the title would remain at Highbury.

Super Sunday showdown

The League sponsors hailed Sunday 16 May as the Carling Final Countdown and all week the bulletins on Sky Sports News – the twenty-four-hour rolling news service which had launched the previous October largely as a promotional vehicle to bark up the broadcaster's sporting content – presented this as the greatest climax to a championship season ever, even better than the last one. Sky may have failed in its attempt to buy up the main participant, but not to worry. They still owned the delivery of the drama.

The build-up made much of the nature of United's opponents. In a straight race with Arsenal, it was not just that the Mancunian side were due to play the Gunners' loathed north London rivals Tottenham. More intriguingly, the club was now managed by George Graham, the very coach who had been dismissed from Highbury four years previously.

It might have seemed wholly counterintuitive when the chairman

Alan Sugar invited Graham to leave Leeds United and take over at White Hart Lane in 1998. After all, when he first acquired the club, Sugar had engaged in a lengthy battle with Terry Venables, during which the future star of the television reality show *The Apprentice* had accused his manager of all sorts of things, not many of which featured the word 'probity'. Now here he was employing a man who admitted to accepting unauthorized cash (albeit he had returned every penny, with interest). What's more, Graham was a man loathed around White Hart Lane for his long-standing Arsenal connections. What was Sugar playing at? Yet the tycoon's reasoning was instructive. Like Ferguson he saw the motivational merit in a cause. He believed Graham would be a man on a mission; bent on revenge, he would be singularly driven to better Arsenal. And in those days it was evident: better Arsenal and you would win things. Graham, he was sure, would do his utmost to stymie the Gunners. And in the process further the Spurs cause.

Such is the fondness among football fans for a conspiracy theory that all week Sky Sports News was full of angry Arsenal fans predicting that the combination of Graham and Spurs had effectively gifted the title to United. They insisted there was nothing either party would like more than to see Arsenal finish the season without a trophy, with the title heading back to Manchester. One Gooner, interviewed by the channel outside Highbury that week, even went so far as to claim that it was part of a wider plot to do down his club: the FA and Premiership had contrived the fixture in the certain knowledge that it would result in a United win, so depriving Arsenal of what was rightfully theirs. Quite why the Premiership would wish to engineer such a result against the club run by its architect remained unclear. Never mind, too, that Tottenham were the only Premiership side that United had not beaten that season and had knocked them out of the League Cup. The conspiracy theory proved tenacious: Spurs, cajoled by Fergie's good mate Graham, would lie down and allow United easy victory just to spite their north London neighbours.

Indeed, Spurs supporters themselves were divided over whether

Graham ought to instruct his players to do just that. In the absence of any title challenge of their own, here they were in a position to stifle the achievement of their hated rivals. Some thought this golden opportunity should be grasped with both hands and called for a tactical surrender. Lie back and think of Arsenal's misery. But a Tottenham blogger called Brian Judson, writing on the Spurs Odyssey website, called those who harboured such views 'morons'. A true Tottenham fan, he wrote, 'should never wish to see his side lose, regardless of the circumstances of the game'.

Arsenal fans may have been convinced that fate and their previous manager were lining up against them. Some Tottenham fans may have worried about their fellow supporters' sanity. But Sky had no such fears. Sure they were happy to communicate others' worried theories, but the company itself was purring about what lay ahead. For the armchair fan, the fixture offered an irresistible invitation to enjoy someone else's discomfort. It was a nice demonstration of how Sky's technological advances had not simply enabled the delivery of the drama, they had enhanced it. In those pre-smartphone, Twitter-free days, in the stands information on critical developments elsewhere still came via a tortuous system of Chinese whispers, begun by those few who had thought to bring along transistor radios. On television you knew exactly what was happening as it happened. So not being there now meant being closer to the action than being there. How quickly the final day of the league season – and football in general – had become a television event.

And television was there from the start of the day, Sky's cameras stationed on the Old Trafford forecourt and outside Highbury soliciting predictions from fans as they arrived for the Super Sunday showdown. Arsenal supporters hoped that their rivals might do them a favour. Several were even broadcast uttering the blasphemous chant of 'Come on you Spurs!', an irony not lost on blogger Brian Judson: 'They really would sell their souls for a title,' he wrote. 'Pathetic.' Spurs fans were relishing what was effectively a no-lose engagement: if they won or drew the game they could celebrate the accrual of points at the league's least generous away ground. They knew their team's record was not good at Old Trafford (they had not won there since Gary Lineker scored the only goal in a First Division game ten years previously, and hadn't even scored since Darren Caskey got a consolation goal in a 2–1 defeat in 1993). But never mind if they lost. At least they could comfort themselves with the knowledge defeat had scuppered Arsenal's hopes. They were determined to have fun.

In stark contrast, fun was in short supply among the United fans. Sure, there were some who exuded confidence that their team would do the business. But such bravado was rare. Outside the ground as in the stands nerves were frayed. Their team may have been close to a history-making treble, but nothing had been won yet. They had spent most of the season mockingly comparing their position to that of their local rivals, who were about to participate in the Second Division play-offs. But fail here and Man City supporters would make the next day at work or school intolerable.

As kick-off approached, the fans' sense of trepidation was shared in the United dressing room. The fear of failure was articulated by their perfectionist captain, Roy Keane, who wrote in his autobiography:

> We know if we win these three games we have surpassed anything achieved in the game. However, there is an alternative possibility that might prompt a different headline: United Blow Treble Bid or The Nearly Men.

Ferguson, who had seen nervousness thwart ambition before, went round the dressing room quietly telling each player how much he valued their contribution that season, wishing them well. Collectively, he reminded the players that: 'The only way we lose at home is when we beat ourselves.' He told them to forget the broader picture, to win the immediate battle, the one-on-one against their direct opponent. Wear down the spirit of individual players on the opposing side and their collective morale will swiftly crumble, he said. That way victory lies. The captain added just one observation to the manager's speech. 'We're hungrier than they are,' he said. 'We want it more.'

And there was no doubt there was an appetite for this game in the home ranks. Ferguson had picked a team which reflected that. With Keane and Scholes unable to play in the forthcoming Champions League final because of suspension, he selected them both, telling them this was their big moment, their chance to leave a final indelible mark on a historic season. Stam was suffering from a sore Achilles tendon, so was rested in the hope he might be fit for Barcelona; David May played alongside Ronny Johnsen in the centre, with Schmeichel, Gary Neville and Denis Irwin completing the backline. Beckham and Giggs occupied the wings. And up front was the canny Yorke, whose clever movement sharpened United's goal-scoring threat.

Alongside him, Ferguson chose Teddy Sheringham rather than Andy Cole. For most of the season he had used his four strikers in pairs: Cole and Yorke, Sheringham and Solskjaer. But on this occasion he wanted to employ Yorke's finesse and he felt Sheringham might have a personal motivation to perform. He recognized someone with a cause.

Sheringham had been signed from Spurs in the summer of 1997, charged with the impossible task of replacing Eric Cantona. When he arrived in Manchester, the Londoner said he had left the comforts of home in order to win something. Spurs supporters, who regarded him as one of their own, were mortified. How dare their hero desert them in order to fulfil his own ambition? Why not stay at White Hart Lane and try to win something there? And how they relished it when, in his first year at Old Trafford, he found himself unable to fill the holes in his trophy cabinet. When Tottenham had won the 1998–99 season's first trophy – the League Cup – the stands at Wembley had echoed to their now favourite chant: 'Oh Teddy, Teddy, he went to Man United and he won fuck all.' So Sheringham had motivation all right. What better reply to the taunts than scoring the winner here, the goal that secured the title? That would shut them up. And also silence their Arsenal counterparts who had cheerfully adopted the ditty.

Graham, meanwhile, made two changes from the Spurs line-up that had drawn with Chelsea the previous Monday. Justin Edinburgh and Les Ferdinand came in for Mauricio Taricco and Chris Armstrong. Which meant the former Liverpool defender John Scales was available to play only his seventh game of a season bedevilled by a recurrent ankle problem.

Just before the teams came onto the pitch, the Salford-born tenor Russell Watson stoked up the crowd with a spine-tingling unaccompanied rendition of the Italia 90 World Cup theme, 'Nessun dorma'. It was an apt lyrical summary of what was to follow: nobody was going to sleep during the ensuing ninety minutes. Though they were going to be nervous, too nervous to create much of a spontaneous atmosphere. Even Watson's vocal gymnastics had not got the Stretford End singing. It was one of those games that needed action to get the crowd humming. And, thankfully, that action came quickly. Almost as soon as the game started, for watching Arsenal fans it seemed as if their paranoid assumptions of Tottenham capitulation were about to be horribly, inevitably fulfilled. First Spurs' playmaker David Ginola hobbled off after a mere nine minutes on the field. Even as the Frenchman stood on the touchline receiving treatment from a physio, his colleague Sol Campbell played a simple pass back to Ian Walker. It may have appeared a routine defensive manoeuvre, the kind of thing practised endlessly on the training pitch. But the goalkeeper did not see Yorke haring down on him, rapidly closing down his defensible space, and his clearance struck the advancing Tobagan on the back. The ball looped out of Walker's reach, spinning comically towards the goal. Fortunately for the keeper, it hit the post and rolled back slowly along the line. He was able to dive on it. 'That crazy moment could have settled the Championship' was commentator Martin Tyler's summary on Sky.

It was to be Walker's last moment of aberration. Recovering his composure, he saved well from Giggs and stopped a shot from Sheringham, who was offside. Then, with twenty minutes of the game gone, he dispatched a huge punt downfield. Steffen Iversen outjumped

May and headed the ball on. Moving adroitly in anticipation of the flick, Les Ferdinand strode in front of Johnsen and, with the inside of his right boot, sent the ball first time in a high arc towards the United goal. Schmeichel watched it loop over his head. In a desperate scramble, he tried to back-pedal into position to push it away. But he ran out of room and ended up like a big, blond salmon, thrashing around in the back of the net with the ball alongside him for company. It was Ferdinand's first goal of 1999 and it stunned the Stretford End. Behind the goal the United fans were open-mouthed in astonishment. Surely not. Surely the pessimist's view of football, which posits that everything will inevitably turn to dust, was not going to apply here. Not now.

Are you watching, Arsenal?

In the section reserved for Tottenham followers, the visitors from north London immediately sensed the importance of the strike. Never mind the boost it might have for Arsenal, at least if the score stayed like this it meant Sheringham would be prevented from fulfilling his immediate hope. And they relished a noisy rendition of their chant, just to remind him how things stood. Keane, never one anxious to acknowledge others' achievements, even in victory, disparagingly described the goal as a fluke, a perverse and undeserved slice of ill-fortune. But Ferdinand looked as if he had meant to direct the ball goalwards, if nothing else to put it in the mixer and see what happened.

At Highbury news of the goal quickly spread. Never before – or since – had Tottenham success been so rapturously received in Arsenal ranks. As their team were struggling to convert territorial superiority into goal opportunity in their own game, here was hope. Here was possibility. And they too articulated their optimism with a round of Teddy-baiting. Ferguson, meanwhile, was not fretting. While never enjoying an opposition goal, he reasoned at least this one had come early. There were still seventy minutes left to put things right. He stood at the edge of his technical area and encouraged his players to be patient, to play to their strengths, to keep the ball.

Almost from the restart, United pressed their opponents back on their heels. Keane upped the tempo, urging his team-mates to pass the ball quicker, to move into space with more urgency. Chances began to arrive: Scholes had two fierce shots well saved by Walker ('magnificent goalkeeping,' cooed Tyler) while Beckham met a Giggs cross with an unchallenged header, which he sent over the bar. Far from worrying that it might be one of those days, Keane took these efforts as signals of a change of momentum. Keep working, keep trying, keep going forward, he kept yelling.

Then, with five minutes to go before half-time, came reward for their sustained endeavour. Scholes sharply dispossessed Tim Sherwood in midfield and, while the former Blackburn man complained vociferously of being upended, passed out to Giggs. The Welshman returned the ball inside to the advancing Scholes (who later confessed he had a bit of extra speed as he was running away from a fuming Sherwood). He quickly moved it outside to Beckham on the edge of the area. Justin Edinburgh, the Spurs full-back, had been deceived by a darting run by Yorke and had followed him towards the penalty spot. It meant Beckham had space and time to line up his shot as if it were a free kick. Edinburgh, suddenly made aware of what had happened, desperately tried to close him down. But he was nowhere near as Beckham bent the ball away from Walker into the far side of the goal.

'Tottenham don't like it,' said Tyler as Sherwood sprinted to Graham Poll, the referee, to complain about Scholes's spikey challenge which had set the attack in motion. 'But Manchester United love it.' And love it they did. The home section erupted in relief and song. Mind you, the Spurs fans weren't entirely quiet either. Just as the half-time whistle sounded, they could be heard chanting: 'Are you watching, Arsenal?' In the dressing room, Ferguson demonstrated his lynx-eyed ruthlessness. He replaced Sheringham with Cole. He had noticed that John Scales was tiring after his long injury lay-off and reasoned that Cole's pace might trouble the defender. The Londoner was furious. Not only was the manager depriving him of the opportunity to silence his detractors, he was turning to Cole, someone he had no time for. Sheringham unleashed a string of expletives at his manager. Ferguson, though, quickly pacified him, telling him he could still play his part in history over the next ten days. Given Sheringham's forthcoming contributions to both the FA Cup and Champions League finals, it was some prophecy.

More to the point, it was some substitution. Less than five minutes into the second half, as United pressed towards the Stretford End, Gary Neville sent a high, hopeful forward pass from the right wing. Cole, absolutely fulfilling his manager's instruction, left Scales leaden-footed as he sprinted forward into the ball's trajectory. He allowed it to drift over his shoulder, stretched his right leg, controlled it on his laces, flicked it up with his left and volleyed with his right over Walker. What a goal it was, a juggling act of the highest skill. And for Cole it represented real vindication.

Four years previously, in the final game of the 1994–95 season, he had been deemed culpable for United's failure to beat West Ham and secure the title. That afternoon in east London he had seemed anything but the clinical finisher Ferguson thought he had bought from Newcastle. But here at Old Trafford, with the treble now looming large, he did not squander opportunity. He dispatched his first chance with aplomb. 'The chairman mentioned it after the game,' he said of his failure at Upton Park. 'What goes around comes around. It's just fantastic.'

The score may now have been the one Ferguson wanted, but there was still forty minutes to go, nearly an entire half in which to ensure there was no faltering, no mishap, no more of what Keane might deem flukes. To stiffen resistance, Ferguson instructed Beckham and Giggs to tuck inside and sent Butt on to replace Yorke. When Phil Neville trotted on for Giggs, he ended up with five at the back, four in midfield and Cole alone up front. He needed to be sure. Word had reached him that Arsenal had taken the lead against Villa. He recalled the dénouement four years previously at Upton Park. He knew he could not afford a slip-up. He had to win this one. He had to come out on top in the battle with Wenger.

As the games headed towards their conclusion, television screens across the country were split into two boxes. In the one captioned 'Old Trafford', fans in replica United shirts could be seen desperately scanning their watches, whistling for a conclusion. They didn't want any hint of 'Fergie Time' here. In the one captioned 'Highbury', Arsenal followers had transistors pressed to their ears, hoping against hope for news of a miracle.

'Come on you scum' was the chant from the Clock End, the aficionados feeling compromised by the obligation to trust their fortunes to the enemy. Spurs, though, could not conjure up an equalizer. With Graham on the touchline waving his players forward, with just two minutes and forty-one seconds of injury time elapsed, Poll blew the final whistle. At Old Trafford the stands erupted. Even the Spurs section cheered the knowledge of Arsenal failure. At Highbury it was as if the balloon had been emptied of air.

'It has gone all the way to the final whistle of the final game,' observed Tyler, as Ferguson was buried in a celebratory huddle of his coaching staff. And the outpouring of delight was unconfined. With the PA playing Queen's 'We Are The Champions', Neville and Beckham embraced, as did Cole and Yorke, while Schmeichel soaked up the home atmosphere for the last time. 'To finish like this is really fantastic. Me and my family have really enjoyed our stay in Manchester,' he told a television reporter, as the fans chanted 'don't go' in the background.

At Highbury, Sky's cameras picked out in the stands what was to become their defining shot of any season's conclusion: a middle-aged fan blubbing uncontrollably. Sheringham, meanwhile, could not contain his glee, trotting round to where the Tottenham fans were stationed and raising his hands to them. On one hand he held up three fingers, on the other one. Oh Teddy, Teddy: he was on the verge of coming to Man United and winning the lot. Behind him, the television crews buttonholed Ferguson. For once, he was delighted to be interviewed. He summed up the match as follows:

Their central midfield had started to get hold of the ball and it was a hanging-on job. We were hanging on to a whole season of hard work. We deserved the title because we are the best team in the country. We have to take ourselves to the wire all the time but we proved there is something about certain teams that elevates them beyond the rest. We just never give in.

Set to party like it's 1999

What really pleased Ferguson, however, was the manner in which his side had clinched the title. As it happens, United had done it with ten fewer points than they accrued when they came second in 2012. But in 1999, seventy-nine was a total sufficient to better Arsenal. A more instructive illumination of the difference in approach between the two teams was to be found in the goals-for column. United had netted eighty times, twenty-one more than their rivals. For Ferguson this was proof that for all Wenger's supposed sophistication, for all his clever continental ways, it was his United side that played the more progressive football.

It was a discrepancy that was to haunt Wenger that summer. His bullish insistence that his team had completed the season with the best defensive record in Europe notwithstanding, he had been given a stark lesson that it was goals at the other end that won titles. The Frenchman would be obliged to change his outlook, to make his sides more fluent, more persuasive in front of goal. And that gave Ferguson enormous satisfaction, the certain knowledge that he had required his vaunted rival to reconsider his footballing philosophy.

Even better was the fact that, while Wenger was off on holiday, the season was decidedly not over for Ferguson. With two matches to go he was keen that the mood of celebration should not impinge on preparation. He sent his players home from the match with clear instructions that they were to be rewarded with a day off on the Monday in which to relax. But that would be it. They were back to work on Tuesday. There were two cup finals over the next ten days. History was within their grasp. And no booze-up was going to compromise that possibility.

Keane, however, had a more old-fashioned view of what a day off might constitute. After drinking all day that Monday with the former United hero Norman Whiteside in several pubs in Hale, he headed to Manchester city centre to meet up with the rest of the team. He found them in a bar called Mulligan's where he almost immediately became embroiled in an altercation with the only three people in the place more intoxicated than he was. Punches were thrown, a glass was smashed across his forehead. He was arrested and spent the night in a Manchester police cell. Ferguson was fuming. Though his anger somewhat dissipated when it became evident his captain was the victim in the disturbance not the instigator.

At the Cliff that week, as Keane sweated out his hangover on the training pitch below, the manager sat in his office giving an interview to Hugh McIlvanney, the veteran *Sunday Times* man who was in the process of ghost-writing his autobiography. For the fifth time in his managerial career, the Premiership trophy had found its way into his hands. And there was more to come. He was on the verge of rewriting football's history books. Which was something he relished. 'History is important,' he told McIlvanney. 'If we don't know where we've been how can we know where we're going?' And where Ferguson was heading was towards football immortality. He smiled that day when he discovered that McGregor and his staff were wearing round the place their T-shirts with the logo 1 down 2 to go. Then again, maybe it would have been more appropriate if they'd donned the shirts on sale outside Old Trafford that triumphant Premiership day in May 1999. Harking back to that infamous *Evening Standard* headline, the shirts bore a simple legend: 'Arsène Who?'

● ● ● ● ●

FA CARLING PREMIERSHIP

Old Trafford, Manchester

Sunday 16 May 1999

MANCHESTER UNITED   2 – 1   TOTTENHAM HOTSPUR

United scorers: David Beckham 42; Andrew Cole 48

Spurs scorer: Les Ferdinand 24

Attendance: 55,189

Referee: Graham Poll

TEAMS:

MANCHESTER UNITED (4-4-2)

Peter Schmeichel; Gary Neville, David May, Ronnie Johnsen, Denis
Irwin; David Beckham, Roy Keane, Paul Scholes (Nicky Butt 70),
Ryan Giggs (Phil Neville 70); Teddy Sheringham (Andrew Cole 46),
Dwight Yorke

Subs not used: Raimond Van der Gouw; Ole Gunnar Solskjaer

TOTTENHAM HOTSPUR (4-4-2)

Ian Walker; Stephen Carr, Sol Campbell, John Scales (Luke Young 70),
Justin Edinburgh; Darren Anderton, Steffen Freund, Tim Sherwood,
David Ginola (José Dominguez 10; Andy Sinton 77); Les Ferdinand,
Steffen Iversen

Subs not used: Espen Baardsen; Stephen Clemence

Match 5

We won the League at White Hart Lane

TOTTENHAM HOTSPUR v. ARSENAL

White Hart Lane, London

Sunday 25 April 2004

Ally MacLeod was a football manager who seldom allowed grim reality to intrude on his sporting fantasies. The man who, when he took the Scottish national side to the 1978 World Cup, raised levels of tartan expectation to heights not witnessed since the English were poleaxed at the Battle of Bannockburn in 1314, was the very epitome of the football optimist. When he was boss of Ayr United in the early 1970s, the story goes he was sitting with his assistant ahead of the season's start, going through the fixture list. MacLeod ticked off each of the matches in turn. 'We'll win that one, we'll win that one, we'll get a draw there,' he said. And so on, until, still gloriously unbeaten, he reached the climax of the season, a home fixture against Rangers. 'Well, that's maximum points in the bag,' he said cheerfully, crossing Rangers off his list. 'We'll do them for sure. No way we'll do anything but win that one.'

By now, his more cautious assistant had grown a little disturbed at his colleague's unhinged confidence. 'But Ally, this is Rangers you're talking about,' he said. 'They're the champions. You can't be saying we'll beat them just like that.' 'Course I can,' came MacLeod's rejoinder. 'By the time we meet them we'll be miles clear at the top of the league. And not even Rangers will fancy their chances coming to the home of the runaway leaders.'*

Running through an entire season unbeaten is something that generally only occurs in the wilder flights of a football manager's imagination. Reality suggested it was – like eternal youth or Andy Carroll picking up the Ballon d'Or as the world's finest footballer – a functional impossibility. By the beginning of the twenty-first century it had only happened once in England. That was in 1888–89, the inaugural year of league competition, when Preston North End did not lose a single one of their twenty-two fixtures. They were the one and only 'Invincibles'.

At the beginning of the 2002–03 season, however, Arsène Wenger was moved to suggest that he had built a side capable of matching Preston's feat. He was developing his own Invincibles. The previous year his Arsenal had won the double, outpacing and outmanoeuvring the now knighted Sir Alex Ferguson and his treble-winning Manchester United. So certain was Wenger that something was stirring at Highbury that, ahead of the season-opening Charity Shield, he had an Ally MacLeod moment. He said in an interview with the *Daily Mirror* that he had the team to do one better than merely winning the title as they had the previous term: they could go through the whole fixture list unbeaten. We can do it, he insisted, if we get the attitude right.

'I remember it being mentioned, it kind of went public,' recalls Martin Keown, Wenger's indomitable centre-back. 'I remember thinking he's put us under pressure, I think he was trying to set us goals. But he felt the team was capable of doing it.' Capable maybe. But doing it was somewhat harder. When, in early October 2002, Arsenal were beaten by a stunning goal from Everton's teenaged sensation of a striker – 'remember the name: Wayne Rooney,' cooed Clive Tyldesley on the television commentary – his remarks took on more than a hint

* In each of Ally MacLeod's six seasons (1969–75) as manager of Ayr in the old Scottish First Division, the club finished 14th, 14th, 12th, 6th, 7th and 7th.

of hubris. And when Manchester United overhauled an eight-point gap at the top of the table in the spring of 2003 to steal the title from his grasp, Wenger was widely mocked for his wilful tempting of fate.

From that point on, he kept his predictions of invincibility to himself. Though according to Bob Wilson, the former double-winner who was goalkeeping coach at Arsenal at the time, the manager's focus was always on a less tangible if more glorious ambition than the mere avoidance of defeat:

> Look, he hates to lose, Arsène, really loathes it. But what he most wants is for the fan to feel, after paying to watch a game, that it was worth the money. Win, lose or draw, his mission is to give people a sense that they have been transported, taken to another place. He sees football very much as an art form, like the theatre or the opera, he wants people to be moved by what they see. His priority is always to try to outplay the opposition and play in an attractive way. It's not always the winning that counts. That's probably where he differs from the fans. They want to see victories. Though what everyone saw in 2004 was the happy coincidence of both priorities: wonderful, uplifting football that was also winning football.

Boring, boring Arsenal?

Wonderful, uplifting: those were not adjectives anyone would have chosen to describe the club Wenger inherited in 1996. Arsenal had twice recently won the title (in 1989 and 1991) embracing a cagey, careful, frill-free approach. The Gunners' fans revelled in their team's reputation for grittily eschewing the embrace of a concept as soft as entertainment. '1–0 to the Arsenal' was the soundtrack from the Highbury terraces as Arsenal clocked up unspectacular victories with metronomic regularity. While Wenger's ideal would be a team that could always outscore the opposition, George Graham had believed that, if you get the defence right, one goal should always be sufficient. Sod the glory game, his was the winning game.

The irony is, if Graham had embraced as unostentatious an

approach to personal finance as he had to his football, he might have remained in his job, continuing to grind out results in the Premiership. But he preferred to line his pockets (see Match 3, page 86) and, after a brief interregnum featuring Bruce Rioch, bookended by even briefer caretaker managerial spells by Stewart Houston and Pat Rice, Wenger was invited to bring his methodology to Highbury.

It may have been the product of a mindset diametrically opposed to his own, but the Frenchman was pragmatic enough when he first arrived to accept that the team he took over had its good points. Principally its magnificently solid backline. Building around the defence of David Seaman, Lee Dixon, Nigel Winterburn, Steve Bould and Tony Adams, plus, in reserve, the equally redoubtable, if somewhat younger, Keown, Wenger won the double in 1997–98 and again in 2001–02. But not even his regime of pre-match stretching and post-match cool-downs, pasta and vitamin injections was enough to keep the old guard playing on forever. Eventually they had to go. And by the 2003–04 season Keown – by now approaching his swan-song – found himself in a very different club from the one dominated by the old-time back five. 'I was the only one left,' he recalls. 'And my role changed. I'd vowed because of my own experience that I'd always help the next generation when my time came. So much of my effort that season was helping Kolo Touré to take my place. The gaffer had created this learning environment and I just followed suit. That was the way he encouraged us to behave, nudging people in the right direction.'

As the old guard exited the stage, Wenger had created his own team, one that reflected his own priorities: cerebral, imaginative and, like him, imbued with a distaste for defeat that bordered on the pathological. It was, furthermore, a team that was a product of its era. 'Could he have built this side in the Football League days? Possibly,' says Alex Fynn, the advertising executive involved in the origins of the Premier League and the author of *Arsenal: The Making of a Super Club*. 'But there is no question the Premier League facilitated his skill. Because he was a pioneer, he was able to tap the overseas markets that others hadn't. But it was because of the revenues generated by the Premier League that he had the money to go out and buy experienced players on that market.'

Before the Premier League, English clubs could not match the salaries on offer in Italy, Spain and Germany. The old English First Division was vulnerable to football's brain drain, its best players – Gary Lineker, Trevor Francis, David Platt, Des Walker, Ian Rush, Mark Hughes, Paul Gascoigne – quitting the fields of home to play over there. Now, when Wenger went to negotiate with someone plying his trade in Milan or Madrid, they were more than attracted by the Premier League-driven returns he could promise.

Wenger was also able to exploit a particular advantage he had in those early days: because of his background he was comfortably familiar with the overseas market, while his rivals were taking only the first tentative steps into this new area. He knew French players, obviously, but also those from Africa and South America. This knowledge enabled him to launch a footballing recruitment drive on a worldwide scale, bringing to Highbury an international brigade of players – a foreign legion destined to make a seismic impact on the English game.

Arsène's foreign legion

Alex Fynn says of the group of players assembled by Wenger by the summer of 2003: 'It was his creation in its entirety. It was created in his image, an attacking team. Dixon and Winterburn were the epitome of tenacious English full-backs and he replaced them by [the Cameroonian] Lauren and Ashley Cole. They were not as rigorous defensively, but were much better at moving forward.' According to Fynn, the lesson he had learned from his tussles with Ferguson had left its mark on Wenger's thinking. Arsenal had been caught out in 1999 by a shortage of goals. He wouldn't let that happen again: 'Everything was now done with the idea of outscoring the opposition.'

Knowing the market is one thing, however, getting the best from it another. Fynn says that at this stage of his career Wenger was a brilliant

As this touchline collision in 2004 suggests, Arsène Wenger and Sir Alex Ferguson were never likely to exchange Christmas cards.

Old school: Bryan Robson, the one member of Manchester United's fearsome drinking school to survive Alex Ferguson's purge, celebrates victory in 1993 with a favoured method of rehydration.

The man who won the 1992–93 Premiership: Steve Bruce, the uncomplicated, resolute stopper who became Manchester United's unlikely saviour with his two late goals against Sheffield Wednesday. After retiring as a player he enjoyed a significant career as a Premier League manager at Wigan, Sunderland and Hull City.

Eric Cantona is restrained after attacking a spectator at Selhurst Park, 25 January 1995. He had just provided the image that made the Premier League worldwide news.

Older, though not necessarily wiser, Cantona – now engaged in a second career as a screen actor – enjoys a 2011 reunion with Sir Alex Ferguson, the man who did not abandon him at his point of crisis.

Jack Walker strides across Ewood Park. A pioneer of the Premier League, he was the first man to appreciate that success was now the preserve of those with the deepest pockets.

Wallop: the prodigious Alan Shearer, the man whose goals won the title, wheels away with his familiar celebration after blasting Blackburn into the lead at Anfield, 13 May 1995.

The heartbeat of the treble: Beckham, Scholes, Giggs, Butt and the Nevilles (plus a couple of interlopers) celebrate another title, 1997. Several members of the 'Class of '92' reunited briefly to steer United through the post-Moyes managerial hiatus in May 2014.

Teddy Sheringham with the Premiership trophy, 16 May 1999.

The professor: when he arrived at Highbury in 1996 Arsène Wenger changed the face of English football. By 2004 he was convinced he had a team that could not be beaten.

Arsenal fans at White Hart Lane offer a succinct summary of why Sol Campbell had left Tottenham to join the Gunners. The talent drain was soon to switch direction.

WHY DID SOL
LEAVE THE LANE?
ARSENAL
CHAMPIONS!
43 YEARS AND
YOUR STILL WAITING

Arsenal's veteran centre-back Martin Keown offers a gentle word of condolence after United's Ruud van Nistelrooy misses the penalty that would have defeated the Invincibles, 21 September 2003.

People's hero: Alan Smith kisses the badge on his Leeds shirt in a teary display of fealty to his home-town club, 8 May 2004. Two weeks later, he signed for Manchester United.

Former Leeds United chairman Peter Ridsdale enjoys the good times at Elland Road. They were not to last long.

buyer. 'My definition of a great manager is he who makes the fewest mistakes in acquiring players,' he believes. 'By that criterion Arsène obviously was, though not necessarily any longer is, a great manager.'

Even when his players moved on to more lucrative pastures, Wenger was able to find suitable replacements. When such crucial squad members as Emmanuel Petit, Marc Overmars and Nicolas Anelka – all from his first double-winning squad – agitated for a money-spinning transfer, they were all sold for a sizeable profit. And in their stead he brought in better players for less outlay: Overmars was sold to Barcelona for £25 million in 2000; his replacement Robert Pirès cost just £6 million. From the manager who had a degree in economics it looked like the very epitome of good football business.

'The bottom line is to recruit the right players,' explains Bob Wilson. 'Arsène in those days was the master. He may not have been a great player himself – I can relate to that – but he knows what one looks like. I remember him saying of Jack Wilshere "the game speaks to him". That's a great quote. It sums up his ability to recognize what makes the best.'

Nowhere was that ability better illustrated than in the player Wenger regards as the finest he has ever coached, an Arsenal legend latterly immortalized in bronze outside the Emirates Stadium. When he arrived in north London, Thierry Henry was not an unknown quantity. This was not some scruff plucked from a crumbling Parisian *banlieue*. He was a French international, playing for Juventus. Even so, there were not many observers who could detect in his skittish performance any hint of the world-class footballer into which he was to develop under Wenger's tutelage.

'I saw Thierry in 1998 at the World Cup when I was working for ITV,' recalls Wilson. 'I thought, bloody hell – he's quick! But you got a real sense he didn't know what he was doing. Literally, there were times when he was dashing down the wing having left the ball behind, forgetting to take it with him. But what he became was something extraordinary.' Martin Keown agrees that Henry deserves his permanent place in the Emirates forecourt. 'He was the icing on the cake,' he says. 'The thing was he wasn't just skilful and quick, he was driven. He played with a ferocity and focus that you rarely see. He was defiant.'

Initially, when he arrived in 1999, Wenger utilized Henry where he had always been played: on the right wing. He didn't score for his first nine games in north London. Then the manager moved him inside, into the position previously occupied by Ian Wright. It was not an immediately obvious fit. The comedian Ian Stone, a lifelong Gooner, recalls watching from the stands as Henry missed plenty of chances in early games as he tried to get to grips with his new central role. 'I thought ooh-er,' says Stone. 'I was glad he [Wenger] could see something there because I'm not sure we could.' But Wenger persevered. And by the beginning of the 2003–04 season he was reaping the full reward for his patience with a player of quite breathtaking panache, as dynamic on the pitch as he was cool off it.

'I remember Arsène once telling me that in the history of the game there have only been four or five players who could pick up the ball in the defensive third, carry it through the middle third, into the attacking third and score,' says Wilson. 'He believed Henry was one of them. Henry could change the course of a game in one second. And for that reason Arsène thought him the best player he has ever worked with.'

Stone does not disagree:

Someone once asked me when I've been happiest in my life. And there are three occasions. One was a particular time messing about with my kids. One was when I was on the Comedy Store stage talking nonsense. And one was watching Thierry Henry put Gary Neville on his arse, absolutely leaving him for dead. I've never seen a sight like him. My eldest son is a dancer and he always said Henry had the air and physicality of the ballet dancer. He was poetry in motion.

For Arsenal fans, the great thing about that 2003–04 side was that

Henry was not alone. Alongside him he had colleagues of dash and skill: Pirès, bought from Marseilles in the summer of 2000; Freddie Ljungberg, who cost £3 million from the Swedish club Halmstads BK in 1998; and the incomparable Dennis Bergkamp.

The Dutchman was another player Wenger had found on the premises when he arrived at Highbury. Rioch had signed him from Internazionale in 1995, although there are those who insist the Frenchman was privately consulted about his recruitment by his friend David Dein a year ahead of his arrival in London. If so, Wenger knew what he was talking about. If not quite to the same degree as the manager, Bergkamp changed the mindset at Highbury, subtly altering the tactical thinking of players used to Graham's more robust approach. Though sometimes he was not that subtle.

'I remember watching a session with Dennis quite early on,' recalls Wilson. 'And he got quite shirty with Ray Parlour. "Just hit me with the fucking ball," he shouted. "Just give me the ball and move." He changed the way of playing by showing them what to do in training. They got used to passing it in to him really quickly, then moving into space for the return.' And Bergkamp's return passes sometimes defied all known footballing geometry. 'Dennis could find a pass like no one else,' says Stone. 'Sometimes you'd see him hit one and you'd think, well where's that to? What are you doing, man? Then you'd realize: oh blimey, there's a player there, running into that space. It's perfect.'

Attack, however, was only part of Wenger's constructive excellence. His defence, too, was a thing of substance. He played a very modern 4-2-3-1 formation, with Henry the spearhead, in advance of the fluid, forever interchanging, difficult-to-pin-down trio of Pirès, Ljungberg and Bergkamp. Behind that front four patrolled Patrick Vieira and Gilberto Silva. Chelsea's Claude Makélélé might argue, but these two have a strong claim to be the best defensive midfielders of the Premier League era.

Vieira was a giant of aggression and power, happy to mix it whatever the circumstances. 'I remember being in the tunnel when he kicked off with all the Man United lads,' says Wilson. 'It was him

against them. Hilarious looking back on it. But by God he was fearless.'
After joining Arsenal from AC Milan in August 1996, Vieira adapted
perfectly to the English game, his muscularity the ideal weapon.
Indeed, by 2003–04, he had come to be regarded almost as a home-
grown player by his Highbury team-mates. 'We saw Patrick as pretty
much English,' says Keown. 'From the moment he arrived, he was just
one of those guys you wanted alongside you in the dressing room. He
was never going to hide.' The Brazilian Silva too was absolutely crucial
to the team's success. As the statistics demonstrate: of the three cup
games Arsenal lost that season, Silva was missing from two of them.

In the backline, Wenger mixed the English attitude of the young
Cole and the unsmiling former Tottenham stalwart Sol Campbell
with the African physique of Keown's protégé Touré and Lauren. And
behind them barked the keeper known in the Highbury stands as
'The Mad German', Jens Lehmann. An eccentric, he had a reputation
for overreacting to criticism, flinging himself theatrically to the turf
after the most minor altercation with an opponent. He once stole the
glasses from a fan who confronted him after a game and refused to
return them until the man apologized. Not that he seemed that self-
conscious: he gained widespread notoriety after he left Arsenal when
he was caught short in the middle of a match playing for Stuttgart.
Footage of him nipping behind the advertising hoardings to relieve
himself still attracts a steady stream of viewers on YouTube. But
fellow keeper Bob Wilson, who worked with him every day, was most
decidedly a fan:

> For all his strange habits, for all everyone said about him, Jens was
> a great goalie. The rest of the players were terrified of him. If any-
> one turned up late for training, he collected the fines. Boy, you did
> not mess with Jens. He'd get the money from them, no matter who
> they were, or how few seconds they were late. That was the com-
> petitive nature of him.

The key to success, however, was that Wenger's first-choice eleven lined up in almost every game. Keown, Parlour, the young full-back Gaël Clichy and the French centre-back Pascal Cygan had an occasional run-out, while the expensively acquired Spanish winger José Antonio Reyes played seven times. But through the season Wenger preferred to rely on the same group, time after time. It was a side absolutely at the peak of its collective powers. The average age of that team was 28.3, bang in keeping with the statistical insistence that a footballer's best years – when physical strength and resilience mix with mental toughness and growing knowledge of the game – is between twenty-seven and twenty-nine. Fitness and experience, seen-it-all-before resolve and muscles like steel: this was a team equipped in every way for the task in hand.

Strength in depth

In sticking with the old-fashioned principle of never changing a winning side, the Frenchman also went against the growing managerial trend which suggested the only way to win the Premiership was by rotating a sizeable squad. 'Strength in depth' was the mantra from the *Match of the Day* sofa or behind the technical gizmos on Sky's *Monday Night Football*. You can't do it without class cover in every position was the wisdom then current. Sir Alex Ferguson had won the treble five years previously by mixing and matching four strikers, a policy which had come to be seen as essential. In Henry, Wenger effectively had just the one. Down the road at Chelsea, Claudio Ranieri was developing such a reputation for constantly interchanging his resources he had earned the nickname 'The Tinkerman'. At Stamford Bridge it was said nobody knew the best line-up. And that was assumed to be the modern way. Wenger, however, eschewed such thinking. In game after game, he played his first choice, knowing they had the blend to achieve everything he wanted. 'In my head, when I look back, it's just the eleven of them,' says Ian Stone. 'I don't remember any personnel changes. It was the same bunch, every time. But then to do that, to keep picking the same guys, you do need luck.'

And Arsenal had luck. Although there were the occasional

absences through suspension (usually involving Vieira), all season long injuries were barely an issue. For Wenger's class of 2003–04 there were none of the debilitating long-term lay-offs that would afflict a later generation of Arsenal players like Jack Wilshere, Abou Diaby or Tomáš Rosicky. As each weekend came around, with everyone fit and ready, he was able to supply the same team sheet to the match officials.

Arsenal fans had their first inkling that something special was brewing in a match against the champions at Old Trafford on 21 September 2003. They had approached it on the back of a string of wins, gloriously achieved in the late summer. This, though, was a cantankerous game, full of spit and fury, largely lacking in the aesthetic finer points Wenger claimed to cherish. Vieira against Roy Keane, Silva against Paul Scholes, everywhere on the pitch the personal animosity between the two managers seemed to be reflected in the tackles. Nowhere more so than in the sparky duel between Keown and Ruud van Nistelrooy. It reached a head right at the last, when van Nistelrooy earned a penalty for the home side.

Arsenal's players were already furious with the Dutchman for what they felt was his elaborate dive which had led to Vieira – not for the first time in his career – being sent off earlier in the game and they were fuming when van Nistelrooy ran up to take the kick. So when he missed, crashing what would have been the match-winner against the underside of Lehmann's bar, they could not hide their visceral delight. Cole, Lauren, Ray Parlour all mocked him. Keown performed a dervish whirl round the United man, his face twisted in malevolent triumph.

It was a reaction Keown subsequently came to regret. He was more than a touch embarrassed, he now admits, that his sons – one of whom was to become a handy young prospect at Reading – were able to see him behave like that. But for Ian Stone and many an Arsenal fan, Keown's war dance wasn't remotely childish. It spoke volumes about the team.

I was watching in a bar in South Africa. And when that United person missed that pen, this massive roar filled the place. I couldn't work out where it was coming from as almost all the other drinkers in there were supporting United. Then I realized it was me. I was screaming the place down, ranting at the television, yelling at it. And what I was saying was: 'these guys will not be beaten. They just refuse to lose.' And I was right.

Arsenal hadn't been beaten, in fact, since Leeds won 3–2 at Highbury at the tail end of the 2002–03 season, when the visiting manager Peter Reid had played five in midfield, instructing his players to defend deep and attack on the break. And Wenger had learned from that experience, telling Silva and Vieira not to charge forward simultaneously, to keep the cover and remain patient. Staying faithful to that method, after the watershed game against United, Arsenal's unbeaten run in the league lengthened. Across Christmas it continued, remaining intact even after Arsenal were defeated by Middlesbrough in the League Cup semi-final. Through the New Year and beyond it went on, United and Chelsea slipping further and further behind as they carried on clocking up defeats just as the north Londoners simply carried on winning. Even as spring beckoned, the column in the league table denoting the number of Arsenal losses remained defiantly empty. And the possibility of escaping defeat all year became the main topic of discussion at Wenger's press conferences. 'Can it be done? It can,' he would reply, before perhaps remembering his previous MacLeod moment. 'Will it be done? Let us wait and see. But our priority is to win the league. Everything else is just a bonus.'

Could this Arsenal side be the next Invincibles? For most observers, the real test came in early April 2004. In the course of a week, Wenger's team were scheduled to play the semi-final of the FA Cup against United, the second leg of their Champions League quarter-final with Chelsea, and a home Premiership fixture with Liverpool, then sitting fourth in the table. Were his team good enough to emulate United's treble-winners? It was reckoned to be the make-or-break eight days for Wenger's campaign, an echo of the dénouement of the 1999 season when he had so frustratingly lost to Ferguson's side in the Cup semi-final and subsequently seen his league chances fizzle away at the last (see Match 4, page 129).

It could not have started worse for the manager's ambition. First United won the Cup game at Villa Park on Saturday 3 April, then Chelsea knocked Arsenal out of the Champions League at Highbury three days later. Then, adding to the sense that defeat was a contagion, at half-time in the league fixture on Friday 9 April, Liverpool led 2–1. 'Was the season going to fall apart in a week?' Stone remembers thinking as he sought a reassuring drink during that depressing fifteen-minute break. 'Well, it looked like it.' Martin Keown, though, had other ideas. In the dressing room during the interval he made an impassioned call to arms. 'The Gaffer encouraged us to speak our mind, he created this amazing environment. He gave me the licence, really. So I gave it the full works. These were special players, special people, I didn't want to see it all go to dust. After I'd finished, the Gaffer thanked me for what I had to say. But we all played a part.'

Thierry Henry led the Keown-inspired charge. He launched the recovery with two second-half goals to claim a hat-trick and Arsenal cruised the rest of the game, winning 4–2. 'Instead of going home to drown my sorrows,' recalls Stone, 'I went home thinking: this is a team.' That psychological hurdle vaulted, Arsenal were nearing the finish line, which hove into view far earlier than it had in any previous Premier League campaign. When Chelsea lost at Newcastle in the televised lunchtime kick-off on Sunday 25 April, it meant Arsenal needed just a point from fifteen available in five remaining games to secure the title. It was a run-in of unfathomable luxury.

Engaging with the old enemy

Wenger and his team had confirmation of the Chelsea defeat even as they arrived for the first game of that sequence, at Tottenham. It was the 134th time London's two great footballing rivals had met, though in the early days their encounters had involved more travel, as Arsenal were based south of the river in Woolwich until their move to Highbury in 1913.

Not since Arsenal's double-winning season of 1970–71 had there been so much riding on the derby. That year, when Bob Wilson was in goal, George Armstrong on the wing and John Radford up front, they travelled the four and a bit miles from Islington to the Borough of Haringey with a similar goal: they were looking for the victory that would secure the Football League championship trophy. On that May Saturday the crowds arriving at the ground, hoping to pay their way in at the turnstiles, were so dense that Spurs' Alan Mullery could not get anywhere close in his car.

Fearing he might not make the kick-off, he abandoned his motor somewhere on Tottenham High Road and pushed his way through on foot. Only to discover, when he arrived, that every entrance was by now locked. Already a sell-out, with a huge crowd baying inside, the Spurs stewards had decided that no one else should be allowed in. So, as the locked-out swarms heaved and swayed behind him, Mullery found himself obliged to bang on the bolted front door of the stadium's reception. 'Let me in,' he pleaded. 'I'm the skipper.' Eventually they did, though Mullery might have wished they hadn't. Arsenal won the game with an eighty-eighth minute goal by Ray Kennedy – and with it the title.

Thirty-three years on, Wenger did his best to play down the local rivalry. 'The quicker we win the title the better, no matter where it is,' he said as he was intercepted by reporters on his way into White Hart Lane. 'As long as you don't win it, there's always a chance of tension creeping in. That's the reason I want to win it at Spurs, not because it would be humiliating to their fans. I will remind the players that we still have a job to do.'

He may have been claiming, in the managerial cliché, that this was just another game, but his players saw it differently. Many of them relished the idea of inflicting humiliation on Spurs supporters. Ashley Cole revealed much about his long Arsenal heritage when – in those days the England centurion still condescended to speak to the media –

he told pressmen at the door of White Hart Lane: 'It would be a dream for us to win it here. It was brilliant when we did it at Old Trafford two years ago but for me it would be unbelievable to do it at Spurs.'

Cole was voicing the majority feeling in the dressing room. This may have been the international brigade, but they were all acutely aware of the meaning of local dispute. Freddie Ljungberg remembers his new team-mates impressing upon him – virtually from the moment he signed for the club in 1998 – the critical importance of the Arsenal–Tottenham derby. 'It's extremely special,' he says:

> When I first got to Arsenal the English players like Tony Adams, Dixon, Winterburn, a month before the game came about they were all like: 'this is the game we need to win to walk the street in London.' And they really pumped it into you to win it. That was special, I never had experienced that before I got here.

It wasn't just the Arsenal players who were fired up about the prospect. In the Spurs ranks that day, about to make his debut in the fixture, was the young midfielder Johnnie Jackson, whose experiences show the enduring nature of club allegiance. Despite playing with a cockerel on his chest, Jackson – at the time of writing, club captain at Charlton – had been brought up an Arsenal supporter.

'Yes, people knew,' he told the Online Gooner website of his Arsenal attachment. 'I remember Arsenal were playing Villarreal in the Champions League semi final second leg [in the 2005–06 competition]. The game was into its second half when we got on the Spurs reserve-team coach after a game of our own. We had it on the TV. Arsenal conceded a late penalty. This triggered our manager at the time, Clive Allen, to come running down the coach waving his fists in my face with delight. I remained calm... until Jens Lehmann saved the penalty. Then I erupted and duly returned the favour, screaming right in Clive's face. My emotions got the better of me once in a derby at White Hart Lane. I wasn't part of the Spurs squad so was watching from the stands. Freddie Ljungberg went down under a strong Noé

Pamarot tackle and I jumped up appealing for a penalty. I quickly realized where I was, so pretended I was accusing Ljungberg of diving and sat back down again sharpish.'

Whatever the strength of the rivalry, however much Tottenham figures like Gary Mabbutt talked before the game about any result being possible in a derby, if Wenger wanted to accrue his point quickly he could not have chosen more compliant rivals. Tottenham were having a woeful season. David Pleat was acting as stand-in manager following Glenn Hoddle's sacking in the autumn and he had presided over a recent series of miserable results. While Arsenal were hoovering up the victories, Pleat had taken just one point from the previous six games. It was mathematically possible – if somewhat unlikely – that Tottenham could still be relegated. Arsenal, meanwhile, were enjoying their best-ever run against their not-so-noisy neighbours; they were unbeaten in eight north London derbies, including the one earlier in the season at Highbury which they had won 2–1.

It did not, however, require any recourse to statistics immediately to appreciate which was the better side. A glance at the team sheets told you all you needed to know about the prevailing balance of power in north London. In the red corner were Henry, Pirès, Bergkamp, Vieira, Campbell and Cole. In the white were Mauricio Taricco, Stephen Kelly, Anthony Gardner, Simon Davies and the young Johnnie Jackson. Wenger's point was surely a formality. It could only be Arsenal who would go marching on.

Like the 1971 game, this too was a sell-out. For Arsenal fans it is always tough to find a seat in the rivals' domain. This time it was almost impossible. With every Gooner wanting to be there, you would require the services of Willy Wonka to lay hands on a golden ticket. Neither Alex Fynn nor Ian Stone were there, obliged to watch live coverage on Sky. Martin Keown was present, however. He was named as one of the substitutes. And Bob Wilson was there. Back at the scene of his greatest moment in an Arsenal shirt, he recalls being much calmer than when he played, confident in the team Wenger had built. 'I had this feeling all season when I saw those boys go out on the pitch,' he says. 'I just thought: no one can beat this team.'

Lining up in the tunnel before the game, with the police helicopters whirring overhead and the atmosphere bubbling and broiling in the stands, Johnnie Jackson remembers an odd sensation overwhelming him. 'It was my first and last senior north London derby,' he recalls. 'I was sort of both nervous and excited beforehand. But I was also surprised how much I wanted to win this one. Looking down that Arsenal line, your idols quickly became just another eleven men that you want to beat.'

There had been a rumour circulating beforehand that, in the event of Arsenal winning the title, the home fans would applaud them off the field at the end of the match. It was not clear where such wishful thinking came from; it was obvious from the noise filling the stadium that there was never any chance of that. As the players walked from the tunnel onto the pitch, they stepped into an atmosphere charged with bile, a rancorous cacophony of scorn pouring down from the stands onto the heads of the Arsenal team. And a particular target of the home fans' loathing was Sol Campbell. The man who had walked out on Tottenham in 2001 to sign for the enemy was a hated figure hereabouts, his every touch of the ball booed to distraction, the chants questioning his sexuality as contemptible as they were slanderous.

In such a cauldron, Wenger appeared surprisingly calm. After shaking hands with Pleat – who as always bore the look of a depressed science teacher at a failing comprehensive – he took his place on the bench, dapper, angular, somewhat vinegary of mien. He was flanked by his two assistants: Pat Rice, whose photochromatic lenses soon darkened in the spring sunshine, and Vic Akers, his face like an undertaker bearing bad news. The uninitiated outsider looking at the demeanour of Arsenal's managerial triumvirate would find no possible clue that these hangdog, world-weary-looking men were responsible for some of the most uplifting entertainment in world sport. Frankly, they looked a miserable bunch.

First strike to the Gunners

Though their gloomy countenance was not to endure. Three minutes into the game and Tottenham won a corner. Jackson – the only Gooner in the place hoping to witness an Arsenal defeat – took it, swinging the ball into the midst of the visitors' penalty area. However, a poor header by Anthony Gardner allowed the ball to fall to Henry. He took control, turned and galloped forward, all seemingly in the same liquid movement. He dashed on into the space ahead, side-stepping Simon Davies and sliding the ball down the line to Bergkamp, who was lurking near the edge of the Tottenham area. That was always the first rule of this Arsenal team: give the ball to Dennis at the earliest opportunity and then run on. Bergkamp took a touch before squaring the ball across to Vieira who had sprinted eighty yards to be there (in his case that represented about ten strides). The Frenchman went to ground as he slid into the goalmouth, extending a seemingly telescopic leg to brush the ball past Kasey Keller into the empty goal. Fifteen seconds was all that had elapsed between Henry taking possession and the ball nestling in the net at the other end of the pitch. Fifteen seconds to demonstrate Arsenal's surgical ability to slice through a defence. 'Take a note, record this,' said Andy Gray on the Sky commentary. 'This is what has made Arsenal champions of this country.'

The goal brought Wenger to his feet: he dashed across his technical area, fists pumping, his face etched with delight. Behind him, Rice was dancing, the whole Arsenal bench standing in celebration. And it didn't stop there. Half an hour later, Bergkamp and Vieira again combined in the middle of the pitch, finding each other as if by radar. Vieira's pass forward deflected off a hapless Stephen Kelly into the path of Pirès, who angled the ball into the net from eight yards out. It was another exhibition of world-class passing, further evidence of Arsenal's cool-headed mastery of positional play. And it was Pirès's nineteenth goal of the season. He and Henry had now netted forty-four between the two of them, the same total as Spurs' entire squad.

As Pirès, Cole, Bergkamp, Vieira and Henry gathered in the corner, whooping with delight as they celebrated the goal, a brooding silence enveloped White Hart Lane. Everywhere the home fans were working out how to respond to opponents that they loathed but who were evidently playing the game at a new level. These weren't cheats or thugs or bullies; if they were, the Spurs fans would have known how to react to them. Rather this was a team playing the game in the smooth, efficient, endlessly attractive manner that Tottenham had espoused in their glory, glory days of the early 1960s. At least in the George Graham era, when Arsenal were winning through grim pragmatism, the Spurs fans could assume the moral high ground. Now there was not even that thin consolation. There was nowhere to go. The easiest thing seemed to be to greet the Gunners' masterclass with silence. Thick, unhappy silence.

The section of White Hart Lane that housed the visiting Arsenal fans, however, was ringing with what sounded very much like laughter. 'It probably was laughter,' says Stone. 'I remember during that season, the football was at times so good, you'd get 38,000 people at Highbury properly laughing. It was the only response: you'd piss yourself. I'd remember the football we used to watch under George and I'd think: "Fuck me, things have changed round here, we're the best team around."'

In the Sky commentary box, Martin Tyler agreed, albeit less profanely. As Pirès slid the ball home, he rhapsodized: 'What you're seeing here is what we've seen all season: the sheer class of Arsenal.' Alongside him, Gray took up the theme: 'A masterclass. The way they worked the ball around Tottenham in the central area was just fantastic. Well, "a masterclass" doesn't do it justice: it's football from another planet.'

A game of two halves

At the half-time break, there was a sense in the Arsenal dressing room that they had already secured the league title. This was not a team that squandered a 2–0 half-time advantage. There was no need for a Keown half-time rabble-rouser of a speech: that league-winning point was surely coming, and in their high fives and back slaps and grins, the players knew it. No matter how much Wenger told them to stayed focused, not to throw away opportunity, they knew they were there.

As for Pleat, well, what could he say? Start praying seemed to be the best advice he could give. For Johnnie Jackson, though, it was over. In such vaunted company he had struggled. And Pleat replaced him at half-time with the electric-heeled young forward Jermain Defoe. Jackson remembers sitting in the dressing room after he had been told he was substituted, realizing that his moment sharing the pitch with the greatest side he had ever seen was over. He had been out of his depth. 'The game didn't go to plan personally,' he admits now. 'I was glad I'd arranged before we went out to swap shirts with Dennis Bergkamp. I've got his framed on my wall. I'm sure he's got mine.'

But as he sat watching from the bench, Jackson, like everyone else in the stadium, could see that for all Wenger's urging them not to lose focus, the Arsenal players couldn't help it. Their minds had already settled on the title celebrations. And after an hour, their waning concentration got its first comeuppance. Defoe gambolled down the left side of the Arsenal defence and played the ball back to Michael Brown. The midfielder eased it to his right, into the path of Jamie Redknapp. As had been the case nine years earlier when he was at Liverpool playing Blackburn, Redknapp found himself part of the supporting act in a championship-deciding match. And again he made his mark with a thumping goal, searing from his right foot to the top left-hand corner of the net from about thirty yards. It was a fine strike, a reminder of what a player he might have been had injury not undermined so much of his career.

Still, with the score now standing at 2–1, Pirès had the chance to calm any fraying Arsenal nerves. But he hit the middle of the bar with a sharp shot. Then, with full-time approaching, Touré was ruled to have fouled Frédéric Kanouté just outside the Arsenal area. From the free kick Lehmann, with an overdramatic flourish, pushed Defoe's shot over the bar. Spurs were fighting to the last. As the corner was signalled, the crowd responded to their effort, baying them forward. And on the touchline, Pat Rice called the fourth official over to notify him Arsenal were to make a time-consuming substitution. Martin Keown was about to come on. 'It was a sentimental thing to do,' recalls Keown. 'I think the Gaffer wanted me to be out there as a thank-you.'

But he never got his chance. Referee Mark Halsey's attention had been caught by something that had just happened as the corner was about to be taken. Jens Lehmann had intervened to stymie Keown's curtain call. The German's critics had warned all season that his chippy behaviour could have destructive consequences, potentially stalling Arsenal's progress. As Brown took the corner and Lehmann flapped the ball away from under the bar, Halsey's whistle had already stopped play. Players from both sides surrounded the official, with the argument appearing to centre on a goal-line confrontation between Tottenham's striker Robbie Keane and the Arsenal goalie as Brown had shaped to take the corner. There was a lot of finger-jabbing, a flurry of accusations, a push-me-pull-you of frothing complaint.

Lehmann, swigging from a bottle he had picked up from the back of his goal, remonstrated with the linesman Martin Yerby. Meanwhile the other assistant came onto the pitch to help the referee restore order. Halsey indicated to players to calm down and move away from him while he consulted Yerby. The two were in discussion, hands over their mouths to prevent the players eavesdropping, for some time.

Then, as the Spurs fans chanted 'same old Arsenal, always cheating', Halsey reached a decision. A huge cheer filled the ground as the referee pointed to the penalty spot. Television replays showed that when Keane, fed up with the goalkeeper's presence, had pushed Lehmann in the chest, provoking a comedy tumble from the German of a kind Norman Wisdom might have employed in his arthritic dotage, he was merely reacting. The keeper had shoved Keane first. Halsey had got it right. A penalty it was.

'This was always going to cost Jens Lehmann at some stage this season,' said Gray on the Sky commentary. 'It's not going to cost Arsenal – apart from pride, assuming Tottenham get the goal. But this was always going to be a costly thing. People have known about it: he overreacts to any sort of pressure. And my goodness, he's a big enough lump to look after himself, in there against people the size of Robbie Keane. An act of stupidity.' It would not be his last. In Arsenal's 2006 Champions League final against Barcelona, Lehmann's irritability really did cost his side when he was sent off within twenty minutes of the start. That all lay in the future, though. Here, his misdemeanour would barely matter. Keane took the penalty himself. He shot high to the right, the ball fizzing over Lehmann's shoulder as he dived low. 'Keane rattled the goalkeeper, then he rattled the back of the net,' said Tyler.

Bob Wilson, however, refuses to accept Gray's argument that Lehmann was the weak link of that Arsenal team, carried to glory by the efforts of his team-mates, the Ringo Starr of Wenger's great side. 'Don't ever believe he was anything other than a great keeper,' insists Wilson:

> No other keeper in the modern game has gone through a season and not been on the losing side once. I know what that takes psychologically. I know from my own experience when you've gone six games without losing, you wake up and think: 'oh shit, will it be today?' You are in such a position of responsibility you think: 'will I be the one who blows the record?' To go on and on as he did, you have to contribute something enormous as a goalkeeper.

Halsey blew the whistle moments later – there was no chance for Keown to be involved. Not that he minded: Arsenal were champions, thirteen points clear of Chelsea with four games to go. They were untouchable. For Spurs, though, the point was vital. It provided final reassurance that they could not be relegated. Rarely has a north London derby ended in such a happy distribution of the spoils. Not that the Spurs fans had any intention of hanging around to share the happy moment. The last thing they wanted to do was witness Arsenal celebrations.

As the public-address system blared out music to drown out the Gunners' delirium, the visiting players ran to the corner to be with their supporters, Henry waving his shirt above his head, the conductor of the Highbury orchestra. A banner was unfurled which reflected the local significance of the game: 'Why did Sol leave the Lane?' it read. 'Arsenal champions! 43 years and you're still waiting.'

Campbell did not see it. He did not join his exulting team-mates, choosing instead to walk straight down the tunnel to the dressing room, the jeers of the Tottenham fans still filling the stands as he did so. 'One reason I walked off was because I didn't want to provoke anyone,' he says. 'I needed to rise above the situation. I had to be a gentleman and behave in a graceful manner.' Lehmann too strode straight off the pitch. But probably for a different reason. He was still fuming about the penalty. 'I remember Jens was distraught,' says Stone. 'He knew we should have won that game. But hell, we won the league at White Hart Lane. I think there's a song in that somewhere.'

The New Invincibles

The trophy was not presented to Arsenal that day: that would have been a humiliation too far for their hosts. It was handed over at Highbury at the last game of the season, against Leicester City on 15 May. But for the Arsenal players, after they had left the stadium, there was to be no excessive celebration. For them, the job was not yet complete. There was the small matter of matching Preston's achievement. They wanted to become the second Invincibles.

'I remember when we lost in the Cup, Bobby Robson [then Newcastle manager] said that we needed to learn to lose,' recalls Martin Keown. 'And I remember defiantly thinking, "yeah, well we won't be losing again". Once it was in the bag at Tottenham, it became imperative. We couldn't lose. When you're playing for that record, you're very proud. Not picking the ball out of the back of the net too often, that's something you dream of as a defender.'

Ian Stone recalls that the urge to go through the season unbeaten became an obsession among the fans. 'Get the league, sure, obviously that was the main thing,' he says. 'But once we got the title, then you're thinking: can you go unbeaten? I remember a previous time we'd won the league, after doing it, they all relaxed. We lost to Liverpool and someone shouted at Lee Dixon as he huffed and puffed down the wing "are you lot still pissed from the celebration?"And he shouted back: "is it that obvious?"'

The sports pages of the newspapers were filled with speculation as to whether Arsenal could achieve their ambition. Bob Wilson remembers that, after the Tottenham game, Wenger talked about little else. 'After we'd won the league, we wanted that unbeaten record,' he says. 'That team had too much pride, too much ability not to let it happen.'

And happen it duly did. They not only completed the thirty-eight matches of the 2003–04 season unbeaten, they extended the run for another eleven games into the next. Before losing it in a 2–0 defeat at Old Trafford the following October in the acrimonious 'Battle of the Buffet', a match that ended not with a bang but with a pizza – flung at the Manchester United manager by Arsenal's midfield prodigy Cesc Fàbregas.

But the infantile fracas that was 'Pizzagate' lay in the future. In the early summer of 2004 it seemed as if Wenger had achieved a foot-balling ultimate: he had built a team that not only entertained, they could not be beaten. The eulogies were extensive. Henry won the PFA Player of the Year for the second season in succession; Wenger him-self was the manager of the year. And there was a sense around the club that such success would breed success. It would go on and on.

Wenger was bullish about what lay ahead. 'I know there are things we can improve in the team,' he said soon after the title was won. 'I'm convinced we have the best attack and that we have the best defence. That's a good basis – and I think this team is still going up. We have many young players with a lot more to give. That's why we will not be big spenders. You can forget that. We have already spent our big money on José Antonio Reyes. The major buying has been done.'

End of a Golden Age

At the time, no one could quite sense the import of what Wenger had said. But he was right. The spending on the team was over. Now there was another financial priority at Arsenal: building a new stadium. The move from Highbury across the railway line and past the old council recycling yard into the glorious curved sweep of the Emirates Stadium was not an act of folly. It made absolute monetary sense. This was the grandest of new stadiums, situated close to the heart of the capital, where 60,000 premium-priced seats and whole swathes of corporate salons could bring in sufficient revenues to allow Arsenal to match the biggest spenders of Europe. Within a month of moving in in October 2006, Arsenal announced they were now accruing more in matchday income than any other club in the country, including United, with their 77,000-seat Trafford monolith.

All the same, such pre-eminence came at a cost: Highbury could be sold on, lucratively, for a housing development, but even so, the outlay required to build Arsenal's new home was enormous – something north of £300 million. And the club's board was anxious that the debt thereby accrued should be removed from its books with the greatest of dispatch. To do that, spending on the team had to be reduced if not curtailed: paying for the stadium was the absolute priority.

Wenger was convinced he had the internal resources to cope with the more rigorous transfer budget that was imposed upon him. He believed in the club, believed in the stadium and was anxious to play his part in its delivery. He spent hours poring over the plans, working with the architects on the fine details of player accommodation, and talking them through exactly what was required of the playing area. The Frenchman loved Arsenal truly, madly, deeply – of that there could be no doubt.

And he assumed his players would share his affection for the club. But what he did not take into account was how they might succumb to the predatory actions of his rivals. Over the coming years, his best players were to be plucked off one by one by clubs offering them greater rewards; no matter how much he used emotional blackmail in the attempt to make them stay. Cole, Campbell, Lauren, Ljungberg,

Silva and Henry all left in the period 2006–07. And whereas in the past he had always been able to replace his stalwarts with better players, he not only no longer had the cash but others had outflanked him on the contacts. Liverpool signed Fernando Torres from Atletico Madrid, Chelsea bought Michael Essien from Lyon, Manchester United snapped up Patrice Evra from Monaco: these were the kind of players Wenger once had first refusal on. Now others, better financed than him, with ever-improving links to the market, were overtaking him. No more so than down the road at Stamford Bridge, where, according to the newspaper headlines in the days after Arsenal had won the title, José Mourinho was soon to establish his court.

So it turned out that what looked like the start of something untouchable on the pitch at White Hart Lane was in fact something ephemeral. And when Vieira scored the winning penalty in a shoot-out to secure the FA Cup the following season – and then promptly left for Juventus – little did Gooners fans realize that it would be nine long years before Wenger's Arsenal enjoyed similar success.

'Looking back, it really does seem like a golden age now,' says Ian Stone, growing close to moist-eyed at the memory of the Invincibles. 'I know everybody always thinks things were better in the past. But in this case they unquestionably were. When we have discussions about today's Arsenal team [that of 2012–13] we always ask which of them would get in the Invincibles. In all honesty, none of them would.'

Since the glories of his unbeaten season, the man honoured in the banner which hangs at the Emirates with the simple legend 'In Arsène We Trust' has faced increasing discontent. He may have propelled Arsenal to the Champions League for fourteen successive seasons, but his failure to land any silverware for nearly a decade after the 2005 Cup win inevitably rankled. Fourth place began to appear the extent of the club's ambition. I recall at one match in the 2012–13 season hearing him being pilloried by the home supporters with the graceless chant of 'you don't know what you're doing'. For Wenger, the man who had delivered so much, to be thus criticized by the very people whose lives he had strived to enrich was painful to witness.

'I think Arsène will only be truly appreciated when he is gone,' says Bob Wilson:

I'm amazed he takes the stick he does, given what he has achieved. When you get to know him he is an incredibly humane man. He really doesn't like confrontation. And he has a loyalty that sometimes is detrimental, it means he backs off from the tough decisions. But when you think about what he achieved with the Invincibles, it was just amazing. We're lucky to have been around to enjoy what he gave us. You'd think it should be feasible for anyone these days, if they've got the backing. Buy the best players and you get the results, surely. But it doesn't work like that. You need to be Arsène to make it work. And I've got a feeling I won't see it again. To think it went from Preston in 1889 to Arsenal in 2004. I wouldn't be surprised if it took that long to happen again.

●●●●●

Barclaycard Premiership

White Hart Lane, London

Sunday 25 April 2004

Tottenham Hotspur 2 – 2 Arsenal

Spurs scorers: Jamie Redknapp 62; Robbie Keane (pen) 90

Arsenal scorers: Patrick Vieira 3; Robert Pirès 35

Attendance: 36,097

Referee: Mark Halsey

Teams:

Tottenham Hotspur (4-4-2)

Kasey Keller; Stephen Kelly (Gustavo Poyet 79), Anthony Gardner, Ledley King, Mauricio Taricco (Goran Bunjevčevič 90); Johnnie Jackson (Jermain Defoe 45), Jamie Redknapp, Michael Brown, Simon Davies; Robbie Keane, Frédéric Kanouté

Subs not used: Lars Hirshfeld (gk), Rohan Ricketts

Arsenal (4-2-3-1)

Jens Lehmann; Etame-Mayer Lauren, Sol Campbell, Kolo Touré, Ashley Cole; Patrick Vieira, Gilberto Silva; Robert Pirès, Dennis Bergkamp (José Antonio Reyes 80), Ray Parlour (Edu 68); Thierry Henry

Subs not used: Graham Stack (gk), Gaël Clichy, Martin Keown

Match 6

Marching on together

LEEDS UNITED V. CHARLTON ATHLETIC

Elland Road, Leeds

Saturday 8 May 2004

When he was working as Fabio Capello's assistant during the Italian's time as coach of the England team between 2008 and 2012, Franco Baldini watched Premier League matches by the score. Week in week out he would trudge round the grounds in the fond hope he might be able to report back to his boss the discovery of a gem, a home-grown superstar. From all those afternoons and evenings watching he knew what he was talking about when analysing the game's strengths and weaknesses in its motherland. Unlike Capello, he spoke rather more than 100 words of English and when I chatted with him at an FA lunch in 2010, he told me something I'd never appreciated about the unique appeal of the Premier League.

When I asked him what the main difference was between football in England and Italy, I had expected him to mention tactics, skills, technique. In fact, he had found those pretty similar: English players, he said, were not obviously less skilled or intelligent; with a ball at their feet they could roughly do what their Italian counterparts could. No, he reckoned the biggest contrast was in spectator behaviour. He talked with amazement of what he'd seen during the last game of the 2008–09 season at Newcastle's St James's Park, at the end of which the home team had been relegated. He could not believe the reaction of the crowd: the players had done a lap of honour and had been cheered off the pitch. Such a show of magnanimity would never happen in Italy, France, Spain or anywhere else, he suggested. He recalled once being involved in a relegation scrap himself when he was a player, at his club's home ground. And after demotion had been confirmed the players had been forced to dash for the safety of the dressing room as the missiles rained down from the terraces. Once there they had locked themselves in, seeking refuge from a mob outside threatening to lynch them. And there they'd stayed until after midnight, when it was finally thought safe enough for them to emerge. As they left for home, they were told by the club chairman that for their own safety they should under no circumstances show their faces around town for at least a month. It would take some time for the locals to forgive them their complicity in civic humiliation.

That, Baldini said, was what made the English game so singular: the incredible loyalty of the fans, prepared to cheer even as their team went down. If he is right, then what happened at Leeds United's Elland Road stadium on 8 May 2004 would not have unfolded had the game been staged anywhere else in the world. That afternoon those in attendance were witness to an astonishing display of unswerving devotion. From one of the parties involved, at least.

Leeds were already relegated before kick-off. A humiliating hammering at Bolton the Sunday before had confirmed that they were about to slip out of the Premiership into what had just been rebranded the 'Football League Championship' (formerly the First Division and before that the old, pre-Premier League, Second Division). Whatever the nomenclature, however, everyone in the ground that day knew the second tier was no place for a club of Leeds' stature. So the last home game in the top flight had, from the kick-off, taken on the qualities of a wake; more than 38,000 people had turned up to watch the last rites. In Italy, in the same circumstances, Leeds would have been lucky to draw more than a few hundred. In Spain the white handkerchiefs would have been flapping. In France the place would have resounded to catcalls and derisive whistling.

Local hero?

But here, when the final whistle was blown, a gaggle of home support-ers who had been gathering by the pitch side for the last ten minutes forced their way onto the playing area. At first it was just a couple of dozen who evaded the stewards and charged onto the turf. But the trickle turned almost instantly into a flood. Within moments, hun-dreds were out there, and the stewards had quite given up the attempt to hold back the flow. This wasn't, however, a protest. As Baldini would have spotted, the thousands now pouring from the stands onto the pitch had a very different purpose in mind. They weren't doing this in order to assault the players. Far from it. What they wanted to do was acknowledge the team's efforts, thank them for trying, demonstrate that together they – the fans and their heroes – would soon be march-ing on together, as their favourite chant had it, back to the top. 'Leeds First Division 2005: champions elect' read one optimistic banner be-ing flourished in the centre circle.

There was one player in particular with whom the invaders wanted to commune. Hundreds of supporters quickly surrounded the twenty-three-year-old centre-forward Alan Smith, the local lad who had expended so much energy in the Leeds cause throughout the season, the player who always enjoyed joining in with the fans' chants after games. He was likely to be sold over the summer to plug the gaping hole in the club's accounts, and before he left the supporters just wanted to thank him. For them he was the very physical embodiment of what Leeds should be: effortful, aggressive, unyielding.

For a moment Smith was submerged in the host of well-wishers, who grabbed and tugged at him, trying to pull the shirt off his back. Then his peroxide spikes reappeared, as he was lifted up onto the shoulders of his admirers. He was carried around the pitch, waving to the crowd, pulling at the club crest on his shirt, his fist pumping in a gesture of solidarity, his name chanted to the echo.

'Everyone knows he loves the club and of course the fans are sorry to see him go,' said the Leeds caretaker manager Eddie Gray of the ovation. 'He's a terrific player and a local hero so you'd expect a good send-off, but I've not seen sights like that before.' Gray was right there: it was an amazing scene. It took more than twenty minutes before Smith was finally deposited at the players' tunnel, where, to huge acclaim, he turned and gave one final punch of the air. The report by Paul McInnes in *The Guardian*, noting its intoxicating mix of hero worship and faith, likened Smith's goodbye to an Ayatollah's funeral in Tehran. For those romantics who railed against the game's growing commercialization, it was a heartening sight: a suggestion that whatever the burgeoning wealth in the game, still at its heart was the bond between those on the pitch and those in the stands. Unity was all. Old-fashioned values still held sway. It was a gladdening reaffirmation of the true meaning of the game. And Smith was close to overwhelmed. 'I never imagined I'd get a send-off like that,' he said. 'It was unbelievable, beyond my wildest dreams. It just shows how much the fans feel about this club. And I care every bit as much as them.'

A fortnight later Smith demonstrated how much he cared by signing for Manchester United, the fans' most loathed opponents. As a Leeds native, it was something he had said he would never do. Interviewed the previous year on Sky's Saturday morning chat show *Soccer AM*, he had been asked if there was any club he would never under any circumstances join. And – to an almost audible cheer emanating from the West Riding – he had replied: 'Yeah, Man United.'

John Mann, the Labour MP for Bassetlaw and a lifelong Leeds follower, had witnessed the adulation of Smith from his seat in the Don Revie Stand. He was as flabbergasted as his fellow fans:

> We'd known we were going down all season and that when we did there'd be a fire sale of our best players. That last match there was a predictable defiance. Smith was fêted by the fans because he'd remained loyal. Little did we know what lay round the corner.

When the news broke of where exactly Smith was heading there was a brief flurry of protest. The phone-ins rang hot with disappointment, there was plenty of reference to an interview published the previous year in which the player had talked of 'a better type of person' who 'doesn't run away after relegation, but stays and fights'. A couple of fans made a bonfire of their 'Smith 17' shirts alongside the statue of Billy Bremner outside Elland Road. But there were no lynch mobs of the sort Baldini had encountered. Mostly what the move induced was a shrug. Because, by the summer of 2004, Leeds United supporters had grown accustomed to a metaphorical kick in the teeth. Anything of any value that was not screwed to the floor of the stadium was being sold off to anyone with a functioning cheque-book. Smith was simply going the way of everything else at Leeds.

Living the Ridsdale dream

The horrible coincidence for those fans about this, the last game in their club's association with the Premier League, was that it fell precisely three years after the most exalted moment in their recent history. On 8 May 2001 they were defeated by Valencia in the semi-final of the Champions League. Just thirty-six months prior to relegation, then, Leeds had been one of the four best clubs in Europe, restoring the pride of a club whose supporters still hark back to the 1970s glory days by chanting: 'We are the champions, the champions of Europe.' Though coincidence is the wrong word. The two incidents were inextricably linked: the demise of Leeds was the inevitable corollary of their Champions League ambition.

Two days after what turned out to be the very summit of the club's modern achievement in May 2001, I had gone to Leeds to interview the club's then chairman Peter Ridsdale. Things were hectic, but he was perfectly willing to speak to the media. Always happy to talk Leeds, he said. A United fan all his life, he had made some money in the fashion business and had been delighted to join the board of the club that was his childhood obsession. Once there, he told me, he had done no more than apply the normal rules of business to the football game. The company was a plc, floated on the London stock exchange, and he had used its position to facilitate loans. Speculate to accumulate, he said, was the way forward. He was supplying the manager with the funds to buy better players and they in turn would deliver regular participation in the Champions League. This would bring sufficient revenue not only to pay off the borrowing taken out to buy them in the first place, but to improve the side yet further. It was a benevolent circle of investment. He spoke of it as a carefully thought-through strategy that might well serve as a wider model for the game. As for the disappointment of losing to Valencia, he said that would soon pass. There would be many more semi-finals to come. A few finals too, he hoped.

After spending an hour in his company, there were many terms I could have used to describe Peter Ridsdale: smug, complacent, a self-publicist shamelessly placing himself at the centre of Leeds' achievement were but three. But 'deluded' was not a word I'd have added to the charge sheet. In fact, I actually thought he might be on to something. After all, things were progressing exactly as he had mapped out.

Under their manager David O'Leary, who had succeeded George Graham in October 1998 following the latter's departure for Tottenham, Leeds had built a powerful young side, they had just played in the Champions League semi, they were up there, mixing it with the game's superpowers. Ridsdale's manner may have been self-congratulatory, but his vision didn't seem unhinged to me.

Also, I thought at the time, nobody could accuse him of profligacy. His office, for instance, was hardly grand. It was above a shop in the parade opposite the ground, a modest, unshowy administrative base. I had spotted a sizeable aquarium in the lounge outside his door, which gave it the appearance of a dentist's waiting room, but nobody, I reckoned, could accuse Ridsdale of squandering the club's money on soft furnishings.

'Everything is geared to the football here,' he said. 'There is no down side.' And as he spoke, I thought he seemed very plausible. In fact, I pronounced in print that he was precisely the sort of chairman a fan would wish for their club. A man prepared to invest in the team, prepared to go for it, prepared to be bold. He was the embodiment of the new Premier League. Enormously popular with the Leeds supporters, always out there acknowledging their applause after a victory, what he was doing was proving that in football you can buy love. 'We're living the dream,' he told me. It was the catchphrase he used promiscuously that season. And it was to become the mocking epitaph of his chairmanship.

Looking back, it had become clear by May 2004 that I – along with tens of thousands of Leeds supporters – had been hoodwinked. I'm not proud to say I had been fooled by a policy whose stupidity should have been evident from the outset. What Ridsdale was in fact presenting was a footballing Ponzi scheme. The rewards looked unprecedented in their scope and scale. The only trouble was the whole thing was predicated on a gamble. Ridsdale's strategy was on the same level of sophistication as a mug punter staking the housekeeping money on the 4.15 at Market Rasen. A brilliant system if your horse won. But a tad problematic if it fell at the first hurdle.

And that's exactly what happened at Leeds. Ridsdale borrowed heavily to provide O'Leary with the funds to construct a fine team. In the three years between 1999 and 2001, £120 million was paid out to bring in players of the calibre of Rio Ferdinand, Mark Viduka, Olivier Dacourt and Robbie Keane. The loans were guaranteed by future broadcast and ticket income. While the standard method of budgeting for a football club was to regard the rewards accruing from cup competitions as a welcome additional extra, with Leeds the £25 million-plus bonus from Champions League qualification became a must. Ridsdale saw no problem with that: with this team, surely, gaining entry to Europe's top competition would be a cinch.

Yet as he soon discovered, in football nothing comes that easy. At the conclusion of the 2001–02 Premiership season, the one immediately after their glorious dash to the Champions League semi-final, Leeds finished fifth. With O'Leary's blarney wearing thin in the dressing room, with their progress hamstrung by the crisis that enveloped them after two of their better players – Jonathan Woodgate and Lee Bowyer – were charged with racially aggravated GBH when an Asian student was battered unconscious outside a city-centre nightclub (both men were cleared, though Woodgate was found guilty of affray), they ended up five points behind fourth-placed Newcastle, well outside the promised land. There would be no more Champions League football. Leeds had to make do with the lesser glory and significantly smaller financial rewards of the UEFA Cup. Ridsdale's horse had gone lame.

But the debts still had to be met. So, in order to pay off the creditors, the sales began. With O'Leary sacked in the summer of 2002 and replaced by Terry Venables, Rio Ferdinand was sold to Manchester United for £30 million, and Woodgate to Newcastle for £12 million. The books needed to be balanced and those two sales produced healthy profits. The trouble was, according to John Mann, they proved to be the exception:

> Even in the madness, there was a flicker of logic. In the sale of Ferdinand, there was a model of what could be done. Buy very good players at high prices, but make a profit selling them on. It was the same with Jimmy Floyd Hasselbaink [who was sold to Atletico Madrid for £12 million in 1999, £10 million more than he originally cost when he was bought from the Portuguese club Boavista]. If you have a massive asset, then cash flow becomes less of a problem. As a strategy it is fine, provided you buy good players. The problems arise when you accumulate players not of that standard and find you can't sell them on.

This, Mann contends, was the nightmare lurking within Ridsdale's dream. The huge swill of borrowed money sloshing around engendered a sort of recklessness that ultimately proved self-destructive. Despite what I'd thought during my brief meeting with Ridsdale, there was in fact a huge delusion about the place. The club appeared to be labouring under the misapprehension that it was now in a position where it could spend without risk. 'We had all sorts of journeymen who were bought as if they were superstar assets,' Mann asserts. 'They weren't. They were OK players we overpaid for, who got superstar wages. Economically it made no sense at all.'

Economically illiterate

The poster boy of that policy, and the one who came to symbolize its muddle-headedness, was Seth Johnson. A reasonable young player with a decent left foot, he was bought by O'Leary from Derby County in the summer of 2001. A sensible buy for the future, improving the squad, buffing up the club's playing resources, was the claim at the time. Except O'Leary paid £10 million for Johnson, a transfer fee that raised eyebrows throughout the game. The manager argued there was no gamble involved in the signing: he was convinced the player would go on to have a long, distinguished international career; he would prove to be worth every penny. Which shows how much he knew: compromised by injury almost from the start, Johnson's international career stalled after the one cap (against Italy) he had won while still at Derby. Proof positive that a footballer should never be counted a sound business asset; the pitfalls of the profession are simply too many and varied.

But it was when Johnson's agent Leon Angel was negotiating his salary that it became clear how far the Leeds dream had detached itself from reality. The representative was determined he was going to strike a hefty deal and girded himself for a tough couple of hours' bargaining. However, some accounts of the meeting claim he was so astonished by the generous scale of Ridsdale's opening offer he audibly gasped. Ridsdale took this to be a snort of derision and immediately offered to up it by £10,000 a week. The pair shook on a deal way more substantial than the agent expected, close to five times what the player was on at Derby. Or at least that was the story. Angel now insists there was no gasp, no consequent upping of the offer. 'It was an ordinary negotiation,' he says. Nonetheless, whether it was arrived at by happenstance or not, Johnson's wage – well north of £1 million a year for five years – came to define Leeds' folly. Ordinary players on extraordinary money: it spoke of economic illiteracy.

For Mann, however, it was another player acquisition that marked the point when sanity finally vacated Elland Road.

> The moment I knew we were in trouble was when [the Liverpool striker] Robbie Fowler was bought [in the summer of 2001 for £15 million]. Everyone with two eyes knew what we needed at the time was another central midfielder. I remember a group of us from the Supporters' Trust having a meeting with Ridsdale where we told him this repeatedly. And who did he go out and buy? Robbie Fowler, who was already past his sell-by date. He was the bauble on the Christmas tree, the look-at-us-we're-so-clever luxury item.

This is the politician's principal charge against Ridsdale: that under him a collective assumption took hold that the mere spending of money was in itself enough to generate success. 'There was a madness around,' he says. 'I remember queuing up to buy tickets for a cup tie at Scunthorpe and Ridsdale showing up and he started offering to have everyone in the queue chauffeured to the game. Most peculiar. The mindset was clearly that they had to show they lived the high life in order to aspire to remain in it. "Look at us, look at what we can do".'

And the financial recklessness went far beyond the playing budget. In 2001 £70,000 was spent on private jets for directors to fly to games they had previously driven to. The salaries of administrative staff bore no relation to their job description: the man who booked the first-team travel was on more than £150,000 a year. As for Ridsdale himself, he was paid £645,450 in 2001 alone. Which would have been fine if it was the earned surplus of a profitable enterprise. But it wasn't. Almost every penny was borrowed. At some point it had to be paid back. And that point arrived with the dispatch of an express train.

Ten years on from the height of his folly, Ridsdale was interviewed by *The Sun* newspaper. After dabbling at Barnsley, Plymouth and Cardiff, by the end of 2011 he was chairman of Preston North End (where sceptical fans nicknamed him 'P-Riddy'). The man who had been so keen to take personal credit for Leeds' rise when I had met him in 2001 seemed anxious after its fall to invoke collective responsibility. It wasn't him, he insisted, it was everybody else:

> The perception is I sank Leeds United but that mostly stems from an interview with my successor, Professor John McKenzie. It was specifically designed to make out that things were going wrong because of Peter Ridsdale and not the board of Leeds United. That interview included the famous reference to the goldfish tank in my office, which actually worked in my favour. It cost a couple of hundred quid a year, and that was the worst example of 'largesse' they could find? There was definitely a campaign to rubbish my time at Leeds United. It succeeded and that has followed me ever since. Our strategy was endorsed unanimously by the board and the shareholders, and the fans were saying spend, spend, spend. But everyone still says it was Peter Ridsdale's fault. Our strategy was based on the club being in the Premier League top six, so we'd get all the cash.

A year after that interview, in October 2012, Ridsdale's insistence on his own probity was somewhat compromised when he was banned from being a company director for seven and a half years. His company, WH Sports Group, had just folded owing over £400,000, much of it to Her Majesty's Revenue and Customs. It transpired that during the previous couple of years he had channelled nearly £350,000 of payments into his personal account, rather than going through the company. Nevertheless, while Ridsdale may have been mendacious in his claim that he bore no responsibility for Leeds' demise, while he may have been cavalier in his personal accounting, when he made the following observation he had a point: 'I left in March 2003,' he told *The Sun*. 'There is no way the team I left should have been relegated a year later.'

When he departed Elland Road, dispatched from the building by a rising tide of some £103 million debt, Leeds maintained a team fully capable of remaining in the Premiership. In their ranks they still boasted players of the quality of Mark Viduka, David Batty and Harry Kewell. Under their manager Peter Reid, who had taken over from Terry Venables in March 2003, they put together a spirited run to avoid relegation in 2003. It included a thumping 6–1 victory over Charlton Athletic at The Valley on 5 April 2003. The Australian Viduka in particular was brilliantly effective that day, his touch and vision eloquent evidence of a superior talent. With him still on board, the embarrassment of battling against relegation would surely only be temporary. Ahead of the 2003–04 season, Leeds were still in the top flight, still with access to the growing booty from the broadcasting deals and still in possession of their best player for a generation. Indeed, it was a position that prompted Ridsdale's successor, the new chairman Professor John McKenzie, to be florid in his optimism:

Two years ago we were struggling to swim against the current. Now we are treading water. In a year's time I hope to have one foot on the sand, which is where we want to be as quickly as possible. And following that I would hope to be on the sand running with a beautiful blonde.

Side on the slide

Whatever the Prof's desert-island-paradise analogies, the sale of players had to continue. Over the close season Viduka saw the quality around him diminish further when his fellow Aussie Kewell went to Liverpool for £5 million, Dacourt to Roma for £3.5 million and the goalkeeper Nigel Martyn to Everton for a knock-down £500,000. There was no money to give Reid a transfer budget so he was obliged to make do with loans. Most came from France. Didier Domi, Zoumana Camara, Lamine Sakho, Salomon Olembé and Cyril Chapuis were all brought in on season-long deals, to provide a bit of ballast to the squad. None of them were in Viduka's class.

Roque Júnior, on the other hand, looked as if he might be. Borrowed from Milan, he arrived in Leeds in August 2003 and was immediately fêted as the club's first-ever Brazilian international and a man with both a World Cup and a Champions League winner's medal in his collection. 'Rocky', as he was quickly christened in Yorkshire, however, proved to be anything but the anchoring point around which the club could re-form. Flaky, ill-disciplined and clearly not enamoured with life in the damp West Riding, he was sent off in just his second game, a defeat by Birmingham. And that was the highlight of a Leeds career which encompassed only five first-team starts.

'It was a real peculiar mixture,' says Mann of Reid's squad. 'There were these dozens of loanees who were absolutely not up to the job alongside those on high wages we couldn't get rid of because everyone else in the game recognized what no one at Leeds did: they weren't good enough.' Reid soon discovered it wasn't a winning mix. And in November 2003, after a horrible 6–1 defeat at newly promoted Portsmouth, he was sacked. He was replaced by a club hero, Eddie Gray, the tricky Scottish winger who had illuminated Don Revie's championship-winning sides of the 1970s. For a while Gray managed to counteract the downward spiral. Results improved. Viduka – whom he had restored to the side after the player had fallen out with Reid – scored a few crucial goals. Hope began to flicker once more. But it was to be all too fleeting.

At the end of 2003 McKenzie too said his farewells. His departure was precipitated by his announcement that, despite his promise of a beachy, sun-kissed future, Leeds had sustained a loss of £49.5 million in the previous financial year. It was a record for a British football club. It meant each and every week at Elland Road, £952,000 was heading through the exits and out into the ether. After McKenzie – and a brief cameo from Trevor Birch – came Gerald Krasner, the public face of a local consortium buying into the club. There appeared to be something in the water at Elland Road which led its chairmen, against all available evidence, to exude positivity and assurance.

'Mr Ridsdale had spent a bit too much money and they were £103 million in debt,' Krasner says now about his takeover. 'Someone told me that Leeds were going to go bust and there was nothing that could be done, but I'm a bit stubborn that way, so together with some clients,

I bought the club and we reduced the debt to £22 million.' His view of his position was not without moments of humour: 'I remember my first match as chairman was Manchester City at home and we won one–nil,' he says. 'I thought about whether I should resign and become the first chairman of a Premier League team never to lose a match but I decided to follow it through.'

Krasner was a liquidity practitioner: he had made his money from crisis. And Leeds was a crisis all right. He brought in as his chief adviser Geoffrey Richmond, the former chairman of Bradford City. It was like hiring an alcoholic to run a pub. At Valley Parade, Richmond had presided over his own version of the Ridsdale method. In the failed attempt to maintain City in the Premier League following their promotion from the First Division in 1999, he had signed the Italian player Benito Carbone on a five-year contract worth £40,000 a week. When City were relegated after a two-year stay in 2001, the debts almost finished them off. Twelve years on from the Carbone-induced insanity, Bradford, by now in League Two, progressed to the 2013 League Cup final paying less to their entire first-team squad combined than Richmond had paid his luxury Italian import.

But for now, with Leeds again plunged into a relegation struggle that threatened the principal source of their income – Premier League status – Richmond was developing policy at Elland Road. Or at least he was until 26 April 2004 when he was declared bankrupt, owing £3.3 million to the taxman, and was no longer able to function as a director. Leeds being steered by a bankrupt: there was something ghoulishly appropriate in that. Which is why John Mann, for one, does not solely blame Ridsdale for the club's ultimate demise:

It was a spectacular disintegration. The supporters were always irrationally optimistic. What we hadn't got a grip on was the degree to which the board could foul things up. It was crap management from top to bottom. Bad players, a downward spiral, everyone in office seemed bewildered at what had been going on and absolutely incapable of plotting a sound route forward.

The season 2003–04, Mann says, was a particularly dire one for Leeds, with one missed opportunity after another, and the chance to retain their place in the Premiership squandered by ineptitude. And that wasn't all: 'We'd bought nobody and brought in a whole series of duds on loan for reasons that were inexplicable unless you thought carefully about what motivation there might have been for those involved in bringing them on board. I can't say more for reasons of libel.'

If, when they started takeover proceedings in the winter of 2003–04 (they took full control in March 2004), Krasner and Richmond had a plan, it seemed to be this: bleed the patient in the hope that might prompt a revival. They discovered there were eighteen players on the books earning more than £1 million a year; the total wage bill was £40 million. In attempting to reduce his outgoings, Krasner insisted some of the higher earners were loaned out. But he soon discovered the loan system is not that helpful; in most cases the club that owns a player's registration is obliged to continue meeting much of his wages. Effectively, as they attempted to pass on some of their heavy earners like Fowler, Leeds were still paying players to play for someone else.

Dressing-room revolt

So, in the January transfer window, another round of fire sales was launched. But the buying clubs, all too aware that Leeds were by now desperate, drove hard bargains. Assets were stripped for less than their true value. Eventually the training ground and the vacant land around the stadium were sold off at knock-down prices. For those left in the dressing room it was a fractious time. 'The whole season we were struggling, there was so much going on off the field,' says Michael Duberry, the centre-back who joined the club in 1999, a £6 million O'Leary signing from Chelsea. 'One thing I'll say, we always got paid. My mate was at Bradford and he didn't get paid, which was hard.'

But Duberry believes the crisis that enfolded the club only gave excuses to those in the dressing room who were looking for them.

He continues: 'I think the main distraction came from the fact it was always mentioned. Every week you'd get the same question: is it a distraction? We were batting off the question, it was thrown at you all the time. But once you're on the pitch, it's football. It's the one safe place to get away from it all, get away from the problems. Yeah, there was a disruption from players going, managers changing. But that's only a get-out if you want it to be. For me, there was opportunity too. With Rio and Woody going, it was the chance to get into something. I was always third man behind them, now I thought let me nail this. I didn't think this is a sinking ship I have to jump off. I thought this is my chance.'

Relations between those in charge and those in the dressing room, however, were about to take a serious turn for the worse. In January 2004, the board announced that it was looking to impose a 25 per cent reduction in the wages of senior players, including Duberry. David Batty was the players' shop steward, leading the negotiations. And, advised by the Professional Footballers' Association, his stance was that the players should not be obliged to suffer the consequence of directorial incompetence. They were not prepared voluntarily to take a cut.

In the middle of the month, as negotiations became ever more tricky, the *Yorkshire Post* printed on its front page a rogues' gallery of four players – Nick Barmby, Ian Harte, Gary Kelly and Duberry – who were said to be earning £5 million a year between them and were refusing to co-operate with the board's cost-cutting regimen. The implication in the article below was that their greed was bringing the club down.

'It did get personal,' says Duberry. 'That time with my picture on the front page that was not good. There was a bit of animosity in that sense, and you can understand why. Leeds fans are working-class people paying out their own hard-earned money and they're told we're earning that sort of sum.' He wasn't, however, often personally challenged about the issue. He cannot recall much recrimination from the fans directed at him; after all, this was Leeds, not Italy. 'Walking in the town centre there might be passing comment,' he says. 'But looking back it was never too negative or aggressive. If Twitter had been around in them days, mind, I'm sure I'd have got it big time.'

Eventually a compromise was reached: the players took a hit, deferring some payments, but nothing like the scale of reduction the board was seeking. And however much Duberry insists that the squad maintained its focus on performance despite the gathering calamity, the results did not suggest a harmonious enterprise. From the turn of 2004, even as the squeeze was imposed, Leeds lost six league games on the bounce. They were deep in trouble.

'I had a meeting round then with [board member] Allan Leighton on behalf of the Supporters' Trust,' recalls Mann. 'I suggested he hand over the club in its entirety to us. Our strategy would have been sell the sellable players, forget the crap loanees, bring in the juniors. Yes, we probably would have been relegated anyhow, but it would have been a sustainable model. Not surprisingly we got absolutely no response.'

What was remarkable about Leeds' precipitous fall was that the crowds kept on coming. No fewer than 40,153 packed Elland Road for the trans-Pennine hate-fest with Manchester United on 18 October 2003. The trouble was that not even turnouts of that magnitude could make a dent in the mountain of debt. The money generated had already been accounted for, Ridsdale having launched his spending spree by mortgaging off future takings. The cashflow was moribund. In an attempt to bring in some funds, Krasner launched a twenty-year debenture scheme. Two-decade season tickets were put on sale. Clearly nervous about the long-term sustainability of any plan produced by the board, the fans largely ignored the opportunity to invest in the club's future. Krasner sold fewer than 100 such tickets.

By early March 2004, the Premiership table revealed that Leeds were a long way from safety and sinking fast. Along with Leicester and Wolves, they were a mile behind seventeenth-placed Everton. A mood of grim inevitability began to settle over the stands. Gallows humour held sway. A series of calamitous performances (including a 5–0 defeat at champions-elect Arsenal on 16 April) culminated in the

4–1 defeat at Bolton on 2 May that sealed their fate. At the Reebok, Viduka, the one remaining beacon from the past, was sent off. It was his sole involvement in a game in which he had shown precious little interest or commitment. By this point in the season, the attitude of the club's best player appeared to be the most obvious symptom of the miserable failure of O'Leary and Ridsdale's grand delusion. Viduka came across as a mercenary with no understanding of the emotional context in which he worked, a player simply biding his time until he was sold on. His departure at the Reebok was the moment the dream turned irrevocably into a nightmare.

Leeds, loud and proud

The final home game of the season arrived with no hope of reprieve. It was already over. For the fans, however, it presented an opportunity. They wished to demonstrate to the watching world that the fundamental values of their club remained intact. The directors may have derailed the enterprise, some of the senior players may have expressed little interest in the fight, but the collective will of the fans insisted that a club that had won the league title as recently as 1992 would soon emerge from the doldrums and recapture past glory. Outside the stadium the Bremner statue was buried under a tsunami of scarves and shirts. The ground seemed to rock to an anthem of hope, born of the fans' refusal to be cowed by circumstance.

A noisy and prolonged protest against the board took place before kick-off. Beach-balls were punted around the stands, banners were flourished. One read:

YOU CAN TAKE OUR MONEY, YOU CAN $ELL OUR PLAYERS
BUT THE FANS WILL ALWAYS BE UNITED

Peter Lorimer, the club's all-time leading scorer, stalwart of the Don Revie era and since March 2004 invited by Krasner onto the board in a vain effort to create a sense of continuity with the past, had clearly picked up on the mood. He wrote in the matchday programme:

Alan Smith and [goalkeeper] Paul Robinson were pictured with tears rolling down their cheeks after the match at Bolton which sent us down. They were genuinely hurt at the confirmation that Leeds will be playing in Division One next season. If every player had the attitude of Smith, we would be a great team to watch. We always used to have Alan's attitude as players, but unfortunately nowadays, it is a rarity and that is why he stands out. I am not saying our players haven't been trying, because there are lots of them who have tried very hard this season. But when you see some of the more gifted ones strolling around at times, you know that isn't how it should be.

Everyone knew who he meant. Lorimer's words accurately reflected the mood at Elland Road. Never mind the selfishness of the modern footballing mercenaries who were taking monetary advantage of the club when it was in dire financial straits, in its hour of need Leeds United and its fans would be sustained by the spirit of past greatness, the spirit of Revie and Bremner, Lorimer and Norman Hunter.

Gray had picked a team, too, which reflected the club's core purpose. O'Leary may have spent over £100 million on players, but only two of those stepping out for the final game of the 2003–04 season – Duberry and Dominic Matteo – remained from the Irishman's spree. The young winger Jermaine Pennant had been loaned from Arsenal. With Viduka suspended, the rest – all eight of them – were products of Paul Hart's enlightened youth-development programme, local boys with a passion for the club. They were the torch-bearers of the real Leeds. As they walked out alongside their south-east London opponents, the packed stands greeted them with a raucous fanfare. 'It was very emotional,' remembers Duberry. 'Leeds were a massive club. Look where they had been not that long before and now they're here, about to be relegated. No one wants to be part of a team that gets relegated. There's so much glory in a club like Leeds, you want to be part of the glory times. Not the bad times. Those aren't the times you want to be remembered for.'

Lining up against them were Charlton, at the time generally considered to be the common-sense opposite of Leeds. Careful, modest, refusing to embrace unsustainable ambition, since being promoted to the Premiership in 1998 they had been steered by their long-standing manager Alan Curbishley to mid-table consolidation. The slow build was their methodology, not for them dangerous, loadsamoney dreams. It was their sixth season in the league and, even though they were going to lose their best player Scott Parker to Chelsea during the summer, they looked at that time as if they were going to be a Premiership fixture for a while longer.

The skipper Matt Holland epitomized the Charlton way: he didn't cost much, but he played well. Bright, intelligent, undemonstrative, the Bury-born Ireland international opened the scoring with a whipping, swerving, bending long-range shot that dipped past young Paul Robinson at the last second. For a moment, as the small knot of fans who had journeyed up from south London celebrated, an air of defeatism filled the rest of the stadium.

It was not to last long. Leeds were driven by the kind of spirit Lorimer could only wish they had shown all season. Now finally free of the overpriced baubles foisted on them by the Ridsdale experiment, this was a team bristling with determination, exuding a fierce pride in their home club. Up front in particular the pairing of the effervescent Smith with the eighteen-year-old James Milner was a revelation. What a change from Viduka's seemingly uninterested languor. Perspiration had replaced indifference. These two buzzed furiously and irritatingly at Charlton like a pair of attack wasps. The duo – backed by a growing crescendo in the stands – were unrelenting as Leeds took control of the game. Charlton's defenders were simply battered into submission. First Matthew Kilgallon slid in onto Stephen McPhail's free kick to equalize. Then, to a glorious explosion of noise from the stands, came the best goal of the game, in truth one of the best goals seen at Elland Road all season. The ever-busy Milner and Smith smoothly, instinctively, as if they had been playing together for years, exchanged passes, drawing the attention of the Charlton backline. The ball was played to Pennant, unmarked and unnoticed, who smacked home a goal.

After half-time, things got even better for Leeds. A hint of times past shone through the free-flowing, passing football of Milner, Smith and Pennant. And when Duberry was fouled in the Charlton area by Jonathan Fortune, the crowd was delivered their moment. Smith, given the penalty duties for the day in the hope one might be awarded, drove home the resulting spot kick. He celebrated by kissing the club crest on his shirt, pointing to his captain's armband and punching the air in salute to each of the four stands in turn. His demonstration was as poignant as it was powerful. A banner was waved heartily in the stand: 'THANKS ALAN: 100% LEEDS.'

For a few minutes the crowd could properly dream. Not in the Ridsdale way, but in the traditional, authentic footballing fashion. Dream of a future Leeds regrouping and redeveloping on its own home-grown talent. Dream of a Leeds building a sustainable team around the likes of Smith and Milner. 'Leeds had a great youth system under Paul Hart,' says Mann. 'If that had been properly protected it would have rooted the club in the community. It should have given us a future. It was staring you in the face what the way ahead was: invest in youth. Unfortunately those in charge decided to look in the opposite direction.'

Indeed, the rhythm of the final game reflected Mann's narrative. The youth took the team to the very point of success. Then the old guard intervened. This was Leeds, after all, still trapped in the downward vortex. The chance of Leeds exiting the Premiership on a note of optimism, with a heartening win that promised a brighter future, was never likely to be sustained. Like the hope that the Champions League would provide the club with an endless source of revenue, there was a certain inevitability that this game would disappoint.

As Gray put it, silly goals cost them dear. Poor Duberry – never wholly accepted by the crowd because of his Chelsea origins – had a hand in both, gifting Charlton a route back into the match in three traumatic minutes. First he fouled Jason Euell for a penalty the striker duly converted. And then, just 180 seconds later, he became haplessly embroiled in a bout of penalty-area pinball. Which Euell calmly ended by stroking the ball into the net.

There were still ten minutes to go, but Charlton's professionalism stood the test, not least because, exhausted by the emotions of it all, Smith and Milner had run themselves into the ground. Charlton had the point they required in pursuit of the highest placing they had ever achieved in the Premiership. They were to finish seventh; consolidation was their reward. They would still be there, feeding on the rich pastures of English football's uplands as Leeds slipped unstoppably into the financial mire. They would be participating the next season in what was then the biggest share-out of television revenue in British sporting history. Leeds would not.

'It starts sinking in even as you make your way off the pitch at the end that that badge on your sleeve isn't going to be there any more,' recalls Duberry. 'Next season you're not going to be playing at Old Trafford, Stamford Bridge and Anfield. Next season you're not going to be Premiership. As a professional, that's a hard blow to take.'

When the final whistle blew, however, the fans were determined to enjoy their last moment in the top flight. The ovation lasted longer than any Duberry can remember in his career. 'The crowd was brilliant, incredible,' he says. 'They stood there cheering and clapping us off for ages. You could hear it in the dressing room. Though to be fair there wasn't a lot of noise in there. We just sat in silence with our own thoughts, the noise coming in from outside. You just thought: what have we lost here?'

Unlike Smith, Duberry did not hang around long enough to join in the wake in the stands:

I just went home. I can't remember if we were in training the next day. All I remember is what a miserable summer that was. The Premiership is the motherland. It's where you want to be. A couple of weeks later, you look at the play-off final and you think 'they're going up, taking our place'. Across the summer it sinks in. You don't want to be part of that. Players have to move on. It sounds harsh, but this is a short career. You need exposure. And you don't get that in the Championship.

The deadly embrace of Bates

After the final game of the season – a defeat by Leeds' hated old foes Chelsea at Stamford Bridge – the deconstruction began. First Gray was removed from his office, ejected with barely a thank-you for his efforts *in extremis*. He was replaced by Kevin Blackwell, Leeds' fifth manager in just under two seasons, who was informed there would be no transfer budget to rebuild for the Championship campaign. Worse still, the sales continued stripping the club of its remaining assets. First Smith went, the transfer fee some £9 million.

'I owed it to myself to make that decision,' Smith says now of his departure across the Pennines. 'It was difficult because I knew. I'd been a Leeds fan, seen different people leave, I'd seen [Eric] Cantona leave and seen the reaction he'd got and mine will probably be even worse, because of the connection between me and Leeds United. That'll always live with me. My feelings for Leeds will never change; I've never tried to hide that when I went to Manchester. I've thought about it [going back to Elland Road] so many times, to be honest.'

He never did. In 2011 there was a chance he might have been signed on loan from Newcastle, where he had been transferred in 2007 after three seasons at Old Trafford. But the deal fell through over who would pay the majority of his wages. Instead, in 2012 he went to MK Dons, the renamed, Milton Keynes-based avatar of the old Wimbledon FC, and a club that hadn't even existed when Smith made his Leeds debut.

After Smith's defection, the summer just became one long bulletin of bad news for Leeds fans. Milner was sold to Newcastle for £3.6 million. Robinson, too, was on his way – to Tottenham. As was the whippet-quick, sixteen-year-old substitute Aaron Lennon. All went on to have significant Premier League careers. Just not with their home-town club. Mark Viduka also continued his Premier League business, swapping shirts and disappearing up the road to Leeds' North Yorkshire rivals Middlesbrough for £4.5 million.

But the incoming transfer revenue did nothing to reverse the rising tide of debt. Now ejected from the Premiership and with the parachute payments already put aside to fund interest owed, Krasner found himself hamstrung. He attempted to sell on to a Florida-based consortium, but the deal fell through (perhaps at the point the Americans studied the books). Any inspection of the accounts would reveal a motley bunch of former players and managers to whom sizeable sums were still due. These included Robbie Fowler (owed £2,106,000), Danny Mills (£1,841,000,) Nick Barmby (£1,055,000), David O'Leary (£356,000) and Peter Reid (£355,000). Even the very sales required to reduce the club's costs brought associated debt: Leeds paid out £1.6 million in agents' fees in six months up to 31 December 2004 just to facilitate the fire sale. Less than a month after that, in January 2005, Krasner himself left, condemned by his failure to right the listing vessel.

'How can I have any regrets?' he says now of his tenure. 'How many people can say they've been the chairman of the team they've supported all their life? I couldn't be a fan as a chairman. I had to take that hat off and be serious about what was going on. Football is unlike any other business. It does not obey the law of the land and it does not obey the laws of physics.'

Though it might be suggested that Leeds precisely fulfilled the laws of physics, or at least that law which suggests any object relentlessly pumped full of garbage will inevitably sink. Just before Krasner left the building, it appeared Leeds would go out of business altogether. A notice to liquidate was served. 'It was a terrible day, with staff crying all around me,' recalls manager Blackwell. 'The doors were going to be closed on the Monday. We'd all had e-mails, saying we wouldn't be paid. The wages had only been paid in December because I sold [reserve goalkeeper] Scott Carson to Liverpool.'

John Mann looked on in horror as the object of his lifelong affection teetered on the brink. 'People were talking extinction. But that was never going to happen. There was too much money still sloshing around. There were plenty of people attracted still to squeeze and grab the cash.' Mann's cynical assessment was to be borne out by what happened next. At precisely 2.27 a.m. on Friday 21 January 2005, an apparent saviour appeared on the horizon. The Geneva-based Sports Forward Fund (SFF) bought 25 per cent of the club and took on the liabilities. Just for a moment, supporters' hopes stirred. Just for a moment they could look on the bright side. And then it was revealed who was behind the SFF. Step forward Ken Bates, the abrasive erstwhile chairman of Chelsea, and a man about as welcome to Leeds fans as a sexually transmitted disease. 'I would rather we started afresh in the Conference than have him [Bates] in charge,' thundered Simon Jose, of the Leeds United Independent Fans' Association. 'It's like the four horsemen of the apocalypse selling to Lucifer. We need a clean sweep and a fresh start. This is like putting King Herod in charge of babysitting.'

John Mann, albeit speaking in less apocalyptic terms, expressed similar misgivings about the arrival at Elland Road of the man who had made a fortune selling Chelsea to Roman Abramovich in 2003. 'One thing that could be guaranteed the moment Ken Bates took over is that this club would struggle for years to come,' the MP states. 'Its main asset had been the youth system. Nurture that and you have a sound economic model: you are creating players who have a value you can realize. Woodgate, Robinson, Lennon, Carson, Milner, Smith, Micah Richards, Fabien Delph: what a continual source of income that lot represented. So what's the first thing Bates did? Starve the youth system of resources. It was absolutely predictable. And absolutely mad.'

What Bates was certainly never going to do was risk his own money in righting Leeds. Quite the opposite. In May 2007 he put the club into administration, offering the still lengthy list of creditors 1p in the pound to resolve their outstanding issues. Never mind that the ten points deduction would send Leeds plunging to the third tier of English football, it served Bates's purpose. As administration was completed, he then bought a majority stake in a club now artfully, and some might say artificially, finally cleared of debt. Five years later, with Leeds still marooned a long way from the Premier League, with the manager's dug-out still hosting a seemingly endless game of musical chairs, with Bates mortgaging two years' worth of season-ticket income yet again in order this time to upgrade the hospitality facilities in the east stand, the purpose behind the owner's Leeds strategy was revealed. In November 2012 he did a deal with a Bahraini-based consortium called Gulf Finance House. It was worth £44 million, of which £32 million reportedly went to Bates. That is what you call living the dream.

Watching Bates depart with his bank account plumped, Mann remains despondent. 'There needs to be legislation,' he says. 'I stood by and watched a community asset being destroyed. If I were in charge, I'd legislate to protect youth systems. I'd like to see them isolated in law, to protect the grant aid and tax breaks which routinely are used to fund them. In my ideal world, the fans and local community would own a club's stadium and youth structure. The first team and glory bits could then be franchised out to an owner.' In the meantime, the MP is insistent that Leeds need to find a way back into the Premier League as soon as possible:

I think Leeds are now in a very treacherous position. They have not got much longer out of the limelight before their international reputation goes. As an MP I do a lot of travelling abroad and I see Arsenal, Chelsea and Manchester United shirts everywhere. Leeds have to get back in the televised market very quickly to pick up on that reputation. Because whatever we had from the glory days is being very rapidly lost.

That is the thing about the Premier League as it embarks on its third decade. As Leeds have discovered to their cost, if you want to be counted amongst the élite, if you want to live with the giants of the present rather than living on the memory of once bestriding the past, if you want to be a football club that is getting on in the world, the Premier League is the only place to be.

BARCLAYCARD PREMIERSHIP

Elland Road, Leeds

Saturday 8 May 2004

LEEDS UNITED 3 – 3 CHARLTON ATHLETIC

Leeds scorers: Matthew Kilgallon 29; Jermaine Pennant 41; Alan Smith 69 (pen)

Charlton scorers: Matt Holland 11; Jason Euell 76 (pen) 79

Attendance: 38,986

Referee: Mark Halsey

TEAMS:

LEEDS UNITED (4-4-2)

Paul Robinson; Gary Kelly (Jason Wilcox 73), Michael Duberry, Dominic Matteo, Ian Harte; Jermaine Pennant, Matthew Kilgallon, Stephen McPhail, Frazer Richardson (Lucas Radebe 82); James Milner, Alan Smith

Subs not used: Scott Carson (gk), Nick Barmby, Jamie Winter

CHARLTON ATHLETIC (4-4-2)

Dean Kiely; Luke Young, Hermann Hreidarsson, Jonathan Fortune, Chris Powell (Chris Perry 60); Graham Stuart (Radostin Kishishev 60), Matt Holland, Jonatan Johansson, Paul Konchesky; Jason Euell, Paolo Di Canio (Shaun Bartlett 60)

Subs not used: Sérgio Leite (gk), Mark Fish

Match 7

Taking the rest to the cleaners

BOLTON WANDERERS V. CHELSEA

Reebok Stadium, Bolton

Saturday 30 April 2005

As they entered the visitors' dressing room at the Reebok Stadium on May Day morning 2005, Bolton Wanderers' club cleaners quickly realized that the place required a bit more work than the standard tidy-up they were used to doing. 'Sticky' does not begin to describe the condition of the room after Chelsea's players and staff had finished with it. A skip was brought in to haul away the dozens of empty champagne bottles, an industrial steam cleaner used to de-tack the walls, and a mop the width of Lancashire to soak up the bubbly still lapping at the skirting boards. It was evident from the detritus that some serious shindig had taken place the day before. Still, there was one good thing to be said: as the cleaners set about hiring specialist equipment and calculating the amount of overtime needed to sort the place out, they knew that when it came to paying, those who had caused the mess could afford it.

And, like Rod Stewart getting his people to compensate a 1970s US hotel owner whose premises had just been redecorated by him and The Faces, Chelsea made good the damage caused. No problem at all. The reason behind the celebrations made the mess worth every penny. After all, it is not every day that you win English football's most prestigious title for the first time in half a century. And in the club's centenary season at that. 'It's a new era,' BBC commentator Steve Wilson said over the television pictures as the players who had just made Chelsea the fourth club to win the Premiership title bounced around the Bolton pitch. 'It's a blue era.'

If you want to know how it was that this April evening in Lancashire concluded in a rip tide of blue-tinted champagne flowing across the Reebok, then the answer lies some seventeen miles to the south-east. There, at Manchester United's Old Trafford ground just over two years earlier, the seeds of the unconfined joy that would be unleashed on the Reebok's visitors' dressing room that spring evening in 2005 had been sown. Although the club had already been in existence then for ninety-eight years, in many ways Chelsea's modern history can be said to have begun on St George's Day 2003, when Manchester United entertained Real Madrid in a Champions League quarter-final. And in the process – though no one involved had the slightest inkling at the time – they changed the very fabric of English football.

Madrid back then was the team of the *galácticos*. This stellar side was the collective result of a policy of borrowing heavily to hire the world's finest talent, in the expectation that their prowess would generate sufficient revenue to repay the investment. Think Leeds, but with a realistic chance that the gamble would pay off. The starting line-up included Zinédine Zidane, Raul and Ronaldo (the original Ronaldo, that is, the one with the teeth and the burger habit). Steve McManaman was also in their team, perhaps to demonstrate that even the great have feet of clay. United were not without their own sprinkling of stardust, either, provided by pricey imports like Ruud van Nistelrooy and Juan Sebastián Verón (later of Chelsea), plus the home-grown lustre of David Beckham, the handsome pin-up of British sport who was said at the time to have fallen out with his manager and, after receiving a boot in the face during a dressing-room altercation, was seeking to reposition his brand elsewhere. Even in Madrid, it was rumoured.

Rise of the Roman empire

The clash between the world's two most followed clubs, sides fabled for their attacking verve, it was the tie everyone wanted to attend, a must-see event for every big-game hunter. Among the 66,708 spectators filling United's ever-expanding home was a thirty-six-year-old Russian billionaire called Roman Abramovich. An enthusiast for the game since childhood, how he loved what he saw from his box seat in the south stand. The high-stakes ping-pong, the romping, bravura but ultimately insufficient 4–3 victory to United, the moment when Ronaldo, having scored a hat-trick, was substituted in the second half and the entire home crowd rose as one to salute his contribution: Abramovich wanted more of this, the grandest of football occasions. Indeed, he wanted it so badly, as he left the stadium, he made a call to one of his staff. He was keen to know this: how could he buy Manchester United? He had the money all right, with more funds in his current account than in the central bank of many a Eurozone state. And this looked like the most fun way to spend it. He issued the simple instruction to his people: make it happen.

In Britain back then, we were not yet familiar with the word 'oligarch'. At the time the closest we had to someone of Abramovich's happy coincidence of youth and wealth was the Easyjet founder Stelios Haji-Ioannou. And frankly, the Russian could have bought Easyjet with his small change. Assuming – in his world of Titanic-scale yachts, stables of pricey Italian cars and squadrons of private aircraft – he even knew what Easyjet was. This was a man so loaded he could later state in court that 'it's really difficult for me to say what is a wealthy person and what is not a wealthy person'. And mean it. He was a billionaire, moreover, whose reserves of cash had been accumulated with all the dispatch of a lottery winner. Until 1995, he had been a moderately successful wheeler-dealer, doing nicely as he patrolled the fringes of the Wild West capitalism unleashed by Russia's new embrace of free-market economics, making a rouble or ten in businesses as diverse as tyre retreading and bodyguard recruitment.

Then, on 24 August 1995, just as the Pre-mier League embarked on its fourth season, Abramovich got his hands on Sibneft, the state oil company, which was being offloaded in the fire sale that was the post-Soviet Union privatization programme. He was abetted by his then associate, the late Boris Berezovsky, who was a favourite of President Boris Yeltsin and knew his way around both the Kremlin and the president's thinking. And what Yeltsin needed at that moment was quick cash in order to tighten his slackening hold on the economy. Berezovsky told the president he knew people who could get him some readies all right. Just leave it to him.

Berezovsky subsequently confessed that he had rigged the auction for Sibneft in his and Abramovich's favour. Even so, the younger man's investment in the company has been estimated at $100 million. Where he had got his hands on that sort of money has long been a subject of speculation: Berezovsky, who admitted to being connected to Chechen warlords, once claimed that no one could make money in modern Russia without links to the underworld. But wherever the funds came from, they were well spent. The morning after the deal, Sibneft was worth – at a conservative estimate – twenty times more than Abramovich paid for it. That's what you call a tidy profit.

But even this sweetheart deal wasn't enough to keep the two former business associates on speaking terms. They fell out spectacularly, their relationship unravelling in legal recrimination. In a London court case brought by Berezovsky the year before his death in 2013, Abramovich insisted he had come by his enormous wealth through a process of 'hard work and by taking risks associated with doing business in Russia'. The sort of thing he meant by that, he later admitted in the same case, was paying hefty bribes to government officials and securing protection from gangsters.

Perhaps fearing he might not have it for long, Abramovich did not sit on his money. He moved into the business of acquiring Russia's lucrative aluminium assets as they were being privatized. This was dangerous territory. In 1998 it was said that someone was being murdered every three days in the fractious disputes over aluminium mining rights. Abramovich, though, surfed the mayhem, safely completing a $575 million deal to acquire a majority stake in RusAl in March 2000.

Through the delicate intricacies inherent in accumulating his wealth, Abramovich had acquired a potent collection of political and economic adversaries. In the business circles in which he moved, falling out could have fatal consequences. Given his circumstances, Britain – already popular with Russian money – seemed a much safer place to reside than Moscow. After he came to London in 2002, he showed a fondness for security which led him to buy only properties with at least two exit routes. His requirements were probably not the product of paranoia. Neither was the idea of buying himself a Premier League football club one solely propelled by a wish to immerse himself in the beautiful game. A prominent position in a Western democracy was a sensible safety precaution: his logic was that foes would think twice before taking out the owner of a historic British sporting institution.

One thing we can say about Abramovich's business dealings that will not prick the ears of his lawyers is this: he does not like to hang about. After that game against Madrid had whetted his appetite, his advisers were put to work to ascertain how quickly a deal could be sorted to buy out United. And what he was told about the great Mancunian operation was that, as a then-plc with any number of shareholders to track down and buy out, it would take a good nine months to effect a takeover. That was too long for a man of Abramovich's limited reserves of patience. Besides, as he couldn't help noticing after that Madrid game, when he took a limo to his waiting helicopter, Manchester was not in London. And he preferred to be in or close to the capital, where the other wealthy Russian émigrés congregated. Something about always keeping your enemies in plain sight…

After Manchester United, the next club he looked at was Tottenham. But again, this was not a business officially for sale. Besides, Joe Lewis, their Bahamas-based tax-exile owner, had never been keen on undervaluing his assets: Spurs would not come cheap. But presently, Abramovich's people sniffed out one club – in London, in the Premier League – where a deal might well be quickly done. An operation, moreover, in urgent need of some Russian money, no matter what its provenance.

Reviving the glory days

In 2003 Chelsea FC were in trouble. Not that that was an unfamiliar predicament. In 1982, the businessman Ken Bates had bought the club, then in the Second Division, for just £1, plus so much debt that a more appropriate nickname than 'the Blues' would have been the 'In-the-Reds'. Back then, the club had paid the penalty for an injudicious piece of stadium development at their home ground of Stamford Bridge. Their east stand – a tottering, three-tiered monument to hubris – had cost them so much in interest payments it had plunged the owners previous to Bates, Marler Estates, into insolvency.

Bates may have been brusque, acid-tongued and about as charming as root-canal work, but he was the shrewdest of operators. An early proponent of the Premier League, he saw within it the chance to do something no one had done with Chelsea in a generation: make money. What he mainly appreciated was the real-estate value of his asset: he had acquired a huge tract of land in the middle of the capital's most desirable postcode. Taking advantage of the Taylor Report's insistence on sprucing up stadiums, he rebuilt the ground, absorbing the rusting monolith of the east stand into a Las Vegas-like development of hotels and bars. And he understood that in order to fill the new hospitality facilities blooming across the forecourt of his self-styled Chelsea Village, he needed a successful team.

Under his watch as club chairman, the playing side was transformed. From being a club that had recently yoyo-ed between the top two divisions, he turned it into a team that won trophies, qualified for the Champions League and recruited superstar talent. As they had in the 1960s, under Bates Chelsea once more reflected their fashionable location, embracing in the early days of the Premier League the new trend for foreign players and managers. Under Gianluca Vialli, in a match against Southampton on 26 December 1999, they became the first club in British football history to field a team without a single British-born player in their starting line-up: Ed de Goey (Netherlands); Albert Ferrer (Spain); Emerson Thome (Brazil); Franck Leboeuf (France); Celestine Babayaro (Nigeria); Dan

Petrescu (Romania); Didier Deschamps (France); Roberto Di Matteo (Italy); Gabriele Ambrosetti (Italy); Gus Poyet (Uruguay); Tore André Flo (Norway). But all those salaries, not to mention Bates's ambitious property redevelopment, came at a cost. The chairman was a gambler, largely staking other people's money on the proposition that a winning team based in the swankier end of the capital would eventually hit pay dirt. He had floated the business on the alternative stock market, the AIM, in 1996 in order to raise funds for expansion. And for a time in the mid-1990s, he was backed by a wealthy Blues fan called Matthew Harding. But the pair fell out. And after Harding's death in a helicopter crash in October 1996, Bates was obliged to seek the banks' assistance. He borrowed more and more. By 2003, he was staring down the barrel of some £80 million of debt.

Even so, Bates contended that this was not an impossible position. Loosen the tightening noose of borrowing from around the club's throat and this was a business with real potential. Bates's problem was that far from relaxing, the grip of mounting debt was close to choking the life out of the entire enterprise. The banks were starting to get fidgety, anxious to see their stake returned with interest. Bates, who had seen what had happened to those at Leeds United whose ambition outpaced their ability to pacify the banks, was looking for help. And soon.

We can only imagine how thrilled he was, then, to receive a phone call in June 2003 from the representatives of a man said to be significantly richer than Croesus. A man, moreover, who did not believe in credit notes or hire purchase, who went about his business paying upfront and in full. When Ken met Roman, frankly he couldn't do the deal fast enough. Abramovich agreed to purchase Bates's stake in Chelsea Village for £18 million – not a bad return for an original investment of just a quid. Over the following weeks, the Russian bought out most of the remaining 12,000 shareholders at 35 pence per share, including the Matthew Harding estate, BSkyB (who owned nine per cent, plus a lease on Bates's most expensive hospitality box) and various anonymous offshore trusts. After passing the 90 per cent share threshold, Abramovich took the club back into private hands, de-listing it from the AIM on 22 August 2003. He also took responsibility for the club's debt, immediately paying most of it back to the banks, converting it into soft loans to himself. Within four months of seeing that game in Manchester he now owned a football club in the Premiership. Chelsea was his. The total bill – including paying off the debt – was £140 million.

This organization does not tolerate failure

With the purchase, Abramovich sealed his exit from much of his Russian business. A few months after concluding his deal with Bates, he sold RusAl for £920 million, and then Sibneft for a reported £8 billion, leaving him plenty of money to buy the odd full-back. That same year he bought the 420-acre Fyning Hill estate in West Sussex. By sheer coincidence, this glorious swooping property with views across half of southern England was a stone's throw from the final resting place of Frederick Parker, the man whose vision had first convinced landowner Gus Mears to create Chelsea Football Club in 1905.

Whatever could be gleaned from his business strategy, this much was evident about Roman Abramovich: he was not in football to mess about. Chelsea was no vanity purchase. Spurning all media approaches, he showed absolutely no interest in using the club as a vehicle for self-promotion. He was not in it for social leverage either; he didn't enjoy pressing the flesh, refusing rival directors' hospitality at away grounds, while at the Bridge he avoided the superannuated luvvies in the boardroom, fans like Dickie Attenborough who used the club like, well, a club.

He preferred his own company in an executive box where his bodyguards could keep an eye on the exits. Unlike his predecessor Bates, he did not use a column in the matchday programme to air robust political opinions. No, what he wanted from Chelsea was more straightforward: a winning team, competing at the top in Europe, an asset which would give him the pleasure of knowing he owned the best. And he wanted it now. Or even sooner.

In effect, what Abramovich had done was take the idea first made flesh by Jack Walker – that money could buy the Premier League – and inflated it to fit the pricier parameters of the competition as it entered its second, ever more financially muscular, decade. Where Walker had done it for tens of millions, the price of entry had doubled in less than ten years. This was now a seriously rich man's game. An oligarch's game.

But – as Jack Hayward discovered as he lost much of the proceeds of his pickle inheritance failing to turn Wolverhampton Wanderers into world beaters, and as Lakshmi Mittal found out as he hurled his steel assets into the unfathomable money-pit that was Queens Park Rangers – in football a rich man needs the right kind of assistance to spend his cash effectively. When the Russian arrived in west London such assistance was not instantly apparent.

He had inherited from Bates the Italian Claudio 'Tinkerman' Ranieri as head coach. But whatever the nickname, Abramovich was prepared to give the manager a chance to build a superstar-infused, championship-winning, Europe-busting Chelsea. At their first meeting, he told the Tinkerman whatever money was required to fulfil those requirements would be forthcoming. The Italian assumed he must have died and gone to heaven: suddenly in a world previously constrained by budget, money was no object. After dealing with the Santa-lookalike Bates, he appeared to have met the real thing.

Jimmy Floyd Hasselbaink, the club's centre-forward at the time, recalls that the effect of the sudden cash injection was quickly felt in the dressing room. The manager was like a child given unexpected access to keys of a sweet-shop:

A couple of weeks after Abramovich had taken over, Ranieri called in me and Eidur [Gudjohnsen, his strike partner]. We'd just had this really good season, scoring forty odd goals between us, and he said to us: 'we're going to buy two bigger, better strikers than you. [Adrian] Mutu and [Hernán] Crespo, they'll be my number one and two. If you want to go, tell me now.' I said 'I want to stay and fight for a place'. I think he was surprised. I thought: 'I'm going to give you a problem.' In the end, it never kicked off for Crespo and Mutu and he had to come back to me and Eidur.

That was Ranieri's problem in a nutshell. He spent Abramovich's money with gusto (he handed over £111 million for new players in 2003 alone). But many of his glitzier purchases – Mutu, Crespo, Glen Johnson, Wayne Bridge, even Verón from that Madrid-beating United line-up – failed to improve the team enough for the owner's liking. And though, in Abramovich's debut season in control, Ranieri took Chelsea to their highest league position since 1955 (they were runners-up) and steered them to the Champions League semi-final, though he had previously brought in the likes of Frank Lampard and Joe Cole from West Ham and promoted John Terry from the youth team, the new owner was not satisfied. He wanted more than second, he wanted more than semi-finals.

And so, on 31 May 2004, the Tinkerman became the first of a phenomenon that was soon to become familiar in English football: a well-travelled, much-liked Chelsea manager who did not meet his employer's demanding requirements. As Ranieri left the building, however, he was not complaining about the terms of his sacking. Though he might have felt slighted that he had not been fired directly by Abramovich (the owner had people to do that sort of thing), at least his contract was paid up in full and on the spot. Failure in Abramovich World, it immediately became clear, had its compensations. Taking soundings from advisers like the super-agent Pini Zahavi and his long-term associates Piet de Visser and Eugene Tenenbaum, plus Peter Kenyon, the chief executive he had recruited from Manchester United in 2003 for a tidy annual salary with a brief to make the club more businesslike, Abramovich was keen to bring in the brightest and the best to run his team. Price would be no object. He wanted the top man and was prepared to pay whatever salary was necessary to lure him. If it seems a simple instruction, it was not easily fulfilled. A clumsy attempt to lure Sven-Göran Eriksson from the England job was exposed in a tabloid sting. And efforts to dangle large wads in the direction of Arsenal's Arsène Wenger met with little success.

The answer finally came in late June 2004, when the young Portuguese manager who had just taken Porto to victory in the Champions League was unveiled as the new Chelsea head coach. José Mourinho had announced himself to the British public with his uninhibited touchline celebration when his team had knocked United out of the competition in the quarter-final that March. Sliding on his knees across the muddy turf to ruin what looked like a pricey suit, his arms spread wide in triumph, it was some introduction. Young, dynamic, good-looking, comfortable in half a dozen languages but especially fluent in football, the man who had first become involved in the game as Bobby Robson's interpreter and assistant at Barcelona in the 1990s was identified by Abramovich's sources as a manager who could not only build a football team, but could also create a dynasty.

Reign of the Special One

He was some character, too. Jorge Mendes, Mourinho's agent, once told me that when Abramovich held a meeting with his client soon after his appointment, he showed him a list of players he would love to see in Chelsea blue. Mourinho, Mendes recalled, merely shook his head as he read through the list. This confused the Russian, who said: 'But you don't understand, Mr Mourinho. I want us to win everything and to make sure that happens I will buy you Zidane, I will buy you Shevchenko, I will buy you Beckham, I will buy you every superstar on the planet.' Mourinho's response was: 'No, it is you who don't understand, Mr Abramovich. To win everything you only need one superstar: me.'

It was a riposte that neatly summarized the new man's approach. The son of a successful professional goalkeeper, Mourinho had failed to make the grade as a player. Instead, he dedicated his considerable intellect to mastering the art and science of coaching; by eighteen he was running the youth team at his father's club in Setúbal, south of Lisbon. Driven by an urge to prove himself potent in the game he loved, his ambition was to elevate the coach's role to the most important in the business. A trained teacher, his real genius lay in team-building. Not for him success through the simple expedient of employing superstar players. As he had done at Porto, he sought to create an impregnable dressing-room culture that would elevate the talented to the level of the untouchable.

A follower of the Brian Clough philosophy of unity of purpose ('we talk with one voice; my voice'), unlike his new employer he was happy to put himself into the glare of press attention in order to deflect the pressure from his players. His facility with the media was evident from the moment of his unveiling in the Stamford Bridge press room, where, in perfect English, he informed the watching world that he was no ordinary manager. 'Please don't call me arrogant, but I am not one out of the bottle. I'm European champion,' he said. 'And I think I'm a special one.' He subsequently made it clear his use of the indefinite article was intended to suggest he was not unique. But such grammatical nuance was ignored. From then on he was known by a soubriquet slightly more distinguished than the Tinkerman: he was called The Special One. Not least in the Stamford Bridge dressing room. Here his attention to detail, the precision of his preparation, the thoroughness of his planning were quickly noted. What ambitious professional footballers most admire in a manager is someone who they believe will improve them, individually and collectively. Chelsea's players were immediately convinced that under Mourinho they would get better. 'I remember our first training session,' recalls Gudjohnsen. 'He told us how long each routine would take and when we were going to finish. And it went exactly as he said, it finished to the dot on time. We all looked at each other and thought: aye aye.'

As he strode into his new terrain, Mourinho betrayed few nerves. He quickly proved himself a master of the flourishing managerial trick of the Premier League era, perfected by Alex Ferguson, known as the mind game. Before matches he would raise issues designed to get under the skin of a rival coach. One of his favourite tricks was to name the other side's team line-up, the intention to cast doubt in his opposite number about his subsequent choice. 'Do I think a match can be won in the press conference?' he once remarked to me.

'No. But what a manager can do is make the other side think. Always make them think.'

If it wasn't the coach, it was the referee or a rival player he targeted. There was not a word wasted in his deliberations: everything had meaning and purpose. It meant his press conferences quickly became major events; a source of drama, intrigue and controversy. Under his direction, Chelsea became the centre of the Premiership orbit, the story every reporter wanted to cover.

None of that is to suggest that he was remotely shy of spending the boss's money. Within a year of arriving at the Bridge – and taking possession of the magnificent new Cobham training facility Abramovich had built in Surrey's gin-and-Jaguar belt – he had spent £95.8 million on players. But the interesting thing was who he bought. These were not the superstars the Russian had craved to see in a blue shirt. He showed no interest in Beckham, Zidane, even – for now – Shevchenko. Instead, he brought in players with hunger and desire, players who might grab the opportunity offered by the new manager, then give their all to ensure it was realized. Players like his Porto colleague Ricardo Carvalho, the powerful Ghanaian Michael Essien and a young bull of a striker from Ivory Coast via Paris called Didier Drogba.

Lean, mean winning machine

What he wanted above all was not simply players. He wanted a team. And he wanted improvement. Hasselbaink, for instance, he regarded as inferior to Drogba. So he showed him the door without demur. 'I had no relationship with Mourinho whatsoever,' Hasselbaink recalls. 'He let me go before we were even introduced.'

Along with Hasselbaink, he moved on thirteen others from Ranieri's personnel. Bringing in only nine, he wanted his squad to be leaner, tighter, more cohesive. His chosen newcomers were added to those few left in the dressing room he had already identified as his kind of footballer. They would join a team built around Lampard and Terry, competitors strong of sinew and even stronger of mind. Plus,

Ranieri's two parting gifts. Claude Makélélé, the defensive midfielder, had come from Real Madrid soon after Abramovich had taken over. When his contract in Spain came to an end, the Frenchman had been able to take his pick of employer across the continent. But he was hugely impressed by the vision Ranieri had sold him of a club on the verge of greatness. It was that, he insisted, rather than the financial reward that swung his choice. 'I know when I came for the pre-season, a lot of people said: "he came for money",' Makélélé says. 'Money is important. But if it was only money, I would have gone for another club. When I wanted to leave Real Madrid, Chelsea told me they had a big project and had ambition. I like this.'

Then there was the player Ranieri had signed but who had never played for him. The goalkeeper Petr Cech was bought from Rennes for £7 million just as the Italian was let go by Chelsea. Ranieri's idea was that he would act as second choice to Carlo Cudicini. Mourinho had other, better plans for him.

The new man was shrewd in his choice of backroom staff too. He brought with him three of his helpers from Porto, including the young André Villas-Boas employed as opposition scout, his role simply to identify strengths and weaknesses in rival teams (an appointment indicative of the new man's thoroughness). But he wanted his assistant to be somebody imbued with the spirit of the club, who could help him ensure he fitted into its history and continuity. So he promoted from the academy staff the former full-back Steve Clarke, who was part of the Chelsea side that had had a spurt of cup-winning success in the late 1990s, bringing a strange muscle rictus later identified as a smile to Ken Bates's face as they won the FA, League and European Cup Winners' Cups in the space of three years.

Even as he refashioned the team to his liking, Mourinho spent the summer ahead of his first season studying, studying and studying again his new working environment. And one thing he noted was the number of times other managers referred to the Premiership title as a marathon, not a sprint. He sensed a degree of complacency in that observation; he saw that there was almost an acceptance of errors and defeats early in the season because they might be rectified later. Under Ferguson, Manchester United, for instance, were renowned as sluggish starters, never seeming to hit peak performance until after Christmas, often falling to spectacular defeat in the autumn before going on to win the title the following spring. As far as Mourinho understood mathematics, however, three points won in August are worth as much as three gleaned in May. So his approach would be different: he would get his team to sprint from the start. Hit the ground running, charge to the top of the table and stay there, disappearing over the horizon before his opponents had woken up to the threat they posed.

His approach would require hard work in the close season: get the players fit, get them ready, applying the latest sports science to tailor training regimens to individual needs; big lads would work in a different way from whippets and everyone would be encouraged to hit the gym. And he worked closely with those like Joe Cole, Damien Duff and Arjen Robben, encouraging them to ally work rate to their prodigious creative skills.

As a strategy, it proved almost flawless. Once the season started, from the moment they beat United at home in their first game, Chelsea were away and gone like greyhounds from the trap. Fitter, faster, more powerful than any of their rivals, they brooked no opposition, bulldozing all aside; Mourinho's favoured tactical style was more bludgeon than rapier. He was cautious too: this was a manager who would always prefer to win a game 1–0 than 5–4. Which placed him at the opposite end of the aesthetic spectrum from his employer, who relished swash and buckle. But any friction between them over this philosophical divide was not in evidence as Chelsea stormed the Premiership that autumn; there is no more unifying device in football than victory.

At home the new man's Chelsea were immediately invincible, just as Porto had been under his stewardship (from 23 February 2002 to 16 February 2011 as he coached successively Porto, Chelsea, Internazionale and Real Madrid, Mourinho did not lose a home match; his record run encompassed 150 games). And away they were pretty tough to better, too. With a defence built around Terry, Carvalho and Cech, shielded by Makélélé, they were the antithesis of the soft southern Chelsea of traditional assumption. No more were they the team that once cheerfully fitted the music-hall stereotype of self-absorbed London makeweights. Wet, windy Wednesdays in Wigan held no fears for Mourinho's lads. Indeed, after a chill February night's victory at Blackburn, the manager instructed his players to chuck their shirts into the crowd. As the team made their way back to the dressing room bare-chested, he was sending out a signal to his rivals, a demonstration that these were no pushovers, hiding behind gloves and snood. In fact there was one thing you couldn't help noticing as Lampard, Terry and the rest high-fived each other in mutual congratulation: my, those boys were stacked. Even Joe Cole, the light-footed playmaker and once a player who might fear the consequences of exposure to a stiff northerly breeze, looked as if he were auditioning for a role as Arnold Schwarzenegger's body double.

So powerful were they, they lost only once in the league all season – at Manchester City on 1 October. On the way they set a bucketful of Premier League records. Across the term, they let in the smallest number of goals (15), kept the most clean sheets (25), recorded the most wins (29), and accrued the most points (95) anyone had in the league's dozen-year history.

In the wake of such results trophies inevitably follow. The first reward of his owner's faith came in February, when Chelsea beat Liverpool in the League Cup final in Cardiff. Not for Mourinho the habit of Ferguson and Arsène Wenger of using the competition as a training ground for young talent, or as an opportunity to give squad members a run-out in the first team. He played his strongest side available, sensing he could catch his principal rivals napping (as indeed he did in the two-legged semi-final, beating United away after seemingly ceding advantage by only drawing the first at the Bridge). The competition might not represent his ultimate goal. But what it did offer was the chance to forge trophy-gathering momentum. This, the sixth piece of silverware in his short and astonishingly accumulative career, was indicative of what was being built under Mourinho's stewardship: a team of winners.

In the Champions League, too, progress was ominous. After Barcelona and Bayern Munich had been dispatched in the knock-out rounds, the semi-final was reached for the second year in succession. And this time the opponents were Liverpool, already vanquished in the League Cup, beaten twice in the Premier League. Abramovich's cup appeared to be about to flow over.

Indeed, by the spring of 2005, the principal sense abroad was that what was being witnessed was the start of something huge. Chelsea were re writing the Premiership rulebook. The alignment of substantial investment, managerial expertise and good players was not just hoovering up silverware, it was shifting the competition's centre of gravity. Mourinho's timing was perfect. In Manchester, Ferguson appeared to be in decline, recently rescinding a regrettable decision to retire and now distracted by a row over the ownership of a racehorse. Arsenal had gone through the previous season unbeaten to win the title, but they remained still at Highbury, constrained by their surroundings, yet to enjoy the income benefits of a move to the less claustrophobic Emirates Stadium. Ominously – as Mourinho would soon note in the case of their left-back Ashley Cole – some of their best players were already restless for moves to more financially beneficient employers. Chelsea, by contrast, had it all. Particularly in the dug-out.

That spring, all eyes were on Mourinho. Many of them female. 'This intelligent, witty, charismatic and exceptionally good-looking young pipsqueak' is how Marina Hyde described him in *The Guardian*. In his smart overcoat, he cut a far more modern figure on the touchline than his rivals: compelling, handsome, a mischievous sparkle in his eye. As noted by fashion editors as he was by sportswriters, he was the sexy new thing. And the point about him was he had the results to back up the looks. This was no empty vessel, no mere coat-hanger: this was the future of football. 'The suit is pure stealth wealth, the shirt is a baby blue and button-down with elegant preppiness, even the socks have a certain minimalist luxe,' panted Polly Vernon in *The Observer Sports Monthly*. While Professor Manuel Sergio of the University of Lisbon insisted he was 'the ultimate post-modern soccer coach... he spends his time reading contemporary European philosophy: Karl Popper, Edgar Morin and Thomas Kuhn'.

But perhaps what most boosted Mourinho's gathering renown was that he made the game look easy. He not only knew what he was doing, he told us in advance what he was up to. In November 2004, he predicted that the game when Chelsea would win the Premiership title would be the one away at Bolton Wanderers on 30 April. Then, with the trophy tucked in the Stamford Bridge safe, he could concentrate on his campaign of furthering his European domination. Arriving in Lancashire that Saturday was a man on the march.

Clash of cultures

It was a busy time for Chelsea. The fixture was squeezed between the two legs of the Champions League semi-final against Liverpool. The first had taken place at the Bridge three days earlier. Blues fans in the SoBar, a noisy pub close to the ground, had been amazed to see Michael Howard – the leader of the Conservative Party and a renowned Liverpool fan – stroll in with a police guard. The moment he was spotted, the fans launched into a chant of 'PM, you'll never be PM'. He quickly sought an alternative watering hole. There in one incident was evidence of how much the Premier League had changed not just football but society: fifteen years previously, when he was rising to prominence under Margaret Thatcher, Howard would have risked his future political advancement by admitting to watching football on the telly, let alone turning up to witness a match in person.

Mourinho was not remotely worried about the goalless draw Howard witnessed. He was convinced it was a sound result. Not conceding was always his priority. And, as he had proved in beating United in the League Cup semi, the obligation for the opposition to score at home in the second leg might well leave them vulnerable to the kind of counterattack at which his team excelled. He was relishing the return match at Anfield. As far as he was concerned, it couldn't come quick enough.

Before that, however, there was the small matter of the league game at Bolton. A win there would confirm Chelsea as champions with some three fixtures still to play. Mourinho needed no reminding that this would be the club's first title since Ted Drake led them to the old First Division championship in 1955, fifty long years ago. Here's how lost in the mists of time that was: Sir Winston Churchill had resigned as prime minister soon after that victory was confirmed. Though that may have been a coincidence of timing. Convinced they were on the verge of witnessing history, en route to Bolton, Chelsea fans stocked up on bottles of champagne and bags of ice at supermarkets they passed on their way north. In keeping with one of English football's weirder club traditions, they also came armed with a plentiful supply of celery stalks to hurl about the Reebok stands.*

Mourinho was taking no chances. He understood what Chelsea were up against: a powerful, organized team that, under Sam Allardyce's stewardship, was pursuing a place in the following season's UEFA Cup and needed to finish sixth in order to do so. This was a side for whom this game mattered; a side, moreover, equipped to take on anybody in a physical challenge. Consequently, he gave the night off to his two flimsier wide men, Duff and Robben, who were both carrying slight knocks from the Champions League game, and left Cole on the bench. His selection, he knew, would require a toughness of sinew to challenge Bolton on their own turf. So he played a diamond formation, flooding the centre of the pitch, determined not to relinquish any ground to his square-jawed opponents.

Robust though they were, Allardyce's side was far from being devoid of inventiveness. Phil Brown, his assistant who was later to become a Premiership boss in his own right at Hull City, recalls the

---

* Blues fans had been bringing celery to matches since the 1980s, in homage to a ribald terrace chant. Celery was banned from Stamford Bridge by CFC following the 2007 League Cup final, when Arsenal players complained of being hit by the vegetable.

astute manner in which the manager had converted Fernando Hierro, the former Real Madrid centre-back, into a defensive midfielder:

When he arrived at ours, he was 36-odd, basically his legs had gone. But he had more than 500 games playing at the top for Madrid in his head. That's the kind of knowledge that's priceless. So we moved him forward, got him to sit in front of the back four, spraying out those passes. He didn't have to move far to be able to dictate the pattern of a game.

Hierro's presence in a side like Bolton – and that of Jay-Jay Okocha, the Nigerian playmaker flitting around alongside him – was testament to the Premiership's ever more magnetic drawing power. The money and the opportunity now available in England had made even its less fashionable outposts attractive to foreign players of real renown seeking to buff up their pension. And Brown reckons the presence of the likes of Hierro substantially altered the horizons of the English players too. 'We had Kevin Nolan as a 19-year-old in that side,' says Brown. 'He was sharing a dressing room with someone who had won everything with Madrid. He learned from him not just how to behave as a professional, but how to become a winner.'

And in the game with Chelsea, Hierro's influence was immediately evident. As the action began, with the Chelsea fans offering up an insistent fanfare to their heroes from the visitors' section, the Spaniard's shrewd use of possession stifled much of the putative champions' forward momentum. Every time Chelsea attacked, he seemed to be there, predicting where a pass would go, always at least three steps ahead in his ability to intercept.

Watching up in the stand, Abramovich looked more nervous than a basketload of kittens as the game progressed. He appeared to be living every pass, feeling every tackle, suffering every missed opportunity; this was a fan all right. Alongside him, incidentally, was Bruce Buck, Chelsea's chairman. Despite owning the club outright, Abramovich didn't call himself chairman, or indeed anything. The only title he was interested in was the one being fought over on the Reebok pitch.

Down on the touchline, his principal employee Mourinho looked less alarmed. To the disappointment of his growing army of female supporters, he had not come in his coat. There was no handsome suit or pricey suede shoes. Instead, fearing that spraying of champagne might be involved in the game's aftermath, he was wearing a club tracksuit, topped by an undistinguished branded rain jacket. As with everything else, when it came to tailoring arrangements he was one step ahead.

There may have been no nerves evident in his demeanour, but as he sat in the away team's dug-out watching Bolton dominate the first half, with Kevin Davies spurning the best chance when he failed to make adequate contact and planted a free header in Petr Cech's embrace, Mourinho was writing prodigious notes in his little black book. This piece of stationery, he maintained, was the repository of his managerial know-how; within its pages lay all his secrets. And what he had written during the first forty-five minutes was about to be revealed in the dressing room.

As Allardyce a few yards away assured his players that if they maintained their control the rewards would be forthcoming, Mourinho unleashed both verbal barrels. His team talk was brusque, direct and to the point. It was also delivered with a bravura flourish of humour. As Steve Clarke recalls:

We knew the team was tired. We were limping along, we were missing key players and we needed to win it there and kill it. It was just motivation. It was, 'I need more from you.' How you choose to get that effort out of players is down to different managers. José's way was: 'give Stevie [Clarke] a jersey, give [assistant manager Baltemar] Brito a jersey and for five minutes we will show you the passion needed to win a game like this'. He did also say 'and after five minutes you can call an ambulance,' but that wasn't reported.

Gudjohnsen too suggests that Mourinho's honest, funny appraisal was just what the team required to sort itself out and deliver. 'We were not good enough in the first half and he made that very clear to us and we responded.' And, as they came out first onto the Reebok pitch, encouraging each other in a bouncing, shouting, teeth-gritted demonstration of *esprit de corps* which could be heard from the stands, the talk appeared to have worked. What was evident almost immediately was the shift of control in the centre of the field. While Hierro might have been able to dictate play for forty-five minutes, his stamina was not sufficient to corral Chelsea's number eight for much longer.

Lampard in his pomp

Frank Lampard was enjoying the season of his life. A player of immense power – tall, strong, physically dominant – he was also in possession of a good brain. Unusually well educated for a professional footballer (he remains the only regular in the Premier League to have achieved a GCSE in Latin – and with an A grade at that), Lampard had an innate understanding of the geometry of the game. He could time his runs like few others, perfectly arriving in the right place at the right time. Already as good a player as England had produced in a generation (indeed, along with Alan Shearer, Paul Scholes and Steven Gerrard, he has a claim to be as the most influential Englishman of the Premier League era), he had enjoyed a superb European championship in Portugal the previous summer.

But under Mourinho he had blossomed yet further. Unlike some of the other foreign coaches coming into the Premiership (indeed unlike some of his predecessors at the Bridge), the Portuguese valued Englishness as a footballing concept. And he saw in Lampard its perfect embodiment. Rarely if ever injured, always up for it, an assiduous trainer determined to make the most of his gifts, he was also a superb reader of a game. Few of his contemporaries were as capable of seizing the momentum as effectively.

And on the hour of this game, Bolton Wonderers were given a lesson in that season's most singular football development: Lampardism.

A long ball was floated towards the Bolton area. It was flicked on by Jiří Jarošík to Didier Drogba, who rose above Hierro and headed it on again. Lampard, always lurking where he could do most damage, was first to the ball as it bounced, heading it forward into his own path, the perfect first touch. Vincent Candela, the Bolton full-back, attempted to intervene, but Lampard, now with the scent of goal in his nostrils, simply brushed him out of the way, bouncing him to the turf. He then stepped inside a leaden-footed Bruno N'Gotty and smacked the ball past Jussi Jääskeläinen into the corner of the Bolton goal.

For a moment there was a silence in the Reebok, as the Chelsea fans drew breath. Then a roar engulfed the away stand. Lampard ran celebrating to the blue corner, pursued by his team-mates. Caught and bundled to the ground, he found himself at the base of a human pyramid forming behind the Bolton goal. It was a noisy bundle. The wordless yelps of celebration caught by the pitch-side microphones were eloquent expressions of the Chelsea players' joy. Mourinho too was in ecstatic mood, running from his seat across the technical area, arms apart, fists pumping. And up in the stands, Abramovich could be seen sporting a wide grin. It was the smile of a man convinced he had bought the future. 'That could be the championship,' exclaimed Steve Wilson on the BBC commentary. 'They are in touching distance now. Chelsea are half an hour from the title.'

The Bolton camp was rather less ecstatic. Allardyce and Brown were incandescent, yelling at the fourth official on the touchline. Their gripe was that one of their players had been fouled in the lead-up to the goal. In what might be cited by future football historians as the perfect example of a growing trend among Premier League managers – blaming the officials for your own shortcomings – Allardyce put his complaint like this:

The referee has won them this game. He failed on a major decision, with Jarošík's foul on Hierro. There was nothing more blatant than that you can see in the game. Hierro was going to win the header but

Jarošík just barged into him. The referee waved play on and Frank Lampard got in to score. It's just not on. That's cost us the game, as well as ourselves not punishing them in the first half, when we were hugely on top. We're hugely disappointed at the standard of the refereeing. There's no question that he had a major contribution in today's result. That cost us very dearly at the 0–0 stage.

Exhorted by a visibly fuming Allardyce, Bolton were now obliged to attack, to find the goals to further their pursuit of a European place. And when Gary Speed unleashed a trademark long throw into the Chelsea area, Petr Cech showed that titles are as much won by dogged goalkeepers as they are by fancy-dan forwards. As the ball looped across right on to the penalty spot, the Cameroonian Geremi – playing only his fourth game of the season at full-back – attempted to head the ball clear. Unfortunately his header went precisely in the opposite direction from the one intended and was on course for the bottom corner of the Chelsea net. But Cech, showing astonishing athleticism, dived down to his right and pushed the ball out for a corner. In doing so he collided heavily with the post. 'A quite stunning save' was Wilson's commentary, as Cech was seen grasping at the ball with his extended right hand. It was the kind of save that gives players belief. Bolton, though, perhaps fearing the explosion in their own dressing room if they failed to do so, kept pressing. Davies, Okocha and the young, galloping Nolan who came on as substitute, refused to be cowed, constantly testing the Chelsea rearguard. Not that the Chelsea backline had much sight of the ball, given that Makélélé was at his most obstructive, belligerent best.

But still Bolton pressed. In the seventy-eighth minute they won a corner, which Speed arced across the Chelsea area. It evaded every head and landed at the feet of Gudjohnsen, lurking at the far post. He charged to the edge of his penalty area and fired the ball quickly forward to Makélélé up on the halfway line. He spotted Lampard tearing through the middle on the counterattack, completely unattended by Bolton defenders. The Frenchman's pass was perfect and Lampard in that sort of mood was not inclined to pass to Carvalho, galloping up alongside him. 'I joked afterwards about not passing to Ricky but the truth is, looking back, I didn't really have any idea that he was actually there with me,' recalls Lampard. 'I was so concentrated on taking the ball on, getting it past the keeper and into the net.' Instead of passing he scored what was his eighteenth goal of the season. Not a bad return for a midfielder. And indicative of Mourinho's no-star policy. When the most down-to-earth, roll-your-sleeves-up-and-graft member of your squad is contributing that sort of return, what need is there of Abramovich's wish-list of superstars?

With Chelsea 2–0 up, the result was no longer in doubt. That was another thing about Mourinho's team: they didn't blow winning positions. The next fifteen minutes of the match passed in a blue-tinged blur. In the stands the celebrations had already started. Champagne corks and celery alike were flying across the seating. On the touchline, the Chelsea substitutes lined up, linking arms with the technical staff: this was one united squad. The substitute keeper Cudicini could be heard above the raucous mayhem repeatedly shouting out the one word: 'Frankie'. It was an apt summary of the game. As Allardyce put it at the post-match press conference:

> The best player in the world at the moment has to be Frank
> Lampard. There's no question about that. To play as many games
> as he does, with the distances he runs and the finishing power
> he has, it's wonderful.

Ending fifty years of hurt

At the final whistle, Mourinho's caution in not wearing his renowned coat proved well founded. As Abramovich high-fived his cohorts in the stands, as Allardyce and Brown delivered their congratulations and, as was now customary on such occasions, the players were handed their celebratory championship-winning T-shirts, Barclays, the Premiership's sponsors, generously handed out bottle after bottle of champagne. And the spraying started.

Fifty years is a long time to wait. Abramovich had delivered what Chelsea fans most desired. The trophy would not be presented until their next game at Charlton (and there was the delicious sight of Manchester United's players forming a congratulatory guard of honour at Old Trafford to come) but this was the moment the past was buried and the future welcomed. As Steve Clarke recalls:

> For me, having been associated with the club for so long, it was incredible, to be involved when we won the league after fifty years was so special. We'd won some trophies, but that was the one everybody wanted to win. It was a statement because Mr Abramovich had come in, put his money in the club, some of the buys had worked, some hadn't. The club had to be careful it wasn't one of those which just buy players but don't win anything. And I think the appointment of José made sure we had a leader who could take the group forward and get the trophies. As a coach it was the best. I enjoyed it. Working with José was fantastic.

This was the point. Chelsea were an amalgam of investment and execution, Abramovich and Mourinho in perfect harmony. On the pitch, the players were quick to pay credit to their boss. 'He's worked on spirit, worked on the confidence of the lads, made every player feel important,' said Lampard. 'He's a real leader of men, he's a winner.' Analysing from the BBC studio, Alan Hansen agreed. 'Everyone focuses on Abramovich's money,' he concluded. 'But if you want a reason why they won, you'd say what a team. The goalkeeper, the centre-backs and the holding player: that's why they don't concede. The skipper has been truly inspirational. Brilliant in the air, tremendous captain. Then Makélélé, there to protect, awesome, so much protection in front of the back four, that's why they concede so few goals. As for Lampard: strength, pace, technique, absolutely magnificent. But all great teams need a great manager, he's the real deal. He knows how to pick a player.'

Mourinho himself admitted he was concerned that the assumptions about money might dilute the achievement:

That was the risk that I know I was going to have in a club like Chelsea, because you come, you change things, you work a lot, you do, in my opinion, a very good work, and in the end of the day some people can still think that with Abramovich behind him it's easy. I don't say it's easy, I say it is easier. It's easier you know, you need you buy. Make it work maybe faster. But I keep saying, the most difficult thing in football today is to lead the stars. So what people think is the easiest job because you are in a big club and you have the big players, I say is the worst job, the most difficult job because you have to lead and you have to lead the stars.

For once, however, even at the moment of triumph, Mourinho was not keen to hold the centre of attention. 'It is time for me to disappear. It is time for them, they are the men,' he said, indicating his players. While they jigged and danced in front of the travelling fans, wrapping themselves in flags and club scarves, the manager sat quietly in the dug-out, on the phone to his wife, beamingly talking her through the events of the momentous day. Even Abramovich was more involved in the celebrations than the manager. He was seen with his arms round Lampard and Terry as the pair led the crowd in an orchestrated chant of 'there's only one Roman Abramovich'. The owner's vague, distant smile suggested he did not fully understand the tenor of the lyrics.

From there, the players eventually made their way to the away dressing room, where the champagne was stacked to the ceiling. Very little of it was drunk. Steve Clarke recalls most of the bubbly ended up on the Reebok floor. 'We had loads of champagne in the dressing room, left the place in a terrible mess, I expect the club got a big bill for that,' he says. 'But on the bus there wasn't any drinking because we were going on to the Champions League semi-final with Liverpool. Maybe with hindsight, given what happened there, we might have been better enjoying the moment. Maybe we'd have got a better result there.'

Drink or no drink, the players were hardly restrained. As the celebrations raged around Stamford Bridge, two hundred miles to the south, with thousands who hadn't made it to Bolton filling Fulham Broadway with a tooting, yelling, chanting Bank Holiday fervour, things got pretty overexcited on the team bus too. Joe Cole and Didier Drogba climbed through the skylight onto the roof and, as the coach stood outside the Reebok surrounded by delirious Chelsea fans, conducted them in a chorus of 'One Man Went To Mow'. Abramovich, too, was mobbed as he was driven out in his Mercedes, with dozens of fans clambering onto the bonnet. Despite the fact that the last thing on the Chelsea fans' minds was to do the man who had delivered their dreams any harm, the oligarch's twitchy-looking minders quickly cleared a path.

What seemed absolutely certain to everyone lucky enough to watch the celebrations was this: even as history was being made, they were being gifted a sight of the future. Fuelled by a seemingly endless supply of Russian finance, Chelsea were redefining what the Premier League was about. And this was the point that much of the post-match analysis dwelt on.

'What has happened this season is a remarkable achievement,' said the club chief executive Peter Kenyon. 'But there's nothing with the team or the set-up that suggests it's a one-off. The key for us is that it's sustainable.' Alan Hansen concurred: 'I don't think there's ever been a side better equipped to roll and roll and roll like this Chelsea side.'

Even Mourinho, a man whose ambition hardly seemed containable in a single institution, appeared smitten, insisting in the after-glow of title achievement that he wanted to stay in west London for the rest of his life. 'This group is so special that maybe I will have to stay longer than my current contract,' he said. 'My heart is with them, and this club.'

What was happening on the Bolton pitch and in the dressing room afterwards did seem like the birth of a dynasty. A skilfully manipulated juggernaut that would brook no opposition, Chelsea were the new kings of the Premiership, orchestrated by a genius of a coach. Events the following season appeared to bear this out. Although they lost by what Mourinho described as a 'ghost goal' at Liverpool in the 2005

Champions League semi-final, in 2005–06 his team went on to win the Premiership title again, this time more emphatically.

But in football appearances are invariably deceptive. The cult of the coach instituted by Mourinho came to a shuddering halt when he was fired in the autumn of 2007. There seemed to be little coherent explanation for his sacking beyond the proposition that his employer had grown tired of him. Thereafter, Abramovich instituted a system at the club which could only be described as anti-coach, firing the occupant of the dug-out with a regularity that soon became monotonous. Seven managers – among them World Cup and Champions League-winning coaches – attempted to fill the Portuguese's suede boots. Yet, whatever the benefits of stability demonstrated elsewhere under Sir Alex Ferguson, Arsène Wenger and David Moyes, the perpetual Russian revolution at Stamford Bridge had little negative effect on the haul of trophies. Chelsea won the FA Cup under Guus Hiddink (2009), the double under Carlo Ancelotti (2010), the Europa League under Rafa Benítez (2013) and, grandest of all, the Champions League under Roberto Di Matteo (2012). None of it was sufficient to maintain any of Mourinho's many successors in their position for more than a few months. Abramovich tired of managers like Zsa Zsa Gabor tired of husbands, and moved them on with the dispatch of a serial killer.

Eventually he ran out of plausible alternatives, and, after failing to persuade Pep Guardiola to decamp to west London, turned back again to Mourinho. After a spell winning the Champions League with Internazionale and blitzing La Liga with Real Madrid, in June 2013 the Special One returned to the job he so artfully filled in the mid-noughties. Renewing what he described as his marriage vows, this time he called himself The Happy One. Though even as he was presented with the razzmatazz of a Hollywood star to 250-plus journalists and more than fifty television crews filling the Harris Suite at the Bridge, there was nobody gathered in the room who really believed he would be seeing out the four-year contract he had just signed. In truth, not even him.

BARCLAYS PREMIERSHIP

Reebok Stadium, Bolton

Saturday 30 April 2005

BOLTON WANDERERS   0 – 2   **CHELSEA**

Chelsea scorer: Frank Lampard 60, 76

Attendance: 27,653

Referee: Steve Dunn

TEAMS:

BOLTON WANDERERS (4-4-2)

Jussi Jääskeläinen; Vincent Candela (Radhi Jaidi 77), Bruno N'Gotty, Tal Ben Haim, Ricardo Gardner; Fernando Hierro, Stelios Gianna-kopoulos (Henrik Pedersen 63), Jay-Jay Okocha (Kevin Nolan 63), Gary Speed; El Hadji Diouf, Kevin Davies

Subs not used: Kevin Poole (gk), Khalilou Fadiga

CHELSEA (4-1-2-1-2)

Petr Cech; Geremi Njitap, Ricardo Carvalho, John Terry, William Gallas; Claude Makélélé (Alexey Smertin 90); Jiří Jarošík, Tiago Mendes; Frank Lampard; Didier Drogba (Robert Huth 65), Eidur Gudjohnsen (Joe Cole 85)

Subs not used: Carlo Cudicini (gk), Mateja Kežman

Match 8

Top, top entertainment

PORTSMOUTH V. READING

Fratton Park, Portsmouth

Saturday 29 September 2007

As Chelsea sacked the finest manager in their history, as Arsenal began to lose their best players to a rapacious transfer market, as Liverpool contested two Champions League finals in three seasons (2004–05; 2006–07), you might think the place to look for entertainment in the mid-noughties was at the top of the Premiership. Watch Manchester United regroup and reassemble around the finest player in a generation, the young Portuguese winger Cristiano Ronaldo, the man bought to replace David Beckham: that was where the action was, surely. Keep your eyes on the prizes.

Harry Redknapp, for one, was not inclined to agree. After this early-season encounter with Reading the manager of Porstmouth was loudly insisting he had just staged the perfect exhibition of what the Barclays Premier League was all about. What an advert, he crowed. Blimey, this was entertainment of the most delightful sort; proper escapism, evidence of the value for money that was still available even in the modern world. This was top, top stuff. 'I would rather win 7–4 than 1–0, personally,' Redknapp chortled, his face awash with barely concealed delight as he addressed the media in Fratton Park's cramped little press room. 'People have had a great day out. They have seen goals and good football. What more could you want?'

The Reading left-back Nicky Shorey, however, did not view his afternoon's work with quite the same beaming equanimity. For him, what had just taken place was little short of desperate. Being on the wrong end of a 7–4 scoreline was simply miserable. He wore a face that suggested he had just been subject to ninety minutes of humiliation of a kind Torquemada might be loath to inflict. 'I feel embarrassed,' Shorey scowled at a reporter who caught up with him as he left the stadium. 'That was the worst game I've ever been involved in. It was a joke game and it's gutting to have to say I was involved in it.' To the victor the grinning, to the loser the misery: some things never change in football.

But the truth is, for all its energy and rhythm, for all its attacking zest, the game that Redknapp and Shorey had been involved in was one whose real significance was not to be found in its record-breaking scoreline (the biggest aggregate tally in the Premier League's two decades). Nor indeed did it reside in its comedy defending, or in the number of goals an under-eights team with a modicum of organizational skill might have prevented. Nor was it Redknapp's gloating or Shorey's grumping that hinted at the true undertow of this match. No, what makes this encounter matter in the story of the Premier League is that it represents the high noon of a member club in the midst of perhaps the most self-deluded period of maladministration in the game's chequered history. This was not a tale – as had been the case at Leeds half a dozen years before (see Match 6, page 164) – of optimistically 'living the dream'. What Portsmouth were doing, even as the record books were being rewritten to accommodate this freakish game, was something even more reckless: they were living a lie. A lie that was to unravel spectacularly swiftly. Within three years of this apparently carefree exhibition, within just three seasons of moving to fifth in the Barclays Premier League table, Pompey would be in ruins, the manager unpaid, the players recruited on a match-by-match basis, and the club secretary obliged to ring round to find which local park pitch might be available for the next day's training. This match was the preface to misery. But at the time it felt like the very apogee of a good time.

Poor Old Pompey

'Play Up Pompey, Pompey Play Up' had filled the ground as the referee blew the final whistle. The Pompey Chimes, as the chant is known, is one of the grand sounds of English football. And how they chimed that day. No one any longer sings the next line of the old song: 'Just one more goal. Make tracks. What ho.' And anyway, to have done so in these circumstances would have seemed a touch greedy: eleven goals in one game was surely enough sustenance for even the most spoiled palate. In an era of spit and bile, of whistling disdain and self-righteous fury, to hear the Chimes in full flow, rolling across the Fratton Park pitch, is to be transported back to another time and place. The moment you hear them you are back in an era of rattles and woolly scarves and gentlemen sporting ties and trilbies. Never mind that these days the fans singing the chant are led by a bloke wearing a blue and white acrylic wig, shaking a bell and baring his heavily tattooed chest, a man who changed his name by deed poll to John Portsmouth Football Club Westwood. Quaint, homely, modest, the chant is the aural equivalent of being handed a steaming cup of Bovril. It induces instant nostalgia.

If the chant encourages us to hark back fondly to an earlier age, it would be a misplaced wistfulness to assume that all was wine and roses in football's days of yore. Certainly not in the boardroom. Looking back over the history of the game in England, it is impossible to discern anything remotely resembling a golden age of club administration. Almost up until the moment the Premier League came into being, players throughout the professional game were chronically underpaid, spectators were treated with disdain, and football's broader social responsibilities were rarely recognized. Meanwhile the cash income through the turnstile frequently went improperly declared, laundering the proceeds of many an illegal enterprise. From the moment professionalism was introduced in 1885 and money entered the frame, football has been a happy hunting ground for crooks and swindlers.

But even in a business with a long tradition of widespread corruption and cack-handed maladministration, even by the shabby moral standards of the thieves and jokers who have occupied the club boardrooms of English football, Portsmouth seem to have had it worse than others. Far worse...

The ten-year period in the club's history leading up to this match is not one that could be mistaken for an era of probity. In 1997 Terry Venables, the man who had steered England to the semi-final of Euro 96 and had long harboured ambitions to own a football club, bought 51 per cent of the shares in Portsmouth from the administrators for just £1 and installed himself as chairman. Within months of his takeover, however, a Department of Trade and Industry investigation was launched into how he had acquired his stake in Tottenham earlier in the 1990s, in the days before his stewardship of England. Charges ensued of bribery, deception, manipulation of figures, failing to keep proper accounts and allowing a bankrupt to manage his companies. As a result Venables was banned from holding a directorship for three years and was thus obliged to vacate the Fratton Park chairman's lounge pronto (he would later earn a living briefly steering Leeds United closer to oblivion).

Venables may not have been long in charge, but, in the couple of months he had control, he gave a hint of the sort of chairman he might have become. During his brief tenure he arranged the sale of Portsmouth's then most significant asset, its centre-forward Lee Bradbury, who went to Manchester City for £3 million. After the transfer was completed, the chairman immediately billed the club for a personal 'performance fee' of £300,000 (though Venables later denied there was any connection between his fee and the sale).

With its recently departed chairman declared an unfit person to run a business, the club was pitched into receivership in its centenary season of 1998–99. There it remained until, in May 1999, the Serbian-American Milan Mandarić – who had founded the San José Earthquakes in 1974 before moving back to Europe and taking over FC Nice – bought the place. With him he brought not only a sizeable pile of cash from the fortune he had acquired supplying hardware to Apple, but also something not frequently associated with Portsmouth: a sense of optimism and uplift.

That feel-good factor was reflected in his appointment of Harry Redknapp, first as director of football in the summer of 2001, then, from March 2002, as manager. It was quite a coup for Portsmouth; Redknapp was a talented coach whose previous employment, from 1994 until 2001, had been in the more exalted environs of West Ham. And it was a positive move for the ever-enthusiastic Redknapp also, one that cut several hours from his daily commute to London's East End from his desirable Sandbanks home near Bournemouth. Nor was he unhappy with the terms Mandarić offered him: his contract was initially worth £3 million rising to £4.2 million a year. But what pleased Redknapp most was that his new best friend seemed to be a man who shared his long-held belief about football: that if you are going to get anywhere you need to spend big. With Mandarić providing the resources to sign up such expensively remunerated talents as Paul Merson, Tim Sherwood and Teddy Sheringham, Redknapp delivered promotion to the Premiership in 2004.

Redknapp recalls of his early days at Fratton Park:

When I went to Portsmouth that first year I was lucky that quite a lot of players were out of contract and I could change things around. And I brought characters into the club. People like Arjan de Zeeuw, the centre-half, who was an absolute leader of men. I took Paul Merson for £5,000 a week. Villa were paying the rest of his wages and he changed the club around with his ability and wanting to play and his enthusiasm.

As they set about revitalizing the club, Portsmouth's presiding twosome had a combative relationship. Details revealed in a court case brought against the pair by Her Majesty's Revenue and Customs in February 2012 suggested they engaged in continuous robust verbal jousting, mainly about money (though obviously, as the case established, everything the duo did was totally and completely above board and legal). After one such row in November 2004, which came about when

Mandarić installed Velimir Zajec as director of football to oversee Redknapp's behaviour, 'Arry flounced out of Fratton Park, heading a few miles west to become manager of Pompey's bitter local rivals Southampton, then in trouble near the bottom of the Premiership. This, the Pompey fans would insist, was the right place to be for the despised 'Scummers'.*

If Redknapp's plan was to inflict revenge on his former partner by securing South Coast domination, however, his scheme quickly unravelled. To the huge chagrin of the Saints' fans, he failed to prevent Southampton being relegated from the top flight for the first time in twenty-seven years. He then walked out to rejoin Portsmouth in December 2005. He and Mandarić had been reconciled: the director of football departed and the returning manager extracted from the owner the promise of further investment.

Investment is a limited term in Redknapp's way of thinking. He liked his chairmen to spend money on what he regarded as the business end of the operation, on the first team. And with players to be bought and paid, there was not much left over to fund other important areas of Portsmouth's development. Like its stadium, for example. Atmospheric Fratton Park may be, a cosy throwback with its half-timbered entrance and tight little stands; the tiny dressing rooms could fit in the store cupboard at the Emirates. Its 20,000-odd capacity, however, was 5,000 short of the number of seats reckoned the minimum requirement to run a sustainable business in the Premier League. It was a full 15,000 fewer than the capacity of St Mary's, the new stadium that had been recently built up the road in Southampton, a club then, after Redknapp's hasty departure, in the midst of a tailspin

_____

* According to one possibly apocryphal story, so named after dockers from the city were brought in to break a strike in Portsmouth; SCUM supposedly stands for 'Southampton Corporation Union Men'. The counter-insult by Saints' fans to Pompey supporters is 'Skates' – a scurrilous allusion to the flat fish that Royal Navy sailors from the port allegedly used for 'comfort' on long, lonely voyages. Southampton supporters also delight in the fact that the name of Pompey's ground can be reversed to read: 'NOTTARF KRAP'. Few footballing rivalries are as venomous as this.

down to English football's third tier. An additional financial downside of Fratton's antediluvian stadium was its absence of anything remotely resembling proper corporate entertainment facilities. The smartest lounge in the place was about as inviting as the staffroom of an inner-city comprehensive. In short, Portsmouth Football Club lacked the material infrastructure required for Premier League money-making.

There was talk of a new ground, but an appropriate location could not be secured. In any case, even if the council had been more helpful in granting planning permission elsewhere, the existing stadium, sited in the midst of what was once a railway marshalling yard, hardly represented prime real estate. Mandarić was finding it impossible to make the sums work on any future move. So Pompey stayed where they were, in their cramped and crumbling home. To add to the sense of a club without real assets, they did not even own their training facility; that had been sold long ago in a pre-Venables period of cutbacks. Space was first rented at Southampton University's sports ground, then Redknapp moved the tenancy to King Edward VI School, a Southampton public school, where Portsmouth's expensively acquired internationals found themselves sharing the turf with spindly-legged adolescents in aertex polo shirts feebly chucking around a rugby ball.

Money men

Somehow – largely by getting the chairman to subsidize the wage bill and transfer budget – Redknapp kept the club in the Premiership at the end of the 2005–06 season (relegation being avoided in Pompey's penultimate game with a victory at Wigan). Then in September 2006, Mandarić, perhaps sensing where this was all heading, moved on, first to Leicester City, then to Sheffield Wednesday. Alexandre Gaydamak, a young French businessman of Israeli-Russian descent based in Paris, bought his shares. Mandarić – never a man to be left short in any business deal – trousered more than £47 million in the transaction. It was the sort of cash return that must still keep Venables awake at night.

Where Gaydamak found such money to fund his purchase was not entirely clear. Still only in his late twenties, he had surely not had time to acquire such depth of wealth. Yet he vehemently denied that he was merely the front man for his father Arcadi, an international wheeler-dealer who owned football clubs in Israel and was on the run from several police forces anxious to investigate illegal arms dealing. The only thing that was clear about Gaydamak's ownership, fogged as it was in a series of offshore holdings, was that it came through a company registered in the British Virgin Islands called Devondale Investments. As to who – if anyone – had invested in Devondale, it was impossible to fathom.

As far as Redknapp was concerned, however, Gaydamak was great news. By the start of the 2006–07 season, the manager was setting ambitious targets for the club. Mere survival in the Premiership was no longer enough, his aim was a place in Europe for the following season. Whatever loose shackles Mandarić had imposed on spending were instantly removed. In his ambition to become the manager of a top, top club, Redknapp easily persuaded the new chairman to finance a spree. Some £30 million worth of deals had been done during the summer transfer window. First-class players like Sylvain Distin, Glen Johnson, Lassana Diarra, and Kanu arrived at Fratton Park, all of them attracted by princely retainers. They joined the England stalwarts David James and Sol Campbell dodging the public schoolboys on the training pitch. As a statement of intent, it was eloquent.

But as Redknapp buffed and honed his squad, no one seemed to worry that this was a business with few viable assets beyond its roster of players. Nor did anybody seem too concerned that Chelsea and Arsenal were soon querying when the money for Johnson and Diarra's moves might eventually reach their current accounts. Certainly not Redknapp. As he often said, it wasn't his job to sort out the financial side of things. That was up to the chairman. And Gaydamak – as far as the manager could see – was 'as good as gold'.

More sober analysis might have spotted that the chairman was presiding over a club that had sprung a leak in its accounts, and from which money had begun to gush in an uncontrolled torrent. The annual pre-tax loss had spiralled from £912,397 in 2006 under Mandarić to over £23.4 million twelve months later. The wage bill alone now accounted for more than 106 per cent of income – hardly a surprise given that some players were so handsomely rewarded their pay slips would have turned Donald Trump dollar-bill-green with envy. This truth went largely unremarked upon: by September 2007, when their goal-spattered encounter with Reading took place, Pompey was a business perched on a tottering pile of rapidly fragmenting financial chicanery.

What a stark contrast, then, to the club's opponents on that warm, sun-speckled early-autumn afternoon. Reading had approached their second season in the Premiership by forking out for £3.1 million worth of new players over the summer, a tenth of the amount Redknapp had spent. But that tallied with the club's financial approach. This was not a business run like Portsmouth. For a start, some might say, it was actually run like a business. 'It was a brilliant club,' says its then centre-back Michael Duberry. 'It had good foundations in every department, from the board downwards. You can see those foundations have really stood it in good stead: everything just works there.'

Its chairman John Madejski had bought Reading in 1990. When the crooked publisher Robert Maxwell had owned the place in the mid-1980s, Madejski, who made his fortune from starting *Auto Trader* magazine, had offered him £5 per share. But the Bouncing Czech had dismissed the bid as laughably undervaluing its town-centre location of Elm Park. Long after Maxwell had departed the scene, Madejski later paid just ten pence a share when he picked it up from the administrators. 'A funny old life, isn't it?' he says, still smiling about the deal years later.

As was evident in his purchase, Madejski had not become one of the country's richest men by being reckless with his cash. Reading Football Club might be a pleasant hobby, a place where he could entertain his celebrity chums like Chris Tarrant and Cilla Black, but he was not prepared to suffer any personal loss in its cause. The books had to balance, and spending had to be controlled. His managers were obliged to work within a budget Redknapp would have considered an insult. And, unlike those in charge at Portsmouth, Madejski appreciated that the business could not progress in its old surroundings. So in 1998, after selling Elm Park as the site for a supermarket, he built the club a new home. Which, given that he had ploughed £25 million of his own capital into its construction, he reckoned it was only appropriate to call the Madejski Stadium. And in the 2005–06 season Reading achieved something as bright and shiny as their gleaming new stadium – they won the Championship to gain promotion to English football's top division for the first time in their history.

The Madejski Stadium may not have been as atmospheric as Fratton Park – in fact, it was a rare thing to hear so much as a chant struck up in its polite interiors – but the ironically nicknamed Mad Stad was a very modern piece of out-of-town property development. Alongside it was a retail park and a hotel, which during the week utilized the same car-parking facilities that were available for spectators on match days. With 24,161 seats and the potential to rise to 38,000, it bristled with hospitality suites, offering pricey corporate packages to the wealthy companies of the Thames Valley. During the week the place thrummed with conferences and meetings. On those weekends when the football club did not have a home fixture, crowds poured in to watch London Irish play rugby there, the semi-artificial pitch ensuring the maintenance of a level playing field. The Madejski Stadium was a cash-generating machine. And, with matchday income almost twice that at Fratton Park, after its first season in the Premiership, the club had posted pre-tax profits of £6.6 million. Madejski made it look easy. And in a sense it was: control your costs, sit back and watch the money roll in was his modus operandi.

But even with Reading FC apparently thriving, Madejski was happy to admit that if the club were to advance and join the Premiership élite, then he was not the man to take them there. He would need to sell to an owner with an even more substantially upholstered bank account. 'The brand is getting stronger all the time and if there is a billionaire who wants a nice accessory down the M4 then come and talk to me,' he said in an interview published at the beginning of the 2006–07 season. 'I'll listen to sensible offers. But from billionaires only. Millionaires need not apply.' In January 2012, incidentally, he found his billionaire, selling the club to the Russian paper magnate Anton Zingarevich for £40 million.

But never mind billionaires, on Planet Pompey no one could be entirely sure Gaydamak was even a millionaire. Nor indeed was there any immediate indication of what he sought from his association with Portsmouth. Was it prestige? Was it social advancement? Was it to build a long-term operation? Or was it simply to provide some sort of concrete business proposition for his father? Nobody knew. But in September 2007 nobody seemed too concerned about his intentions. Portsmouth were riding a rip tide of Redknapp-inspired achievement. When Reading arrived at Fratton on the 29th of that month, Pompey's expensively accumulated first team had lost only one of their previous five Premiership fixtures and were fresh from success in the early rounds of the Carling Cup. They were sitting pretty just below mid-table in the league, in eleventh place, a good position from which to mount the European challenge Redknapp insisted was possible. A decent win would pitch them up to fifth, right up there with the big boys.

Madness and mayhem

Reading's season, by contrast, had been slow to take off. Three losses in their previous five games hinted at decline, leaving them in sixteenth position, just above the drop zone. They had yet to register an away win. In their second season in the Premiership, some of their fans worried that the stalwart players who had won promotion and then managed to survive that first year had run out of the adrenalin that had carried them so far. 'I'm not sure I believe in all that second-season syndrome stuff people chucked at us,' says Michael Duberry. 'The problem was we struggled for consistency. We just couldn't string the results together like we had the previous year. It was frustrating because nothing had changed. The gaffer was still a good gaffer, there was good discipline, we played as a team. But we couldn't get those results.'

'The gaffer' was the laconic former Manchester United winger Steve Coppell. A thoughtful, undemonstrative man, he admitted he was finding the Premiership a little too all-consuming for his tastes. When I interviewed him during the course of that season, he expressed astonishment at the intensity of media scrutiny that had accompanied elevation to the top division:

In the Championship, matches last basically a day. In terms of the media interest, the noise that surrounds them, it's all over in twenty-four hours. In the Premiership they last a week. You have three days' build-up, the match day itself, then three days of post-mortem. The interest is that much bigger.

Coppell did not seem to enjoy the greater attention. A man who had walked out on Manchester City after discovering quite what a task management of a big club was, he found the spotlight an uneasy place in which to operate. How unlike his counterpart. Redknapp thrived in the harum-scarum rush of the Premiership soap opera. It was, he reckoned, the only territory in which a manager could properly be judged. It was where he was born to be.

It was no surprise then that before the game kicked off the bald-headed Coppell had taken himself away from the bear pit of the touch-line and headed for the stands. There, his face inscrutable, he remained throughout the game, blending in with the crowd, demonstrating little emotion as the action jack-knifed down on the pitch.

Redknapp, meanwhile, was there in the thick of things, the television cameras homing in on his every twitch. As usual he was surrounded by his cohort of trusted lieutenants. There was Joe Jordan, the former Leeds and Manchester United centre-forward and about as scary a minder as you could wish for. There was the great Arsenal stalwart Tony Adams, now in charge of Portsmouth's defence, which, presumably, he spent hours choreographing to ensure they stuck their arms in the air simultaneously in the appeal for offside. And all of Harry's men, crowding the home dug-out like it was a bus shelter in rush hour, seemed to have something to say as the game went duly crackers.

The madness was first unleashed after just seven minutes, when Portsmouth scored a goal that spoke volumes about the new international flavour of the Premiership. The Ghanaian Sulley Muntari unleashed a bruising challenge in midfield, won the ball and found John Utaka with a crisp forward pass. The Nigerian glanced up before picking out Benjani Mwaruwari, unmarked, unattended and unnoticed by the Reading defence, lurking in front of their goal. The slim, dreadlocked Zimbabwean striker duly scored. It was a goal made in Africa, a continent where at least fifty million people would be watching this game on television. That was what the Premiership had become by this stage: an international offering, its product flashed around the globe, a regular moment of broadcasting imperialism.

The African audience would have been ever more thrilled when Benjani struck a second within the half hour. He was leading the line in place of another African, the Nigerian veteran Kanu, who had been obliged to withdraw from the game after painkilling injections had failed to resolve knee and thigh problems. And Benjani, a man previously thought by many who had watched him incapable of kicking his way out of a damp paper bag, was taking his opportunity. He ran at the Reading defence, brushed aside the half-hearted challenge of Ívar Ingimarsson, a man whose Icelandic homeland lay some 6,500 miles to the north of Benjani's, and sizzled a shot into the corner of the Reading net. It was a fine finish, which he celebrated by trotting across to the excited home crowd and pointing at them while shaking his hips, as if possessed by the spirit of Elvis's trousers. It was another goal made possible by some limp defending. 'As a defender,' admits Michael Duberry, 'it's not the sort of game I look back on with much pleasure. Or pride.' As Fratton Park purred, and an excited Redknapp tried to remain impassive, Coppell swept his hand across his shaven head in a gesture of impotence. Never mind three days, it would take a month to conduct a thorough autopsy of the disaster that was unfolding before his eyes.

But then, just before half-time, unexpectedly given both the run of play and the disproportionate weight of resources behind the respective line-ups, Reading pulled a goal back. It was not a classic. Kevin Doyle set up Liam Rosenior, whose shot hit the bar and bounced down. Even as the linesman flagged that the ball had crossed the line for a goal, a scramble ensued in the Portsmouth goalmouth. First Dave Kitson's shot was blocked by David James, then the ball bounced up to Stephen Hunt, who followed up to make sure with a header. The goal, though, was subsequently awarded to Rosenior for his earlier strike off the woodwork. And with that, the players made their way to the sanctuary of the dressing room, where they had the opportunity of fifteen minutes' pause to reflect on the mayhem. Michael Duberry takes up the story:

Coppell was never one to give your spitting-in-the-face, shouting-type team talk. He never used the hair dryer. It was always controlled, very measured. He wasn't panicking and to be fair there was no reason to, they weren't running away with it. It was still quite close. I can't remember exactly what he said, but basically he wanted us to up it and take control, keep control. And make sure there was no more lapse in our concentration. That's what he went on about: concentration.

A hatful of goals

The manager's words appeared to have an immediate effect. Within three minutes of the restart, Reading had an equalizer. Though it was gifted to them. In fact, of all the goals on this goal-drenched afternoon, this was the most comical. As he trotted back towards the Portsmouth area, shadowing Reading's flame-haired centre-forward Kitson as he pursued what looked like an aimless through-ball dispatched by Shorey, Portsmouth's grand old defender Sol Campbell – a one-time Arsenal 'Invincible' – seemed to slow down. Apparently under the impression that his goalkeeper James was going to come out of his area and sweep up the ball, he appeared to be running in sand. But it quickly became clear James had set off too late to make it. With Campbell suddenly obliged to back-pedal in an urgent flurry, Kitson arrived at the ball first, flicked it beyond James's onrushing reach, and, from an unlikely angle on the edge of the area, shot into the now unprotected net. This was two-fifths of England's recent international backline displaying the kind of defending more usually seen in a primary-school playground. It made you wonder what Adams did all day in his role as defence coach.

In the stand, Reading's manager remained unmoved by the equalizer. As Kitson turned and trotted away grinning at his good fortune, Coppell merely wiped his hand across his head once more and looked uncomfortable. He might have been a little happier had Reading taken advantage of another gift-wrapped opportunity handed to them five minutes later. The giant Senegalese Papa Bouba Diop, another of Portsmouth's African contingent, was reckoned by the referee Mark Halsey to have handled the ball in the area. The Portsmouth players were furious, surrounding the official to complain. On the touchline, Redknapp and his coaching posse made their views immediately known to the fourth official. But the award stood. Shorey stepped forward and struck the spot kick firmly. Making amends for his howler a few minutes earlier, James leapt vigorously to his right and palmed the ball to safety. It was a fine save, one of the match's rare moments of defensive competence. No wonder Shorey was so deflated afterwards: had he scored, Coppell was convinced it would have changed the momentum of the game. If that penalty had gone in, the tide would have turned in their favour.

Well, it might have done. In truth, the match was beginning to acquire a crazy momentum of its own, as the defending slipped well below Premiership standards. Goals started arriving with the frequency of points in a basketball match. Every attack seemed to result in a score. First Hermann Hreidarsson put Pompey back in front (to give an indication of how easy it was to score a goal in this game, it was his first in three seasons). Then Benjani completed his hat-trick with a solo goal that put the home side 4–2 up. Niko Kranjčar kept up the goal-fest by heading home a Sean Davis cross to make it 5–2 before Shane Long replied for Reading from a position Redknapp and his posse angrily gesticulated had been offside. The strike stood. Then Davis smacked a screamer from thirty yards that deflected in off Ingimarsson for Pompey's sixth and best goal, before Muntari made it seven in stoppage time with a penalty after Kranjčar was tripped. Reading, though, had the last word, as Shorey's shot was deflected in with the final kick of the game. The young player's temper might have improved if his strike had not been adjudged an own goal by Campbell.

What a game it was. What an extraordinary amalgam of mistake and ineptitude. As James embraced his opposite number Marcus Hahnemann at the end, it was clear he was struggling to make sense of it. He was laughing. Not just smiling, he was giggling, his shoulders rocking at the absurdity of what had just unfolded.

And it was bonkers: a cavalcade of error that launched the home supporters into a flurry of excitement. In the crowd you could see fans on their mobiles texting or ringing friends, relatives and Southampton fans, telling them that they'd never believe what had just happened. For the visiting team, particularly its defenders, there was less to be so perky about. Even now, for Michael Duberry the memory jars. 'I remember going home thinking: I can't watch *Match of the Day*, I'm not going to pick up a paper tomorrow either,' he recalls. 'You don't like conceding seven goals in a five-a-side game, never mind in the Premiership. After four you just want the game to end. But, looking back I guess even I've got to admit, for neutrals it must have been a great spectacle. Be fair: who wouldn't want to watch a game like that?'

Spend, spend, spend

While the Reading players climbed aboard their coach ahead of their journey back north along the A34, heads down to hide their embarrassment, Fratton Park was left basking in happy astonishment at what it had just witnessed. Of the smiles about the place, Redknapp's

Roman Abramovich was not interested in social advancement or political posturing, or indeed a new wardrobe, when he bought Chelsea in 2004. His ambition was a simple one: to own the finest football club in the world.

José Mourinho and his coat patrol the touchline, January 2005. 'This intelligent, witty, charismatic and exceptionally good-looking young pipsqueak,' swooned the *Guardian*'s Marina Hyde, one of his growing cohort of female admirers.

Half an hour from the title: Frank Lampard enjoys the first of his brace of goals at Bolton, 30 April 2005, with William Gallas and Didier Drogba.

According to John Anthony Portsmouth Football Club Westwood, the club's least shy supporter, winning the FA Cup in 2008 was worth the financial fall-out that followed.

The man who changed the game: a smiling Sheikh Mansour relishes his one and only visit to his prime asset, Manchester City, 25 August 2010.

Why always him? City's great eccentric Mario Balotelli makes his point during the Manchester derby demolition of United at Old Trafford, 23 October 2011.

Carlos Tévez ponders life on the bench, September 2011.

Worth the forty-four-year wait: Vincent Kompany, Manchester City's urbane, intelligent Belgian captain, lifts the trophy that marks his club's first championship in a generation.

Not waving but drowning: after eleven years of steady management at Everton, David Moyes lasted no more than eleven months as Sir Alex Ferguson's chosen successor at Old Trafford.

'The Engineer' engineers his way to the title: the normally undemonstrative Chilean Manuel Pellegrini gets unusually animated as he negotiates Manchester City to the summit of the Premier League in his first season in charge, 2013–14. In the background are the unmistakable brown shoes of Everton's Roberto Martínez, one half of Merseyside's progressive new management pairing.

was the broadest. Try as he might to look restrained and dignified, he couldn't stop grinning as he addressed the media afterwards, comparing the scoreline to the greatest of all club matches, Real Madrid's 7–3 European Cup final win over Eintracht Frankfurt at Hampden Park in 1960. He joked that some of his players had now put themselves in the same category as the legends of Madrid. 'Francisco Gento, Alfredo Di Stefano, Ferenc Puskás, José Santamaría… Sean Davis, Sulley Muntari,' he chortled. 'I mentioned it to Tony Adams, but he wasn't happy we let in four, because he's boring, boring Arsenal.'

Even Coppell, never someone prone to unnecessary displays of levity, admitted in his post-match press conference that this had been an unusual event. He could see the positives, he said. 'Four goals away from home. I don't think many teams will come here and score four goals,' he suggested. 'You know, we played a full part in the game today. At half-time I felt we were very, very passive and at the end of the game I felt a lot better, even though we were beaten by such a high scoreline.' Or at least he could see the positives for a moment or two. What quickly changed his mood – and exposed his barely concealed frustrations – was a follow-up question from a reporter who asked if this match was final demonstration that Reading were suffering from second-season syndrome. Coppell's studied calm shattered.

'I'm fed up with this thing,' he spat. 'I've had seventeen million questions about it. It's just as hard whether it's first season, second season or third season. Listen, Ferraris and McLarens wins Grand Prix races, the rest just compete. In football, if you spend a lot of money you're going to win games. It's just the fact that in terms of this division we're not investors. That was a decision I made. We could have invested more but I decided not to. I've got to live with that.'

Indeed, that was the conclusion of many watching this game: the difference between the two sides was that Portsmouth had speculated to accumulate and Reading hadn't. Even the most loyal of Royals supporters bridled at the gap in aspiration between the two exposed in the different level of funding, and now in the scoreline.

'The lack of investment in the club and inability of so-called directors to sign new players has created a situation that has put the club and its small squad under severe pressure this season, which in turn has resulted in a total confidence breakdown in the players who take to the field,' wrote 'Nick Newbury' on the Reading fansite HobNobAnyone that evening. Another Reading regular, 'Nick Tilehurst', posted this:

> A final word about Pompey. Let's not forget that for a few seasons they have flirted with the lower reaches of the Premiership and only now have begun to buy in a decent team and produce some good results. It's about hanging in there and seeking to improve step by step.

So that was Portsmouth, according to rival fans: an admirable institution which had prudently planned for the future, improving by steady increments, whereas Reading's parsimony was putting their very survival at risk. Fiscal largesse was now assumed by many to be the way of the Premiership: spend or die. And the truth of this assumption was not immediately challenged by subsequent events. While Pompey finished the season comfortable in the middle of the table, Reading were relegated. Gallingly they went down by goal difference behind Fulham. And the gap between the two clubs? Three goals. Effectively the defeat at Portsmouth in September 2007 – or at least the extra goals conceded there – sent Reading back into the Championship.

As the Fratton massacre was picked over in the papers, nobody was querying Portsmouth's financial strategy. Quite the opposite, in fact: they were getting it right, everyone reckoned. Certainly at the time, Redknapp appeared to be under the impression he was engaged in a long-term process on the South Coast. It was not his place to cavil. He was given money and he duly spent it. Or rather invested it, to use the preferred euphemism.

Nor were Redknapp's players questioning what was going on. They purred away from the match in their pricey examples of German and Italian engineering, stopping momentarily to lean through the open window and sign their names on blue Portsmouth shirts proffered by fans, which would soon be put up for sale on eBay. As for the home supporters, they seemed more preoccupied with ringing BBC Radio Five Live's phone-in *606* to insist that the BBC's institutional bias against Pompey would finally be exposed if this game was not shown first on *Match of the Day* that evening.

The next morning's headlines shouted about goal feasts and inept backlines, about cosmopolitan forwards and attacking vigour, about happy Harry and his band of African buccaneers. No one saw the storm clouds banking above the creaking stands at Fratton Park. And no one, in the midst of all the self-congratulation, sought to ask this simple question: where was the money coming from to pay for all this investment?

So it went on at Portsmouth for another footballing season. After paying Tottenham £6 million for Jermain Defoe in the 2008 January transfer window, Redknapp steered them to victory in the FA Cup final in May of that year, their 1–0 win over Cardiff coming through a Kanu goal. How the Chimes filled Wembley in celebration of the club's first trophy since 1939. The hated Scummers were scudding round the basement of the Championship, and had only avoided relegation to League One by the skin of their teeth (they went down next season); by contrast Pompey were flying high and had silverware in the cabinet – could life get any better? Then, in July 2008, ahead of Portsmouth's debut in European competition, Redknapp signed Peter Crouch from Liverpool for £11 million, the most the club had ever spent in the transfer market. It was, he said, a bold statement of their determination to kick on. In Reading, no doubt, the geographically named posters on the fan website cursed their own board for its stinginess. Why couldn't they be more like Pompey?

A mortgaged future

And then reality broke down the door and shattered the reverie. In September 2008 the world's banks suffered cardiac arrest. The entire international banking system turned out to have been constructed on the jelly-like foundation of sub-prime debt. In a scrambling desperation to balance their books, the banks began to call in their loans. At the same time they immediately ceased making any more money available to borrowers. Credit, which had been so promiscuously available during the preceding years of boom, suddenly dried up.

At first, it was not clear how this would affect the Premiership clubs. For a month or so the banking trauma looked like it was confined to the trailer parks of Wisconsin, where sub-prime mortgages were being wound up in a flurry of repossessions. At Portsmouth, the only blot on the landscape that autumn was the announcement by Redknapp that he was off to become manager of Tottenham.

Demonstrating his unfathomable reserves of chutzpah, just a week after he had walked out on the club, Redknapp turned up at a ceremony in Portsmouth town hall to receive the freedom of the city, a long-planned official thank-you for delivering the FA Cup. I was there that day and was witness to the endearing fickleness of the football supporter. Dozens of Pompey fans had gathered in their blue shirts to boo the former hero now regarded as a traitor. When he arrived in the hall, one man in the balcony stood up and yelled obscenities at Redknapp. The mayor of Portsmouth then made a speech asking for the audience to forget Harry's – he called him Harry – defection to Spurs and recall instead what he had delivered to the city with the Cup win. Harry deserved to be praised and remembered for that wonderful achievement, thanked for how he had cheered up everyone in the area. When the mayor finished, the man on the balcony, who minutes earlier had been frothing at the mouth in anger, started applauding vigorously, nodding in agreement. Bang on, he shouted, Harry deserved respect.

That day, even as the world's financial markets were in meltdown, still nobody seemed remotely concerned about Portsmouth's wider future. Tony Adams had been made caretaker manager alongside Joe Jordan, the club was in Europe, Spurs had even kindly agreed to pay Pompey a seven-figure sum's worth of compensation for the peripatetic Redknapp's latest flit: what was there to fret about?

But within weeks the tone had changed. Things took a turn for the pessimistic. It became clear that Gaydamak had made little capital investment of his own in the club. He had borrowed from Standard Bank and Barclays, who now demanded urgent repayment of some £50 million of loans. Well, that should have been a simple enough thing to do: swallow hard and sell a couple of players. But that was not the end of it. As Portsmouth had no substantial assets he could use as collateral, in order to secure these and other loans in the first place the owner had used the one guarantee he could rely upon: the future income from the Premier League television revenues and season-ticket sales. Just like at Leeds seven years before, the club's next few years had been mortgaged. When it came to paying back what had been borrowed, any income was already accounted for. And, while it was not available to pay back the debt, it was also not available to meet the club's absurdly inflated day-to-day running costs either. Effectively, as the banks sought to secure their debt, Portsmouth had no income. It was the footballing equivalent of sub-prime.

In the past, banks had been reluctant to foreclose on football clubs. There was too much negative publicity inherent in being the ones who called time on the objects of their customers' allegiance. Barclays preferred to be seen as the benevolent sponsors of the Premiership, not the enforcers spoiling the fun. But times were changing. And Gaydamak did not exactly present the most steadfast of debtors. Though Gaydamak had argued that his father was not directly involved in Portsmouth, his old man was on the run from several police forces. And now, long after they had lent him the money in the first place, the banks started to voice concern.

With what was coming in going straight out to pay off previous loans and with the chairman no longer able to source the easy credit he had used to keep the place going in the past, Portsmouth was in a hole that was deepening by the second. The house of cards was tumbling. There was only one thing that could be done: find a buyer quickly who had funds of a sufficient scale to plug the gaping breach in the business plan.

Amazingly, by May 2009, Gaydamak had found one. Or at least, he found a buyer who claimed he had money. Indeed, he looked as though he had money. The Abu Dhabi businessman Sulaiman al-Fahim, who had just announced the depth of his football knowledge by arranging for Manchester City to buy Robinho immediately after they had been taken over by his friend Sheikh Mansour, breezed through the Premier League's Fit and Proper Person Test and took control of the club in August.

As it turned out, al-Fahim had nothing like the readies he claimed. Worse, if the Abu Dhabi wannabe football tycoon thought he was buying his passport to the big time, he soon discovered he had inherited a basket case. With all the future revenues already accounted for to pay off debts, the club's one true asset – its most valuable players – now needed to be liquidated. In July Johnson went to Liverpool for £18 million and Crouch to Tottenham for £9 million. Over the summer Distin and Kranjčar were both sold. Redknapp's team of all the talents was being dismantled before the fans' eyes, the man himself happy to help himself to a couple of bargains. But the sales did not stem the crisis. By October, the players were not receiving their wages, and the Premier League had issued an embargo on future signings until Chelsea and Arsenal had been fully paid off for the sales of Johnson and Diarra.

It appears several of Redknapp's buys had not been completed: a deposit had been forthcoming, but subsequent agreed payments had been stalled. It meant that even as the players were being sold, the money was not going to the main creditors, it was just meeting debts that had not been settled in the first place. It got worse: the Premier League diverted £5 million worth of broadcast revenues to other clubs owed money for transfers. Franz Kafka would have been hard put to construct a scenario as nightmarishly labyrinthine as the one into which Pompey now found themselves plunged. The more they sold, the less they had to pay off those now seeking payment. With every penny required elsewhere, the club had no income whatsoever. Even the emergency loan of £17 million from a Hong

Kong speculator called Balram Chainrai vanished in a single stroke of an accountant's pen. Pompey supporter Rob Dunford, author of the GoodFeetForABigMan.com blog, sums up the club's financial misery:

> The FA cup-winning team cost a total of £27 million. The sales of Diarra and Johnson alone recouped £30 million, with the sales of Muntari, [Pedro] Mendes, and compensation for Redknapp's departure adding a further £26 million. Reports suggested that the club were losing £15 million a year during Gaydamak's three-year reign as owner. The sales of Crouch, Distin, Defoe, Kranjčar, [Younus] Kaboul and [Asmir] Begović should have wiped most of those out. Yet somehow, it just seemed to get worse instead of better and the club found itself in over a £120 million of debt.

By now the chairman's office had started to resemble a merry-go-round. Al-Fahim sold his shares to someone called Ali Al Faraj, who was in control for – well, no time at all. Across the dismal season of 2009–10 there were four owners who all passed the Premier League's Fit and Proper Person Test.

Skates on Skid Row

By the turn of 2010, Fratton Park was engulfed by crisis. Its chief executive Peter Storrie resembled a juggler suddenly required to keep a dozen balls in the air at once with his hands tied behind his back while wearing a blindfold. Every penny in income was seized by creditors. Her Majesty's Revenue and Customs issued a winding-up order over non-payment of tax and national insurance. The super-agent Pini Zahavi was among a group of players' representatives seeking more than £9 million in unpaid fees over transfer dealings. Astonishingly, Arcadi Gaydamak weighed in with a demand for £31 million, owed to him, apparently, for personal loans he had given the club. So much for his son's claim that his father had nothing to do with the business.

What was quite clear was that at Portsmouth everything was predicated on future income, on the assumption that as long as they kept running in the Premiership, the money would somehow follow. The credit crunch had completely scuppered this most risky of strategies. Gaydamak's approach relied on a steady supply of easy money. Now none was available, and with no income to pacify the growing army of existing creditors, the debts just kept accelerating. Debts that should have been paid off in the good times piled up alongside debts accumulated in the bad. Portsmouth was being flattened by the unpaid bill of hubris.

In the end, there was only one place they could go: on 26 February 2010 a weeping Storrie announced that Pompey had become the first club in Premier League history to go into administration. They were bust. And the list of creditors stretched all the way round Fratton Park. Some – like Distin, who was owed over £300,000 – were categorized as 'footballing creditors', so would be paid in full. Others would be lucky to get 20p in the pound. These included not just the big boys like HMRC. King Edward VI School was owed £41,000 in rent for the training facility; the local St John Ambulance were £2,700 out of pocket after providing a season's worth of first aid; the club even owed the local boy scouts £697 (using the cubs as your bank: that was classy). For many a local operation, Portsmouth's demise was a catastrophe.

There was no end to the bad news. With ten points immediately deducted from their league total as punishment, the prospect was only going to get worse. Portsmouth were now certain to be ejected from the exclusive club that was its major source of income (income, of course, that it had already spent): the Premiership.

There was little sympathy from the League officials. The chairman Dave Richards said: 'We always thought the kind of money the Premier League was supplying to the clubs was sufficient.' Richard Scudamore, the chief executive, greeted the news of Portsmouth's demise with a shrug. Any club which went into administration while still playing in the Premiership was simply badly managed, he said. With £50 million in guaranteed income, it was only rank incompetence that could squander such resources. A harsh assessment it may have been. But he had a point.

240

As soon as he had recovered from his first examination of the books, the incoming administrator Andrew Androniko fired eighty-five Portsmouth employees. Cooks, cleaners and groundsmen all suffered the consequence of all that investment. Fratton Park quickly resembled a ghost town, the souvenir shops boarded up, the bars empty, the ticket office manned only spasmodically. Astonishingly, somehow, even as the place was going into meltdown around him, the manager Avram Grant, who had taken over from Adams in February 2010, managed to steer the team once again to the FA Cup final in May. There had been a brief hint of catharsis in the semi-final, when Redknapp's Tottenham were beaten on penalties. But at Wembley at the final, as Pompey lost 1–0 to Chelsea, there was an overwhelming sense of a wake. The money earned from the cup run did nothing to stem the losses, it simply disappeared into the ever-widening black hole. With the reopening of the transfer window, most of the players who had got the club to the final had to be sold. Not that the fire sale appeased the creditors: HMRC alone claimed £37 million was still owed.

The following October, by which time Portsmouth were in the Championship, Chainrai became chairman and negotiated the club out of administration. It was but a temporary release from the nightmare. In June 2011 he sold his stake on to a London-based Russian called Vladimir Antonov. This was no Roman Abramovich. In fact, Antonov made Venables look like the Governor of the Bank of England. By November an arrest warrant had been issued in Lithuania: he was wanted on charges of forgery. At the time of writing he was awaiting an extradition trial in London. He denied all the charges against him. But, as a consequence of the action, the holding company that owned the club went bust. And with the Revenue again trying to close the place down, in February 2012 Portsmouth was once again pitched into administration. Once more points were deducted, which this time would ensure the club's relegation from the Championship to League One. In September 2012 the administrators revealed that, despite being stripped of every valuable playing asset, despite shedding virtually every staff job, despite using its youth team for league fixtures, the club had accumulated debts now standing at over £58 million. The accountants suggested it might not be able to carry on unless some sort of deal was reached with its creditors.

Portsmouth was in ruins, pitched there by Gaydamak's reckless investment. The young Frenchman has been variously dismissed as a fantasist, an asset stripper and a puppet front man for his suspect father. He may have been a bit of all three. There may even be some Pompey fans who agreed with John Portsmouth Football Club Westwood, who told the journalist Ian Ridley in an interview that victory in the FA Cup was worth the Faustian price of multiple administrations. He seemed quite content that at least in those intoxicated times he had got to witness games like Portsmouth 7 Reading 4.

Stopping the rot?

But of one thing about Gaydamak's tenure we can be sure: his timing was woeful. Had the credit crash happened even a year later, he might have been in receipt of sufficient funds from Premier League membership to make his gamble work. But it didn't and his business plan unravelled quicker than a Jermain Defoe run. Rather than being criminally irresponsible, he may well simply be the unluckiest man in Premier League history.

After Pompey had inevitably, horribly crashed and burned and were now sitting at the bottom of the third tier, unable to pay a bill, with their supporters rattling collection buckets outside the ground in a bid to scramble together the players' wages every week, I had breakfast with Dan Johnson, the Premier League's director of communications. He said that the club's precipitous collapse had been far and away the most troubling episode in the competition's timespan. Yes, they may have been matter of fact at first, but the Premier League's officials had been more than chastened by what had happened subsequently. When one of the members of the world's richest football competition had somehow managed to find itself facing oblivion, it had brought them up short.

How, they wondered, could they ensure it didn't happen again? Clearly simply relying on the assumption that the huge income that came with membership should be sufficient to keep any club afloat was not enough. So the League has strengthened its procedures. In February 2013 it introduced the Owners and Directors Test, a Means and Abilities Test and insisted upon future financial information, HMRC quarterly reporting and regular directors' reports. New financial regulation would restrict losses, seek to cap wages and introduce penalties for those who spent beyond their means. What they had learned through Portsmouth's unhappy demise was that not everything was always as it appeared on the surface. Greater scrutiny and transparency was needed. For the first time in football history, directors would be obliged to prove they had access to funds to meet outgoings. Thanks to Gaydamak, what went on in the boardroom would now be much more transparent.

Ultimately, however, Johnson said it was not the job of the Premier League to prevent a club failing. Even if there were twenty brilliantly administered clubs in the league, every year three of them would – by definition – be deemed to fail through the system of relegation. Each season three of them would be dismissed from the money-spinning heart of the game. What was vital was to ensure that none of those thus ejected were destroyed as a result of demotion. It all sounds sensible, proper, appropriate. Responsibility required, transparency insisted upon, risk restricted though not entirely removed. Just a pity it all came way too late for poor old Pompey.

But even in its darkest hour, there is a glimmer of light in the Portsmouth story. The Football League, finally cottoning on to the fact that the succession of putative owners lining up outside the administrator's office did not have the club's best interest at heart, insisted in February 2013 that the only organization it deemed sufficiently responsible to take Pompey out of administration was the

Pompey Supporters' Trust (PST). They will be entrusted with bringing a little bit of sanity back to Fratton Park.

And maybe now they are in charge, the supporters might seek a different model for their club's future. One based not on the head-down embrace of ambition, but the adoption of fiscal prudence. Let us hope that now they have experienced the consequences of flying too close to the sun, they will see the merit in the kind of approach that allows a club to be relegated but not torn asunder, that keeps it solvent until it can rally and bounce back, regaining its place in the Premier League where it can benefit from the increased revenues and subsequently flourish. Maybe the PST will now model their phoenix club on a more plausible footballing business, such as – well, to pluck a name at random out of the ether – Reading FC.

BARCLAYCARD PREMIERSHIP

Fratton Park, Portsmouth

Saturday 29 September 2007

PORTSMOUTH 7 – 4 READING

Portsmouth scorers: Benjani Mwaruwari 7, 37, 70; Hermann Hreidarsson 55; Niko Kranjčar 75; Ívar Ingimarsson 81 (og); Sulley Muntari 88 (pen)

Reading scorers: Liam Rosenior 45, Dave Kitson 48, Shane Long 79, Sol Campbell 90 (og)

Attendance: 20,102

Referee: Mark Halsey

TEAMS:

PORTSMOUTH (4-3-3)

David James; Glen Johnson, Sylvain Distin, Sol Campbell, Sean Davis; Hermann Hreidarsson, Sulley Muntari, Papa Bouba Diop; John Utaka, Benjani Mwaruwari (David Nugent 80), Niko Kranjčar

Subs not used: Jamie Ashdown (gk), Noé Pamarot, Matthew Taylor, Pedro Mendes

READING (4-4-2)

Marcus Hahnemann; Graeme Murty (Shane Long 77), Michael Duberry, Ívar Ingimarsson, Nicky Shorey; Liam Rosenior, Brynjar Gunnarsson (Emerse Faé 77), James Harper, Stephen Hunt; Kevin Doyle, Dave Kitson

Subs not used: Adam Federici (gk), André Bikey, Leroy Lita

The game set a new Premier League record cumulative score of eleven goals, surpassing the previous record of nine, recorded eight times up to that point:

NORWICH CITY 4 SOUTHAMPTON 5

9 April 1994

MANCHESTER UNITED 9 IPSWICH TOWN 0

4 March 1995

SOUTHAMPTON 6 MANCHESTER UNITED 3

26 October 1996

BLACKBURN ROVERS 7 SHEFFIELD WEDNESDAY 2

25 August 1997

NOTTINGHAM FOREST 1 MANCHESTER UNITED 8

6 February 1999

WEST HAM UNITED 5 BRADFORD CITY 4

12 February 2000

TOTTENHAM HOTSPUR 7 SOUTHAMPTON 2

11 March 2000

TOTTENHAM HOTSPUR 4 ARSENAL 5

12 November 2004

Alex Ferguson's last game in charge of Manchester United, at the Hawthorns at the close of the 2012–13 season, ended in the scoreline:

WEST BROMWICH ALBION 5 MANCHESTER UNITED 5

19 May 2013

Match 9

Fourth is the new first

MANCHESTER CITY V. TOTTENHAM HOTSPUR

City of Manchester Stadium

Wednesday 5 May 2010

To say that there was a lot riding on this game would have been to re-define the term 'understatement'. A cool £20 million to the winner. As Manchester City took on Spurs, that was the anticipated reward for securing the last place reserved for a representative of the Barclays Premier League in the Champions League for the following season. This was indication of how the Premier League had grown in its near twenty years of existence: not just a money-spinner in its own right, now it was the passport to even greater wealth available in competitions which had copied its relentless marketing drive. Twenty million quid: no trifling amount, that.

Unless, of course, you happened to be the owner of a leading Premier League club. Then, provided you didn't behave with the sort of financial illiteracy that sank Pompey (and Leeds), that sum might seem thin pickings. There used to be an old joke that posed this question: how do you make a small fortune in football? To which – stitch my aching sides – the answer was: start with a large one then buy a football club.

But no one tells that gag any more. The Premier League changed all that. Never mind small fortunes, get it right in the new world of football and substantial wealth is up for grabs. Here is a by-no-means-comprehensive list of those who, in the last decade, have pocketed very large bounties indeed out of selling their stake in leading clubs:

Lady Nina Bracewell-Smith, who made £116 million for her shares in Arsenal; David Dein, who saw a £292,000 investment bought in 1983 in the same club blossom into £75 million by 2011; Doug Ellis, who received £63 million for Aston Villa; David Moores, who graciously accepted £88 million for his shares in Liverpool; Martin Edwards, who banked £84 million for his stake in Manchester United; and John Madejski, who walked away with £40 million when he sold up at Reading.

Madejski apart, most of those vigorously reupholstering their nests did so by the simple expedient of sitting on their asset until someone came along and made their day. These were not risk-takers. They did not put their hand in their wallet to fund the purchase of players or to refurbish a stadium. They were not there writing a cheque on their current account to pacify the taxman or to ensure the electricity bill was paid in time to keep the floodlights blazing. They did not flirt with personal bankruptcy in order to keep the object of their obsession in business. They simply found themselves able to reap the happy consequence of being in the right place at the right time.

Sure, there were those who messed up the opportunity the League offered. Simon Jordan at Crystal Palace, Steve Morgan at Wolves, the Venkys at Blackburn: all lost vast amounts by misjudging their footballing investment. But some did very nicely. And without question the most handsomely rewarded member of the Premier League owners' club, the man who accrued the biggest return through the least effort in the shortest period of time, was Thaksin Shinawatra. He was the ultimate winner in the Premier League lottery. A telecoms entrepreneur and former prime minister of Thailand, he bought Manchester City and sold it on after owning it for just fifteen months, making himself more than £90 million profit in the process. Now that is what you call football finance.

Thai take-away

Shinawatra arrived in Manchester as a man on the run from his homeland, after having been accused of systematic corruption, tax evasion and using the state police force as a private army to intimidate his political enemies. He bought City for £81.6 million on 21 June 2007, using a small proportion of the resources he had managed to squirrel out of Bangkok as collateral. At the time the Premier League had at its disposal the so-called 'Fit and Proper Person Test', which it employed to assess the suitability of putative owners. But, as was evident with the dream-chasers at Leeds United (see Match 6, page 164) and more particularly as was all too painfully obvious in the imploding mess that was the ownership of Portsmouth (see Match 8, page 223), this was not a piece of judicial scrutiny that remotely lived up to its name.

The test seemed to be applied as a measure not of moral fitness but of financial clout, and even in this respect was not used to any useful critical purpose. The way the rule was breezily by-passed, a cynic might suggest that a Premier League official would have cheerfully held open the door for Saddam Hussein and Slobodan Milošević had they wished to join the ownership party. Provided they had the readies. In fact – as was proved by the Glazer family who took over Manchester United in 2005 by the simple expedient of foisting a huge mortgage on the club, paid off out of the fans' pockets via the gate receipts and merchandise revenues – you didn't even need the readies.

Incredibly, then, Shinawatra was deemed entirely above board by the powers that be. Far from being shocked that a man with no apparent respect for the values regarded as desirable in British public life should be thought a legitimate custodian of one of the country's leading sporting institutions, Garry Cook, the club's chief executive, seemed surprised that anyone should even question the new owner's presence in Manchester City's directors' box.

'Is he a nice guy?' Cook asked of Shinawatra soon after he had arrived. 'Yes. Is he a great guy to play golf with? Yes. Does he have plenty of money to run a football club? Yes. I really only care about those three things. Whether he is guilty of something over in Thailand, I can't worry. My role is to run a football club.'

So that was all right then. Provided the bloke could stand his round in the golf club bar, who was to gainsay his right to own a

Premier League football club? Cook later retracted his endorsement, admitting he was mortified by his own crass insensitivity. But by then it was too late: at the time of Shinawatra's takeover, he had prostrated himself as a welcome mat at the door of the club. For his part, it was pretty obvious why the Thai wanted to buy into the competition. And it was very different from the reasons of bolstering local social standing that lay behind many a chairman's purchase of his football club in times gone by. It wasn't quite the same as Jack Walker's mission to restore local pride at Blackburn (see Match 3, page 75). This was a man who saw football as a geopolitical weapon.

By 2007, the Premier League had become Thailand's most watched televised sporting event. From Bangkok to Chiang Mai, tens of thousands gathered round their sets every weekend to follow Liverpool, Arsenal and Manchester United with a fanaticism that bordered on the obsessive. Regular pre-season tours to the country by English clubs provoked the kind of overexcited response more suited to the arrival of a boy band. In exile, pursued by his political enemies, the disgraced former premier would, by buying Manchester City, be able to remind his erstwhile supporters that he continued to thrive, that he was still a man of influence, exercising control over their most cherished sporting event. I've not gone away, Shinawatra was saying when cameras picked him out cheering on his team, I'm still standing. By 2007, it was clear by his intervention, the Premier League had become a vehicle for statements of intent that could be heard across the globe. By a nice coincidence, it was this, the very quality which first attracted him, that would ultimately so enrich him.

The footballing authorities might not have minded, but for some observers, the alacrity with which Shinawatra was welcomed to east Manchester was all the more alarming given the relationship between the club he was taking over and the local taxpayer. Observers like David Conn, the investigative reporter, lifelong Blue and author of *Richer Than God: Manchester City, Modern Football and Growing Up* (2012), suggest the club's recent history is unlike that of any other. Manchester City was put into the position it now finds itself by the taxpayers of the place in which it plied its trade, who unwittingly abetted the fiscal advancement of a dodgy despot. When I spoke to Conn, he gave a damning verdict on Shinawatra:

> By the time he sold his stake in City, he was a convicted criminal on the run, and he always had major questions over his human rights record. When the stadium was given to City and the club's owners, there should have been a clawback of the public money if any owner subsequently sold at a profit. That it was Thaksin who ultimately made £90 million for himself, with nothing to Manchester council tax payers or Sport England, illustrates the point spectacularly.

Regenerating Eastlands

The relationship between Thaksin Shinawatra and the council tax payers of Manchester went like this... In 2002 the city, after fruitlessly attempting to land the Olympics, staged the Commonwealth Games. As a centrepiece for the event, it built the City of Manchester Stadium, a sporting arena that cost £127 million, £49 million of which came from Manchester council, the rest from the National Lottery via Sport England. In justifying its investment, the council's thinking was similar to that which would inform the hosting of the Olympics in Stratford, east London, a decade later: here was the opportunity to spruce up a run-down part of town, and to use sport as the engine to regenerate a wasteland.

And the part of east Manchester in which their stadium was to be built was a wasteland all right. Once a crucible of the Industrial Revolution, it had stumbled and shambled its way through much of the twentieth century, its railway yards, collieries and chemical works closing one by one and, by the 1980s, falling into dereliction. With nothing arriving to replace its heavy industry, by the turn of the century its seven boroughs – Newton Heath, Harpurhey, Gorton South, Gorton North, Charlestown, Ardwick and Bradford – were the seven most deprived in Manchester, together forming the fourth-poorest urban area in England. This was a tattered, worn-out place where opportunity was sparse, 32 per cent of the population were on benefits and the education provision minimal (no local school had so much as a sixth form). Around 150,000 jobs had vanished from the area since the mid-1950s. Its building land was poisoned by the toxic legacy of industry, its transport connections woeful, its future bleak. In a city attempting to reinvent itself in the post-industrial age, it was the forgotten quarter, the zone without prospect. This was the council's argument in summary: without taxpayers' subvention, the chances of revival there were minimal. The Commonwealth Games, they said, would transform the place. And they made a bold first step.

As promised, the 2002 Games did turn out to be a grand success for the city planners. World-class sporting facilities sprang up and gleamed in the omnipresent Manchester rain. The town's self-confidence was bolstered by the hundreds of smiling, helpful local volunteers who flooded the streets. For a couple of weeks in August 2002, depressed old east Manchester was, if not quite the centre of the universe, then at least the centre of the Commonwealth.

The trouble was, though, that the Games lasted only a fortnight. And the good burghers of the town hall appreciated even before they began construction that a grand stadium was of little use to the city if it fell into disuse after the event. What they were desperate to avoid was the legacy of the Games turning out to be a white elephant. As their counterparts in London would later reluctantly concede in the case of their Olympic stadium, they quickly accepted that, if it were to have a future, the only viable tenant would be a football club. With United busy expanding their home in Old Trafford and so not interested in such a move, the councillors approached City to take it on.

The club's then owners could barely conceal their astonishment at such good fortune coming their way; such luck had not been so forthcoming in City's recent history. Though they insisted in negotiations that all conversion costs of removing the running track, completing the stadium symmetry and fitting a new tier of seats would be met by the council, the subsequent deal was beneficial to both sides. City would bequeath their old higgledy-piggledy, architectural mess of a ground at Maine Road to the council – which would be demolished and housing built on the site – and roughly £2 million a year would make its way into the town-hall coffers by way of rent. What's more the stadium would fortnightly attract huge numbers of people into east Manchester, bringing with them – it was hoped – jobs. The club, meanwhile, would enjoy a state-of-the-art new home, without the obligation of funding its construction.

And the most immediately tangible benefit of that was soon become apparent. Unlike, say, Everton or Liverpool, City had a freshly built facility, one from which the marketing opportunities of the Premier League could be all the better exploited. It meant any new owner coming in would not be obliged to fork out to build a functioning modern stadium. The council had done that work for them. Suddenly the club – despite spending the previous fifteen years withering in the shadow of its neighbour, despite oscillating between the divisions, despite at times resembling a paradigm of cack-handed maladministration – looked like a delicious business opportunity. The City of Manchester Stadium put Manchester City on the investment map.

The council was keen, too, that the stadium would provide a wider benefit for the people who paid for it than merely hosting a football match once a fortnight. In the rental agreement, it insisted on a clause to ensure that City used the place to foster community relations. The club's outreach department was already adept at that and relished their new space, immediately opening it up every day to local people, hosting all sorts of functions from education sessions and fitness clubs to tea dances for the elderly. These, much to the fluttering excitement of the regulars, were often later graced by the club's manager Sven-Göran Eriksson.

Football as an engine of urban regeneration: it was a grand ambition. Unfortunately, it was not Manchester's most deprived citizens who were the principal beneficiaries of the new stadium. The unhappy unintended consequence was that a corrupt former politician from South-east Asia did very nicely thank you out of the attempt at social engineering.

After less than fourteen months of increasingly unimpressive stewardship of the Sky Blues, Shinawatra received some interesting news from Garry Cook.

With his political enemies closing in, Shinawatra's assets had been frozen back home and he was looking to free up some cash from the one asset he had in England: Manchester City Football Club. Accordingly, he had instructed Cook to find a buyer. The departure was not unwelcome. Conn describes the former Thai premier's year of ownership of City as one of the 'most miserable' even by the standards of the club's recent history of underachievement. A derby victory at Old Trafford was the one highlight of twelve months of on-the-hoof, knee-jerk administration and broken promises, which included the harsh sacking of the popular Eriksson in June 2008. A succession of substandard players were bought, the once vibrant youth system squeezed of resources, the community work threatened. Vicky Kloss, now City's director of communications, expands: 'It was a very painful time. As a City fan, working within the organization, I had insight into how bad it was. And it was terrible: under him [Shinawatra] we were literally heading for disaster.'

Shinawatra's legacy may well have been dismal. But that would not be reflected in the price he extracted for the club. His reward was to be immense. Through an intermediary called Amanda Staveley, Cook had been contacted by a putative investor in the Middle East who had identified the Premier League as the most interesting opportunity in the world of sport. This group had an intriguing requirement: they wanted a club which, although not yet dominant, had the potential to produce rapid improvement from their involvement and become an international brand. They had looked at Newcastle and Everton, Arsenal too. But Cook persuaded them that the Premier League club that fitted their ambition most snugly was Manchester City. Apart from the name – which, thanks to the neighbours, was already half way to being an internationally known brand – there are no prizes for guessing that other, rather attractive aspect of the club that Cook was happy to communicate to its Middle Eastern suitors. Of the many areas that required major investment at Eastlands, the stadium was not among them. Thanks to the local council's largesse, that work had been done. City were already poised on the very lip of breakthrough.

Full of Middle Eastern promise

Thus it was that Sheikh Mansour Bin Zayed Al Nayhan, scion of the Abu Dhabi ruling family and heir to a further century's worth of the world's most valuable natural resource sitting under the sands of his homeland, handed over £213 million to take over Manchester City in August 2008. None of that money, incidentally, went to the people who had funded the asset that had so attracted the Sheikh and his advisers. Manchester City Council's coffers remained unvisited by his largesse. Thaksin Shinawatra, on the other hand, took the lot. Allowing him, after paying off debt and expenses, to withdraw from the club with the princely reward of £90 million profit in fourteen months. That meant that during his period of ownership of City, the disgraced Thai had earned nigh on £215,000 a day, more than enough to fund the drinks at Garry Cook's golf club.

David Conn insists that the manner of the sale of the City of Manchester Stadium robbed the public of their rightful share in the profits accruing:

> Whatever the argument for giving the stadium to City, I always believed the council should have insisted on a future deal. That's what the Olympic authorities concluded they had to do in negotiations with West Ham about the Olympic stadium. They said to the club's owners, if you sell the club on at an enhanced profit because of this great gift of a new stadium built with public money, the public must have a large share of that profit. The stadium was crucial; there is no way Sheikh Mansour would have bought City if they were still at Maine Road.

255

There was no doubt the council had helped the club move on. And, from the mire towards which Thaksin Shinawatra was leading them, they had landed in a bed of very fragrant roses. Because when it came to a fit and proper person to run a football club, not even the most forensic of investigations could find fault with Sheikh Mansour Bin Zayed Al Nayhan. There were no alarming skeletons rattling around in his furniture. As well as being – in the description Conn heard during a visit to Abu Dhabi – 'richer than God', reports suggested he was well-read, thoughtful and lacking in self-aggrandisement. Although he and his family had come by their wealth by geographic happenstance rather than personal innovation, the Sheikh had demonstrated some imagination in his investment portfolio. Through wise purchase of Western assets as varied as restaurants and banks, his fortune was expanding by the day. Moreover, he would also prove to have considerable reserves of something not frequently associated with football-club owners: patience.

Though we might not have appreciated all that in his first appointment as City's owner. A man who prefers to keep himself away from public attention, the Sheikh selected as his spokesman in Manchester another prominent Abu Dhabi citizen, Sulaiman al-Fahim. A character who makes Piers Morgan look chronically afflicted by self-doubt, the voluble al-Fahim announced the Sheikh's takeover in the most flamboyant way possible. On the first day of the new ownership, 31 August 2008 – which also happened to be the last day of the summer transfer window – he facilitated the purchase of Robinho from Real Madrid for £32.5 million.

The Brazilian had been expected to sign for Roman Abramovich at Chelsea, but al-Fahim derailed the negotiations by offering him a small fortune to come to Manchester, reputedly £10 million a year. The move signalled in the brashest manner possible that Abramovich was no longer the richest man in the Premier League. The big boys had moved in. It was a moment of high drama, if not high confusion. As Robinho explained in a press conference to mark his signing: 'On the last day, Chelsea made a great proposal and I accepted.' A reporter queried him: 'You mean Manchester, right?' 'Yeah, Manchester, sorry!' he replied.

If this was a piece of transfer business intended to make a statement, it certainly did that. Trouble was, the statement it made appeared to be: this club's new owner has more money than sense. As was evident by the look on the face of the recently installed manager Mark Hughes at Robinho's unveiling, it might have helped had al-Fahim consulted those who knew something about the football business before acting with such dispatch.

'I remember sitting in the office thinking: out of the frying pan into the fire,' recalls Vicky Kloss. 'Only this time there's going to be more cash.' Hughes may have had a shopping list of priorities rather more compelling than a flaky young Brazilian who had never quite lived up to the stellar reputation acquired in his youth, but Robinho was, for better or worse, the first signing of the Sheikh Mansour era. And as City's supporters quickly denuded the local fancy-dress hire shops of Arab head-dresses to celebrate their new owner (and his money), it was he who was expected to lead the Manchester City revolution, to try to stem the red tide down the road, and to score the goals that made the difference. Which, it became quickly evident, were just three of the things that were beyond his capabilities.

Whether it was the Robinho transfer or the fact he had given his mobile number to every pressman who asked and was subsequently leaking information like a rusting Manchester Ship Canal tug, within three months al-Fahim had been eased out of the operation... and was attempting to buy Portsmouth FC. Some clubs get all the luck.

In al-Fahim's place, the Sheikh appointed his old friend and trusted adviser Khaldoon al-Mubarak as chairman. Suddenly the volume was turned down, the tone became notably less noisy and the plan much, much more coherent. Vicky Kloss recalls al-Mubarak's arrival:

The chairman's adviser Simon Pearce came over just before him and set up a series of meetings at the club. I was one of the people he spoke to, along with Gary James, the club historian, and old players like Mike Summerbee, insiders who knew the club's fabric. It enabled the new chairman to get a grasp pretty quickly of what the club was about, what it meant to people.

In fact, so much more coherent was the plan, it was no longer referred to as a mere plan. No, al-Mubarak insisted in his every public pronouncement, what the Abu Dhabi people were doing at Manchester City was to be described as 'a project'. And investment in the project was quickly evident. Finding little was quite as glamorous as had been anticipated, the new regime ordered money to be spent everywhere: at the stadium a new pitch was laid, offices built for administrative staff, cover provided for those queuing at the ticket office, the corporate hospitality facilities upgraded, the concrete greyness of the public areas softened by the incorporation of imagery reflecting the club's heritage. The Abu Dhabi group appeared to be living up to the promise issued to season-ticket holders the day they took over: that they would listen to the fans' concerns and that their intention was to make City great in every way.

Even as the lot of the supporter was addressed, however, the fundamental purpose of the takeover was visible in the new electronic billboards that were soon installed around the new pitch. These flicked through a roster of advertisements rather different from the notices for meat pies and ale that were traditionally carried in a football match programme. As City took on Wigan or Blackburn, they promoted the virtues of the Abu Dhabi national air carrier Etihad, of the Abu Dhabi Grand Prix, of holidays in Abu Dhabi. There was a certain recurring theme apparent in these promotions.

Although he insisted that he was acting as an individual rather than a representative of the Abu Dhabi government, it was clear the Sheikh wanted to use his new investment as a vehicle to promote his homeland. Like Shinawatra, he appreciated that his was an asset that might speak volumes across the world, using the global television audience tuning in to watch the Premier League. So much so that within a year he had changed the name of the stadium to reflect the club's new direction. Etihad – the family airline - became its name sponsors. And in a shrewd bit of local politics, £2 million a year of the fee for the naming rights was given to Manchester City Council. This was in addition to a £3 million new annual rent deal. No wonder the city was evidently grateful for his presence. A banner was soon hung in the stands at the Etihad which carried a simple message reflecting local feeling beyond the Sky Blue support. 'Manchester thanks Sheikh Mansour,' it read. The joy that one of the world's richest men had arrived to start investing in the city's eastern quarter was not misplaced. Soon plans were unveiled for 'The Etihad Campus' – a £170 million development in training facilities, with community access, which would be built on the wasteland surrounding the stadium.

'The council hit the jackpot with Sheikh Mansour' is David Conn's assessment:

> He is continuing the redevelopment work they started in the area. When it's finished, it will be a huge improvement on what was there when he arrived. My major doubts are about the rhetoric, which suggests that the sporting economy can be a basis for replacing the industrial one which was allowed to die. East Manchester lost 150,000 jobs. However exciting the new City is, I feel Manchester, and the country, should not delude itself that this kind of regeneration is an answer to the massive de-industrialization which is still the underlying cause of so much poverty and deprivation in the neighbourhoods right around the new stadium.

But whatever the long-term result of the Sheikh's association, of this there is no doubt: without the broadcasting reach of the football club's product, the Sheikh and his unfathomably deep pockets would never have ventured anywhere near Manchester M11. Maybe the banner should be thanking the Premier League. The Sheikh himself, though, has had scant opportunity to view the banner in person. The Premier League's worldwide popularity means he has no need to venture from his home in the Gulf to keep tabs on his investment. With al-Mubarak doing the honours in the directors' box, to date the owner has watched his team in the flesh only once, when his expensively assembled side beat Liverpool 3–0 in August 2010. He did so without flourish or fanfare. Introduced to the crowd at the start of the game, to a huge ovation, he stood up and waved shyly. He looked thrilled to be there, grinning sheepishly, like a schoolboy who has just been gifted the world's swankiest train set.

But there was one thing that was immediately clear about the Sheikh: if he was smiling, it wasn't about City's wider reputation. As he immersed himself in the place's history, he found little to amuse him. Which was ironic, because for the past thirty years or so this was a club that had increasingly come to be known for a brand of self-deprecating humour. It was a sort of defensive reflex to help it cope with the massive imbalance of power in the local football rivalry: as United swanked, City sniggered.

A cure for City-itis?

Mind you, as a City fan you had to laugh. Otherwise you'd have cried. As the club bungled and bumbled their way through a succession of managers, sacking the good and hiring in their stead the weak, the inadequate and the chairman's mates (sometimes all three at once), the jokes did the rounds. There was the one about the erstwhile chairman Francis Lee arriving at work one day and seeing an old lady struggling with her shopping. 'Can you manage, love?' Lee says through the window of his car. 'Yes,' she replies. 'But I'll want a three-year contract and complete control of transfer negotiations.' And he signs her up on the spot.

Sometimes though, the fiction couldn't match the reality. Lee, for instance, had engaged in a long-time civil war from the late 1980s on with the previous chairman Peter Swales, which resulted in the two men not exchanging a single word for many years. At board meetings they blanked each other. Eventually, other directors approached Howard Davies, the leading economist and a lifelong City fan, in the hope he might broker a rapprochement. Davies wondered what had caused such a problem between the two men in the first place. Was it a financial dispute he might help resolve? He was told it was slightly more mundane than that: the two men had fallen out over who had the better parking space at Mere Golf Club. At that news, Davies politely declined the invitation to get involved.

Such was the club's unfailing ability over the past three decades to snatch defeat from the jaws of victory, it seemed almost pathological. Indeed Joe Royle, the former City striker who managed the club from 1998 to 2001, gifted the condition a name. The manager who pulled the club up from its lowest ebb, relegation to the third tier in 1998, christened it 'City-itis'. The fans had seen little in the intervening time to alter the perception that City-itis was embedded in the club's DNA. And if that was the case, the best way to cope was to laugh. They did a lot of that in the stands. When they weren't shaking their heads in dismay.

The Sheikh, though, wasn't interested in City-itis. An association with failure, albeit greeted with a philosophical shrug and a smile, did not fit with his ambition. He wanted Abu Dhabi to be projected round the world on the back of success, of modernity, of the very epitome of sporting excellence. There was nothing aspirational about City-itis. He wanted it excised from the club's soul. And quickly.

But it soon became apparent that to do so would take significant investment on the pitch. Even as he modernized everywhere, making the playing staff fit for purpose was essential. If his new brand was to make the noise he wanted around the world, then the team had to sing. At first the responsibility for rapid upgrade in the quality of the personnel was entrusted to Mark Hughes. He may not have been the Sheikh's appointment, but Garry Cook – who had persuaded the former United hero and former Blackburn manager to step across the Manchester divide – spoke highly of the Welshman's professionalism and intelligence. The Sheikh was impressed by Hughes on meeting him, and liked the reports he heard of the manager keenly involving himself in the broader business development meetings at the club. As well intentioned as he was well briefed, he too seemed eager to rid the club of City-itis. So he was granted the resources to start things moving. At the training ground he had £350,000 worth of improvements immediately nodded through, he bought in assistance from sports scientists, bolstered the medical team, hired specialist fitness consultants. And then he went to work in the transfer market.

Eschewing the notion that there was no value available in the January window, the moment the New Year turned in 2009 he bought the following players: Wayne Bridge, Shay Given, Craig Bellamy and Nigel de Jong. The following summer, Gareth Barry, Roque Santa Cruz, Kolo Touré, Emmanuel Adebayor, Joleon Lescott and Sylvinho joined them. Within a year of taking over, Hughes had persuaded the Sheikh to fund more than £150 million in transfer fees, with the concomitant inflation in the club's wage bill. He meant business all right.

But the deal which perhaps signalled City's intent more than any other (certainly more than their brief flirtation with Robinho) was when Hughes signed Carlos Tévez from Manchester United in July 2009. Tévez had not enjoyed the smoothest of rides since he arrived in England from the Brazilian club Corinthians in 2006. His problems were not on the pitch: there he had proved magnificent, a relentless, barrelling combination of skill and determination for West Ham and then United. Rather, his problem was one of ownership.

With the wages being paid, to describe football as a slave economy in the Premier League era may seem far-fetched. But nevertheless there was something ante-bellum about the fact that Tévez was apparently owned by someone. And no one was quite sure who. As West Ham discovered when they were obliged to pay compensation after his goals had kept them in the Premiership in his first season (2007), it wasn't them who owned him. Nor was it Corinthians. It turned out his registration belonged to a group of South American businessmen represented in Europe by an Iranian financier called

Kia Joorabchian, who, by a neat coincidence, was also Mark Hughes's agent. Tévez had gone on loan to United for two seasons, winning the Champions League with the Reds and playing every week to a chorus from the club's followers of 'Fergie sign him up'.

But Sir Alex Ferguson had not taken to Joorabchian's pushy insistence and thought the price demanded for the Argentinian's signature too high. So Joorabchian did the one thing he thought most likely to provoke Ferguson into action, by offering the player to his client Hughes at City. By now the Premier League had introduced rules on third-party ownership of players. Joorabchian's deal was simple: in order to take Tévez on, and so unravel the fisherman's knot of registration issues, City would have to pay £47 million. When they agreed to do so without demur, and further acquiesced to his demand that a line be inserted in Tévez's contract that he must always be the highest-paid player at the club – starting on an eye-watering £190,000 a week – there was no need for Joorabchian to return to Old Trafford and see what might be on offer there. He had hit pay dirt. He was laughing.

And so were City. So thrilled were they by the transfer, the club's kit provider Umbro arranged for it to be announced through a poster, sited on Deansgate, on the route into Manchester city centre from United's Trafford headquarters. It featured Tévez in familiar arm-spread goal celebration, but now wearing the sky-blue shirt of City. Below the picture were the words 'Welcome to Manchester'.

Mischievous perhaps. Clearly tongue-in-cheek. But the reaction it elicited was telling. Sir Alex was furious about it, thundering at a press conference about a club without respect. That seemed a little rich coming from a man who every week for the previous fifteen years had said nothing about the sneering banner hung by fans at the Stretford End, showing a digital clock that counted the years since City had won a trophy. But for Fergie this poster was a bit of banter too far. Privately, even as the object of his ire was quietly removed, many at City were delighted by Ferguson's overreaction. It proved, if nothing else, that this was a signing he would dearly have loved to make.

Blue Moon rising

With Tévez immediately in rampant form, Hughes's revamped team won the first four games of the 2009–10 season without so much as conceding a goal. It was a soaring sequence topped off by a 4–2 win over Arsenal, a proper team of the kind City needed to outflank if the owner's ambition was to be achieved. But then things started to unravel, beginning with defeat in the Manchester derby. On 20 September, United won a pulsating game at Old Trafford 4–3 with the winner coming in typical fashion in added time, from their veteran substitute Michael Owen. As an exultant Ferguson described the game as 'probably the best derby of all time', the home crowd were left to question loud and long: who needs Tévez?

And that defeat seemed to undermine Hughes's determination to unburden City of their all-enveloping sense of inferiority. There had been much talk before the game that the 'Blue Moon' was rising, that City were on the march and would assume ascendancy over home territory en route to global domination. Players who had been part of City's last championship-winning side like Mike Summerbee were brought out to shout up their club's arrival in the big time. Things were changing. Instead, after the defeat at Old Trafford, Hughes's side embarked on a dismal run of seven successive draws. He had now spent over £200 million of the Sheikh's money forging a team of his own and here they were stuttering and stalling. True, he managed to notch up a couple of firsts during that autumn – a first win over Chelsea in five years, plus a place in a cup semi-final for the first time since 1981. But it was not enough.

At the beginning of December 2009, City lost 3–0 at Tottenham, another of the sides who really needed to be bested if the new owner's governing ambition was to be realized. It was a dismal showing. Spurs won by the simple tactical expedient of attacking City's unprotected left flank, where the hapless Robinho offered scant cover for the ageing Sylvinho. Hughes failed to intervene until the hour, when he finally withdrew Robinho and sent on Roque Santa Cruz. By then it was too late: City were 2–0 down. This was simply not the sort of return that the plutocrats of Abu Dhabi expected from their massive investment.

After that game, a worried al-Mubarak, who had been in constant communication with the club's paymaster, called Hughes into his office. He asked him what he intended to do. Hughes's response was roughly: 'We've been unlucky. We'll keep trying.' Such fatalism did not sit well with the project. What it required from the team was clear demonstration that getting involved with Abu Dhabi produces evident benefits. Al-Mubarak suggested that additional defensive coaching expertise might help. Hughes said he would soldier on.

There would be no chance for that. Two wins in his last eleven Premier League matches had sealed his fate. Even as Hughes presided over the next game, a 4–2 home win over Sunderland, Cook and al-Mubarak had already signed up a replacement. They had tried for José Mourinho. But, after taking a year's sabbatical following his precipitate dismissal by Chelsea, he had only just arrived at Internazionale and was loath to leave Milan so soon. However his predecessor at the San Siro, Roberto Mancini – so inside gossip went – had for some time made it clear that if he were offered Hughes's job he would be happy to take it. And that was a proposition the City hierarchy could not afford to pass up.

Unfortunately, suggesting that all hint of City-itis had yet to be eradicated from the club's system, news of Hughes's defenestration and Mancini's appointment had leaked out before the man himself had been informed. As he stood on the touchline that December afternoon, he was a dead manager walking. His wave to the crowd at the end of the game struck a valedictory note: everyone knew he was a goner.

It was a shabby way to conduct a change in personnel and the goalkeeper Shay Given led a deputation of players to remonstrate with Cook about the sacking. Poorly handled as it may have been, the logic of the move was self-evident. Mancini – unlike Mourinho, a wonderful player before he took to coaching – came with some managerial record. He had won seven trophies in seven years in Italy.

In a decade as a manager with Wales, Blackburn and now City, Hughes had won nothing. What Cook and al-Mubarak hoped they were doing with Mancini's appointment was injecting a winning mentality into the club, just as Jack Walker had done employing Kenny Dalglish as Blackburn manager nearly twenty years previously. It didn't come cheap, the Italian signed a contract that was worth £7 million a year if he hit certain performance targets. But there was no better way, it was felt, to excise City-itis than to employ the serially successful.

Suave, handsome, stylish, the forty-five-year-old Mancini was an immediate hit with the fans. Not least because of the way he knotted a sky-blue scarf around his neck the first time he stepped out to take charge of the team, animatedly pacing the touchline.

'Mancini woe-oh Mancini: he came from Italy to manage Man City' was the chorus from the stands. It made a change. In the past, City managers had tended to come from the chairman's immediate circle of mates. This was an appointment of a different order for a club now with a new mindset. And the new man showed his authority by immediately sending Robinho back to South America on loan. This was not a manager who would be told who to buy or who to play. Indeed, one former associate warned anyone in England who might be misled by Mancini's debonair appearance into thinking he was a soft touch that he was 'the hardest bastard you could ever meet'.

Mancini on a mission

Whatever his level of self-confidence, it was immediately made clear to Mancini what his new task entailed. It was there enshrined in one of his potential bonus payments: the minimum requirement as he got to grips with the scale of his new job was to qualify for the Champions League. If he did so he would earn a personal bonus of £1 million.

From the turn of the century, when UEFA changed its criteria to open up the Champions League to a larger group of participants, the top four clubs in the Premier League qualified for the competition. And from that moment, getting into that select group of invitees became the definition of a successful season: Arsène Wenger maintained his job at Arsenal during that club's trophy-less years post-2005 largely because he always managed to come at least fourth in the Premier League. And what was so good about Europe? Winning domestic silverware simply could not compare with the rewards available in the continent's senior competition. From 2011, the base fee for just making it into the group stage was £8.6 million. Every victory in the group brought a further £1 million, even a draw was worth £500,000. And that's without even factoring in the television income, which generally doubles the return. Manchester United earned over £55 million for their run to the final in 2011. That's big money in anyone's language.

Though for the Abu Dhabi contingent, the attractions lay not so much in the money (even if getting something back for a change would be no bad thing) as in the further exposure it gave the brand. City playing in the same competition as Barcelona and Real Madrid would be the ultimate endorsement, proof that the Emirate's backing had propelled the club into the big time. Hughes had spent over £200 million of their money and had singularly failed to deliver on that fundamental. Now it was Mancini's turn.

Unlike Hughes, though, the Italian didn't do much in his first January transfer window, adding just two players to his squad. Alongside the quick and exciting young Adam Johnson from Middlesbrough, his other January signing was Patrick Vieira, the former Arsenal behemoth who had been a stalwart for him at Inter. Mancini's thinking was clear. It was not so much the Frenchman's – undoubtedly waning – presence on the pitch he was investing in, it was the experience and sense of certainty he might impart to the dressing room. Vieira had a winner's mentality, and that was what Mancini wanted him to convey to the rest of the squad.

No sooner had he arrived in east Manchester than Mancini was given a sobering lesson in the power of single-minded belief. City were drawn to meet the old enemy in a boisterous League Cup semi-final. Despite being given a 2–1 first-leg lead by the pugnacious Tévez, City lost the second 3–1. It was Ferguson's welcome present to the latest pretender. And it was not a happy result for Gary James, a lifelong Blue and author of *Manchester: The City Years* (2012): 'When we lost to United, after all the boasts following the first leg, there was a feeling that we are always going to be the bridesmaids.'

In the League, though, things were much more hopeful. Mancini successfully persuaded his players to break the drawing habit and win their first four league matches under his charge. Defensively coherent, with Hughes's Belgian signing Vincent Kompany, bought from Hamburg, excelling at centre-back, they allied work rate and technique to Tévez's forward nous. The momentum was sustained. By mid-April, when they thrashed lowly Burnley 6–1 at Turf Moor, the stuttering autumn was becoming a distant memory. Sure, there might still not be any silverware. Sure, the first three places in the division looked as though they would be carved up by those serial Champions League qualifiers Man United, Chelsea and Arsenal. But that first, important target seemed within reach: they were looking good for Europe. Fourth, as the late Brian Moore would have had it, was up for grabs.

City weren't alone in casting covetous glances at the new holy grail of the game. On Merseyside Liverpool were anxious to get back into the competition in which they had so recently excelled. In Birmingham, Martin O'Neill had given Aston Villa a belief that they might be good enough to qualify. But it was from north London that the real challenge appeared to be coming.

What a transformation had taken place at Tottenham Hotspur. In the autumn of 2008 they were at the bottom of the Premier League, looking more likely to be playing away at Barnsley and Middlesbrough the following season than at Barcelona and Madrid. Their taciturn Spanish manager Juande Ramos had managed to win just two points from their first eight games when he was let go in October 2008, just a year after taking charge. In his place came Harry Redknapp, fresh from galvanizing Portsmouth, bringing along his small army of touchline assistants and his bustling, old-school bonhomie.

He had left Pompey just as he was about to be given the freedom of the city for leading the club to FA Cup success and the rate he was going in his new job, the freedom of Tottenham would soon be his too. At last, after a career patrolling the game's less luminous byways, the champion wheeler-dealer had taken control of a big-budget club. He arrived blowing a gale of energy through the corridors. His presence revivified Spurs. In his first season they recovered to finish in the top half of the table, as well as making it to the League Cup final, where they lost on penalties to United.

The 2009–10 campaign was Redknapp's first full season in charge and he was moulding the team into the sort of shape he wanted, loving his moment. He had sold Darren Bent in the summer after observing tartly that his wife might have scored some of the chances the striker spurned. He had plucked his old collaborators Jermain Defoe, Peter Crouch and Nico Kranjčar from the rapidly decaying corpse of Portsmouth, and had brought the tenacious Wilson Palacios from Wigan. How he was loving it, even if it did entail driving up from Bournemouth every day, stopping only at the training ground gates to address the Sky Sports News cameras through the window of his Range Rover, telling them that if he had any news to impart, they would be the first to know.

After starting the campaign with four consecutive wins, Spurs had remained effective, serious and focused. It was, after all, Redknapp's team who had seen off Mark Hughes at City. As the season progressed, the ambition of the chairman Daniel Levy was beginning to look as if it might be realized. He ran the club for the tax-exile owner Joe Lewis and his goal had long been clear: if the club were to match their neighbours Arsenal, with their huge new stadium and greater flow of cash through the turnstiles, the minimum requirement was a regular supping at the top table. Get into the Champions League and Spurs could enter a perpetual virtuous circle. Money would be made, better players would be attracted, which would mean qualification could become a commonplace.

But for that to happen, they had to get there in the first place.

Spurred on to success

Thus it was that as the season moved towards its climax, the match that mattered, the one that was going to have the most significant effect on its participants did not involve the putative champions. True, Carlo Ancelotti's Chelsea may have been heading towards the title, the first part of a domestic double. But the biggest game, the one that best highlighted Premier League priorities, was the one that the fixture computer had thrown up for the penultimate weekend of the season. Manchester City were to entertain Spurs in an encounter that quickly became billed by an excited Sky Sports News as the '£20-million Match'. This was the new phenomenon of the Premier League era: the Fourth Place Cup Final.

Mancini described it as 'the most important game for this club for many years'. Though there were some who felt that the importance of this game might have been reduced had Mancini been a touch more ambitious in the season's latter stages. Had he instructed his team to give it a go against an injury-weakened Arsenal a fortnight earlier, for instance, the tension around this match would have been reduced. Both Wigan and Blackburn had beaten Wenger's team by embracing attack. But Mancini, an Italian to the tips of his handmade shoes, counselled caution, coming away with just one point from a 0–0 draw. Three points gained and things would have been very different.

Instead it meant Spurs could emerge from the game with but a draw to ensure their elevated status. City had to win. Otherwise, £200 million spent on the team notwithstanding, the glories of fourth would be beyond them.

It was a cool, dank and unappealing Wednesday night in east Manchester. Spring might have arrived elsewhere, but the rain-soaked Ashton New Road looked marooned in an unending winter. For the City fans turning up in their thousands, this was a strange sensation: for the first time in a generation their side could be found at the business end of the season in contention for the important issues rather than locked in a basement scuffle to avoid demotion. They had a good team, made up of the likes of Kompany, Barry, Tévez and Bellamy, players who had real heart. More to the point, they had a good manager. They had much to thank the new owner for.

Yet even in the build-up to the game the possibility that this was still a club capable of shooting itself in the foot hung heavy in the air. The goalkeeper Shay Given had dislocated his shoulder in the game against Arsenal. Back in the summer, Hughes had dispatched his young understudy Joe Hart on a season-long loan to Birmingham City. With the third-choice keeper Stuart Taylor also unavailable, Mancini had been obliged to make an emergency loan signing of the Hungarian Márton Fülöp from Sunderland. Thus were the club about to compete in their most significant game in a generation fielding a keeper surplus to requirements at Sunderland. It did not inflate the lungs with confidence.

But never mind that. The City fans roared their team out onto the beautiful City of Manchester Stadium playing surface with a defiant chorus of 'Blue Moon'. The Sheikh wasn't there; he was one of a global television audience of millions, gripped by the unyielding tension of a match that really, really mattered.

City looked elegant in their retro-style light-blue shirts, a uniform awash with visual echoes of the last time they had contended for league honours back in the 1970s. Spurs, their white shirts besmirched with luminous yellow flashes under the arms, were less sartorially distinguished. But whatever the aesthetics of the tailoring, it was Spurs who had the more adventurous cut to their formation. Mancini sent out his team in the favoured Italian fashion. Barry and de Jong were the holding players in front of the back four. Ahead of them Bellamy, Tévez and Johnson were tasked with finding space, while Adebayor was a lone striker. Redknapp, for whom a draw would have been fine, selected a far more audacious line-up. Ahead of a creative central midfield pairing of Tom Huddlestone and Luka Modrić, he selected two strikers: the speedy Jermain Defoe and the tricky, gangly Peter Crouch. They were to be supplied by crosses from perhaps the quickest wide men in the Premier League, the emerging Gareth Bale and Aaron Lennon – the latter playing his first game since December. 'I took a big gamble and played an attacking team,' says Redknapp of his selection. 'We went for it. People probably thought I was mad going away from home like that – all the top teams only play with one up front now.'

Redknapp targeted his final words in the dressing room on the inspirational possibilities of attack. He had picked a side to win, he told his players, now it was up to them to do just that. As the Spurs team gathered in a huddle before kick-off, their captain Ledley King reminded them of their manager's stirring belief in their attacking prowess. 'We can do this,' he said. 'Just believe.'

Once it started, if the Sheikh had any fingernails left after his second season owning the club, he would have chewed them to the quick as he watched from Abu Dhabi. In the directors' box his representatives Cook and al-Mubarak looked racked with tension. Nearby Levy was a flutter of twitchy nerves. In the stands, every face seemed etched with worry. This was not a game for the frail of constitution. Aggressive, pugnacious, full of gristle and grit, the significance of the prize seemed to infect every tackle, every headed challenge, every dispute over a throw-in. Players snarled and snapped. In the technical area, Mancini appeared to be living every misplaced pass, throwing himself around in increasing animation, his anger growing ever more vivid and transparent.

His impassioned pleas from the touchline to his players didn't help. As the half progressed, with King and his excellent centre-back partner Michael Dawson completely nullifying Adebayor, Tévez was being forced ever deeper in pursuit of the ball. Johnson tried a few dashes, but Bellamy was largely ineffective, his trademark scowl rarely translating itself into purpose.

By half-time, neither side had threatened much, the tension resulting in a mutual smothering. Tévez had had a shot saved by Spurs' keeper Heurelho Gomes, Crouch had hit a post and Defoe had tested Fülöp's nerves. But in a game with so much at stake, goals were always likely to be at a premium. During the interval, in the home stands as the fans sought a drink to calm their nerves, there was a grumbly discontent that the manager had not been more adventurous. City needed to win and yet were adhering to a plan of containment. Many felt that going down in a blaze of glory would be preferable to watching their ambition fizzle out. Bring on Santa Cruz, bring on the home-grown hero Wright-Phillips, they counselled. Besides, if defence was the Italian's priority, how come his left-back was so poor? Because Wayne Bridge was being publicly humiliated by Lennon.

There was to be no respite as the second half picked up much as the first had done. With Tévez seeking to rally his side by charging about the pitch, with Johnson constantly looking to cross with either foot, with Fülöp earning a standing ovation after a finger-tip save from Bale's shot, it was unrelenting, if not exactly elevated. This was what made the Premier League such a compelling media product: pace, fury, unstinting drama.

To the home fans' tutting annoyance, when the fourth official's board was finally held up on instruction from the City bench to signify a substitute, it was not an attacking reinforcement. Instead, Vieira trotted out to replace the injured Barry. Mancini wanted his lieutenant out there, to calm nerves, to ensure there was no regression to old habits. But with so much at stake, tempers continued to fray. Vieira himself was not exactly a calming influence. He tangled with Huddlestone, who was then caught by a bad tackle from de Jong. The Spurs man reacted angrily, just missing with a retaliatory stamp on de Jong and earning a caution. On the touchline, Mancini was apparently seized by a bad case of St Vitus' Dance, yelling and imploring, living every missed opportunity, working himself into a lather.

Then disaster struck for City. Blowing across the stands of their shiny new stadium came evidence that whatever the circumstances, whatever the new owner's reserves of cash, some things never change for those of sky-blue persuasion: disappointment lurks round every corner. With less than ten minutes remaining, Tottenham's Younès Kaboul – another Portsmouth old boy – loped down the wing, evading Bellamy and bundling on towards the byline. Bridge was absent without leave, giving the Spurs full-back time to cross. The ball struck

Bridge as he desperately tried to recover his station. Its change of path then deceived Fülöp, who could only pad it out into the middle of the danger zone in front of his goal at a deliciously inviting height. And there was Crouch, all six foot seven inches of him, to snaffle up the opportunity, stooping and looping the ball off his forehead into the back of the net. The England striker – who had been so well rewarded during his career in football he was said by his agent to employ a personal staff of seven – scored what was without question the most valuable goal of his career. It was the £20 million goal.*

And from it, there was no coming back for City. In *The Guardian*, Daniel Taylor was pointed in his assessment of the home team:

> In the last half an hour City were outpassed, outpaced and very nearly outclassed. Passes were misplaced; far too often for a side that would like to believe it merits a place among that élite group of European clubs. Mancini insisted his team had not deserved to lose and had 'no luck' but he was in a small minority. Tottenham's second-half pressure had been almost unrelenting.

With Spurs fans crowing, the home supporters had a horrible vision of times past. Despite all evidence to the contrary, City-itis still bubbled through the bloodstream. Here they were about to make the great leap forward and yet they had blown it. 'We thought fate's always going to go against us,' as Gary James puts it. Others, though, were less convinced there was anything supernatural in the defeat. More it was to do with the ambition shown by the respective managers. The *Daily Telegraph's* Henry Winter epigrammatically summed it up: 'fortune favoured the brave and the brave now inherit a fortune.'

Dignified and restrained in victory, Redknapp had become the

---

* Though not the best goal of his career. That came two years later, by which time the much-travelled Crouch was playing for Stoke City at the Britannia Stadium, and the opponents were once again Man City. Teeing it up for himself on the corner of the eighteen-yard box, Crouch thumped the sweetest volley you'll ever see into the far top corner of the City net past the despairing full-stretch lunge of keeper Joe Hart.

first Spurs manager to take the club into Europe's senior competition since Bill Nicholson in 1961. They had not been close to the top four since the Premier League had started. No wonder he went on to be acclaimed the Premier League's manager of the year, only the second to win the award without securing the title.

As Spurs players whooped and hollered with their fans, and then soaked Redknapp with a bucket of iced water as he conducted an interview with Sky, a sense of fatalism overwhelmed the City fans. In the directors' box Cook and al-Mubarak looked as if they were preparing for a funeral. And many thought the funeral in question would be that of Mancini's management. After all, he had failed to deliver the assumed minimum requirement of his tenure. However, the Italian himself seemed sure he would be back at work for the pre-season training. 'Why not?' he replied at the press conference when he was asked whether he would still be in Manchester in June:

> I'm confident. I think I will stay here. I have worked here five months and you don't start from the roof but the basement. We have worked very well and we are near the roof now. But I am not a magician and I don't have a magic wand. We wanted this [fourth] place, just like Liverpool and Aston Villa, but this is football.

There would, he said, be other moments. Many of them. They were on the right track. Make no mistake, he insisted, City's time would come. But not many City fans were so sure. Yes, there had been much progress: this was only the team's seventh league defeat, the same number as Manchester United; they finished above Liverpool in the league for only the third time in forty-eight years; they had scored four times in matches against both Arsenal and Chelsea. Yet the prevailing sense was of a mighty let-down, a sinking, hollow disappointment for everyone connected with the club, from Ardwick to Abu Dhabi.

The stadium announcer certainly understood the significance of what had just hwappened. With the ground echoing to the cheery chants of Spurs supporters who were to see their team electrify the San Siro the following season, he reached for the only eulogy that seemed appropriate. As the City fans filed out, anticipating nothing more than yet another excruciating ribbing from glory-sated Red workmates at this latest, devastating manifestation of City-itis, they were serenaded by the perfect song for a Mancunian wake. It was The Smiths' 'Heaven Knows I'm Miserable Now'.

● ● ● ● ●

BARCLAYS PREMIER LEAGUE
City of Manchester Stadium
Wednesday 5 May 2010

MANCHESTER CITY   0 – 1   TOTTENHAM HOTSPUR

Tottenham scorer: Peter Crouch 82

Attendance: 47,730

Referee: Steve Bennett

TEAMS:

MANCHESTER CITY (4-2-3-1):

Márton Fülöp; Pablo Zabaleta, Kolo Touré, Vincent Kompany, Wayne Bridge; Nigel de Jong, Gareth Barry (Patrick Vieira 57); Craig Bellamy (Roque Santa Cruz 84), Carlos Tévez, Michael Johnson (Shaun Wright-Phillips 72); Emmanuel Adebayor

Subs not used: Gunnar Nielsen, Micah Richards, Nedum Onuoha, Sylvinho

TOTTENHAM HOTSPUR (4-4-2):

Heurelho Gomes; Younès Kaboul, Michael Dawson, Ledley King, Benoît Assou-Ekotto; Aaron Lennon (David Bentley 71), Tom Huddlestone, Luka Modrić (Wilson Palacios 89), Gareth Bale; Peter Crouch, Jermain Defoe (Roman Pavlyuchenko 81)

Subs not used: Ben Alnwick, Jermaine Jenas, Eidur Gudjohnsen, Sébastien Bassong

Match 10

Now it's Mancini time

MANCHESTER CITY V. QUEENS PARK RANGERS

Etihad Stadium, Manchester

Sunday 13 May 2012

It was late afternoon on 30 May 1999 when a thick cloud of misery descended over the fading, clapped-out, unfit-for-purpose old Wembley Stadium. With less than ten minutes remaining of their Second Division play-off final against Gillingham, a similarly fading, clapped-out, unfit-for-purpose Manchester City had conceded two late goals. The conviction that their side was destined to remain in the third tier even as their hated neighbours completed the first treble by an English club was a prospect too hurtful for many of the thousands of Blues fans in attendance. As their team seemingly huffed and puffed their way to oblivion, hundreds of them had abandoned hope, left their seats and made their way down Wembley Way to the Underground.

Oh Blues of little faith! As full-time drew near, one group was already on a tube train that was about to depart for central London. One of their number had a transistor radio, which he tuned to the BBC radio commentary. Just as the doors shut and the train began to ease out of the station, the unbelievable news was broadcast: not only had City scored a consolation goal right on ninety minutes, they had also, thanks to the efforts of a diminutive Scot called Paul Dickov, added an equalizer in the final seconds of added time. It was now 2–2. Suddenly half an hour's extra time loomed, if not a penalty shoot-out. From being dead, City's hopes had undergone a Lazarus-like resurgence. Panicking that they were going to miss out on a seminal moment in their club's history, one of the group did what any sane football fan would do in the circumstances: he pulled the emergency communication cord. The train shuddered to a halt. And when the doors opened to enable station staff to investigate what the problem was, the Blues inside legged it off the train and back to the stadium as fast as they could. There, they were witness to what turned out to be a famous footballing resurrection. At the end of 120 minutes of throttling tension, City won promotion back to the First Division (now the Championship) on penalties. And so began their long march back to the summit of the game, a giddying peak they had not occupied since the glory days of Joe Mercer and Malcolm Allison in the late 1960s and early 1970s.

This was a moment which, thirteen years on, should have been uppermost in the minds of their followers as Manchester City approached the most important ninety-four minutes in the one hundred and thirty-two years of its existence. This is not a club that makes life easy for its fans.

From its birth in the autumn of 1880 to that late spring afternoon in the last year of the twentieth century, Manchester City had seized with gusto every possible opportunity to toy sadistically with its supporters' emotions. Though in the tortuous annals of Man City, even that was to pale into insignificance compared to the devilishly, wilfully capricious and climactic final game of the 2011–12 season.

'It was quite ridiculous,' says Michael Baxandall, a lifelong Blue, whose total commitment to the cause was demonstrated when he captained a team of City fans on the BBC television quiz show *Eggheads*. 'I have never experienced the lowest of lows and the highest of highs in such proximity. I will go to my grave and never see anything like that again. Unbelievable.' The game was a perfect microcosm of the twisting, tortuous progress of the entire 2011–12 season: it strained belief to such a degree that the only rational explanation was that its narrative had been contrived in a Hollywood script meeting. What a way to signal the start of the Premier League's third decade: by producing the single most extraordinary afternoon of drama in English football history.

Bread and circuses

As it marked its twentieth season, it was not just the Premier League's plotlines that appeared to be in robust good health. It was clear from the figures its marketing team released during the course of the year-long celebration of its landmark that the Premier League was more than thriving. Those of us who had predicted almost from its birth that the bubble must soon burst and that the new competition would inevitably pay the price for its hubris and crash, Icarus-like, to Earth had been proved wrong, wrong and wrong again. More people were watching live and on television across the globe. More money was coming in, skills were more consummate, pitches smoother, the football quicker. Everything was brighter and more expansive. Not least the players' current accounts: the average salary for a first-team squad member at a Premier League club was, in its twentieth year, considerably more than a million pounds a year. That was the average.

Sure, there was much that was absent from the glowing reports. Writers like David Conn ran extensive investigations throughout the anniversary drawing attention to the other, less positive strand of the Premier League tale. There was the above-inflation increase in admission prices (a ticket for an away fan to watch Southampton at Arsenal at Highbury in 1992 had cost £8; for City supporters heading to the Emirates to watch their team play the Gunners in 2013 it was £62). There were the thirteen clubs that had gone into administration after falling out of the Premier League, undermined by ruinous attempts to buy their way back. There was the collateral damage to England's national team, weakened by the League's influx of foreign players. There was the money leeched out of the game by the parasitical demands of players' agents. Plus there was the manner in which, even as the Premier League dazzled, direct participation

279

in football declined. In 1992, nearly three million adults played the game regularly in England. By 2012 this figure had dropped to just over two million. Over this twenty-year period, more than 900,000 English footballers had hung up their boots. The Premier League was a significant part of a twenty-first-century trend that was turning the nation that invented football from one that kicked a ball into one that watched others doing so.

But hey, such caveats were largely drowned out in the noise of celebration. All season long the trumpets sounded and the pyrotechnics flashed. 'I was there at the start, commentating on Leeds v. Wimbledon in the first week of the League,' says Martin Tyler, Sky's main man with the microphone. 'To come from there to where it is now was an utterly amazing journey for football. And one I don't think anyone could have predicted at that first game. Certainly not me.'

Tyler – the man whose words had formed a constant soundtrack to the League's development – has a point. Everything had changed with the Premier League. Not least the identity of the dominant teams. Of the clubs that had won the title in the twenty years prior to its formation, only Arsenal – Football League champions in 1989 and 1991 – repeated the trick in the Premier League era. Derby County, Aston Villa, Nottingham Forest, Everton and Leeds United – winners all since 1972 – never came closer than Villa's second-place finish in 1993. What was more surprising, given their utter dominance of the previous two decades in which they savoured no fewer than eleven league championships, was that in twenty years Liverpool's best effort was to be runners-up in 2002 and 2009.

Instead, in the Premier League seasons to date (2012–13), Chelsea and Arsenal have taken three titles each and Blackburn one. But it was Manchester United who awoke from a twenty-six-year slumber to dominate the competition, gobbling up thirteen of the twenty titles up for grabs. Peter Hooton, lead singer of the Liverpool-based band The Farm and a long-time season-ticket holder at Anfield, recalls:

I remember around 1992 doing an interview comparing the

Manchester music scene with Liverpool's and I was asked what was the difference between the two cities. I just said the single word: 'trophies'. Because that was what defined the gap. We'd won the title eighteen times, United had done it seven and their last one was ages before. Never in a million years did I think that in just twenty years the bastards would have overtaken us.

The indefatigable Fergie

United's dominance of the competition was marked in the anniversary polls celebrating the milestone. In these, the Premier League's finest goal was deemed to have been scored by a United forward (Wayne Rooney's acrobatic overhead winner in the Manchester derby of 2011); its best player was a United stalwart (Ryan Giggs); and the all-time Premier League dream team had six United representatives in it (Peter Schmeichel, Gary Neville, Nemanja Vidić, Cristiano Ronaldo, Paul Scholes and Giggs joined Tony Adams and Thierry Henry of Arsenal, Ashley Cole of Arsenal and Chelsea, Liverpool's Stephen Gerrard and Alan Shearer of Southampton, Blackburn and Newcastle in the line-up selected by popular vote).

As was intended when those polls were commissioned, in newspaper columns, phone-ins and internet chatrooms the debate around the anniversary was extensive. Who had the best goal celebration? Who sported the worst haircut? Which team wore the least distinguished change strip? There is nothing football fans like more than categorizing and ranking their obsession.*

However, when it came to the answer to one crucial question there was no doubt, no debate, no argument. When asked which was the best-ever Premier League season, indeed which was the most riveting, diverting, extraordinary year of football in living memory, the answer was unfolding even as the candles were being lit on the

* The answers are: Eric Cantona after his goal against Sunderland in 1996; David James's matinée-idol sleek cut of 2006 that looked more like he had been sitting too long under a cow; and Arsenal's bruised-banana acid nightmare of a shirt in 1993.

twentieth birthday cake. As Michael Baxandall and his fellow Blues would concur, there had been nothing to touch 2011–12: 'After that, everything and anything else will be an anti-climax.'

In the anniversary year, as had become customary since 1992–93, driven by their astonishing manager Sir Alex Ferguson, Manchester United were in contention. Ferguson bestrode the Premier League era, he was unquestionably its most distinguished figure. His longevity alone brooked no argument as to his position of pre-eminence. Looking back to his twenty-one rival Premier League managers in 1992, twenty years on only the then QPR boss Gerry Francis was still working in the game (as first-team coach at Stoke). Nor was it just the likes of Southampton's Ian Branfoot or Tottenham's Doug Livermore whom the Scot had seen off. He had also accelerated the departure of managerial titans such as Kenny Dalglish, José Mourinho and Carlo Ancelotti from England. He had rescinded his own retirement in 2002 to re-emerge as focused as ever. Now in his seventies, his appetite for the competition showed no sign of being sated. He was still there, still florid of nose and short of fuse, still tapping at his watch on the touchline, still bitterly bringing up from the unfathomable depth of his elephantine memory a failure by a linesman to award his team a throw-in four years previously.

Andy Mitten, founding editor of the fanzine United We Stand, watched the man at work from the first season of the Premier League:

Ferguson's personality is multi-faceted. He's developed to survive in a world he's suspicious of, despite his success. To the cleaning ladies at United's training ground in Carrington, he's the greatest man alive. To the journalists who go to Carrington, he's anything but. Yet even they love him sometimes. He has far more friends than enemies. He talks like a socialist, yet acts like a capitalist. Says he understands fans, yet was compromised when the fans wanted his support. For the vast majority, he'll be judged by what his teams do. And his teams win top-level trophies with unmatched consistency in the history of world football.

282

Mitten is right. Whatever his flaws – bullying, avarice, a touchline view a Cyclops might consider a little narrow in its focus – Ferguson possesses the one characteristic that matters most in his profession: he knows how to build a football team. At a rough count, as the League's anniversary season began he was on his fifth United side. No one would claim the 2012 vintage a match for his coruscating 2008 Champions League-winning side, or the resilient double-winning tough guys of 1994, or those who scooped the treble in 1999. There were obvious weaknesses in goal (where the young Spaniard David De Gea spent the season learning to fill the gloves of Edwin van der Sar), at full-back (where Gary Neville was sorely missed), in central midfield (where their successors struggled to match Paul Scholes and Roy Keane), and up front (where the departure of Ronaldo to Real Madrid for a record £80 million in 2009 had been a defining moment).

But Ferguson had the knack – unseen since Bob Paisley was manager at Anfield – of making his team competitive even as he reconstructed it. You might be able to see the scaffolding, but the building inside was more than functional: Giggs, Rooney, Rio Ferdinand and Michael Carrick provided the foundation as the next generation of David De Gea, Phil Jones, Chris Smalling, Rafael da Silva, Javier Hernández and Danny Welbeck were blooded. Thus it was that his perspicacity and steel ensured a young, developing United would be scrapping and scrabbling for the twentieth-anniversary title. It would not be easy. In 2012 Ferguson faced what he himself described as the most significant challenge of his ever-lengthening tenure.

That challenge didn't come, as might have been predicted five years earlier, from Chelsea. At the Bridge, Roman Abramovich had continued his thus-far vain pursuit of an adequate replacement for the manager he had so hastily let go in 2007, José Mourinho. Many a club chairman might have thought the urbane, trophy-accumulating Italian Carlo Ancelotti worth keeping. After all, he had won Chelsea their first double in 2010. But Abramovich reckoned otherwise. By now, he presided over an institution that increasingly resembled a medieval fiefdom, full of barons jostling for favour by second-guessing the monarch's unspoken wishes. Or a Bond villain's lair, where the latest minion to fall short of the evil Master's expectations is dropped at the flick of a switch into a pool of ravening piranhas. Abramovich sacked Ancelotti in the summer of 2011 and brought in André Villas-Boas, a former member of Mourinho's backroom staff at the Bridge, a manager talked up as the next Portuguese 'Special One'. AVB, as he liked to be known, had shown his potential by winning the Europa League with Porto the previous summer.

As was growing ever more characteristic of Abramovich's reign, however, the appointment was given little time to prove its worth. By Christmas Chelsea were riven with internecine feuding. By February the senior players were said to be in open revolt, plotting against the manager's attempted reform of the squad. By March, AVB had been jettisoned. The former Chelsea player – and Villas-Boas's assistant – Roberto Di Matteo was given the task of righting the listing vessel. Something he accomplished with such aplomb that the Blues won both the FA Cup and Champions League under his stewardship (though even that towering achievement would not ultimately save him from the chop). But in the Premier League, Di Matteo could not bring about a dramatic enough turnaround; by the spring Chelsea were not even in the top four.

Challenge out of the Blue

Nor were Arsenal the force they had been. Arsène Wenger now found himself running a feeder club for others' ambitions, presiding over a talent drain that saw players schooled under his watchful eye – Ashley Cole, Cesc Fàbregas, Kolo Touré, Emmanuel Adebayor, Samir Nasri, Alex Song, even, eventually, the irreplaceable Robin van Persie – all heading for more lucrative employment.

While Newcastle offered a fleeting challenge, and Tottenham looked occasionally handsome under Harry Redknapp, the identity of the side who really threatened Ferguson's supremacy not only in the anniversary season, but into the future, would have astonished anyone looking forward in 1992. Back then, Michael Baxandall would never have imagined it could be his team, Manchester City.

I have known Bax since we were at school together. We have long stood on opposing sides of the Manchester football divide. And Bax really did stand there. When rival fans chant at City supporters in the modern era of Arab money 'where were you when you were shit?', I know where he was because he took great pride in telling me. He was at Doncaster and Shrewsbury supporting his team. He was there when City played in the division below Oldham, Stockport and Bury, a masochist to the Blue cause, taking perverse pride in their incompetence and seemingly limitless capacity for self-destruction. Not unsurprisingly, Bax's perspective changed when City suddenly found themselves projected by their Abu Dhabi paymasters into contention at the top of the game.

In May 2011, when they lifted the FA Cup at Wembley, Roberto Mancini's side had obliged United's followers to take down the countdown-clock banner at the Stretford End totting up the years since City had last won a trophy. But for the owner Sheikh Mansour, that represented no more than a start: it was the Premier League he felt would best announce his side's arrival to the watching world.

In order to land the trophy, Mancini spent the summer of 2011 strengthening what was already the most substantial squad in the country. By the simple expedient of offering the Frenchman £20,000 a week more than United had, he snaffled Nasri from under Ferguson's nose as the two jostled to sign him from Arsenal. To reinforce the notion that the Gunners were now City's feeder club, the full-back Gaël Clichy was signed too. But his real transfer coup was when he added to his already formidable forward line by paying Atletico Madrid £34 million for Diego Maradona's son-in-law Sergio Agüero, 'a proper player', according to Tyler. With his compatriot Carlos Tévez, the Argentine duo now offered the paciest front partnership in the division, a dynamic combination of pace, panache and perspiration.

From the early exchanges of the season it looked a masterstroke of a buy. City began the term by spanking five past Tottenham at White Hart Lane, and beating Villa, Blackburn and Swansea by four.

When they went to Old Trafford in late October, they had won seven and drawn one of their opening league games. Mourinho's tactic of turning the championship into a sprint was being borrowed unashamedly: City were hurtling over the horizon. Not content with entertaining on the pitch, they even had an in-house clown prince to provide after-hours pratfalls. Their live-wire Italian forward Mario Balotelli was fast becoming a one-man content provider for the League's soap opera diversions. He may subsequently have denied most of them ever happened, but his bizarre interventions into Manchester life – popping into a school one day to use the toilet, buying up a lorry-load of toys on a shopping trip for kitchenware, handing over his casino winnings of £14,000 to a homeless person – became legend. In the week of the derby, Balotelli surpassed even his high stan-dards of buffoonery by letting off fireworks in his own bathroom and setting fire to his house, an escapade that required the attendance of the fire brigade.

At Old Trafford on 23 October Balotelli continued to make head-lines – and this time at least in part for footballing reasons. When he opened the scoring in what was to prove a traumatic derby for United, he lifted his shirt to reveal the message 'Why Always Me?' em-blazoned on his undershirt. It was a phrase that was to be heard a lot that season.

With United weakened by the long-term injury to their defensive anchor Vidić, City now sent their followers into raptures. Balotelli scored again, and Edin Džeko struck twice before David Silva and Agüero ground salt into United's wounds with late strikes. Ferguson's disbelief was etched on his face. As United fans drifted towards the exits, dazed and confused, the band of travelling City followers joyously launched into their now-familiar celebratory dance. Turning their backs to the pitch, with arms round each other's shoulders, they bounced in unison. They named the jig in homage to the fans of the Polish club FC Poznań, whom they had seen perform this strange ritual during their recent Europa Cup run. And the 'Poznań' was to get plenty of outings in 2011–12.

The 6–1 defeat was not only the worst Ferguson had suffered in twenty-five years of managing United and the biggest home reverse the club had experienced since Huddersfield Town stuck six past them without reply in 1930, it had more immediate mathematical resonance. Those five more goals City scored that afternoon were to have a profound bearing on the season's final outcome.

There was just one consolation for United fans: at least the player they had once worshipped – and who, through his decision to join their rivals, had since become their pantomime villain – had not scored. Carlos Tévez was otherwise detained during the derby victory. He was playing golf in Argentina.

The Tévez furore

One of the certainties as the Premier League reached its twenties was that crisis was now a weekly event. The breathless reporting across hours of Sky Sports News and pages of tabloid and broadsheet, stoked up in internet blogs and fan chatrooms, transformed many a minor event at our leading clubs into a catastrophe. An altercation in training, an injudicious comment caught by the television cameras, a couple of unexpected defeats: these and similar storms in teacups were reported as calamities. It became part of a manager's working brief that he would be obliged at least once a season to find himself in the midst of a media-fomented whirlwind of crisis.

So it was that, when Tévez, sitting on the bench during City's un-successful Champions League game away at Bayern Munich on 27 September 2011, refused to follow his manager's instruction to warm up ready to go on the pitch, the incident was inflated into one that threatened to push the club to the brink of disaster.

True, the fevered temperature of the reporting was hardly helped by Roberto Mancini's post-match comments. Tévez, he thundered, was finished with City and would never play again for them while he was manager. As was demonstrated in many a touchline meltdown, Mancini's fuse was shorter even than his star player's. And it later transpired that Tévez – hardly the world's most gifted linguist (after five years in England he could barely order a pizza in the local tongue) – may have been the victim of a mistranslation.

Nevertheless, as he headed into temporary exile in Argentina, for football's crisis-promotion industry this was manna from heaven. As the forward skulked and sulked in Buenos Aires, telling anyone who would listen that he was finished with Mancini and would never ever go back to Manchester, a town he likened to the fourth circle of Hell, there was little sympathy for him in England. The newspapers were full of vituperative assaults on his reputation. He was portrayed as the worst exemplar of the mercenary footballer: selfish, venal and utterly unprepared to make personal sacrifice for the team effort. Never mind that this view didn't seem to tally with a player who invariably gave his all on the pitch, the character assassination was comprehensive.

And the crisis was assumed to signal the end of City's challenge. Many surmised that, since Mancini was clearly incapable of corralling his mercenaries, he was paying the inevitable price for trying to shortcut success with a cheque-book. It was a nice theory. Except that on the pitch, despite their diminutive scrabbler being AWOL in South America, City kept winning. Agüero more than adequately occupied the Tévez-sized hole. David Silva was majestic, Vincent Kompany and Joleon Lescott defensively solid, the young goalkeeper Joe Hart often spectacular. Mancini too showed shrewd judgment in a minor tactical switch that paid enormous dividends. For the anniversary season, he moved his defensive midfield titan Yaya Touré further forward, giving him licence to join in attacks. The giant Ivorian tore through rival defences, resembling more and more one of the stomping tree Ents in *The Lord of the Rings*, an unstoppable force of nature.

Their defeat by City, meanwhile, plunged United in turn into crisis. This was reckoned Ferguson's weakest ever Premier League side and its limitations were adduced as evidence of his declining powers. It was over, his detractors insisted, better he step aside now and let Mourinho or Pep Guardiola take over while there was still a chance for United to catch their local rivals.

Quieter voices pointed out that Ferguson and United had suffered similar autumnal embarrassment before. In the Premier League era they had lost 5–0 at Newcastle (20 October 1996), 6–3 at Southampton (26 October 1996) and 5–0 at Chelsea (3 October 1999). And what was common to those defeats? All three had occurred in seasons when United went on to triumph in the league.

United resurgent

Ferguson responded to calamity in his customary fashion: by presiding over immediate recovery. As City won, so did United. With both clubs ejected early from Europe, the Premier League became the priority. The two teams swapped the lead promiscuously. Until, in mid-March 2012, the labyrinthine plot of the 2011–12 Premier League season took what looked like its final twist.

City, with Touré absent throughout January on Africa Cup of Nations duty for Ivory Coast, Silva tiring and Balotelli growing ever more detached from any connection with reality, suffered defeats at Sunderland, Arsenal and Swansea. United on the other hand, bolstered by their hero Scholes who, Ferguson-like, had reversed his retirement the previous summer to return to the fray in January, kept winning. With only six games to go, the Reds had managed to fashion an eight-point lead at the top. And there was one thing everyone could agree on about Ferguson's United: in twenty years of Premier League dominance, his sides – whether classic Red or of more ordinary vintage – never relinquished their advantage at such a late point in the season. From here on in, they knew how to become champions.

With six games left, the joys of autumn were a distant memory for City. When they lost at Arsenal on 7 April and Balotelli was sent off, their defeat coincided with the disruption of the University Boat Race by a swimming protester. A visual mash-up of the two incidents immediately did the rounds on social networks. It showed the two rowing boats, with Balotelli's superimposed head apparently bobbing up between them. The headline read: 'Lone Nutter Wrecks Title Race.' There were not many, even in the Blue quarters of

Manchester, who did not believe that the satirical barb might prove horribly prescient.

Certainly Mancini himself gave the impression of having surrendered the title. At every press conference he claimed there was nothing he could do: United had won it. It was a counterintuitive strategy, one that went against the grain of standard managerial practice, which required the gaffer to rage against the dying of the light. But it was one which, arrived at after discussion with senior figures at City, was designed to defuse tension. It was one Mancini stuck to resolutely. Even after City hammered West Bromwich on the night of 11 April when United lost away at Wigan – something Ferguson had never done in his career – he still ceded eventual Premier League victory to his rival. It was too little too late, he insisted.

That night we reporters at the Etihad were left scratching our heads. Why was Mancini being so publicly defeatist? What was his purpose? Surely, with City but five points adrift and the two teams still to play each other for a second time, he should now acknowledge he had a chance. So intent were we on asking such questions, we barely noticed the identity of City's substitute: Carlos Tévez. Now that was a sight worthy of comment. The player who had vowed never to return to Manchester, whose manager had said would never play for the club again, trotted out onto the pitch midway through the second half. Ferguson called the move confirmation of City's desperation. Others saw it as evidence of Mancini's pragmatism. This was a manager prepared to do whatever was necessary to win the title, even to go back on his word. And, with Agüero suffering from injury and Balotelli threatening finally to lose all contact with planet Earth, how he needed Tévez to provide some impetus to the wilting Blue challenge. So, after City executives spent weeks reconciling the player and his shirty agent to the idea of a return to Manchester, Mancini gulped, took a deep breath and welcomed him back.

Not that it altered his public insistence about the title being United-bound. Even as the Reds drew at home with Everton on a night when the swag workers were selling 'Champions' souvenir scarves on the streets around Old Trafford, he kept up the rhetoric. Even as United threw away a 4–2 lead in an act of thoroughly un-Ferguson-like self-destruction, even as City returned to winning ways, he kept banging on about how United couldn't lose it. By now, reporters were beginning to see the tactic for what it was: a cunning piece of managerial subterfuge, whose aim was to relieve the pressure on his own players and heap it upon his rivals.

And so it was, when United came to the Etihad for the return derby, a 1–0 home victory in which the Reds did not achieve a single shot on target, the rollercoaster switchbacks of the season placed City once again on top of the table. Rarely in Ferguson's time had he sent out a team as unimaginative and static as on this occasion. His timidity got its just deserts. To the astonishment of City's followers, with the climax now in sight, as long as they won their remaining two games, with their superior goal difference, there was nothing United could do: there would be Blue ribbons on the trophy. What a turnaround that represented.

Nail-biting finale

After City duly won away at Newcastle and United beat Swansea, the final destination of the 2011–12 Premier League trophy came down to the last day of the season. How Sky relished a plot like this. It was the sort of climax of which their dreams – and thousands of new subscribers – are made. In Olympic year, with the Games due to electrify the country, here was an eloquent reminder of the reasons why Premier League football remained the sporting activity that kept most viewers glued to their televisions. What a conclusion had been delivered. The two Manchester clubs had the same number of points at the top of the table: if both won, it would be a matter of goal difference. And thanks to that thumping win over United in October, City's was notably superior.

While United were playing away at Sunderland, the Blues were at home to Queens Park Rangers, a side that had not won a single away game all season. The Londoners were a club in trouble, jostling frantically to avoid the drop. Despite millions invested by the Malaysian entrepreneur Tony Fernandes, they were just a point ahead of Bolton, looking primed for the final relegation place, a shapeless agglomeration of expensively assembled mercenaries. A bit like Manchester City, a cynic might say. Except with forty-nine fewer points.

In the press, in the pub and in the chat-rooms the assumption was that the game would be a formality: City could not fail. Two days before the dénouement, Samir Nasri received a text from his French international team-mate, United's Patrice Evra, congratulating him on winning the title.

'I sent him one back saying "Nothing's over yet",' Nasri recalls. 'But he said: "Stop it, if you don't beat QPR, if you're not champions this year then you'll never be".' The pair had made a bet. Whoever lost the title would clean the other's car. Evra's final text was: 'Anyway, you'll be champions and I'm gutted. I bought some Kärcher to wash your car with.'

Vicky Kloss, the club's director of communications, who sat on the committee that prepared the celebrations, spoke of her trepidation as the Blues organized their Premier League champions party:

I'm 42, which is about as old as you could be without ever having seen City win anything. As a fan, it was horrendous planning ahead. I was so worried we were tempting fate, at meetings I'd put my fingers in my ears and go 'I'm not listening'. But as a club we had to. United would have had a bus decorated and ready to go the same as us. You've got to be ready.

I was dispatched by the *Daily Telegraph* up to the Stadium of Light to report on United's game against Sunderland. Even as I drove up the A1 that morning, I assumed I was on my way to write an obituary of United's chances: we all knew there was no way they could win the title from here. Ferguson had – against all prediction – blown it. The weather seemed to reflect the shift in football's balance of power. After a week of rain, the sun was shining on Manchester; it was warm, a harbinger of the sporting season to come. In Sunderland, however, winter was refusing to relinquish its grip; a thick jumper, scarf and overcoat were required to counter the grey chill parked over Wearside. And over United's immediate prospects.

Still, whatever the rational assumption, there were City fans – Vicky Kloss among them – who couldn't dispel their worries. In part they agonized about the identity of their opponents. QPR were managed by Mark Hughes, the manager latterly spurned by City. He had at his disposal several City alumni, including Shaun Wright-Phillips, Nedum Onuoha and Joey Barton, the snarling former jailbird who had spent much of the season ludicrously attempting to reposition himself as football's lost intellectual by tweeting sayings from Aristotle, Virgil, Orwell and Nietzsche (the latter generally misspelt). There was ample motivation among their ranks for revenge.

Mainly, though, City fans worried about their own club's oft-demonstrated ability to snatch defeat from the jaws of victory. Martin Tyler had seen enough over the years to ensure he arrived at the Etihad Stadium not entirely convinced events were going to be straightforward. 'Take it out of context and it looked like a case of dotting the i's and crossing the t's,' he recalls. 'But it was never a formality. In my preparations for the game, I'd taken account of City's history. It had crossed my mind that I might have to say something if they messed it up.'

Oddly, given that he had been there at Wembley in 1999, Michael Baxandall did not share that worry. As he took up his position in the stands with his student son Jonathan, who arrived only just in time after being stuck in a vast traffic jam on the M56, he was convinced he was going to be rewarded for thirty-four years of pain:

My attitude was pretty much: this is done and dusted. I thought having bagged the FA Cup the previous season the old City, the one which consistently shot itself in the foot, had been consigned to history. No more City-itis. Ha! If only I'd known.

Mancini picked what was unquestionably his strongest line-up. Tévez and Agüero played together, ahead of a midfield of Touré, Silva, Nasri and Gareth Barry. Lescott and Kompany anchored the back four between Clichy and Pablo Zabaleta. Behind them all, Hart patrolled the goal-line. Of that line-up, Hughes had been responsible for recruiting five players, Mancini six. As for his own new side, Hughes went with an aggressive line-up, with Djibril Cissé, Bobby Zamora, Wright-Phillips and Jamie Mackie all expected to test Hart's reflexes. 'They were going to have a go,' recalls Tyler. 'You wouldn't expect a Mark Hughes team to do anything else.'

The action at both the Etihad and Stadium of Light started simultaneously. As was its custom, Sky had cameras at all the grounds for the final-day drama. The only logistical issue was where the trophy should be located. Clearly, it was more likely to be required in Manchester. But just in case there should be a final twist in the plot, a helicopter was chartered to whisk it up to Sunderland if things looked like they weren't obeying the expected script.

At City, there was a strange sense of lethargy in the air. The game got underway with the feel of a testimonial, rather than an impassioned tilt for the title. Beach-balls and inflatable bananas were lobbed around the crowd. Blue-and-white tickertape streamed down. QPR made little attempt to press. It was like the first exchanges of a boxing match, except without any punches being thrown. The nerves were evident everywhere, from stand to pitch.

The first twist in the plot came 23 minutes in, when Wayne Rooney scored at Sunderland. His celebration was muted, matter-of-fact. He clearly assumed it wasn't going to be enough. In the stands, I saw United followers barely watching events unfold in front of them. Instead, they pored over their mobiles, following the action at City on Twitter, wondering what was the significance of Rooney's strike. Catching the goal on his monitor, Tyler had a flicker of worry that he was in the wrong place. 'I thought of the huge operation Sky had constructed at the Etihad – the cameras, the whole operation,' he says. 'I just hoped we had all the same paraphernalia up at Sunderland.'

Those City fans spooked by Rooney's early contribution, however, did not have long to panic. On forty minutes Zabaleta galloped forward and shot powerfully at the QPR goal. Paddy Kenny, the Hoops' permanently dishevelled-looking keeper, misjudged the flight and allowed the ball to spin over his hands: 1–0. Though, as the half-time whistle sounded, it was not enough to unravel the knot of worry still occupying City stomachs. Jonathan Baxandall takes up the narrative:

Normally they have some naff half-time entertainment at the Etihad. There wasn't any laid on that day. We could have done with some. It was eerily quiet. Everyone was still very tense, me and dad especially. There was just this thought: it can always blow up at any point.

In the visitors' dressing room below where father and son were stationed, Hughes was delivering an impassioned half-time speech. He was pointing out to the QPR players that only victory would suffice for them. And that victory was not impossible, given the manner in which they had contained the home side in the first half. 'Just believe in yourselves and attack' was his final instruction as the players headed out for the second half. 'It's up to you now to make sure this isn't your last forty-five minutes in the Premier League.'

Within just three minutes of the restart, Hughes's rousing call to arms got its reward. Lescott, who up to that point had enjoyed an almost error-free season of authority and power, misdirected a headed clearance straight to Djibril Cissé, who, from no range at all, knocked the ball past Hart to equalize. It was a strike that sent the intrepid band of QPR followers, who had come north in the unhappy expectation of bearing witness to someone else's triumph, loopy. In Sunderland, the news spreading from mobile to mobile through the United section was greeted with no less enthusiasm. The Reds were back in the ascendant. 'At that point I was thinking of a different career elsewhere,' admits Hart. 'Maybe cricket or something.'

Six minutes later, however, QPR's chances of holding on to their spoils appeared to be holed below the waterline. Barton, demonstrating that his newly buffed image as cutting-edge contemporary thinker was about as substantial as his chances of becoming a UN peace envoy, tangled with Tévez on the edge of the QPR area. Television replays suggested that Tévez may have got his retaliation in first. But Barton, never slow to take offence, immediately exacerbated the hostility by thrusting his hand into the Argentine's face. On the QPR bench Hughes shook his head as referee Mike Dean pulled the red card from his pocket.

Barton, though, was not finished. As he went, he kneed Agüero in the thigh and aimed a headbutt at Kompany, quickly escalating things. A push-me-pull-you mêlée ensued, with the sweary, gobby Barton at its heart. He was lucky that Micah Richards, the City substitute, who had been an apprentice with him at the club, dashed from the bench to usher him from the field. Barton's motive for his sudden violence, he explained afterwards on his favoured media outlet Twitter, was to try to provoke one of the City players into a red-card response. It was, he said, the professional thing to do. Thank you, Einstein. As Barton headed to the dressing room, accompanied by whistles of derision from Blues supporters who used to value the spirit he brought to their team, it now seemed a straightforward task for City. Half an hour to go, against ten men, a bunch who hadn't won away from home: where was the problem? The problem was soon to make itself known.

With twenty minutes to go, QPR attacked down the left wing. Armand Traoré crossed from the left and Jamie Mackie came flying in with a forceful diving header. For a moment on television it seemed the ball had passed the post. But the look on Hart's face signalled it hadn't. Mackie didn't wait for confirmation, he charged round the back of the goal to celebrate with the now delirious QPR supporters. 'It had been such a tough season for us and the build-up to the game had been incredibly stressful,' Mackie remembers. 'I had hardly slept all week because of the pressure so when I scored and it looked like we were staying up, all the emotion just flooded out. We weren't thinking of City at that point. Although my brother is a United fan, so I did think I had done him a favour.'

Agüerooooooooo!

In Sunderland, the sudden roar from the United followers indicated to the players on the pitch that something momentous, something extraordinary had happened. In Manchester, the QPR section aside, the Etihad lapsed into stunned silence. 'We didn't talk,' says Michael Baxandall. 'Not a word. Though I didn't start panicking, I thought it was retrievable.'

Pretty quickly, though, every remaining vestige of optimism seemed to seep out of City hearts. On the pitch, the players looked spooked, panicking, unable to control the ball or the action. Passes went awry. Nerves seeped into every attempt to gain possession. It was as if some of the finest footballing talent on the planet had suddenly been infected by that scourge of City sides past: the Blue virus of failure. World-class footballers who had arrived in Manchester entirely unaware of the existence of Jamie Pollock, Gerard Wiekens and other forgotten bit-part players in City's miserable 1990s and early 2000s suddenly started playing like them. 'At 2–1 down I was thinking "this is done",' recalls Gareth Barry. 'I looked up and saw a helicopter. I wondered if it was the trophy being flown north. It was unbelievable.'

From his seat parallel to the edge of the QPR area Michael Baxandall reflected bleakly on the extent of the humiliation that seemed to be beckoning for the Blues and their followers:

As we got into the last ten minutes and didn't look like scoring, I turned to Jonathan and said: 'it's gone'. My dominant thought was the absolute tsunami of derision that was going to fall on our heads from United fans. Not so much that they'd won but the manner of our cock-up. It would have been so shattering a blow I don't think we'd have ever recovered from it. Not just blowing the title, but doing it in the last half-hour against a team of no-hopers. It was a new definition of the word misery.

In Sunderland, meanwhile, I watched as United fans prepared to dispatch their derision southwards. The tweets were being drafted, the text messages to Blue mates readied. I watched as Rooney took a corner right in front of the section where they were gathered. Dozens of them yelled the City score at him, excitedly telling him if he just hung on, then the title was his. He looked up at them slightly puzzled, as if uncertain how to respond to so ridiculous a proposition. But at that moment it really did seem as if United were destined to be champions again. Why always them?

As Rooney furrowed his brow, Mancini was turning purple with rage in his technical area. Never slow to demonstrate his annoyance at his players' shortcomings, he was spewing out invective, hurling abuse at them. Even as he yelled, however, he kept one hand in his jacket pocket. In there, he later revealed, was his rosary. Faith and football, he suggested, are natural bedfellows. You just have to believe. But however agitated he appeared, Mancini was sufficiently in control of his emotions to make two telling substitutions. Soon after QPR got their second he sent on Džeko. And with a couple of minutes of normal time remaining, he rolled his dice for the final time: he sent on the bonkers Balotelli to replace the tiring Tévez.

As ninety minutes ticked over at both stadiums, many of the City supporters did not see the board go up to signal that four minutes of time was to be added, mainly accrued by Barton's sending-off. The exodus that had begun with a trickle about ten minutes from full-time was now in full spate. This was not the usual dash for the car parks to beat the traffic. This was a flight from crushing, mind-numbing reality. Reporters in the press box recall those passing them looked ashen, shell-shocked, apparently shaken to the core.

But there was to be no speedy departure for them. Worried that if the gates were opened before the final whistle there might be a surge of ticketless fans desperate to watch the presentation of the trophy, the club officials had ordered that the exits should be kept locked. Thus it was that the huge concourse at the Etihad began to fill with those City fans who had given up hope (and their seats). They wandered around aimlessly, like the living dead, apparently broken by the events they had witnessed.

There are televisions in the Etihad concourse, relaying match highlights. But the fans milling about there didn't need pictures to tell them that something had happened when, moments into added time, a huge roar shook the stadium: Džeko had scored an equalizer. City still needed another goal, but they had given themselves a chance. The zombies of the concourse, suddenly revivified, rushed back to their seats. Jonathan Baxandall, though, who had stayed put in the stand, too distraught to move, wasn't so sure. 'I still had my head in my hands,' he remembers. 'I thought it might just prove to be a cruel twist, to rub yet more salt in our wounds.'

By now, the games elsewhere had concluded. The QPR bench learned that Bolton had lost at Stoke, so their team would avoid relegation whatever the result. They tried to communicate the news to their players, but the noise prevented them being heard by anyone except those closest to the touchline. In Sunderland, too, the game was over. United had won 1–0. Their players remained on the pitch, unsure what the news was from the Etihad. They looked to Ferguson for information, and he in turn scoured the crowd and the press box for clues. 'We went to a split screen to show the United players waiting on the pitch,' says Tyler of the Sky coverage that was beamed around the globe. 'Then the director switched to single-screen back at the Etihad at the exact moment Balotelli received the ball on the edge of the area. You couldn't have post-produced it better.'

At that point, a long ball from out of defence by the substitute Nigel de Jong had landed at Balotelli's feet, via a flick from Agüero. Attempting to turn, Balotelli slipped and appeared to have lost it. But he stuck out a leg and thrust the ball forward to Agüero. The Argentine pushed it on towards goal, trying to evade as he went a lunge from QPR's Taye Taiwo, which caught him on the knee. But he wobbled on. For a split second the stadium held its breath. And up in the television gantry, Tyler gathered his: 'That moment he took a touch gave me the time to get air into my lungs. I knew he wasn't going to go down. I knew he'd want this. What followed wasn't planned. It was a gut reaction.'

And what followed was this: as the City man blasted the ball past Kenny and ran, delirious, across the pitch, whipping his shirt above his head, the crowd behind him doing as close an impression of collective apoplexy as you could ever hope to see, Tyler opened his throat and roared out his name, adding about twenty extra O's to its end. 'Agüeroooooooo!' he yelled, a cry that was to become the ring tone on thousands of City fans' phones. There was nothing else that would have been appropriate. Nothing else that could have summed up the adrenalin rush of the moment. In the days and weeks to come, the City megastore was to run out of O's as fans bought shirts specially printed with all those extra vowels in the Argentinian's name.

Martin Tyler describes the aftermath of Sergio Agüero's Premier League-winning strike:

> Then when I'd said it I let the pictures take over. They spoke far more powerfully than I ever could. The shot of Joe Hart running with his arms spread and having to look over his shoulder to check whether what had happened really had happened: you couldn't better that. Then I said something like: 'drink this in you will never see anything like it again'. And I stand by those words. It felt epochal. I'd been there really all the way through the Premier League. From the first kick of a game between Leeds and Wimbledon to this, the title won with the last kick of the last game of the twentieth season. I don't mind admitting, when we finished, there were tears in my eyes. Not because I'm a City fan, I'm not. But because it was an epic moment and I had something to do with it. It moved me to the core.

If Tyler shed a tear, he was not the only one. As soon as he scored, Agüero was in floods. So were Nasri and Džeko. According to the skipper Kompany, most of his team-mates were too. Everywhere emotions were strained by what had just taken place. Watching from the Sky Sports News studio, with his headphones on, the former Arsenal player Paul Merson shrieked his description of what was unfolding at the anchorman Jeff Stelling. 'They're all cuddling each other,' he yelled of the players' celebrations on the Etihad pitch. 'They've got love bites and everything, Jeff.'

And in the stands: well, it got teary. Right at the last, after seeming to have thrown it all away, City had won the title. What else could they do but scream their happiness. 'In all my time in football I've never heard a noise like it,' says Mark Hughes of the uproar that greeted Agüero's goal. 'It hurt my ears.'

As the reality of City's achievement sank in, one observer described the Etihad as resembling a Billy Graham event, the gangways packed with fans throwing themselves to the floor as if what they had witnessed was a religious happening, an epiphany. Pandemonium continued, drowning out the final whistle which had sounded as soon as QPR kicked off after Agüero's goal. The last kick of the last game: no title race in Premier League history had been so prolonged. 'It was as well it fell to Agüero, he was one of the few I've seen play for City who would have scored,' reckons Michael Baxandall. 'Francis Lee would have finished like that. I just thank God it wasn't Darius Vassell. It showed how far we've come. It's only a few years since we regarded Georgios Samaras as a star striker.'

As the result from Manchester was confirmed on the Stadium of Light's giant screen, Ferguson was notably dignified in his response to the sudden confirmation that he had indeed lost the title in what must now be described as 'Mancini Time'. He merely shrugged, clapped his hands together and shepherded his players to go and acknowledge the travelling supporters.

'It's a cruel way [to lose], but we've experienced many ups and downs,' he said afterwards. 'We've won the title three times on the last day. Congratulations to our neighbours. But these young players will be around in five, six, seven years' time. The history of our club stands us aside, we don't have to worry. It will take them [City] a century to get to our level.'

The previous season when United visited Sunderland there was a burst pipe above the visitors' dressing room and their pricey suits were ruined by a sewage leak. This time the shower of ordure falling on them was entirely metaphorical. But it will have felt far worse. 'We thought we'd done it,' says Phil Jones. 'Then we hadn't – it was crazy. You went from high to low in the space of about ten seconds. I remember the manager telling us after the game: "always remember this experience and don't let it happen again".'

At City, the joy was untrammelled. The players were presented with the Premier League trophy by Tony Book, the last City captain to lift the championship. Then, to huge applause, up on the stadium's giant screen the figure 34 appeared, in the same typeface that had been used on the hated Old Trafford banner. As the fans watched, the numbers span back to nought. A clever, funny little visual touch. 'Umbro had approached us with that idea after the FA Cup win the season before,' explains Vicky Kloss. 'But to me it seemed too early. I didn't want it to appear as if we were crowing prematurely. This seemed right. Especially after the way it was won.'

And the way it was won cheered the heart of every Blue. Even David Conn, a man who worries incessantly about the financial imbalances distorting the values of the game he loves. 'In a sense the ending made it seem like City – mad old City – had won the trophy,' he says. 'It wasn't Abu Dhabi United.' Michael Baxandall agrees: 'The only difficult thing is to come up with superlatives,' he says. 'City being City couldn't just win it at a canter. We couldn't go out there and spank QPR. Oh no. There had to be a walk-on part for the ghost of that hapless-shoot-yourself-in-the-foot-Theatre-of-Base-Comedy City of old. My dad always used to say that 2–0 up just about puts City on equal terms.'

The players, understandably, had a somewhat different take on the last-ditch nature of their victory. Joleon Lescott summed up the prevailing mood:

Everybody kind of looked into themselves, realizing it was a major achievement but knowing how close it had been to disaster. How could we have looked ourselves in the mirror if we'd chucked it all away? United had done everything in their power to lose it but we'd given them chance after chance. I never want to win anything in that way again. It was just too mentally exhausting.

As the fans made their way out of the stadium into Manchester to drink the town dry, Mancini and Kompany took the trophy into the press room, to show it off to those who had chronicled the journey to its final capture. Mancini did not come across as extravagantly happy. A shrewd politician, he was aware that the victory represented substantial leverage to secure his position at the club. His first instinct was to insist he needed the resources to go and strengthen his squad. As Ferguson had done time and again in championship-winning circumstance, he set his sights on greater future achievement even as the success of the present was being celebrated.

Meanwhile, the Premier League chief executive Richard Scudamore was wandering around the Etihad's corporate hospitality sections wearing a grin the width of the M56. Not because he supports City (well, not *that* City, he is a Bristol City fan), but because – with the new television deal yet to be finalized – he knew that the events that had just unfolded provided the best possible showcase for his product. He had on his hands something that would be talked about for years. Never mind the Olympics that were just around the corner, this proved that the Premier League remained the best sporting show in town.

The ever-growing popularity of the product was emphasized by Martin Tyler's description of the match's climax immediately assuming the status of commentary-box classic:

People still come up to me and tell me what they were doing when they heard my commentary. They tell me it was historic. It wasn't. Sergio Agüero was historic. I was just a witness to extraordinary

303

events. My contribution was probably better summed up by Brian McDermott [the then Reading manager]. I bumped into him a few weeks after the game and he congratulated me on being the soundtrack of history. I said it wasn't really that big a deal. He said, 'it was, you could have fucked it up.' And I thought, yeah, that wouldn't make the worst epitaph: 'Martin Tyler, the man who saw history and didn't fuck it up'.

But it was in Sunderland, 150 miles to the north, just as the City celebrations were going into overdrive, that I saw something which told me that whatever the Premier League has done to the game in this country, some things will never change. As the news filtered through of City's preposterous turnaround, United's players were wandering about the pitch wearing the shocked expressions of mugging victims. Jones's face in particular would have served as a perfect template for any actor cast in a movie in which they are obliged to look as if they have just seen a ghost.

And in the home stands, as one, those Sunderland supporters who had stayed on turned their backs to the pitch, linked arms and pointedly did the Poznań. As they did so, it was obvious from those who glanced back over their shoulder to check out the reaction that they were having a great time. Up there in the stands, bouncing away, the locals were laughing loud and long at the misery of their crestfallen visitors. The very bizarreness of celebrating the success of a team you don't support in a match you had not witnessed after your own team has just lost summed up this most bonkers of football seasons. It also demonstrated something more significant: even at a time when money talks louder than ever in English football, some traditions linger on. And at the heart of our game there remains nothing a fan enjoys more than revelling in their rivals' discomfort.

● ● ● ● ●

Barclays Premier League

Etihad Stadium, Manchester

Sunday 13 May 2012

Manchester City 3 – 2 Queens Park Rangers

City scorers: Pablo Zabaleta 39; Edin Džeko 90; Sergio Agüero 90+4

QPR scorers: Djibril Cissé 48; Jamie Mackie 66

Attendance: 47,435

Referee: Mike Dean

Teams:

Manchester City (4-2-3-1):

Joe Hart; Pablo Zabaleta, Joleon Lescott, Vincent Kompany, Gaël Clichy; Gareth Barry (Edin Džeko 69), Yaya Touré (Nigel de Jong 44); Samir Nasri, David Silva, Carlos Tévez (Mario Balotelli 75); Sergio Agüero

Subs not used: Costel Pantilimon, James Milner, Micah Richards, Alexander Kolarov

QPR (4-3-3):

Paddy Kenny; Taye Taiwo, Clint Hill, Anton Ferdinand, Nedum Onuoha; Joey Barton, Shaun Derry, Shaun Wright-Phillips; Djibril Cissé (Armand Traoré 59), Bobby Zamora (Jay Bothroyd 76), Jamie Mackie

Subs not used: Radek Černý, Danny Gabbidon, Adel Taarabt, D.J. Campbell, Ákos Buzsáky

Postscript

To be continued...

Manchester United v. Hull City

Old Trafford Stadium, Manchester

Tuesday 6 May 2014

Two years on from that hazy, crazy, blue-tinged spring afternoon in 2012, everything had changed. Well, maybe not everything: on 11 May 2014, Manchester City were again crowned Premier League champions, albeit this time lifting the trophy in a smoother, altogether less fraught manner than had been the case in 2012, winning their last half dozen matches to stride confidently across the line. The table never lies: City were worthy champions, scoring more than a century of league goals as they demolished Premier League defences with aplomb.

The day after their triumph, Manchester city centre was once more awash with sky blue. The local swag workers, used to churning out their tat in red, simply changed the dye in their presses and, loading up their trollies, offered up a travelling souk of sky-blue t-shirts, flags and hats all announcing that City were champions of Manchester, champions of England. Police reckoned there were up to 40,000 people on the city centre streets, cheering as an open-top bus, filled with their heroes, paraded the trophy. Yaya Touré, the most complete midfielder in England, a player whose power and strength had driven City to the title, was up there on the top deck, filming the joyous scenes on his mobile. Alongside him were David Silva and the oddly coiffured Sergio Agüero, the scheming heart of City's endeavour. Not to mention Vincent Kompany, the elegant captain, whose affection for his adopted club shone out in his goal celebration in the final game of the season. When he scored against West Ham finally to secure the mathematics of victory, the grin the Belgian wore as he slid across the Etihad turf could have lit up the stadium for a month. This, evidently, was a man who loved his work.

Decorated with the single word 'together' (as a description for the concord of supporters, team and management, at City they prefer that word to its synonym, united), the bus drove slowly along the streets as the young, the old and an awful lot in between belted out their affection. 'We're not really here,' they chanted, a reminder of the days – not so long ago – when they used to sing their way through the embarrassment of playing league games at Gillingham, Preston and Tranmere.

In front of the spectacular town hall that is a monument to Manchester's Victorian self-confidence, thousands had gathered in a huge smile of victory. They were there to celebrate the city's twenty-first century symbol of prominence, its victorious football team. Manchester city centre appeared to be the happiest place in England; even if two Premier League titles were the sum total of what Sheikh Mansour's money had bought, it looked to have been a worthy investment. Here was eloquent proof of the power of football to put a spring in the collective step. If you could have bottled the feel-good frenzy that reigned in Manchester that day, the makers of Prozac would have been out of business within a year.

But for all the fun that everyone was having, this time didn't feel quite so epochal as two years before. The fans looked less astonish-ed, less as though they had all simultaneously learned that their numbers had come up in the lottery. In 2012, the streets around Albert Hall resembled the aftermath of a particularly extravagant all-nighter. People were wandering around in an advanced state of shock, as if this sort of thing didn't happen to people like them. And in a sense it didn't. Central Manchester had spent most of the previous twenty-five years turning red in the springtime, in celebration of the tottering Himalaya of trophies accumulated at Old Trafford. Back in 2012, thousands of City fans who had never known what it was like to celebrate a championship victory had turned out, not wholly sure of the routine. They mingled with those of grey and thinning thatch who were around the last time it had happened back in 1968, but were finding it increasingly hard as the years passed to recall the details.

Two years on, the atmosphere was different. It would be wrong to use the word routine, but this time triumph was less extravagantly received. City had changed, they were now the sort of club programmed to be up there, expected to be competing, likely candidates for possession of large shiny objects come the season's end. With all that investment, with the hosepipe of cash gushing constant readies from under desert sands, it would have been odd if they weren't. The Sheikh had not invested such sums to be an also-ran. He hadn't put £150 million into transforming 25 acres of derelict east Manchester into the swanky new training centre known as the Etihad Campus in order to see his team scrape into the Europa League. City were now set up to win. City-itis had been expunged from the club's core. They didn't do failure any more.

But the oddest thing about 2014, the thing that so distinguished it in City minds from the breathless win of 2012, was the nature of the competition. That it didn't come from their suddenly very quiet neighbours was so amazing it almost – almost – stilled the mockery. Manchester United finished the season in seventh place, with an interim manager and a record of league defeats at Old Trafford worse than any season since they were relegated from the top flight in ignominy in 1973. Imagine that for a moment. For the first time in twenty-four years, United were not in contention for a trophy at the end of the season. For the entire lifetime of the four City-supporting lads making their way down Market Street to Albert Square dressed for the occasion in full Arab costume in homage to their club's owner, United had been the dominant force in town. It was them winning the trophies, it was their smug fans taking the mickey at the season's end, it was them the rest of the world was referring to when they used the single word Manchester to talk about a football club.

Now they were nowhere in the Premier League standings, finishing not just behind City, but lower than Spurs and Everton; so far off the pace, in fact, that the United Megastore could have done a good line in branded binoculars to spot the rest heading over the horizon. That had not happened since before Premier League was ripped from the reluctant donor body of the Football League. This was historic failure.

And the incredible thing was the speed of Red decline. Twelve months previously, with an almost identical squad, they had won the title. On 22 April 2013, four matches from the end of the season following City's first win, United had been crowned champions when they beat Aston Villa at Old Trafford. City had come a distant second, only fleetingly suggesting they would defend their hard-won title with anything other than a whimper. It was United's twentieth championship win, their thirteenth since the Premier League had been inaugurated.

The truth – as we were rapidly to discover – was that this was a victory wholly engineered by their manager. United's success in 2013, as it had been so often in the past, was rooted in Sir Alex Ferguson's indomitable will. The triumph of 2013 represented the fifth time he had won back the Premier League title from a rival widely reckoned to be in possession of a stronger hand. Kenny Dalglish at Blackburn, Arsène Wenger at Arsenal, José Mourinho and Carlo Ancelotti at Chelsea and now Roberto Mancini at City, all had seen their apparent domination undermined. On every occasion, a change in the pecking order had been predicted and then immediately proved a will-o'-the-wisp. On every occasion Ferguson soon restored the status quo.

As he conceded the title in the spring of 2013, Mancini admitted that the difference between his side and Ferguson's was one of attitude. Like for like, the Blues were as good as the Reds. Indeed, they had enjoyed a superior record in the derby encounters of late; out of the last four, City had won three. But they had signally failed to convert temporary superiority into long-term domination. United, on the other hand, had a doughty will at their heart that brooked no challenge. And that came from the manager. When faced with an obstacle, he was utterly focused in his urge to navigate round it. Or better still, plough straight over the top of it.

Phil Jones's slack-jawed gurn of distress on the pitch at the Stadium of Light the previous May might have been mocked by City fans, but for Ferguson it was the very source of renewal. He had seen in his young player's abject expression of disappointment the roots of a new cause. On the coach back from Sunderland to Manchester, somewhere on the A19 south of Thirsk, even as City's representatives were whooping in triumph at the Etihad, Ferguson and his players took a vow of vengeance. He told them to remember how awful they felt and to make sure they never felt like that again. Forget the old adage about revenge being a dish best served cold: Sir Alex and his team were intent on serving it up piping-hot and wolfing it down with gusto.

And so it came to pass. United restored the old order with exemplary dispatch. In May 2012, we were witness to the most delayed finish to a season in Premier League history. It was not over until the third minute of added time in the final game. A year on, and things were done and dusted when United were declared champions with twelve points still to be played for. Though there were plenty who suggested the competition was over much earlier than that. There is a logic to the argument that it was finished on 12 August 2012, at the precise moment when Arsenal's prolific striker Robin van Persie decided to sign for Manchester United rather than Manchester City.

The summer after his league win, Mancini tried to sign van Persie. The player's contract had come to an end at Arsenal and it was known that he was seeking a new employer more likely to provide him with something requiring silver polish. When Arsenal signed Sol Campbell from Tottenham in 2001 they had been a club that offered the opportunity to fulfil ambition. Eight years on from the Invincibles, constrained by the economic exigencies of trying to pay for the magnificent Emirates stadium, now they merely provided the raw material for others to accumulate trophies. Samir Nasri, Gaël Clichy, Kolo Touré, Cesc Fàbregas, Alex Song and now the finest of them all, van Persie: they all concluded that success would only be achieved elsewhere. And success is ultimately what a modern player – no less than his historic counterpart – craves. Sure, the money is nice. Yes, the material goods provide pleasant consolation. But, as competitive beasts, what they seek above all is unimpeachable proof that they are better than their peers. After he left north London, Ashley Cole won eight trophies with Chelsea over a nine year period in which Arsenal won nothing at all (until they finally picked up the FA Cup in May 2014): that is the difference.

Mancini told the Dutchman that he would win with City and pick up a weekly cheque of some £300,000 for his efforts. But van Persie was persuaded by Ferguson that he had more chance of accumulating prizes at Old Trafford. 'The little boy within him,' he claimed, had told him to sign for United. It was the veteran manager's single most vital piece of persuasion since he talked Eric Cantona out of quitting the game back in the summer of 1995.

Ferguson wanted van Persie because he had identified precisely where he had lost out the previous season: never again would he allow his team to be beaten on goal difference. Van Persie – driven by a raging personal thirst for something to put in his trophy cabinet – ensured his wish would come true. It was his strikes that meant games that might have been previously drawn were won. United's title-winning haul of victories was accrued through his wand-like left foot.

Van Persie was not the first to have made the difference in Sir Alex Ferguson's astonishing accrual of thirteen Premier League titles. Cantona's sense of certainty won it for him in 1993 and 1996. The former United chairman Martin Edwards reckons the supreme midfield scheming of Paul Scholes was largely responsible for landing the 2003 trophy. Cristiano Ronaldo was the beating heart of the wins in 2008 and 2009. But van Persie's role in turning the second best in the country in 2012 into the runaway champions of 2013 cannot be overstated.

'He has made a fantastic contribution, in terms of impact he has made as big as I can imagine,' said Ferguson after the title had been achieved. 'We had an expectation of him. His performances last year were sensational. Arsène [Wenger] said to me he's a better player than you think. I think he was right.' The simple fact is, if City had signed van Persie, Mancini might well have celebrated his second Premier League title. Instead Ferguson snaffled the prize, maintaining his tradition of not only strengthening his own squad, but simultaneously diminishing that of a rival – and the purchase of van Persie fundamentally emasculated Arsenal. Meanwhile the only forward Mancini signed was Scott Sinclair from Swansea. Worse, in the January transfer window City lost Mario Balotelli, who headed back to Milan after testing his manager's patience once too often. It meant that, while United returned to their old habit of grinding out victories whatever the status of the opponent, the Italian ended up watching far too many drawn games. Head to head his team may have been United's equal, perhaps on paper their better. But the Premier League has never been a competition that pays much heed to such concerns. All that matters is the number of points accrued.

Just as it seemed the old order had been re-established in Manchester and beyond in the spring of 2013, came news that changed everything. It had to happen one day, but nobody was expecting the story that appeared on the front page of the *Daily Telegraph* sports section on Wednesday 8 May 2013. Indeed Pat Crerand, the former United stalwart-turned-commentator for the club's in-house television station, was so convinced that reporter Mark Ogden's scoop was just tittle-tattle, he went on the radio accusing the paper of making the tale up in order to sell more copies. 'Rubbish, nonsense, there's not a jot of truth in it,' he fumed. Ten minutes after his rant was broadcast, word came from Manchester United that Ogden, as he invariably does, had delivered the truth: Sir Alex Ferguson was to retire with immediate effect.

Mind, Crerand can be forgiven for his certainty. Ferguson had long seemed indestructible, the one fixed point around which the British football world had spun for more than twenty-five years. But it was clear he was not, after all, here forever. At seventy-one, Ferguson faced a hip operation. He had always insisted only a diminution in his fearsome good health would make him consider giving up. Now it had come, together with an urgent requirement to spend more time with his wife, who had recently lost her sister. Suddenly and without warning, British football's most distinguished figure was departing the scene.

He had announced his retirement once before: in 2001 he said he would go at the end of the season. But what was intended as a triumphal retreat had proved to be – he said later – an 'absolute disaster'. The air of uncertainty had undermined the team as power bases jostled for position ahead of the appointment of a new boss. After he reneged on his decision to go in February 2002, and stayed on for more than another decade, he said the next time he retired it would be without public notice, without fanfare, to his own timetable.

Never mind that in his programme notes published just three days before his 2013 retirement announcement he insisted he was 'going nowhere', looking back across the season there were clues his mind had been made up to go long before the official announcement of his departure. His hangdog demeanour after United were knocked out of the Champions League by Real Madrid – and he had been comprehensively out-thought by José Mourinho – seemed at the time to be overly disappointed. In retrospect it was clear: Ferguson knew he had just blown his last chance to win the trophy he most coveted. Furthermore, the announcement in March that David Gill was to step down as United's chief executive signalled that an end was coming for the most successful double act in Premier League history. It turned out that both men were heading for the exit.

Most of all, though, the evidence was there in the signing of van Persie. In the past Ferguson had always made his biggest buys for the future: Wayne Rooney, Cristiano Ronaldo, Rio Ferdinand were all young players with their best years ahead of them when he brought them to United. Aged twenty-nine when he put pen to paper, the Dutchman was urgently needed in the present. For Ferguson there was not much future left. He needed his title back.

When it finally came, Ferguson's departure was marked appropriately. Newspapers produced souvenir pull-outs, the radio airwaves filled with eulogies, the academic Richard Dawkins complained that British television was fixated with a 'mere' football manager to the detriment of reporting the world's important news. Then he turned to Al Jazeera and discovered that the Qatar-based channel too was filled with retrospectives of the great man's career. And rightly so. Ferguson has a legitimate claim to be recognized as the most successful individual in British public life in the twenty-first century. Lord Coe enjoyed a magnificent year in 2012, Sir Nicholas Hytner marked an unsurpassed decade in charge of the National Theatre, but Ferguson stayed at the top of a profession more generally characterized by employers' impatience for more than a quarter of a century.

At the last home game against Swansea, the guard of honour, the tearful interviews, the Sinatra tunes booming from the public-address system indicated the esteem in which he was held. Twenty-six years he had ruthlessly held sway at Old Trafford, tolerating no opposition as he deposited thirty-eight trophies in the club museum. It was a record of longevity and achievement unparalleled in the game. Richard Scudamore, the chief executive of the Premier League, got it right when he said that Ferguson 'more than any other figure contributed to the growth and success of the Premier League'.

After that game, as the crowd stayed to acknowledge the success Ferguson had brought into their lives, he addressed them. With the Manchester rain falling in a neat meteorological metaphor of the moment, he stood in the centre circle surveying the stadium his success had constructed. As he spoke, one remark stood out: 'Your job,' he told the fans, 'is to support the new manager.'

The manager who is privileged to choose the time of his own departure is a rarity in football. A couple of weeks after Ferguson announced his retirement, Roberto Mancini was hurried out of the Etihad with a dispatch that redefined the term brutal. Paying the price for failing to retain the title and losing the FA Cup final, Mancini was quickly snapped up by the Turkish side Galatasaray. His place at City was taken by the altogether less abrasive figure of the former Villarreal, Real Madrid and Malaga manager Manuel Pellegrini.

The Chilean was known in Spanish football as 'The Engineer', not just because he had an engineering degree, but for the smooth manner with which he constructed teams. There was much talk of 'projects' at his unveiling. Much talk of 'beautiful moments' ahead.

Ferguson, meanwhile, was not only gifted his choice of exit date, he was handed the unique distinction of choosing his own successor. It was he – and he alone – who would decide who replaced him in the technical area at Old Trafford, who it was who would be standing there opposite the words 'Sir Alex Ferguson' written in ten-foot-high letters across the roof of the north stand.

If it seems extraordinary that a business of the scale of Manchester United would recruit its single most important executive on the say-so of its outgoing boss, if no other company of such size would select a man with so little due diligence or proper research, it is worth recalling what a figure Ferguson cut in the corridors of Old Trafford. After accumulating thirty-eight trophies in twenty-six years, he bestrode the place; it was built in his own image. His word was law. The owning Glazer family deferred entirely – and rightly – to him on football matters. Besides, they found him physically and psychologically intimidating. In truth, what he said had long been the only thing that mattered in M16.

So it was that, despite José Mourinho making an almost comical public pitch for the job with an obsequious show of deference ahead of their Champions League quarter-final, Ferguson dismissed him as a candidate. He considered Mourinho too sizeable an ego, too fractious a political animal, too divisive a figure behind the scenes. He wanted someone more likely to maintain the systems he had established. He wanted someone not prone to rock the boat. He wanted someone in his own image. He tried for Pep Guardiola. But the former Barca man, then taking a sabbatical in New York, had not been able to penetrate Ferguson's Glaswegian brogue when the pair met for lunch in a Manhattan diner, so the opportunity was missed. Ferguson thought, too, about the smooth and charming Carlo Ancelotti. But in the end, his gaze landed on the candidate he felt was most appropriate. He wanted David Moyes, the pragmatic Scot who had efficiently managed Everton for eleven seasons.

There was a nice dynastic circularity to the idea: Moyes was cut from the same cloth as Ferguson; so similar were their backgrounds they had both played for the same Glasgow youth team, under the same coach, albeit a generation apart. True, in his time on Merseyside, Moyes had never won anything, nor had he demonstrated an attacking instinct of the sort demanded by United tradition. But Ferguson believed his favoured candidate had been constricted by monetary circumstance at Goodison. Given time – as Ferguson himself had been – at Old Trafford, he would grow into the role. And Ferguson would be around to ensure time would be given. There was symbolic intent in the six-year contract Moyes was handed.

This appeared to be proper succession planning in action; there was a real romance about the possibilities inherent in Moyes's appointment. Sadly, it turned out to be Ferguson's least successful piece of recruitment in his time at Old Trafford. And that includes the signing of Ralph Milne in 1988 and Eric Djemba-Djemba in 2003. The choice quickly turned into an exercise in misery, not least for Moyes himself.

A conspiracy theory began to circulate that Ferguson had chosen Moyes simply in order to protect his own standing. What better way, the theory posited, to cement a legacy than to promote someone who was incapable of challenging your record. But that belied Ferguson's clear determination to see Moyes succeed. He did his best to clear the way for the new man, removing himself immediately from day-to-day activity at Old Trafford, anxious that his shadow would not smother his successor, as Sir Matt Busby's had forty-four years before. There was a huge amount of goodwill among United followers towards Fergie's choice. A banner was installed in the Stretford End to mark Moyes's arrival. It read: 'The Chosen One', a nice verbal reminder of his place in the succession.

And Moyes tried to reciprocate. When Ferguson was interviewed on stage at the Lowry Centre in Salford to promote his autobiography a couple of months after Moyes's appointment, I sat behind the new man in the stalls. He was more than assiduous in his glad-handing. He stayed behind after the show for an age communing with the fans, signing autographs, posing for pictures, telling everyone that he 'would do his best' to maintain the Ferguson way. But in truth, even as he stood there shaking hands and grinning for the selfies, Moyes looked to be a man out of his comfort zone. He didn't look like someone who thought he belonged.

The reality was that Moyes had been consumed by doubt from the very moment he was appointed. It was back in March 2013 – long before even Mark Ogden was aware of what was happening – that the call came. It was Moyes's day off and he was out shopping with his wife when Ferguson rang him on his mobile. Fergie asked if he was free, and if so could he come round immediately. Moyes told his wife it was 'the boss' on the phone and he had to go. He thought the United manager was going to make a bid for one of his Everton players, probably the brilliant left-back Leighton Baines. He was a little nervous that he was so casually dressed. 'Don't worry,' his wife told him. 'You'll be fine.' He arrived at Ferguson's Macclesfield home to be greeted by the great man with the simple words: 'I'm retiring. And you are the next manager of Manchester United.'

Moyes remembers it took him a couple of moments to recover the power of speech. He never thought he had a chance of landing the biggest job in British football. He never applied for the position. He was not even asked if he wanted it. He was simply told he was the man. For a few seconds he stood in Ferguson's study blinking in astonishment that it had happened to him. Ferguson, however, was insistent. Be yourself, he told his fellow Glaswegian. Trust those instincts that stood you in such good stead at Everton. You'll be fine.

But Moyes was almost immediately overwhelmed by the scale of his new job. On United's pre-season tour of Australia, he suggested to the team that they take a walk together along the beach. He had done this when in Sydney with Everton. It had been a terrific bonding exercise on Bondi, relaxed and unobtrusive. But while the Everton players had been able to walk along the sand almost unnoticed, the moment United's world-renowned crew stepped on to the seafront, they were mobbed. Immediately a huge crowd gathered round them. The press of sightseers wasn't hostile, but as they were getting up close and very personal, Moyes began to panic. Sweating and hugely uncomfortable in the growing human swell, he hurried his players into a beach-front bar, where they were locked in a back room until a security party could be summoned to escort them back to their bus. When he emerged, Moyes looked shell-shocked: he simply had no idea of the scale of United.

And this was his problem from the start: the job he had never sought, the job that had been thrust upon him, was simply too big for him. Following Ferguson's advice, he tried to do things his way. He dispensed with Ferguson's back-room staff and brought in his own trusted lieutenants from Goodison. But the players were used to the skills-based training methodologies of René Meulensteen and Mike Phelan. They had won trophies by the score following their light-touch regimen. Steve Round and Jimmy Lumsden, however, had won nothing, yet here they were introducing dull, repetitive, fitness-oriented drills which seemed designed to stunt creativity. When Moyes suggested to Rio Ferdinand that he study a video of Everton's Phil Jagielka to see how to defend a corner, the veteran centre-back asked a pertinent question: 'so what has he ever won?' Respect was not going to be easily won.

That summer of 2013, every pundit was in agreement: the United board needed to make a marquee signing to reinforce Moyes's appointment. But Gill had gone, taking his contacts with him, leaving the former commercial director Ed Woodward as the club's chief negotiator. Between them, what a hash Moyes and Woodward made of their first foray into the market. Not for nothing was Moyes known as 'Dithering Dave' at Goodison. Lacking Ferguson's gambler's instinct, he prevaricated when he needed to pounce. His judgment of players, too, was odd. He told reporters that he did not rate the brilliant young Atlético Madrid midfielder Koke, who was said to be

318

keen on joining United. Ross Barkley, the gifted young Evertonian many thought he should buy, he confidently predicted 'won't make it'. Wilfried Zaha, the young winger Ferguson had signed from Crystal Palace for £12million, was never given a chance, farmed out on loan to Cardiff. Woodward, meanwhile, tried for players he had no chance of signing, his very public interest used as a negotiating chip to buff up the contracts of Cesc Fàbregas at Barcelona and Gareth Bale, newly arrived at Real Madrid. As the summer transfer window slammed shut, the only new recruit the pair secured was Moyes's old stalwart Marouane Fellaini, Everton's fourth-best player, signed for an eye-wateringly inflated sum of £27.5 million. Baines, incidentally, publicly stated he preferred to stay where he was.

Seeing the busby-haired Belgian in United red was by no means the end of the embarrassment. Van Persie, rumoured to be missing his countryman Meulensteen on the training field, was soon absent after sustaining injury, probably to his pride. And the results quickly turned sour. The away defeats by Liverpool and City in September were bad enough, but Moyes's United started losing at home to teams like Newcastle, Spurs and West Bromwich Albion. Even Everton won at Old Trafford, a feat – their gloating fans were delighted to point out – they had never managed under Moyes's stewardship. By the autumn of 2013, the phone-ins were clogged with fair-weather United fans bemoaning the change in their fortunes, demanding Moyes's removal. Those who attended matches, however, were more inclined to patience. They had seen the problems building over the last couple of seasons, the back four ageing together, the gaping hole where a central midfield should be, the number of mediocre players furring up the squad. They appreciated it would take time and money to rebuild. They felt Moyes should be given both. 'Every single one of us stands by David Moyes,' was the chant that rang out among the United away following.

Whatever its weaknesses, however, this was the same squad that had strolled to the title nine months earlier, now playing like drains. Rumours filled the fanzines of unhappiness in the dressing room. A disaffected Ryan Giggs was said to be planning a coup with his fellow Class of '92 graduates. Ferdinand and van Persie were largely absent. The four-square skipper Nemanja Vidić announced he would be leaving at the end of the season. Everything appeared to be conspiring against the new manager. And what the choice of Moyes did was provide compelling evidence of the huge contribution Ferguson had made. The old manager had papered over the cracks; Moyes merely exposed them.

As Moyes-era United continued to stutter and stall, even the staunchest Ferguson loyalists began to worry about the appointment. On Merseyside, Liverpool and Everton were flying – under progressive, forward-thinking management. Brendan Rodgers and Roberto Martínez were producing teams of fluidity and sophistication. Sound of technique, attacking, intelligent: they were a joy to watch. Across town at City, the club was benefitting hugely from a vigorous summer of recruitment. Under Pellegrini, City had shed Mancini's caution and were hammering in the goals. Arsène Wenger had finally made a major signing and brought in the German Mesut Özil to instigate some coruscating moves by Arsenal. The potent early-season form of Aaron Ramsey lent the Gunners further goal-scoring ammunition. Attack was everywhere in vogue. Except at United.

The thing is, nobody knew what Moyes's philosophy was. It was accepted that United were in transition, but what was he trying to build? Where was he hoping to lead the club? Aside from caution, what did he stand for? At Goodison, he had set out not to lose. Now he was in charge of an institution where the first imperative was to win, he appeared utterly nonplussed. His verbal offerings demonstrated his unease. He called Liverpool 'the favourites' ahead of a fixture at Old Trafford. He said City were a club to which United 'aspired'. Two years earlier, Ferguson had said it would take City a century to reach United's level. Now, under Moyes, City were cast as role models. United fans didn't want to hear that sort of talk from their manager.

In the January transfer window came a brief glimpse of a possible future. Moyes signed the Chelsea number ten Juan Mata, for a club record fee of £35 million. But the optimism his arrival engendered was short-lived. Mata could not stem the decline, could not bring harmony into an increasingly unhappy dressing room. The nadir was reached in successive home defeats to Liverpool and City in March. In both games, United were lucky not to lose by more than 3–0. In the Sky commentary box for the game against Liverpool on 16 March, Gary Neville spotted, within about three minutes of the kick-off, the flaw in United's game plan: the midfield was static and pedestrian and desperately needed reinforcing, while the wingers were allowing the Liverpool full-backs far too much room to initiate attack. Moyes, however, seemed to see nothing. Rather, standing in his technical area, he was channelling the spirit of Alan Partridge in his most uncomfortable moment.

It is one of the funniest, if most excruciatingly painful, episodes in British television comedy. Partridge is making his way across a public car park when he catches sight of an acquaintance in the distance. He shouts out his name. But the man – for reasons too obvious to rehearse here – ignores his calls. Partridge, though, is not to be deterred and keeps shouting out the single name 'Dan! Dan! Dan! Dan! *Dan!*' until it becomes absurd.

As his United side were swamped by Liverpool, technically, tactically and physically, Moyes stood there shouting out names. 'Mike! Mike!' he would yell at Michael Carrick. Or 'Wayne! Wayne! Wayne! *Wayne!*' at Wayne Rooney. Like Partridge, the objects of his attention did not respond. But Moyes did not give up. 'Wayne! Wayne! Wayne! *Mike!*' he went. But they weren't listening. Which was no real surprise as apparently shouting out a name was all he had to contribute. Alongside him, his Liverpool counterpart Brendan Rodgers was assiduously taking notes. He wasn't shouting, he was observing, scheming, planning. As a contrast between a man in control and a man not waving but drowning it could not have been more stark.

It was after that game, it seems, that Ferguson finally realized his mistake. Until then he had been anxious to protect his successor. Far from intimidating the new man, Ferguson's presence behind the scenes had sustained him in the post. But once Fergie's doubts were expressed, Moyes was history; those within the organisation who had long since lost confidence swooped. And, after a horribly symbolic defeat at his old club on Easter Sunday, he was gone, his demise leaked from the dressing room to Mark Ogden and his colleagues in the press before he had been officially informed.

Moyes would undoubtedly point to the fact that his win percentage of 54 per cent was better than any of his successors – including Busby and Ferguson – in their first season in charge. But perhaps a more telling statistic was this: in his 51 games at United, he picked 51 different teams. That does not speak of a man confident in what he was doing.

The timing of his departure was revealing. He was sacked the day after the loss at Goodison had marked the moment when it became mathematically impossible for United to qualify for the following season's Champions League. That enabled the board to invoke a clause in the manager's contract reducing the amount of compensation to which he would be entitled in the event of dismissal. When he signed that clause the previous June, he must have reckoned it a mere formality. Never in a million years could he have thought it would ever be invoked. United not qualify for the Champions League? It had never happened. Until David Moyes arrived.

In his place, United temporarily appointed Ryan Giggs, the Interim One, for the last four games of the season. He in turn, brought in his Class of '92 mates to assist him. Seeing Giggs, Paul Scholes, Nicky Butt and Phil Neville together in the dug-out restored the good cheer around Old Trafford. On social media, a picture of van Persie greeting Giggs with a handshake and a broad grin alongside one of him scowling at Moyes quickly did the rounds. Happy days were here again. Except, as defeat at home to Sunderland proved, not all of the problems within the club had been resolved by Moyes's defenestration.

And in his last home game in charge against Hull City, Giggs sent out a pointed message to his successor about the United way. He selected a forward line of Adnan Januzaj, Tom Lawrence and James Wilson, three young graduates of the United youth system. He then sent himself on for a poignant last hurrah, to demonstrate quite what can be achieved by promoting from within.

'That is what United have always done,' he said in his parting address to the Old Trafford press room. 'As a club, we've always looked forward and always given youth a chance.'

His successor was to be Louis van Gaal, the former Ajax, Bayern and Barcelona coach, a proven winner and a man with no shortage of self-confidence. If Ferguson was worried about Mourinho's ego, the corridors at Old Trafford will need to be widened to accommodate the new man's head. Only time will tell if Dutchman was listening to Giggs's pointed message (and he was good at those, telling reporters at Southampton on the final day to turn off television coverage of City's title celebrations with a brisk 'flippineck').

With United floundering in a David Moyes-inspired fug, the competition to step into the space vacated by the wounded champions was as open and exciting as any in Premier League history. For much of the season there were four teams in with a shout: City, a revived Liverpool, Chelsea and, until they were scuppered by their standard mid-season implosion, Arsenal (who occupied top spot in the League for longer than anyone). At times it was breathtaking. At times the attacking was a ferocious as the competition had ever witnessed.

Twenty-five years on from the Hillsborough disaster, Liverpool surfed a wave of emotion to head the league into early April. Under Rodgers's enlightened stewardship, led by the veteran Steven Gerrard, a cohort of young players were blossoming. Raheem Sterling, Jordan Henderson, Jon Flanagan and Daniel Sturridge were demonstrating that English did not have to equate to hit-and-hope and chuck-it-in-the-mixer. Rodgers encouraged them to be patient, to be intelligent, to be modern. And how they responded.

But whatever the skill of players like that, the reason Rodgers turned Liverpool from outsiders to contenders could be found in the identity of the man he picked up front. He was blessed by the performances of the Uruguayan Luis Suárez. Mixing a velvet touch with a raging desire to win, the man who was to become double footballer of the year was at times unplayable. It was his goals that restored Liverpool to a competitive position they had not occupied in a generation.

And they were almost there, too. When they beat Manchester City at home on 13 April, to go clear at the top, Steven Gerrard was caught by the television cameras giving his young team mates a lecture about not getting carried away. 'Nothing's won yet,' he breathlessly insisted. 'We go on from here.'

But it was Gerrard himself who let it slip. Literally. In the home game against Chelsea on 27 April they needed to win finally to secure their place at the top, his studs fell away under him as he was about to make the most routine of back passes. In stepped Demba Ba to score the first goal in a 2–0 victory. It was a moment repeated in a thousand mocking internet memes, a moment of crushing symbolism, the moment Captain Fantastic himself let slip the title.

And the irony was, Chelsea had gone to Anfield with no intention of winning. They had gone simply not to lose. That was what Chelsea did that year. That and stir up debate. They may not have got the goals, but they were restored to the centre of the national conversation with the appointment of their new manager. After spending six years failing to replace José Mourinho, Roman Abramovich had finally realized there was only one candidate who could successfully fill his shoes: José Mourinho. The Portuguese had tested the patience of the board (and half the dressing room) at Real Madrid and was looking for an escape route. After failing to persuade Ferguson of his qualities, Chelsea seemed the best option. His appointment in June was hugely welcomed, not just by Chelsea fans but by the British press, who relished the return of the headline-writer-in-chief. Though as always with Mourinho, his return came with a health warning. It was issued by Carles Vilarrubí, the vice- president of Barcelona – whom I met at a festival of Catalan culture in, of all places, Salisbury – a few days after the news of the Chelsea appointment had broken.

'It is not good for English football. Chelsea maybe think they had a good time from him in the past. But you will see the real Mourinho now. If he behaves like he did in Spain it will only be an unhappy relationship. A disaster. And at his age he is not going to change,' Vilarrubí told me. He went on to describe the manager's departure from Madrid as 'a scourge being lifted from the face of Spanish football'. Vilarrubí, it is fair to say, was not one of the Ultras in the Bernabeu chanting the manager's name all the way through his final game in charge against Osasuna in Madrid in May 2013.

'My position is not because he was the coach of a rival,' he went on, 'but because of who he is and what he did. His three years in Spain he only creates disagreements, arguments, there is nothing positive he brings. You can learn good things about life from watching people in football, or the circus, or the opera. There was nothing he brought that was good. There was no positive balance. I cannot see anything good about him. Not one thing. In sporting terms, maybe I am not the person to ask. But in cultural terms, he was a disaster. Apart from his aggression to the coach of Barca, the ambience he creates everywhere he goes, the relations with the players, with the press are absolutely terrible. I am happy that he is leaving. And so is everyone in Spanish football.'

Whatever the warning, Mourinho did not disappoint. Despite describing himself at his unveiling press conference as 'The Happy One', he wore a scowl for much of the Premier League season, prowling the touchline not in a handsome designer overcoat, but now in undistinguished tracksuit tops. And boy was he rude about his rival managers. He publicly dismissed Wenger as 'a specialist in failure'; he dismissed Pellegrini, the man he had succeeded at the Bernabeu, as 'programmed to come second'; ahead of a Champions League tie with Galatasaray, he was asked whether he would invite Mancini, the man he had succeeded at Inter, out for dinner. His reply? 'No. Why would I want to do that?' About the only person he had time for was his old protégé Rodgers. Oh, and David Moyes, whom he said should be given more time at United. But then that was what every rival wanted.

And just occasionally he demonstrated what a coach he was. The victories he organized against Liverpool and City were masterclasses of tactical preparation. He took a Chelsea squad bereft of strikers to the semi-final of the Champions League and to within a couple of goals of the Premier League title. The man knows how to manage.

Through it all Pellegrini remained the quantum opposite of Mourinho. Placid, calm, dignified, he appeared to loathe the very concept of controversy, avoiding it as an old lady might a pile of dog mess on the pavement. Happy to be reckoned dull, he quietly went about the business of restoring morale to a dressing room fractured by Mancini's abrasive leadership. He set his squad just the four targets: the Premier League title, the Champions League, the FA Cup and the League Cup. If it seemed overly ambitious, it tallied with his boss's sense of what sort of return he might expect on his investment. And, after picking up the League Cup and Premier League, two out of four wasn't a bad return.

He timed his side's run for the title perfectly. They did not top the table until mid-April, occupying the top slot for a full 100 fewer days than Arsenal. But the point is, they were there when it mattered. Given their opportunity by Gerrard's slip (and Liverpool's absurd inability to win a match at Selhurst Park they were winning 3–0 with twenty minutes to go), they moved in for the kill, ruthlessly exploiting the advantage handed to them.

And for City, the Premier League was the one that counted, that was what brought the thousands on to the streets of Manchester in celebration. As they relished their ascendancy, many of the fans decked out in blue wondered if it could happen again. Not could City win; they were coming to expect that. But could United be as bad as that again?

It seemed unlikely. After all, for the past twenty-five years, United's success had been part of the fabric of Manchester. And with van Gaal in charge things could only get better in the red parts of Manchester. Couldn't they? That is the thing about this astonishing football competition: as always with the story of the Premier League, the next chapter promises to be the most interesting one yet.

● ● ● ● ●

BARCLAYS PREMIER LEAGUE

Old Trafford Stadium, Manchester

Tuesday 6 May 2014

MANCHESTER UNITED   3 – 1   HULL CITY

United scorers: Wilson 31, 61; van Persie 88

Hull scorer: Fryatt 63

Attendance: 75,341

Referee: Craig Pawson

TEAMS:
MANCHESTER UNITED (4-2-3-1)

David de Gea; Antonio Valencia, Chris Smalling, Jones (Vidić 21), Alexander Büttner; Marouane Fellaini, Michael Carrick; Adnan Januzaj, Shinji Kagawa, Tom Lawrence (Giggs 69); James Wilson (Robin van Persie 64)

Subs not used: Ben Amos (gk), Ashley Young, Juan Mata, Michael Keane

HULL CITY (4-5-1)

Eldin Jakupović, Maynor Figueroa, Curtis Davies, Alex Bruce, Liam Rosenior (Yannick Sagbo 45); David Meyler, Ahmed Elmohamady (Jake Livermore 72); Stephen Quinn, Robert Koren, George Boyd; Shane Long (Matty Fryatt 45)

Subs not used: Steve Harper (gk), Tom Huddlestone, Abdoulaye Faye, Nikica Jelavić,

Premier League

Stats and Facts

INDIVIDUAL RECORDS

- **Most Premier League appearances:** 672,
  Ryan Giggs (Manchester United, 15 August 1992 to 19 May 2014)

- **Oldest player:**
  John Burridge, 43 years and 162 days (for Manchester City *v.* Queens Park Rangers, 14 May 1995)

- **Youngest player:**
  Matthew Briggs, 16 years and 65 days (for Fulham *v.* Middlesbrough, 13 May 2007)

- **Most consecutive Premier League appearances:** 310,
  Brad Friedel (14 August 2004 until 7 October 2012)

Goal-scoring Records

- **Most Premier League goals:**
  260, Alan Shearer

- **Most Premier League seasons scored in:**
  22, Ryan Giggs

- **Most goals in a season (42 games):** 34, joint record:
  Andrew Cole (Newcastle United, 1993–94)
  Alan Shearer (Blackburn Rovers, 1994–95)

- **Most goals in a season (38 games):** 31, joint record:
  Alan Shearer (Blackburn Rovers, 1995–96)
  Cristiano Ronaldo (Manchester United, 2007–08)
  Luis Suárez (Liverpool, 2013–14)

- **Most Premier league hat-tricks:**

  11, Alan Shearer

- **Most goals in a game:** 5, joint record:

  Andrew Cole (for Manchester United *v.* Ipswich Town, 4 March 1995) W 9–0

  Alan Shearer (for Newcastle United *v.* Sheffield Wednesday, 19 September 1999) W 8–0

  Jermain Defoe (for Tottenham Hotspur *v.* Wigan Athletic, 22 November 2009) W 9–1

  Dimitar Berbatov (for Manchester United *v.* Blackburn Rovers, 27 November 2010) W 7–1

- **Youngest goal-scorer:**

  James Vaughan, 16 years and 271 days
  (for Everton *v.* Crystal Palace, 10 April 2005)

- **Oldest goal-scorer:**

  Teddy Sheringham, 40 years and 268 days (for West Ham United *v.* Portsmouth, 26 December 2006)

- **Highest number of different clubs to score for:** 6, joint record:

  Andrew Cole (for Newcastle United, Manchester United, Blackburn Rovers, Fulham, Manchester City, Portsmouth)

  Les Ferdinand (for Queens Park Rangers, Newcastle Utd, Tottenham Hotspur, West Ham United, Leicester City, Bolton Wanderers)

  Marcus Bent (for Charlton Athletic, Everton, Ipswich Town, Leicester City, Crystal Palace, Wigan Athletic)

  Nick Barmby (for Liverpool, Everton, Leeds United, Middlesbrough, Tottenham Hotspur, Hull City)

  Craig Bellamy (for Coventry City, Newcastle United, Blackburn Rovers, Liverpool, West Ham United, Manchester City)

  Peter Crouch (for Aston Villa, Southampton, Liverpool, Portsmouth, Tottenham Hotspur, Stoke City)

Robbie Keane (for Aston Villa, Coventry City, Liverpool, Tottenham Hotspur, Leeds United, West Ham United)

- **LONGEST CONSECUTIVE RUN WITHOUT CONCEDING A GOAL:**

  14 games (1,311 minutes), Edwin van der Sar (for Manchester United, 2008–09)

- **LONGEST-RANGE GOAL:**

  Tim Howard – 93 metres (102 yds), Everton *v.* Bolton Wanderers (4 January 2012)

RED CARDS

- **MOST RED CARDS:** 8, joint record:

  Duncan Ferguson
  Patrick Vieira
  Richard Dunne

TEAM RECORDS

- **BIGGEST HOME WIN:**

  9–0, Manchester United *v.* Ipswich Town (4 March 1995)

- **BIGGEST AWAY WIN:**

  1–8, Nottingham Forest *v.* Manchester United (6 February 1999)

- **HIGHEST-SCORING GAME:**

  7–4, Portsmouth *v.* Reading (29 September 2007)

- **HIGHEST-SCORING DRAW:**

  5–5, West Bromwich Albion *v.* Manchester United (19 May 2013)

- **LOWEST FINISH BY THE PREVIOUS SEASON'S CHAMPIONS:**

  7th, Blackburn Rovers (1995–96)
  7th Manchester United (2013–14)
  Leeds United were defending champions in 1992–93 and finished 17th, but they were technically the Division One holders rather than the Premier League holders.

- **HIGHEST FINISH BY A PROMOTED CLUB:** 3rd, joint record:

  Newcastle United (1993–94)

  Nottingham Forest (1994–95)

- **MOST POINTS IN A SEASON:**

  95, Chelsea (2004–05)

- **FEWEST POINTS IN A SEASON:**

  11, Derby County (2007–08)

- **MOST POINTS IN A SEASON WITHOUT WINNING THE LEAGUE:**

  89, Manchester United (2011–12)

- **FEWEST POINTS IN A SEASON WHILE WINNING THE LEAGUE:**

  75, Manchester United (1996–97)

- **MOST POINTS IN A SEASON WHILE BEING RELEGATED:**

  42 games: 49, Crystal Palace (1992–93)

  38 games: 42, West Ham United (2002–03)

- **FEWEST POINTS IN A SEASON WHILE AVOIDING RELEGATION:**

  34, West Bromwich Albion (2004–05)

- **MOST GOALS SCORED IN A SEASON:**

  103, Chelsea (2009–10)

- **FEWEST GOALS SCORED IN A SEASON:**

  20, Derby County (2007–08)

MANAGERIAL RECORDS

- **LONGEST-SERVING MANAGER:**

  Sir Alex Ferguson, 21 years (Manchester United, 1 July 1992 to 19 May 2013)*

- **SHORTEST-SERVING MANAGER (EXCLUDING CARETAKERS):**

  Les Reed, 41 days (Charlton Athletic, 14 November 2006 to 24 December 2006)

* Ferguson's tenure at Old Trafford began on 6 November 1986, before the old First Division became the Premier League.

ATTENDANCES

• HIGHEST ATTENDANCE, SINGLE GAME:

76,398, Manchester United *v.* Blackburn Rovers (at Old Trafford, 31 March 2007)

• LOWEST ATTENDANCE, SINGLE GAME:

3,039, Wimbledon *v.* Everton (at Selhurst Park, 26 January 1993)

MISCELLANEOUS RECORDS

• LONGEST ADDITIONAL TIME:

12 minutes 58 seconds (Arsenal *v.* West Ham United, 23 January 2013)

FINAL PREMIER LEAGUE
TABLES
1992/93–2013/14

1992–93

Pos	Team	Pld	W	D	L	GF	GA	GD	Pts
1	Manchester United	42	24	12	6	67	31	+36	84
2	Aston Villa	42	21	11	10	57	40	+17	74
3	Norwich City	42	21	9	12	61	65	−4	72
4	Blackburn Rovers	42	20	11	11	68	46	+22	71
5	Queens Park Rangers	42	17	12	13	63	55	+8	63
6	Liverpool	42	16	11	15	62	55	+7	59
7	Sheffield Wednesday	42	15	14	13	55	51	+4	59
8	Tottenham Hotspur	42	16	11	15	60	66	−6	59
9	Manchester City	42	15	12	15	56	51	+5	57
10	Arsenal	42	15	11	16	40	38	+2	56
11	Chelsea	42	14	14	14	51	54	−3	56
12	Wimbledon	42	14	12	16	56	55	+1	54
13	Everton	42	15	8	19	53	55	−2	53
14	Sheffield United	42	14	10	18	54	53	+1	52
15	Coventry City	42	13	13	16	52	57	−5	52
16	Ipswich Town	42	12	16	14	50	55	−5	52
17	Leeds United	42	12	15	15	57	62	−5	51
18	Southampton	42	13	11	18	54	61	−7	50
19	Oldham Athletic	42	13	10	19	63	74	−11	49
20	Crystal Palace	42	11	16	15	48	61	−13	49
21	Middlesbrough	42	11	11	20	54	75	−21	44
22	Nottingham Forest	42	10	10	22	41	62	−21	40

Leading Premier League Scorer:

Teddy Sheringham (Nottingham Forest and Tottenham Hotspur) 22

Football Writers Association Footballer of the Year:

Chris Waddle (Sheffield Wednesday)

1993–94

Pos	Team	Pld	W	D	L	GF	GA	GD	Pts
1	MANCHESTER UNITED	42	27	11	4	80	38	+42	92
2	BLACKBURN ROVERS	42	25	9	8	63	36	+27	84
3	NEWCASTLE UNITED	42	23	8	11	82	41	+41	77
4	ARSENAL	42	18	17	7	53	28	+25	71
5	LEEDS UNITED	42	18	16	8	65	39	+26	70
6	WIMBLEDON	42	18	11	13	56	53	+3	65
7	SHEFFIELD WEDNESDAY	42	16	16	10	76	54	+22	64
8	LIVERPOOL	42	17	9	16	59	55	+4	60
9	QUEENS PARK RANGERS	42	16	12	14	62	61	+1	60
10	ASTON VILLA	42	15	12	15	46	50	-4	57
11	COVENTRY CITY	42	14	14	14	43	45	-2	56
12	NORWICH CITY	42	12	17	13	65	61	+4	53
13	WEST HAM UNITED	42	13	13	16	47	58	-11	52
14	CHELSEA	42	13	12	17	49	53	-4	51
15	TOTTENHAM HOTSPUR	42	11	12	19	54	59	-5	45
16	MANCHESTER CITY	42	9	18	15	38	49	-11	45
17	EVERTON	42	12	8	22	42	63	-21	44
18	SOUTHAMPTON	42	12	7	23	49	66	-17	43
19	IPSWICH TOWN	42	9	16	17	35	58	-23	43
20	SHEFFIELD UNITED	42	8	18	16	42	60	-18	42
21	OLDHAM ATHLETIC	42	9	13	20	42	68	-26	40
22	SWINDON TOWN	42	5	15	22	47	100	-53	30

LEADING PREMIER LEAGUE SCORER: ANDREW COLE (NEWCASTLE UNITED) 34

FOOTBALLER OF THE YEAR: ALAN SHEARER (BLACKBURN ROVERS)

1994–95

Pos	Team	Pld	W	D	L	GF	GA	GD	Pts
1	Blackburn Rovers	42	27	8	7	80	39	+41	89
2	Manchester United	42	26	10	6	77	28	+49	88
3	Nottingham Forest	42	22	11	9	72	43	+29	77
4	Liverpool	42	21	11	10	65	37	+28	74
5	Leeds United	42	20	13	9	59	38	+21	73
6	Newcastle United	42	20	12	10	67	47	+20	72
7	Tottenham Hotspur	42	16	14	12	66	58	+8	62
8	Queens Park Rangers	42	17	9	16	61	59	+2	60
9	Wimbledon	42	15	11	16	48	65	–17	56
10	Southampton	42	12	18	12	61	63	–2	54
11	Chelsea	42	13	15	14	50	55	–5	54
12	Arsenal	42	13	12	17	52	49	+3	51
13	Sheffield Wednesday	42	13	12	17	49	57	–8	51
14	West Ham United	42	13	11	18	44	48	–4	50
15	Everton	42	11	17	14	44	51	–7	50
16	Coventry City	42	12	14	16	44	62	–18	50
17	Manchester City	42	12	13	17	53	64	–11	49
18	Aston Villa	42	11	15	16	51	56	–5	48
19	Crystal Palace	42	11	12	19	34	49	–15	45
20	Norwich City	42	10	13	19	37	54	–17	43
21	Leicester City	42	6	11	25	45	80	–35	29
22	Ipswich Town	42	7	6	29	36	93	–57	27

Leading Premier League Scorer: Alan Shearer (Blackburn Rovers) 34

Footballer of the Year: Jürgen Klinsmann

NOTE: At the end of the 1994–95 season, the League was reduced from 22 teams to 20.

1995–96

Pos	Team	Pld	W	D	L	GF	GA	GD	Pts
1	Manchester United	38	25	7	6	73	35	+38	82
2	Newcastle United	38	24	6	8	66	37	+29	78
3	Liverpool	38	20	11	7	70	34	+36	71
4	Aston Villa	38	18	9	11	52	35	+17	63
5	Arsenal	38	17	12	9	49	32	+17	63
6	Everton	38	17	10	11	64	44	+20	61
7	Blackburn Rovers	38	18	7	13	61	47	+14	61
8	Tottenham Hotspur	38	16	13	9	50	38	+12	61
9	Nottingham Forest	38	15	13	10	50	54	-4	58
10	West Ham United	38	14	9	15	43	52	-9	51
11	Chelsea	38	12	14	12	46	44	+2	50
12	Middlesbrough	38	11	10	17	35	50	-15	43
13	Leeds United	38	12	7	19	40	57	-17	43
14	Wimbledon	38	10	11	17	55	70	-15	41
15	Sheffield Wednesday	38	10	10	18	48	61	-13	40
16	Coventry City	38	8	14	16	42	60	-18	38
17	Southampton	38	9	11	18	34	52	-18	38
18	Manchester City	38	9	11	18	33	58	-25	38
19	Queens Park Rangers	38	9	6	23	38	57	-19	33
20	Bolton Wanderers	38	8	5	25	39	71	-32	29

Leading Premier League Scorer: Alan Shearer (Blackburn Rovers) 31

Footballer of the Year: Eric Cantona

1996–97

Pos	Team	Pld	W	D	L	GF	GA	GD	Pts
1	Manchester United	38	21	12	5	76	44	+32	75
2	Newcastle United	38	19	11	8	73	40	+33	68
3	Arsenal	38	19	11	8	62	32	+30	68
4	Liverpool	38	19	11	8	62	37	+25	68
5	Aston Villa	38	17	10	11	47	34	+13	61
6	Chelsea	38	16	11	11	58	55	+3	59
7	Sheffield Wednesday	38	14	15	9	50	51	−1	57
8	Wimbledon	38	15	11	12	49	46	+3	56
9	Leicester City	38	12	11	15	46	54	−8	47
10	Tottenham Hotspur	38	13	7	18	44	51	−7	46
11	Leeds United	38	11	13	14	28	38	−10	46
12	Derby County	38	11	13	14	45	58	−13	46
13	Blackburn Rovers	38	9	15	14	42	43	−1	42
14	West Ham United	38	10	12	16	39	48	−9	42
15	Everton	38	10	12	16	44	57	−13	42
16	Southampton	38	10	11	17	50	56	−6	41
17	Coventry City	38	9	14	15	38	54	−16	41
18	Sunderland	38	10	10	18	35	53	−18	40
19	Middlesbrough	38	10	12	16	51	60	−9	39
20	Nottingham Forest	38	6	16	16	31	59	−28	34

Leading Premier League Scorer: Alan Shearer (Newcastle United) 25

Footballer of the Year: Gianfranco Zola (Chelsea)

1997–98

Pos	Team	Pld	W	D	L	GF	GA	GD	Pts
1	Arsenal	38	23	9	6	68	33	+35	78
2	Manchester United	38	23	8	7	73	26	+47	77
3	Liverpool	38	18	11	9	68	42	+26	65
4	Chelsea	38	20	3	15	71	43	+28	63
5	Leeds United	38	17	8	13	57	46	+11	59
6	Blackburn Rovers	38	16	10	12	57	52	+5	58
7	Aston Villa	38	17	6	15	49	48	+1	57
8	West Ham United	38	16	8	14	56	57	−1	56
9	Derby County	38	16	7	15	52	49	+3	55
10	Leicester City	38	13	14	11	51	41	+10	53
11	Coventry City	38	12	16	10	46	44	+2	52
12	Southampton	38	14	6	18	50	55	−5	48
13	Newcastle United	38	11	11	16	35	44	−9	44
14	Tottenham Hotspur	38	11	11	16	44	56	−12	44
15	Wimbledon	38	10	14	14	34	46	−12	44
16	Sheffield Wednesday	38	12	8	18	52	67	−15	44
17	Everton	38	9	13	16	41	56	−15	40
18	Bolton Wanderers	38	9	13	16	41	61	−20	40
19	Barnsley	38	10	5	23	37	82	−45	35
20	Crystal Palace	38	8	9	21	37	71	−34	33

Leading Premier League Scorers: Dion Dublin (Coventry City), Michael Owen (Liverpool), Chris Sutton (Blackburn Rovers) 18

Footballer of the Year: Dennis Bergkamp (Arsenal)

1998–99

Pos	Team	Pld	W	D	L	GF	GA	GD	Pts
1	MANCHESTER UNITED	38	22	13	3	80	37	+43	79
2	ARSENAL	38	22	12	4	59	17	+42	78
3	CHELSEA	38	20	15	3	57	30	+27	75
4	LEEDS UNITED	38	18	13	7	62	34	+28	67
5	WEST HAM UNITED	38	16	9	13	46	53	−7	57
6	ASTON VILLA	38	15	10	13	51	46	+5	55
7	LIVERPOOL	38	15	9	14	68	49	+19	54
8	DERBY COUNTY	38	13	13	12	40	45	−5	52
9	MIDDLESBROUGH	38	12	15	11	48	54	−6	51
10	LEICESTER CITY	38	12	13	13	40	46	−6	49
11	TOTTENHAM HOTSPUR	38	11	14	13	47	50	−3	47
12	SHEFFIELD WEDNESDAY	38	13	7	18	41	42	−1	46
13	NEWCASTLE UNITED	38	11	13	14	48	54	−6	46
14	EVERTON	38	11	10	17	42	47	−5	43
15	COVENTRY CITY	38	11	9	18	39	51	−12	42
16	WIMBLEDON	38	10	12	16	40	63	−23	42
17	SOUTHAMPTON	38	11	8	19	37	64	−27	41
18	CHARLTON ATHLETIC	38	8	12	18	41	56	−15	36
19	BLACKBURN ROVERS	38	7	14	17	38	52	−14	35
20	NOTTINGHAM FOREST	38	7	9	22	35	69	−34	30

LEADING PREMIER LEAGUE SCORER: JIMMY FLOYD HASSELBAINK (LEEDS UNITED) 18

FOOTBALLER OF THE YEAR: DAVID GINOLA (TOTTENHAM HOTSPUR)

1999–2000

Pos	Team	Pld	W	D	L	GF	GA	GD	Pts
1	Manchester United	38	28	7	3	97	45	+52	91
2	Arsenal	38	22	7	9	73	43	+30	73
3	Leeds United	38	21	6	11	58	43	+15	69
4	Liverpool	38	19	10	9	51	30	+21	67
5	Chelsea	38	18	11	9	53	34	+19	65
6	Aston Villa	38	15	13	10	46	35	+11	58
7	Sunderland	38	16	10	12	57	56	+1	58
8	Leicester City	38	16	7	15	55	55	0	55
9	West Ham United	38	15	10	13	52	53	−1	55
10	Tottenham Hotspur	38	15	8	15	57	49	+8	53
11	Newcastle United	38	14	10	14	63	54	+9	52
12	Middlesbrough	38	14	10	14	46	52	−6	52
13	Everton	38	12	14	12	59	49	+10	50
14	Coventry City	38	12	8	18	47	54	−7	44
15	Southampton	38	12	8	18	45	62	−17	44
16	Derby County	38	9	11	18	44	57	−13	38
17	Bradford City	38	9	9	20	38	68	−30	36
18	Wimbledon	38	7	12	19	46	74	−28	33
19	Sheffield Wednesday	38	8	7	23	38	70	−32	31
20	Watford	38	6	6	26	35	77	−42	24

Leading Premier League Scorer: Kevin Phillips (Sunderland) 30

Footballer of the Year: Roy Keane (Manchester United)

2000–01

Pos	Team	Pld	W	D	L	GF	GA	GD	Pts
1	MANCHESTER UNITED	38	24	8	6	79	31	+48	80
2	ARSENAL	38	20	10	8	63	38	+25	70
3	LIVERPOOL	38	20	9	9	71	39	+32	69
4	LEEDS UNITED	38	20	8	10	64	43	+21	68
5	IPSWICH TOWN	38	20	6	12	57	42	+15	66
6	CHELSEA	38	17	10	11	68	45	+23	61
7	SUNDERLAND	38	15	12	11	46	41	+5	57
8	ASTON VILLA	38	13	15	10	46	43	+3	54
9	CHARLTON ATHLETIC	38	14	10	14	50	57	−7	52
10	SOUTHAMPTON	38	14	10	14	40	48	−8	52
11	NEWCASTLE UNITED	38	14	9	15	44	50	−6	51
12	TOTTENHAM HOTSPUR	38	13	10	15	47	54	−7	49
13	LEICESTER CITY	38	14	6	18	39	51	−12	48
14	MIDDLESBROUGH	38	9	15	14	44	44	0	42
15	WEST HAM UNITED	38	10	12	16	45	50	−5	42
16	EVERTON	38	11	9	18	45	59	−14	42
17	DERBY COUNTY	38	10	12	16	37	59	−22	42
18	MANCHESTER CITY	38	8	10	20	41	65	−24	34
19	COVENTRY CITY	38	8	10	20	36	63	−27	34
20	BRADFORD CITY	38	5	11	22	30	70	−40	26

LEADING PREMIER LEAGUE SCORER: JIMMY FLOYD HASSELBAINK (CHELSEA) 23

FOOTBALLER OF THE YEAR: TEDDY SHERINGHAM (MANCHESTER UNITED)

2001–02

Pos	Team	Pld	W	D	L	GF	GA	GD	Pts
1	Arsenal	38	26	9	3	79	36	+43	87
2	Liverpool	38	24	8	6	67	30	+37	80
3	Manchester United	38	24	5	9	87	45	+42	77
4	Newcastle United	38	21	8	9	74	52	+22	71
5	Leeds United	38	18	12	8	53	37	+16	66
6	Chelsea	38	17	13	8	66	38	+28	64
7	West Ham United	38	15	8	15	48	57	−9	53
8	Aston Villa	38	12	14	12	46	47	−1	50
9	Tottenham Hotspur	38	14	8	16	49	53	−4	50
10	Blackburn Rovers	38	12	10	16	55	51	+4	46
11	Southampton	38	12	9	17	46	54	−8	45
12	Middlesbrough	38	12	9	17	35	47	−12	45
13	Fulham	38	10	14	14	36	44	−8	44
14	Charlton Athletic	38	10	14	14	38	49	−11	44
15	Everton	38	11	10	17	45	57	−12	43
16	Bolton Wanderers	38	9	13	16	44	62	−18	40
17	Sunderland	38	10	10	18	29	51	−22	40
18	Ipswich Town	38	9	9	20	41	64	−23	36
19	Derby County	38	8	6	24	33	63	−30	30
20	Leicester City	38	5	13	20	30	64	−34	28

Leading Premier League Scorer: Thierry Henry (Arsenal) 24

Footballer of the Year: Robert Pirès (Arsenal)

2002–03

Pos	Team	Pld	W	D	L	GF	GA	GD	Pts
1	MANCHESTER UNITED	38	25	8	5	74	34	+40	83
2	ARSENAL	38	23	9	6	85	42	+43	78
3	NEWCASTLE UNITED	38	21	6	11	63	48	+15	69
4	CHELSEA	38	19	10	9	68	38	+30	67
5	LIVERPOOL	38	18	10	10	61	41	+20	64
6	BLACKBURN ROVERS	38	16	12	10	52	43	+9	60
7	EVERTON	38	17	8	13	48	49	−1	59
8	SOUTHAMPTON	38	13	13	12	43	46	−3	52
9	MANCHESTER CITY	38	15	6	17	47	54	−7	51
10	TOTTENHAM HOTSPUR	38	14	8	16	51	62	−11	50
11	MIDDLESBROUGH	38	13	10	15	48	44	+4	49
12	CHARLTON ATHLETIC	38	14	7	17	45	56	−11	49
13	BIRMINGHAM CITY	38	13	9	16	41	49	−8	48
14	FULHAM	38	13	9	16	41	50	−9	48
15	LEEDS UNITED	38	14	5	19	58	57	+1	47
16	ASTON VILLA	38	12	9	17	42	47	−5	45
17	BOLTON WANDERERS	38	10	14	14	41	51	−10	44
18	WEST HAM UNITED	38	10	12	16	42	59	−17	42
19	WEST BROMWICH ALBION	38	6	8	24	29	65	−36	26
20	SUNDERLAND	38	4	7	27	21	65	−44	19

LEADING PREMIER LEAGUE SCORER: RUUD VAN NISTELROOY (MAN. UNITED) 23

FOOTBALLER OF THE YEAR: THIERRY HENRY (ARSENAL)

2003–04

Pos	Team	Pld	W	D	L	GF	GA	GD	Pts
1	ARSENAL	38	26	12	0	73	26	+47	90
2	CHELSEA	38	24	7	7	67	30	+37	79
3	MANCHESTER UNITED	38	23	6	9	64	35	+29	75
4	LIVERPOOL	38	16	12	10	55	37	+18	60
5	NEWCASTLE UNITED	38	13	17	8	52	40	+12	56
6	ASTON VILLA	38	15	11	12	48	44	+4	56
7	CHARLTON ATHLETIC	38	14	11	13	51	51	0	53
8	BOLTON WANDERERS	38	14	11	13	48	56	–8	53
9	FULHAM	38	14	10	14	52	46	+6	52
10	BIRMINGHAM CITY	38	12	14	12	43	48	–5	50
11	MIDDLESBROUGH	38	13	9	16	44	52	–8	48
12	SOUTHAMPTON	38	12	11	15	44	45	–1	47
13	PORTSMOUTH	38	12	9	17	47	54	–7	45
14	TOTTENHAM HOTSPUR	38	13	6	19	47	57	–10	45
15	BLACKBURN ROVERS	38	12	8	18	51	59	–8	44
16	MANCHESTER CITY	38	9	14	15	55	54	+1	41
17	EVERTON	38	9	12	17	45	57	–12	39
18	LEICESTER CITY	38	6	15	17	48	65	–17	33
19	LEEDS UNITED	38	8	9	21	40	79	–39	33
20	WOLVERHAMPTON WANDERERS	38	7	12	19	38	77	–39	33

LEADING PREMIER LEAGUE SCORER: THIERRY HENRY (ARSENAL) 30

FOOTBALLER OF THE YEAR: THIERRY HENRY (ARSENAL)

2004–05

Pos	Team	Pld	W	D	L	GF	GA	GD	Pts
1	Chelsea	38	29	8	1	72	15	+57	95
2	Arsenal	38	25	8	5	87	36	+51	83
3	Manchester United	38	22	11	5	58	26	+32	77
4	Everton	38	18	7	13	45	46	−1	61
5	Liverpool	38	17	7	14	52	41	+11	58
6	Bolton Wanderers	38	16	10	12	49	44	+5	58
7	Middlesbrough	38	14	13	11	53	46	+7	55
8	Manchester City	38	13	13	12	47	39	+8	52
9	Tottenham Hotspur	38	14	10	14	47	41	+6	52
10	Aston Villa	38	12	11	15	45	52	−7	47
11	Charlton Athletic	38	12	10	16	42	58	−16	46
12	Birmingham City	38	11	12	15	40	46	−6	45
13	Fulham	38	12	8	18	42	60	−8	44
14	Newcastle United	38	10	14	14	47	57	−10	44
15	Blackburn Rovers	38	9	15	14	32	43	−11	42
16	Portsmouth	38	10	9	19	43	59	−16	39
17	West Bromwich Albion	38	6	16	16	36	61	−25	34
18	Crystal Palace	38	7	12	19	41	62	−21	33
19	Norwich City	38	7	12	19	42	77	−35	33
20	Southampton	38	6	14	18	45	66	−21	32

Leading Premier League Scorer: Thierry Henry (Arsenal) 25

Footballer of the Year: Frank Lampard (Chelsea)

2005–06

Pos	Team	Pld	W	D	L	GF	GA	GD	Pts
1	Chelsea	38	29	4	5	72	22	+50	91
2	Manchester United	38	25	8	5	72	34	+38	83
3	Liverpool	38	25	7	6	57	25	+32	82
4	Arsenal	38	20	7	11	68	31	+37	67
5	Tottenham Hotspur	38	18	11	9	53	38	+15	65
6	Blackburn Rovers	38	19	6	13	51	42	+9	63
7	Newcastle United	38	17	7	14	47	42	+5	58
8	Bolton Wanderers	38	15	11	12	49	41	+8	56
9	West Ham United	38	16	7	15	52	55	−3	55
10	Wigan Athletic	38	15	6	17	45	52	−7	51
11	Everton	38	14	8	16	34	49	−15	50
12	Fulham	38	14	6	18	48	58	−10	48
13	Charlton Athletic	38	13	8	17	41	55	−14	47
14	Middlesbrough	38	12	9	17	48	58	−10	45
15	Manchester City	38	13	4	21	43	48	−5	43
16	Aston Villa	38	10	12	16	42	55	−13	42
17	Portsmouth	38	10	8	20	37	62	−25	38
18	Birmingham City	38	8	10	20	28	50	−22	34
19	West Bromwich Albion	38	7	9	22	31	58	−27	30
20	Sunderland	38	3	6	29	26	69	−43	15

Leading Premier League Scorer: Thierry Henry (Arsenal) 25

Footballer of the Year: Thierry Henry (Arsenal)

2006–07

Pos	Team	Pld	W	D	L	GF	GA	GD	Pts
1	MANCHESTER UNITED	38	28	5	5	83	27	+56	89
2	CHELSEA	38	24	11	3	64	24	+40	83
3	LIVERPOOL	38	20	8	10	57	27	+30	68
4	ARSENAL	38	19	11	8	63	35	+28	68
5	TOTTENHAM HOTSPUR	38	17	9	12	57	54	+3	60
6	EVERTON	38	15	13	10	52	36	+16	58
7	BOLTON WANDERERS	38	16	8	14	47	52	−5	56
8	READING	38	16	7	15	52	47	+5	55
9	PORTSMOUTH	38	14	12	12	45	42	+3	54
10	BLACKBURN ROVERS	38	15	7	16	52	54	−2	52
11	ASTON VILLA	38	11	17	10	43	41	+2	50
12	MIDDLESBROUGH	38	12	10	16	44	49	−5	46
13	NEWCASTLE UNITED	38	11	10	17	38	47	−9	43
14	MANCHESTER CITY	38	11	9	18	29	44	−15	42
15	WEST HAM UNITED	38	12	5	21	35	59	−24	41
16	FULHAM	38	8	15	15	38	60	−22	39
17	WIGAN ATHLETIC	38	10	8	20	37	59	−22	38
18	SHEFFIELD UNITED	38	10	8	20	32	55	−23	38
19	CHARLTON ATHLETIC	38	8	10	20	34	60	−26	34
20	WATFORD	38	5	13	20	29	59	−30	28

LEADING PREMIER LEAGUE SCORER: DIDIER DROGBA (CHELSEA) 20

FOOTBALLER OF THE YEAR: CRISTIANO RONALDO (MANCHESTER UNITED)

2007–08

Pos	Team	Pld	W	D	L	GF	GA	GD	Pts
1	MANCHESTER UNITED	38	27	6	5	80	22	+58	87
2	CHELSEA	38	25	10	3	65	26	+39	85
3	ARSENAL	38	24	11	3	74	31	+43	83
4	LIVERPOOL	38	21	13	4	67	28	+39	76
5	EVERTON	38	19	8	11	55	33	+22	65
6	ASTON VILLA	38	16	12	10	71	51	+20	60
7	BLACKBURN ROVERS	38	15	13	10	50	48	+2	58
8	PORTSMOUTH	38	16	9	13	48	40	+8	57
9	MANCHESTER CITY	38	15	10	13	45	53	−8	55
10	WEST HAM UNITED	38	13	10	15	42	50	−8	49
11	TOTTENHAM HOTSPUR	38	11	13	14	66	61	+5	46
12	NEWCASTLE UNITED	38	11	10	17	45	65	−20	43
13	MIDDLESBROUGH	38	10	12	16	43	53	−10	42
14	WIGAN ATHLETIC	38	10	10	18	34	51	−17	40
15	SUNDERLAND	38	11	6	21	36	59	−23	39
16	BOLTON WANDERERS	38	9	10	19	36	54	−18	37
17	FULHAM	38	8	12	18	38	60	−22	36
18	READING	38	10	6	22	41	66	−25	36
19	BIRMINGHAM CITY	38	8	11	19	46	62	−16	35
20	DERBY COUNTY	38	1	8	29	20	89	−69	11

LEADING PREMIER LEAGUE SCORER: CRISTIANO RONALDO (MANCHESTER UNITED) 31

FOOTBALLER OF THE YEAR: CRISTIANO RONALDO (MANCHESTER UNITED)

2008–09

Pos	Team	Pld	W	D	L	GF	GA	GD	Pts
1	MANCHESTER UNITED	38	28	6	4	68	24	+44	90
2	LIVERPOOL	38	25	11	2	77	27	+50	86
3	CHELSEA	38	25	8	5	68	24	+44	83
4	ARSENAL	38	20	12	6	68	37	+31	72
5	EVERTON	38	17	12	9	55	37	+18	63
6	ASTON VILLA	38	17	11	10	54	48	+6	62
7	FULHAM	38	14	11	13	39	34	+5	53
8	TOTTENHAM HOTSPUR	38	14	9	15	45	45	0	51
9	WEST HAM UNITED	38	14	9	15	42	45	−3	51
10	MANCHESTER CITY	38	15	5	18	58	50	+8	50
11	WIGAN ATHLETIC	38	12	9	17	34	45	−11	45
12	STOKE CITY	38	12	9	17	38	55	−17	45
13	BOLTON WANDERERS	38	11	8	19	41	53	−12	41
14	PORTSMOUTH	38	10	11	17	38	57	−19	41
15	BLACKBURN ROVERS	38	10	11	17	40	60	−20	41
16	SUNDERLAND	38	9	9	20	34	54	−20	36
17	HULL CITY	38	8	11	19	39	64	−25	35
18	NEWCASTLE UNITED	38	7	13	18	40	59	−19	34
19	MIDDLESBROUGH	38	7	11	20	28	57	−29	32
20	WEST BROMWICH ALBION	38	8	8	22	36	67	−31	32

LEADING PREMIER LEAGUE SCORER: NICOLAS ANELKA (CHELSEA) 19

FOOTBALLER OF THE YEAR: STEVEN GERRARD (LIVERPOOL)

2009–10

Pos	Team	Pld	W	D	L	GF	GA	GD	Pts
1	Chelsea	38	27	5	6	103	32	+71	86
2	Manchester United	38	27	4	7	86	28	+58	85
3	Arsenal	38	23	6	9	83	41	+42	75
4	Tottenham Hotspur	38	21	7	10	67	41	+26	70
5	Manchester City	38	18	13	7	73	45	+28	67
6	Aston Villa	38	17	13	8	52	39	+13	64
7	Liverpool	38	18	9	11	61	35	+26	63
8	Everton	38	16	13	9	60	49	+11	61
9	Birmingham City	38	13	11	14	38	47	-9	50
10	Blackburn Rovers	38	13	11	14	41	55	-14	50
11	Stoke City	38	11	14	13	34	48	-14	47
12	Fulham	38	12	10	16	39	46	-7	46
13	Sunderland	38	11	11	16	48	56	-8	44
14	Bolton Wanderers	38	10	9	19	42	67	-25	39
15	Wolverhampton Wanderers	38	9	11	18	32	56	-24	38
16	Wigan Athletic	38	9	9	20	37	79	-42	36
17	West Ham United	38	8	11	19	47	66	-19	35
18	Burnley	38	8	6	24	42	82	-40	30
19	Hull City	38	6	12	20	34	75	-41	30
20	Portsmouth	38	7	7	24	34	66	-32	19

Leading Premier League Scorer: Didier Drogba (Chelsea) 29

Footballer of the Year: Wayne Rooney (Manchester United)

2010–11

Pos	Team	Pld	W	D	L	GF	GA	GD	Pts
1	MANCHESTER UNITED	38	23	11	4	78	37	+41	80
2	CHELSEA	38	21	8	9	69	33	+36	71
3	MANCHESTER CITY	38	21	8	9	60	33	+27	71
4	ARSENAL	38	19	11	8	72	43	+29	68
5	TOTTENHAM HOTSPUR	38	16	14	8	55	46	+9	62
6	LIVERPOOL	38	17	7	14	59	44	+15	58
7	EVERTON	38	13	15	10	51	45	+6	54
8	FULHAM	38	11	16	11	49	43	+6	49
9	ASTON VILLA	38	12	12	14	48	59	−11	48
10	SUNDERLAND	38	12	11	15	45	56	−11	47
11	WEST BROMWICH ALBION	38	12	11	15	56	71	−15	47
12	NEWCASTLE UNITED	38	11	13	14	56	57	−1	46
13	STOKE CITY	38	13	7	18	46	48	−2	46
14	BOLTON WANDERERS	38	12	10	16	52	56	−4	46
15	BLACKBURN ROVERS	38	11	10	17	46	59	−13	43
16	WIGAN ATHLETIC	38	9	15	14	40	61	−21	42
17	WOLVERHAMPTON WANDERERS	38	11	7	20	46	66	−20	40
18	BIRMINGHAM CITY	38	8	15	15	37	58	−21	39
19	BLACKPOOL	38	10	9	19	55	78	−23	39
20	WEST HAM UNITED	38	7	12	19	43	70	−27	33

LEADING PREMIER LEAGUE SCORERS: DIMITAR BERBATOV (MANCHESTER UNITED), CARLOS TÉVEZ (MANCHESTER CITY) 20

FOOTBALLER OF THE YEAR: SCOTT PARKER (WEST HAM UNITED)

2011–12

Pos	Team	Pld	W	D	L	GF	GA	GD	Pts
1	Manchester City	38	28	5	5	93	29	+64	89
2	Manchester United	38	28	5	5	89	33	+56	89
3	Arsenal	38	21	7	10	74	49	+25	70
4	Tottenham Hotspur	38	20	9	9	66	41	+25	69
5	Newcastle United	38	19	8	11	56	51	+5	65
6	Chelsea	38	18	10	10	65	46	+19	64
7	Everton	38	15	11	12	50	40	+10	56
8	Liverpool	38	14	10	14	47	40	+7	52
9	Fulham	38	14	10	14	48	51	−3	52
10	West Bromwich Albion	38	13	8	17	45	52	−7	47
11	Swansea City	38	12	11	15	44	51	−7	47
12	Norwich City	38	12	11	15	52	66	−14	47
13	Sunderland	38	11	12	15	45	46	−1	45
14	Stoke City	38	11	12	15	36	53	−17	45
15	Wigan Athletic	38	11	10	17	42	62	−20	43
16	Aston Villa	38	7	17	14	37	53	−16	38
17	Queens Park Rangers	38	10	7	21	43	66	−23	37
18	Bolton Wanderers	38	10	6	22	46	77	−31	36
19	Blackburn Rovers	38	8	7	23	48	78	−30	31
20	Wolverhampton Wanderers	38	5	10	23	40	82	−42	25

Leading Premier League Scorer: Robin van Persie (Arsenal) 30

Footballer of the Year: Robin van Persie (Arsenal)

2012–13

Pos	Team	Pld	W	D	L	GF	GA	GD	Pts
1	Manchester United	38	28	5	5	86	43	+43	89
2	Manchester City	38	23	9	6	66	34	+32	78
3	Chelsea	38	22	9	7	75	39	+36	75
4	Arsenal	38	21	10	7	72	37	+35	73
5	Tottenham Hotspur	38	21	9	8	66	46	+20	72
6	Everton	38	16	15	7	55	40	+15	63
7	Liverpool	38	16	13	9	71	43	+28	61
8	West Bromwich Albion	38	14	7	17	53	57	−4	49
9	Swansea City	38	11	13	14	47	51	−4	46
10	West Ham United	38	12	10	16	45	53	−8	46
11	Norwich City	38	10	14	14	41	58	−17	44
12	Fulham	38	11	10	17	50	60	−10	43
13	Stoke City	38	9	15	14	34	45	−11	42
14	Southampton	38	9	14	15	49	60	−11	41
15	Aston Villa	38	10	11	17	47	69	−22	41
16	Newcastle United	38	11	8	19	45	68	−23	41
17	Sunderland	38	9	12	17	41	54	−13	39
18	Wigan Athletic	38	9	9	20	47	73	−26	36
19	Reading	38	6	10	22	43	73	−30	28
20	Queens Park Rangers	38	4	13	21	30	60	−30	25

Leading Premier League Scorer: Robin van Persie (Manchester United) 26

Footballer of the Year: Gareth Bale (Tottenham Hotspur)

2013–14

Pos	Team	Pld	W	D	L	GF	GA	GD	Pts
1	Manchester City	38	27	5	6	102	37	+65	86
2	Liverpool	38	26	6	6	101	50	+51	84
3	Chelsea	38	25	7	6	71	27	+44	82
4	Arsenal	38	24	7	7	68	41	+27	79
5	Everton	38	21	9	8	61	39	+22	72
6	Tottenham Hotspur	38	21	6	11	55	51	+4	69
7	Manchester United	38	19	7	12	64	43	+21	64
8	Southampton	38	15	11	12	54	46	+8	56
9	Stoke City	38	13	11	14	45	52	-7	50
10	Newcastle United	38	15	4	19	43	59	-16	49
11	Crystal Palace	38	13	6	19	33	48	-15	45
12	Swansea City	38	11	9	18	54	54	0	42
13	West Ham United	38	11	7	20	40	51	-11	40
14	Sunderland	38	10	8	20	41	60	-19	38
15	Aston Villa	38	10	8	20	39	61	-22	38
16	Hull City	38	10	7	21	38	53	-15	37
17	West Bromwich Albion	38	7	15	16	43	59	-16	36
18	Norwich City	38	8	9	21	28	62	-34	33
19	Fulham	38	9	5	24	40	85	-45	32
20	Cardiff City	38	7	9	22	32	74	-42	30

Leading Premier League Scorer: Luis Suárez (Liverpool) 31

Footballer of the Year: Luis Suárez (Liverpool)

AND FINALLY...

This is my selection of the team picked from those who have participated in the Premier League across its history, including substitutes. And good luck to whoever it is obliged to tell those on the bench that they won't be starting...

PETR CECH (CHELSEA): 3 PL; 4 FAC; 2 LC; 1 CL; 1 EL

GARY NEVILLE (MANCHESTER UNITED): 8 PL; 2 FAC; 2 LC; 2CL; 1 CLUBWC

TONY ADAMS (ARSENAL): 2 PL; 3 FAC; 2 LC; 1 CUPWC; 2 FL

RIO FERDINAND (WEST HAM, LEEDS, MAN. UNITED): 6 PL; 2 LC; 1 CL; 1 CLUBWC

ASHLEY COLE (ARSENAL, CHELSEA): 3 PL; 7 FAC; 1 LC; 1 CL; 1 EL

CRISTIANO RONALDO (MANCHESTER UNITED): 3 PL; 1 FAC; 2 LC; 1 CL; 1 CLUBWC

STEVEN GERRARD (LIVERPOOL): 2 FAC; 3 LC; 1 CL; 1 UEFAC; 2 ESC

PAUL SCHOLES (MANCHESTER UNITED): 11 PL; 3 FAC; 2 LC; 2 CL; 1 CLUBWC

RYAN GIGGS (MANCHESTER UNITED): 13 PL; 4 FAC; 4 LC; 1 ESC; 1 CLUBWC

ALAN SHEARER (SOUTHAMPTON, BLACKBURN, NEWCASTLE): 1 PL

THIERRY HENRY (ARSENAL): 2 PL; 3 FAC

SUBS:

Peter Schmeichel (Manchester United); John Terry (Chelsea); Roy Keane (Nottingham Forest, Manchester United); Patrick Vieira (Arsenal, Manchester City); Frank Lampard (West Ham, Chelsea); Dennis Bergkamp (Arsenal); Eric Cantona (Manchester United)

The code represents honours won:

PL	Premier League
FAC	FA Cup
LC	League Cup
CL	Champions League
EL	Europa League
CUPWC	European Cup Winners' Cup
UEFAC	UEFA Cup
CLUBWC	Fifa Club World Championship
ESC	European Super Cup
FL	Football League

ACKNOWLEDGEMENTS

This book could not have been written without the stirring deeds of the players and managers involved in the Premier League. Sometimes as reporters we don't appreciate quite what we owe those who play the game. Maybe one day we'll find appropriate thanks.

More to the point, I am extremely grateful to the many who were prepared to talk to me about the games remembered here. Specifically: David Miliband, David Dein, Greg Dyke, Alex Fynn, Martin Tyler, David May, Andrew Cole, Graeme Le Saux, Tim Flowers, Peter Hooton, Martin Keown, Patrick Barclay, John Mann MP, Michael Duberry, Bob Wilson, Ian Stone, Jimmy Floyd Hasselbaink, Gary Neville, Phil Brown, Steve Clarke, Dan Johnson, Vicky Kloss, David Conn, Andy Green, and Michael and Jonathan Baxandall. And thanks to Steve Groves, the excellent BBC producer who I worked with on a Radio 4 documentary to mark the twentieth anniversary of the Premier League.

And I owe a huge debt to my cunning collaborators Rik Glanvill and Jamie Ptaszynski for some stalwart research. Without you, frankly, there would barely be a book. Plus many thanks to Peter Lewis for his meticulous copy-editing, Richard Milbank for his wonderfully enthusiastic help (and for having the idea in the first place), Cat Ledger for sorting everything and to Bols for putting up with it all.

BIBLIOGRAPHY

Football: Bloody Hell, the Biography of Alex Ferguson,
Patrick Barclay (2010)

Game Changer, Mihir Bose (2012)

Richer Than God, David Conn (2012)

The Boss, Michael Crick (2002)

Up Pompey, Chick Culpepper (2011)

My Autobiography, Kenny Dalglish (1996)

Fields of Courage, Max Davidson (2011)

Managing My Life, Sir Alex Ferguson (2000)

Arsenal: The Making of a Superclub, Alex Fynn (2008)

Keane: The Autobiography, Roy Keane (2002)

Manchester City Ruined My Life, Colin Schindler (2012)

*This is the One: Sir Alex Ferguson: The Uncut Story of a
Football Genius*, Danny Taylor (2008)

INDEX